Y0-BIT-982

PITT LATIN AMERICAN SERIES

Latin America's Private
Research Centers and
Nonprofit Development

BUILDING THE
THIRD SECTOR

Daniel C. Levy

University of Pittsburgh Press

Published by the University of Pittsburgh Press, Pittsburgh, Pa. 15260
Copyright © 1996, University of Pittsburgh Press
All rights reserved
Manufactured in the United States of America
Printed on acid-free paper
10 9 8 7 6 5 4 3 2 1

Library of Congress Cataloging-in-Publication Data

Levy, Daniel C.
    Building the third sector : Latin America's private research
centers and nonprofit development / Daniel C. Levy.
        p.   cm. — (Pitt Latin American series)
    Includes bibliographical references and index.
    ISBN 0-8229-3944-4 (cloth : alk. paper). — ISBN 0-8229-5603-9
(pbk. : alk. paper)
    1. Research institutes—Latin America. 2. Social sciences—
Research—Latin America. I. Title. II. Series.
H62.5.L3L49   1996
001.4′098—dc20   95-53045

A CIP catalogue record for this book is available from the British Library

To my mother
for her love and guidance

Contents

Acronyms

Note: Acronyms are translated in English because that is the language of the book and because some readers would not understand Spanish translations while Spanish speakers reading the book will be able to read the English and to translate with the aid of the acronyms. Asterisks indicate the principal site for institutions that are not national, though sometimes the line between national and international is ambiguous. Further points about the acronyms appear near the end of the Preface.

ACLS   American Council of Learned Societies (United States)

ADIPA   Association of Development Research and Training Institutes of Asia and the Pacific (Malaysia)*

AEI   American Enterprise Institute (United States)

AGRARIA   Center for Peasant and Nutritional Development, AHC (Chile)

AHC   Academy of Christian Humanism (Chile)

AID   Agency for International Development (United States)

ALAHUA   Latin American Association for Promotion of Habitation, Urbanism, and Architecture (Ecuador)

ANICS   Nicaraguan Association of Social Scientists (Nicaragua)

ANUIES   National Association of Universities and Institutes of Higher Education (Mexico)

ASIES   Association for Research and Social Studies (Guatemala)

AVANCSO   Association for Social Science Advancement (Guatemala)

AVEDIS   Venezuelan Association for the Development of Health Research (Venezuela)

BASE-IS   BASE-Social Research (BASE is not an acronym) (Paraguay)

CAAP   Andean Center on Popular Arts (Ecuador)

CAIE   Center for Economic Analysis and Research, ITAM (Mexico)

CAMESA   Ajijic Center for Improvement of American Higher Education (Mexico)

CAPES   Commission for Training of Higher Education Personnel (Brazil)

CAPIDE   Counseling and Planning Center for Research and Development (Chile)

CATER   Andean Center for Rural Development (Ecuador)

CATIE   Tropical Agronomy Center of Research and Teaching (Costa Rica)*

CBC   Bartolomé de las Casas Center of Andean Regional Studies (Peru)

CBPF   Brazilian Center of Physics Research (Brazil)

CCE   Entrepreneurial Coordinating Council (Mexico)

CCRP   Regional Corporation Center on Population (Colombia)

CDE   Center of Documentation and Studies (Paraguay)

CEA   Center of Studies on America (Cuba)

CEAP   Center of Studies on Policy Alternatives (Cuba)

CEAS   Center of Studies and Social Action (Brazil)

CEASPA   Center for Social Action Studies of Panama (Panama)

CEBEM   Bolivian Center of Multidisciplinary Studies (Bolivia)

CEBRAP   Brazilian Center for Analysis and Planning (Brazil)

CECI   Center of Scientific Studies (Chile)

CED   Center of Development Studies (Chile)

CEDE   Center of Educational Studies, INTEC (Dominican Republic)

CEDE   Center of Studies on Economic Development, Andes University (Colombia)

CEDEC   Center for Studies of Contemporary Culture (Brazil)

CEDEE   Dominican Center for Educational Studies (Dominican Republic)

CEDEP   Center of Studies for Development and Participation (Peru)

CEDES   Center for the Study of the State and Society (Argentina)

CEDICE   Center for the Diffusion of Economic Knowledge (Venezuela)

CEDLA   Center for Labor Studies (Bolivia)

CEDOES   Documentation Center on Higher Education, AHC (Chile)

CEDOH   Honduran Documentation Center (Honduras)

CEE   Center for Educational Studies (Mexico)

CEESP   Private Sector Center for Economic Studies (Mexico)

CEESTEM   Center for Economic and Social Studies in the Third World (Mexico)

CELA   Center of Latin American Studies (Panama)

CELADE   Latin American Center on Demography (Chile)*

CELADU   Study Center for Uruguayan Democracy (Uruguay)

CEMA   Center for Macroeconomic Studies of Argentina (Argentina)

CEMAT   Meso-American Center for Studies in Appropriate Technology (Guatemala)

CEMLA   Center for Latin American Monetary Studies (Mexico)*

CENDES   Development Studies Center, UCV (Venezuela)

CENDES   Center of Studies for Colombian Social Development (Colombia)

CENECA   Center for Inquiry and Cultural and Artistic Expression (Chile)

CENEP   Center of Population Studies (Argentina)

CENICAFE   Center for Coffee Research (Colombia)

CEOP   Center of Public Opinion Studies (Mexico)

CEP   Center for Public Studies (Chile)

CEPAE   Ecumenical Center of Studies on Planning and Action (Dominican Republic)

CEPAL   Economic Commission for Latin America (Chile)*

CEPAS   Center for Social Action (Costa Rica)

CEPEI   Peruvian Center of International Studies (Peru)

CEPEP   Paraguayan Center of Population Studies (Paraguay)

CEPES   Peruvian Center of Social Studies (Peru)

CEPLAES   Planning and Social Research Center (Ecuador)

CERC   Center for Studies on Contemporary Reality, AHC (Chile)

CEREP   Center for Studies of Puerto Rican Reality (Puerto Rico)

CERES   Center for Studies on Economic and Social Reality (Bolivia)

CERES,   Center for Studies on Economic and Social Reality (Uruguay)

CERESD   Center of Studies of Dominican Social and Economic Reality, UASD (Dominican Republic)

CERPE   Center of Educational Reflexion and Planning (Venezuela)

CES   Center of Social Studies (Uruguay)

CESPO   Center for Social and Population Studies, UCR (Costa Rica)

CESU   Center for Studies on the University, UNAM (Mexico)

CET   Center of Transnational Economics (Argentina)

CETAL   Center for Studies on Appropriate Technology for Latin America (Chile)

CEUR   Center for Urban and Regional Studies (Argentina)

CGIAR   Consultative Group on International Agricultural Research (United States)*

CIA   Central Intelligence Agency (United States)

CIAPA   Center of Research and Political Administrative Guidance (Costa Rica)

CIAT   International Center on Tropical Agriculture (Colombia)*

CIB   Corporation of Biological Research (Colombia)

CIBIMA   Research Center on Marine Biology, UASD (Dominican Republic)

CICE   Center for Research in Educational Science (Argentina)

CICESE   Enseñada Center of Scientific Research and Higher Education (Mexico)

CICSO   Center for Social Research (Argentina)

CIDA   Canadian International Development Agency (Canada)

CIDAC   Center of Research for Development (Mexico)

CIDCA   Center for Research and Documentation of the Atlantic Coast (Nicaragua)

CIDE   Center for Educational Research and Development (Chile)

CIDE   Center for Economic Research and Teaching (Mexico)

CIDEIM   International Medical Research Center (Colombia)

CIDOS   Center of Research and Social Documentation (Dominican Republic)

CIEA   Center of Research and Applied Economics (Dominican Republic)

CIEDUR   Interdisciplinary Center of Development Studies (Uruguay)

CIEF   Center of Research and Family Studies (Uruguay)

CIEN   Center of Economic Research (Guatemala)

CIEPLAN   Corporation of Economic Research for Latin America (Chile)

CIES   Center of Economic and Social Research (Venezuela)

CIESAS   Center of Research and Higher Studies in Social Anthropology (Mexico)

CIESE   Center of Research and Socioeconomic Studies (Ecuador)

CIESU   Center of Information and Studies in Uruguay (Uruguay)

CIF   International Physics Center (Colombia)

CIIH   Center of Interdisciplinary Research in the Humanities, UNAM (Mexico)

CIMAE   Albert Einstein Medical Research Center (Argentina)

CIMMYT   International Center for Improvement of Maize and Wheat (Mexico)*

CINAS   Center of Research and Social Action (El Salvador)

CINCO   Center of Research and Consulting (Bolivia)

CINDA   Inter-University Center for Andean Development (Chile)*

CINDE   Corporation for Development Research (Chile)

CINDE   International Center for Education and Human Development (Colombia)

CINEP   Center for National Research and Popular Education (Colombia)

CINTEFOR   Interamerican Center of Research and Documentation on Professional Development, ILO (Uruguay)*

CINVE   Center for Economic Research (Uruguay)

CINVESTAV   Center of Research and Advanced Studies (Mexico)

CIP   International Potato Center (Peru)*

CIPAF   Research Center for Women's Action (Dominican Republic)

CIPCA   Center of Research for Promotion of the Peasantry (Bolivia)

CIPMA   Center of Environmental Research and Planning (Chile)

CIRD   Information and Resource Center for Development (Paraguay)

CIRMA   Center for Regional Research on Mesoamerica (Guatemala)

CISEA   Center for Social Research on the State and Administration (Argentina)

CISEPA   Center of Sociological, Economic, Political, and Anthropological Research, Catholic University of Peru (Peru)

CISMA   Maya Center for Social Research (Guatemala)

CISOR   Center of Social Research (Venezuela)

CIUDAD   Research Center on Urban Development (Ecuador)

CLACSO   Latin American Social Science Council (Argentina)*

CLADES   Center for Latin American Economic and Social Development (Chile)*

CLAEH   Latin American Center for Humane Economy (Uruguay)

CLAF   Latin American Council on Physics (Brazil)*

CLEPI   Latin American Center of Economics and International Politics (Chile)

CNPQ   National Council of Scientific and Technological Development (Brazil)

CNRS   National Center for Scientific Research (France)

COLMEX   El Colegio de México (Mexico)

CONICIT (and similar abbreviations)   National Science and Technology Council (Most nations)*

COPARMEX   Mexican Employers' Confederation (Mexico)

CPDOC   Center of Research and Documentation of Contemporary Brazilian History, FGV (Brazil)

CPES   Paraguayan Center of Sociological Studies (Paraguay)

CPR   Center for Policy Research (India)

CPU   Corporation for University Promotion (Chile)

CREFAL   Regional Cooperation Center for Adult Education in Latin America and the Caribbean (Mexico)*

CRESALC   Regional Center for Higher Education in Latin America and the Caribbean (Venezuela)*

CRESET   Regional Center of Third World Studies (Colombia)

CRIES   Regional Directorate of Economic and Social Research (Nicaragua)*

CSUCA   Central American University Confederation (Costa Rica)*

DAAD   German Service of Academic Exchange (Germany)

DESCO   Center for the Study and Promotion of Development (Peru)

DESEC   Center for Social and Economic Development (Bolivia)

DIBEN   Office of Social Help and Benefits (Paraguay)

DIE   Department of Educational Research, IPN (Mexico)

EARTH   College of Agriculture for the Humid Tropical Regions (Costa Rica)*

ECIEL   Program of Joint Studies on Latin American Economic Integration (Brazil)

ESCOLATINA   Graduate School of Latin American Economic Studies, UCH (Chile)

EURAL   Center of European–Latin American Research (Argentina)

FAO   UN Food and Agriculture Organization (Italy)*

FDN   Foundation for National Development (Peru)

FEDESARROLLO   Foundation for Higher Education and Development (Colombia)

FES   Foundation for Higher Education (Colombia)

FESCOL   Friedrich Ebert Foundation of Colombia (Colombia)

FIEL   Foundation for Latin American Economic Research (Argentina)

FF   Ford Foundation (United States)

FGV   Getúlio Vargas Foundation (Brazil)

FINEP   Corporation for Financing Students and Projects (Brazil)

FJMA   José María Aragón Foundation (Argentina)

FLACSO   Latin American Faculty of Social Science (Costa Rica)*

FUNDAEC   Foundation for Scientific Application and Teaching (Colombia)

FUNDAJ   Joaquim Nabuco Foundation (Brazil)

GEA   Agro-Regional Studies Group, AHC (Chile)

GIA   Agrarian Research Group, AHC (Chile)

GNP   Gross national product

GRADE   Group of Development Analysis (Peru)

GRC   Government research center

GRECMU   Study Group on the Condition of Uruguayan Women (Uruguay)

IAF   Inter-American Foundation (United States)

IBAFIN   Institute of Banking and Finances (Mexico)

IBGE   Brazilian Institute of Geography and Statistics (Brazil)

ICAL   Alejandro Lipschutz Science Institute (Chile)

ICAP   Central American Institute of Public Administration (Costa Rica)*

ICD   Institute of Communication and Development (Uruguay)

ICEG   International Center for Economic Growth (Panama)*

IDB   Inter-American Development Bank (United States)*

IDEA   International Institute of Advanced Studies (Venezuela)

IDEC   Institute of Contemporary Studies (Argentina)

IDES   Institute of Economic Development (Argentina)

IDESP   São Paulo Institute of Political, Social, and Economic Studies (Brazil)

IDRC   International Development Research Center (Canada)

IEP   Institute of Peruvian Studies (Peru)

IEPRI   Institute of Political Studies and International Relations, National University (Colombia)

IESA   Institute of Advanced Administrative Studies (Venezuela)

IICA   Inter-American Institute for Cooperation on Agriculture (Costa Rica)*

ILADES   Latin American Institute of Doctrine and Social Studies (Chile)

ILD   Institute for Liberty and Democracy (Peru)

ILDIS   Latin American Institute of Social Research (Ecuador)

ILET   Latin American Institute of Transnational Studies (Chile)*

ILO   International Labor Organization (Switzerland)*

ILPES   Latin American Institute for Economic and Social Planning (Chile)*

IME   Mexican Strategic Institute (Mexico)

IMES   Mexican Institute of Sociological Studies (Mexico)

IMF   International Monetary Fund (United States)*

INCAE   Central American Institute of Business Administration (Nicaragua)*

INCAITI   Central American Research and Technical Institute (Guatemala)*

INCAP   Institute of Nutrition of Central America and Panama (Guatemala)*

INIES   Nicaraguan Institute of Economic and Social Research (Nicaragua)

INPROA   Institute of Agrarian Promotion (Chile)

INTEC   Technological Institute of Santo Domingo (Dominican Republic)

IPDE   Panamerican Institute of Advanced Business (Panama)

IPEA   Applied Economic-Social Research Institute (Brazil)

IPN   National Polytechnic Institute (Mexico)

IRC   International research center

ISA   Superior Institute of Agriculture (Dominican Republic)

ISIS   Institute of Strategic and International Studies (Malaysia)

ITAM   Autonomous Technological Institute of Mexico (Mexico)

ITDT   Torcuato Di Tella Institute (Argentina)

IUPERJ   Rio de Janeiro University Research Institute (Brazil)

IVIC   Institute for Scientific Research (Venezuela)

JCLAS   Joint Committee on Latin American Studies (ACLS/SSRC) (United States)*

LASA   Latin American Studies Association (United States)*

NED   National Endowment for Democracy (United States)

NGO   Nongovernment organization

NIH   National Institute of Health (United States)

NOVIB   Netherlands Organization for International Cooperation (Netherlands)

NSF   National Science Foundation (United States)

NUPES   Higher Education Research Group, USP (Brazil)

OAS   Organization of American States (United States)*

OECD   Organization for Economic Cooperation and Development (France)

PDC   Christian Democratic Party (Chile)

PET   Program on Labor Economics, AHC (Chile)

PIIE   Program of Interdisciplinary Research on Education, AHC (Chile)

PISPAL   Program of Social Research on Population in Latin America (United States)*

PONPO   Program on Non-Profit Organizations, Yale University (United States)

PRC   Private research center

PREALC   Regional Program on Employment for Latin America and the Caribbean, ILO (Chile)*

PRI   Institutional Revolutionary Party (Mexico)

PUC   Pontifical Catholic University (Brazil)

RAND   Research and Development (United States)

RIAL   Program of Joint Studies on Latin American International Relations (Chile)*

RIDALC   Regional Interchange Network of Researchers for Latin American and Caribbean Development (Argentina)*

SAPES   South Africa Political Economy Series (Zimbabwe)

SAREC   Swedish Agency for Research Cooperation with Developing Countries (Sweden)

SELA   Latin American Economic System (Venezuela)*

SER   To Be research institute (Colombia)

SNI   National Research System (Mexico)

SOLIDARIOS   Council of American Development Foundations (Dominican Republic)*

SSRC   Social Science Research Council (United States)

SUR   Center of Social and Educational Studies (Chile)

TDRI   Thailand Development Research Institute (Thailand)

TEKHNE   Center for Experimentation in Appropriate Technology (Chile)

THOA   Laboratory for Andean Oral History (Bolivia)

UASD   Autonomous University of Santo Domingo (Dominican Republic)

UBA   University of Buenos Aires (Argentina)

UCH   University of Chile (Chile)

UCR   University of Costa Rica (Costa Rica)

UCV   Central University of Venezuela (Venezuela)

UDAPSO   Analysis Unit on Social Policy (Bolivia)

UDUAL   Union of Latin American Universities (Mexico)*

UNAM   National Autonomous University of Mexico (Mexico)

UNDP   UN Development Program (United States)*

UNESCO   UN Educational, Scientific, and Cultural Organization (France)*

UNICAMP   State University of Campinas (Brazil)

UNICEF   UN Children's Emergency Fund (United States)*

URC   University research center

USIA   U.S. Information Agency (United States)

USP   University of São Paulo (Brazil)

VECTOR   Center of Economic and Social Studies (Chile)

VISA   Industrial Values Company (Mexico)

WHO   World Health Organization (Switzerland)*

Preface

Like the developments it treats, this book was largely unplanned. I had intended to analyze private research centers in one chapter of a book on U.S. assistance programs. But the breadth, diversity, persistence, and impact of these centers proved far greater than I had expected. Increasingly, I realized that the centers are integral to the rise of a large third sector—a nonprofit sector—flanking and interacting with the public and for-profit sectors. Contrasted to the lack of study on these centers specifically, and on Latin America's nonprofit sector generally, their fast-growing importance demanded that they be the subject of a separate book. The book's goal, short of final or exhaustive analysis, is substantial enhancement of our knowledge about this extraordinary privatization.

The intertwining nature of the two book projects affects the acknowledgments. Some grants given for the project on assistance programs also benefited the project on private research centers. I thank the Fulbright-Hays program, the Fulbright Council for the International Exchange of Scholars, the Social Science Research Council, the Aspen Institute, SUNY-Albany, and the Program on Non-Profit Organizations at Yale University. Further grants came directly for the new project. For these I thank the Center for the Study of Philanthropy of the City University of New York, the Spencer Foundation, and again, the Program on Non-Profit Organizations.

The first set of grants helped mainly in the field research in Latin America in 1987 and, especially, in 1988–1989. The grants were essential for the site visits, particularly interviews. Regarding the most extended research periods, in Mexico and Chile, I express special gratitude for research affiliations at El Colegio de México and the Academy of Christian Humanism. I also thank those at universities, private research centers, and other institutions who hosted me in ensuing visits to Argentina, Colombia, Costa Rica, the Dominican Republic, Peru, and Venezuela. The second set of grants facilitated the archival research at donor organizations, communications, data analysis, utilization of pertinent conceptual literature, and writing.

Without colleagues' candor and generosity in discussing institutions and nations they know better than I, little would have been possible. I appreciate the help in interviews and personal correspondence of all those listed in the two appendixes. Those lists partly overlap the following list of those who read sections of the book manuscript and offered useful comments: Eduardo Aldana, Patricia de Arregui, Jorge Balán, José Joaquín Brunner, Julio Cotler, Marcos Cueto, Thomas Eisemon, María de Ibarrola, Paul Di-Maggio, Roger Geiger, Iván Jaksić, Marcela Mollis, Jeffrey Puryear, and Simon Schwartzman. Along with Balán, Mollis, and Schwartzman, others who were most helpful in personal consultations include Virgilio Alvarez, Iván Lavados, María Teresa Lladser, Juan Carlos Navarro, Carlos Ornelas, Luis Rubio, Julio Sánchez, Sol Serrano, Víctor Urquidi, and Hebe Vessuri.

SUNY-Albany provided a supportive environment. If Tony Cresswell, Fred Dembowski, and Mike Green give such kind technical advice in their sponsored project work abroad, I must upgrade my assessment of foreign assistance a notch. Barbara Grubalski provided wonderful secretarial help, and Damaris Carrasco was an exceptional work-study student. Several graduate assistants also helped: Xian-hua Chang, He Huang, Daniel Teoderescu, Jinshui Zhang, and Yan Zheng. Morris Berger and Carlos Santiago were supportive department heads. And the Program on Non-Profit Organizations at Yale University has been a source of continual stimulation for my interests in the third sector.

Colleagues gave constructive reactions to presentations at professional conferences and lectures at universities, including the University of Buenos Aires, Universidad del Salvador, and the Universidad Nacional de Mar del Plata in Argentina; Pontifical Catholic University and the Universidad del Pacífico in Peru; the Universidad de Los Andes in Colombia; INTEC in the Dominican Republic; UNAM in Mexico; and the University of California-Berkeley, Harvard University, Seton Hall, UCLA, the University of New Mexico, and Yale University in the United States. Helpful feedback also followed talks at CRESALC/UNESCO, IESA, the American Council on Education, the Bildner Center of the City University of New York, the Ford Foundation, the Institute of International Education, and various units of the World Bank.

I thank Robert Colasacco and others in the Ford Foundation archives for access to grant files, miscellaneous writings found through the card catalogue, and computer printouts categorized according to my particular requests. Thank you also to those who helped in the libraries at USAID and the Inter-American Development Bank and those who sent computer information on grants from other donors. SAREC and the IDRC, Swedish and Canadian agencies, helped through their practice of sharing their evaluative documents with the public.

I wish to thank, in advance, the readers of this volume. I ask your indulgence for a book that is, in some respects, not easy. Aside from whatever difficulties I have inadvertently added, the book is rather detailed. Its subject matter ranges over many different nations and contexts, and much of that subject matter is new or unfamiliar; the book does not build a neat layer on top of a well-delineated and developed literature. Those whose primary interest is one particular part of the study may want to skim sections that focus on other concerns.

Additionally, the citation format requires an explanation. First, to obey the guidelines of Ford Foundation archives, I avoid quotation—and occasionally even citation—where the point is invidious or sensitive. I received the Inter-American Development Bank's documents only on condition that they not be specifically cited. Nor do I cite the few interviews where the understanding was that the comments were not for attribution. Also omitted are numerous informal yet relevant conversations.

Second, citations could not be simplified beyond the following conventions aimed at limiting intrusiveness. I cite Ford Foundation (FF) and AID documents by their project number, the first two digits of which indicate the year the grant was made. I cite interviews by giving the informant's last name, followed by the letter *i*. A list of interviewees, their position, and the date and place of the interview appears in appendix A. Similarly, I cite personal correspondence (letters, faxes, or e-mail) by giving the informant's last name, followed by the letters *pc*. A list of these communications appears in appendix B. Where the same person is responsible for more than one written communication or interview, the citation is appropriately numbered (e.g., i–2). These conventions save space in the text and save the reader from jumping repeatedly to endnotes to identify the informant.

Third, and most of all, acronyms are inescapable when dealing with private research centers and related institutions. Again I opt for abbreviated form in the text along with a separate listing, this one in the book's front matter. Something is lost where full names are not immediately apparent in the text, but the alternatives seem worse. Spelling out each name in the text would consume considerable space while adding little information; doing so upon the first mention in each chapter would only minimally lessen the problem and would hardly improve one's chances of recognizing an acronym fifteen pages later. In fact, most of the institutions in question are better known and more easily recalled by their acronym than by their full name. Those names would be even less recognizable in English, whereas we can use acronyms in their original form. For the exceptional cases in which a private research center is well known by its name and not its acronym, I use the name, most notably for Argentina's Instituto Torcuato Di Tella, Brazil's Fundação Getúlio Vargas, and Mexico's El Colegio de México (rather than ITDT, FGV, or COLMEX).

In any case, I try to insert the acronyms in clear context, always at least identifying the nation in question. Readers certainly need not look up or memorize all the acronyms. Nor is our perhaps exhausting list exhaustive; any institution mentioned just once and not well known by its acronym is omitted from the list. The most-used acronym is PRC (private research center) and, with it, URC, GRC, and IRC, respectively designating university, government, and international research centers.

Four other acronyms bear special mention. They are AJL, ALL, JML, and MEL, without whom the time completing this study might have been shorter, but less fun.

1 | Breakthroughs

A bold new world of nonprofit organizations has appeared throughout Latin America. This appearance marks a historic break from the dominant belief that social welfare activities—from services for the needy to the advancement of knowledge—are public sector responsibilities. Formerly, although charity could help the destitute and inspired individuals could light a spark of scientific inquiry, major organized action—indeed national development itself—depended on the state and its public institutions. There was little alternative when these institutions performed inadequately. In higher education, private university alternatives have attained importance only in recent decades, and only rarely in research. But as public universities founder and demand for research multiplies, freestanding private nonprofit organizations surge to the research forefront in social fields. These organizations are private research centers (PRCS). They form a crucial part of Latin America's suddenly vigorous nonprofit sector.

PRCS have displaced public universities as the region's leading producers and disseminators of social science and policy research (henceforth, "social research"). They are often more skilled, prolific, and influential than their public counterparts. They employ, without doubt, a disproportional share of the best talent, including many of Latin America's foremost intellectuals. But PRCS do more than pick up the slack for faltering public institutions: they make an astonishing breakthrough in the quantity, quality, and relevance of the region's social research. The point is not that PRCS are more important than universities—they are not—but that PRCS are important and merit serious study, which they have not received.[1]

And PRCS are far more than academic leaders. In socioeconomic terms, PRCS are instrumental in designing and promoting development alternatives to official policies and, with the region's democratization, in designing the official policies themselves. PRCS also directly serve for-profit (business) organizations. Further, they contribute mightily to knowledge, training, information, and studies within the booming nonprofit subsector of social action, comprising "social service," "promotion," or "grassroots" organizations. In fact, no clear line separates these organizations from PRCS; many nonprofits are simultaneously PRCS and social action institutions. Whether or not one chooses to call all PRCS nongovernment organizations (NGOS), the PRC/social action institutions fit the label.[2] And other PRCS at least serve nonprofit organizations. PRCS thus play a crucial role in building the third sector both by their own expanding presence and by their bolstering of other nonprofits.

The policy activities of PRCS are political as well as socioeconomic. Most PRCS are think tanks—creators, molders, or transmitters of ideas for policy—or they are partly think tanks, where other tasks parallel or sustain policy.[3] Although think tanks are spreading well beyond the United States (the only nation where they have been much studied), growth is most spectacular in Latin America. PRCS are excellent examples of how nonprofits are increasingly the institutional workplace worldwide for professional policy advocates (Jenkins 1987).

Furthermore, the net political impact of PRCS is decidedly democratic, both in opposition to authoritarian regimes and in collaboration with the democratic successors of these regimes. PRCS have helped expand the breadth and power of civil society, which includes service to such major institutions as churches and large businesses and to smaller groups, enabling the latter to become stronger and more influential. At the most diffuse level, PRCS both inform public opinion and give it added weight. In sum, PRCS add significantly to pluralism because they themselves are diverse and because they serve other diverse private organizations. For their political impact alone, PRCS would warrant analysis.

Contrary to common impressions, few PRCS are temporary sanctuaries for the protection of social science under military rule, even where they began for that purpose. These organizations do not disappear when military rule disappears. On the contrary, they proliferate with democratization, while existing PRCS assume expanded roles. Additionally, PRCS flourish where military rule has not existed. As we shall see, the "government failure" of repressive rule is only the gravest manifestation of a public sector failure contributing to PRC growth. Public university failure, gauged against both expectations and needed products, is endemic in Latin America. Beyond that, PRCS spread, as nonprofits often do, where they appear to be the institution best suited to assume certain tasks. For example, PRCS do contract research for business, applied research for grassroots organizations, policy research for government, and evaluation research for international agencies. PRCS, in short, establish themselves in a variety of both old and new academic, socioeconomic, and political tasks. The continued strength of these organizations owes much to their adaptability and evolution.

And yet PRCS remain fragile and precarious. They have not attained self-sufficiency; most clearly, they are financially dependent on international philanthropy or domestic governments. Furthermore, they cannot fully escape either the deep problems of higher education and the academic profession or unstable political currents. Deteriorating environments threaten PRCS, but improving conditions, perhaps university recovery, could also reduce or alter the role of PRCS. The decline of individual PRCS, including leading ones, is part of the reality even as new PRCS and kindred institutions evolve.

The policy decisions of many government and private institutions will affect that future. Therefore, policymakers need to understand the nature of PRCS so that their decisions about them are well informed. Donors must consider what degree of support makes sense in situations where PRCS, recently their only option, exist in politically open circumstances where they may be simply the best immediate option; expedient in the short run, PRCS may thwart the arduous reconstruction of public institutions. For example, the World Bank is considering what structural homes, worldwide, are most desirable for research. Domestic governments must, likewise, consider the benefits and costs of their financial, political, and contracting relationships with PRCS. Many of the major dilemmas concern the relationship between PRCS and universities, which resemble other dilemmas about the proper role of nonprofit organizations in newly democratic settings (Piña 1990: 47–51). Most decisions are currently tacit nondecisions, where the dilemma is not perceived, identified, or brought to debate. But debate could become strident, tied to ideological positions regarding private versus public institutions. Some, for example, denounce "the privatization of research" in PRCS' market-driven agenda and the state's abdication of responsibility (Favaloro 1991).

Are PRCS, on balance, positive for higher education and for development in general? Should they be promoted, left alone, mildly regulated, or pointedly curbed? The answers to these questions require analysis and evaluation.

THEMES

This book's basic substantive theme is the importance of PRCS: PRCS transform higher education in crucial respects and they promote broader political-economic tendencies, including building up the nonprofit sector. The main purpose of the book, then, is to establish and analyze this importance. At the conceptual level, the theme is that PRCS are integral to a nonprofit privatization that undermines traditional two-sector development models.[4] Analysis focused on the public sector and the private (for-profit) sector must increasingly yield to trisector analysis that includes the private nonprofit sector: the third sector. This third sector is significant for being outside both the public and for-profit sectors but also for its intense interaction with those two sectors. Despite persistent propensities in both liberal and conservative thought, none of the sectors can be well understood without reference to its interpenetration with the other two (Gidron, Kramer, Salamon 1992).

PRCS are at the heart of emerging trisectoral relationships found in both higher education and the general political economy. Nonprofit privatization, which PRCS epitomize, simultaneously shatters historic notions of state centrality and fits voguish state tendencies to modernize by relying on private action and private-public partnerships. One need not assert that the third sector per se is more important or even as important as the for-profit or public sector to recognize that it is given far too little scholarly attention.

An evaluative theme also develops itself throughout the work: PRC successes outweigh PRC failures. This assessment, of course, responds to the basic policy question on the merit of PRCS. At the same time, the limitations of these organizations raise more difficult policy questions. These successes and limitations largely follow performance patterns characteristic of nonprofit organizations.

The balance of this chapter provides the contexts within which we can understand the PRC's twin historical breakthroughs—in nonprofit privatization and in research.

THE THIRD SECTOR

The Relevant Literature

Emerging literature broadly identifies the nonprofit sector by exclusion: activity outside both the public sector and the private for-profit sector or, more questionably, outside both state and market. A key point involves a "nondistribution" requirement, as profits may not be passed to owners. The broad dual exclusion explains the *third sector* label.[5] Focus sharpens as the core literature—like this study—concentrates on the formal or organized part of the sector while deemphasizing family or membership organizations (Anheier and Knapp 1990: 5). The most common Spanish terminology for nonprofit is *sin fines de lucro* or *sin ánimo de lucro*.[6]

Progress in the literature builds upon so meager a base that it still leaves the third sector seriously underrepresented in study and appreciation.[7] Even in the United States, a literature so impressive for its fast growth underscores the incredible neglect prior to the 1970s and has attained only limited integration into diverse literatures beyond that specifically on nonprofits.

But the problem is especially acute for nonprofits outside the United States. The exceptional size and institutionalization of the U.S. nonprofit sector does not justify the myth that vibrant nonprofits are peculiar to that nation. This is not simply a U.S. parochialism: Like Europeans (Anheier and Seibel 1990a: 2–3), Latin Americans sometimes shun nonprofit concepts even as they develop nonprofit realities. We are far from having a decent descriptive mapping of Latin America's third sector with its religious, educational, health, grassroots, and philanthropic organizations.

This study therefore is part of a belated literature dealing comparatively with the third sector. An optimistic view is that "what began as a trickle of scholarly interest in the 1980s has grown to genuinely global proportions" (Hodgkinson and McCarthy 1992: 2). A more sobering perspective is that the literature remains tiny if we refer to studies that deal with nonprofits qua nonprofits and that take "comparative" to mean consideration of contrasting patterns among nations rather than analysis of nonprofits in a given nation outside the United States.[8]

Education is among the first nonprofit topics researched comparatively, largely because education is prominent among nonprofit activities internationally (James 1989; Levy 1987). This prominence must be qualified in higher education, however. It holds in the United States, and U.S. influence promotes private higher education elsewhere, but many nations that allow private schools have barred or marginalized private higher education. Further, the more we move into the research aspect of higher education the more we see public dominance. Notwithstanding some international parallels to the U.S. practice of allocating public funds for research at private universities, most nations have either no or almost no (e.g., Brazil, Sweden) private research universities. In contrast, a growing PRC presence in the Americas and elsewhere marks a growing nonprofit presence in research.

The value of studying PRCs increases to the extent they allow insights into wider phenomena. Central to our study are (1) characteristics of nonprofit institutions and sectors, (2) pluralism and privatization in Latin American development, and (3) international philanthropy. These three overlapping concerns are taken up just below.

PRCs as Nonprofits: An Overview of the Chapters

Pending the details in chapter 2 (which serves as a tandem introductory chapter for its mapping of the centers and their periphery), suffice it here to say that Latin America's PRCs fit the basic definitional criteria for nonprofit organizations. They are juridically private and do not distribute profits. They also rank high on characteristics that may or may not be part of the definitions per se: nongovernment predominance in both financial source and governance.

Moreover, PRCs display characteristics that are associated with nonprofits but that are never definitionally required of them. Among those substantiated in this study are flexibility, adaptability, and innovation. With greater force, however, I develop the idea of a third sector composed of multitudinous nonprofit institutions that tend to be small, specialized, homogeneous, coherent, and largely autonomous of one another and of the state.

Thus, ensuing chapters emphasize the dynamics of a pluralist nonprofit sector based on differentiation among institutions that are not pluralist internally. PRCs often provide options to minorities that are not provided by the public sector. The narrowness and cohesion of these PRCs allow for harmonious matches with funders. Their diversity of political orientation and their contributions to pluralist democracy contrast to their internal homogeneity and hierarchy. Finally, PRCs usually perform well in their academic and policy tasks, but their selection of specialized tasks leaves many tasks undone, a typical configuration where pluralist systems rely on private institutions that choose their own undertakings.

Thematic use of the basic nonprofit literature goes beyond this institutional-sectoral contrast in pluralism. Each chapter is structured around central concerns, questions, hypotheses, dilemmas, and tendencies elaborated in the literature (Powell 1987). A general concern with international perspectives runs throughout the chapters. So does a general concern with comparisons between nonprofit and other sectors, especially public. Function marks another overarching interest, operationally translated as studies of particular fields; here, the field is mostly research and higher education. Several concerns are thematic to more than one chapter; for example, the relation of nonprofits to the state is more basic to chapters 3–5 than to chapters 6–7.

Other common concerns in nonprofit studies correspond mostly to specific chapters. Concerns about sectoral size and scope form the heart of chapter 2; concerns about why nonprofits develop form the heart of chapter 3. Another major topic in the literature is the source of finance; chapter 4 explores that as well as the degree of control that accompanies it. Issues of nonprofit governance and accountability are thematic to chapter 5, though the chapter also addresses broader political questions, such as the nonprofit role in pluralist democracy, not commonly studied. Finally, concern with nonprofit performance forms the core of chapters 6 and 7, which emphasize academic achievements and limitations, respectively. Of course, these topics are interrelated, and none falls exclusively into only one chapter.

Pluralism and Privatization in Development

The pluralism and privatization built by PRCs connect to basic development patterns. Although a third sector can coexist with state-led corporatism, it would then lack pluralist features such as true privateness, spontaneous creation and growth, multiple organizations, autonomy from government, voluntary association, diverse funders and authorities, interinstitutional competition, and system decentralization. Instead, PRCs would be dependent on an architect state, which would create or at least carefully license, regulate, coordinate, control, and subsidize (Schmitter 1974: 93–94). A historic symbol in Latin American higher education was a single national university, or at least that university's centrality, with other universities modeled after it. Closer examination of public university sectors, especially after decades in which many new institutions emerged, reveals ample pluralism alongside corporatism, and the growth of private universities has tipped the scales to the pluralist side (Levy 1986: 323–28).

The corporatist-pluralist juxtaposition exemplifies this study's connection to comparative politics in general and to state-society relations in particular. Literatures on corporatism (Wiarda 1992), authoritarianism (Malloy 1977), organic statism (A. Stepan 1978), and "bringing the state back in" (Evans, Rueschemeyer, and Skocpol 1985b) all stress, though to different degrees and with different emphases, the dominant role of the state in shaping society. For Latin America, then, state corporatism has been more relevant than the societal corporatism associated with democratic Europe (Schmitter 1974: 103–04). The state-centered literature typically relegates pluralism to marginality. Recent realities of Latin American development have blocked further proliferation of statist concepts. Yet the conflict between these realities and those conceptions should be explicitly identified; and alternative conceptualizations of equal force are yet to be developed.[9] These alternatives must accord a major place to privatization. PRCs mark considerable privatization as they are so extensive, so private in structure, finance, and function, and so linked to wider aspects of privatization.

PRCs are thus part of the incredible privatization sweeping much of the world at the end of the twentieth century. In the 1970s, analysis tied Latin American privatization to the then dominant form of political regime, bureaucratic authoritarian, pledged to rationalized, market economics (Collier 1979). One view is that privatization ran up against statist-nationalist doctrines linked to the regimes' repressive nature (O'Donnell 1988), while an alternative view is that by the 1970s authoritarian regimes were notably neoconservative and proprivatization (Schamis 1991). In any case, privatization soon dominated regardless of regime, and ranged from fading military rule to renewed democracy (in the Southern Cone), to liberalizing authoritarian regimes (Mexico) to formal if problematic democracies (Colombia, Bolivia, and much of Central America), to longer-standing democracies (Costa Rica, the Dominican Republic, Venezuela). Privatization dominated even where populist candidates assumed power.

In Latin America and beyond, most analysts direct attention to for-profit privatization (Collier 1979; Glade 1991; Heath 1990). This privatization includes commercial and physical areas such as telephones, airlines, banking, and manufacturing. Some analysts have recently paid increased attention to privatization in human service areas as well, noting that they are major arenas of public policy change and debate (Gormley 1991b; Kamerman and Kahn 1989). They are also areas in which nonprofit privatization is much more common than in the commercial and physical areas. Alongside the bulk of the literature's evidence from the developed democracies comes evidence of nonprofit growth in a liberalizing Eastern Europe, begun at least a decade before communism's collapse, then intensifying with the collapse itself, and extending to the Third World (Marschall 1990: 277; McCarthy, Hodgkinson, Sumariwalla 1992). Returning to the regime dimension within Latin America, suppositions that nonprofits are tied to the repression and exclusiveness of authoritarian regimes prove misleading: nonprofit privatization has proceeded vigorously under a variety of regimes.

PRCs should be placed within the wider context of Latin America's nonprofit privatization, including an expanded role in religious and charitable associations. As in Africa, this expansion features movement beyond relief and emergency efforts to secular development organizations (Anheier 1990b: 373; Carroll 1992: 2; A. Thompson 1992: 398). Latin Americans who think "for-profit" when they think "private" cling to a notion at odds with both historic and especially contemporaneous reality. Latin America's nonprofits merit study both for their importance within the region as well as for their relevance to worldwide privatization. And this privatization involves dynamics other than just outright conversion of a given organization from public to private status.[10]

No regional data base exists for Latin American nonprofits. Brañes (1991: 73) reports estimates of more than 6,000 Latin American NGOs but emphasizes uncertainty beyond the roughly 100 in his surveyed area. A rough estimate for 1986 was that more than 4,000 Latin American "development nonprofits," 20–40 percent of the Third World total, received support from the First World (B. Smith 1990: 231).[11] These figures refer basically to grassroots nonprofits and thereby exclude nonprofits such as those that serve paying clients in hospitals and schools. Underestimation of the size of the nonprofit world results from tacit identification of nonprofit with just one type of NGO.

Universities, a nonprofit subsector with an unusually inclusive count, furnish a good example of growth. The Latin American privatization of universities has been extremely powerful, notable even within an impressive worldwide shift. From a regional presence limited to just three nations before the 1930s, private universities existed in every nation except Cuba by the 1970s and accounted for more than a third of total enrollment (Levy 1992b; Levy 1986: 1–5). As growth in numerical proportion has since slackened, privatization has proceeded regarding the academic, political, economic, and social weight of private over public universities, including unprecedented public sector reform echoing private sector practice (Levy 1992a).

More common than regional data on a nonprofit subsector are national surveys that aim for sectoral inclusiveness. They provide some sense of size; yet they do not escape the arbitrary variation rooted in different methods and coverage in counting (SOLIDARIOS 1981). While one source reports more than 3,000 Peruvian NGOs, most count about 400 NGOs or promotion centers ("Los ONGS y su papel" 1992; Díaz-Albertini 1990: 3; M. Smith 1992: 25–28). All the numbers reflect the sharp increase since the late 1970s, so that Peru joins Chile, Bolivia, Brazil, and other countries with large nonprofit sectors. Spalding (1991: 31) guesses that the budget for Peruvian NGOs, without Catholic church sources, is $50 million to $60 million a year. A Paraguayan study finds more than 200 NGOs, many in education, but also reports a lack of information on numbers of people and projects and on financial size; furthermore, its definition of NGO is vague—independence from government and church or any organization that can influence its decision making (Duarte 1991: 18–19). A Uruguayan survey finds more than 100 NGOs (Barreiro and Cruz 1991).

The IAF has surveyed NGOs beyond single nations; one of its recent guides, which finds 11,000 NGOs, notes that Brazil and Chile stand well ahead of Argentina and Mexico, with Peru and Colombia in between (Reilly 1994: 13–14). Another survey emphasizes the commonality of huge growth in Argentina, Brazil, and Chile since the 1970s but also the divergence of national categorizations (A. Thompson 1992). Its best data, on Argentina, suggest perhaps 11,000 civil associations, 4,850 cooperatives, 2,000 neighborhood associations, and 1,200 foundations; it also alludes to some 25,000 membership organizations in Chile, and in Brazil about 400 nonprofits in environment, about 200 dealing with women, and more than 500 concerned with blacks. The looser the criteria, the higher the totals.

Research privatization, in the social sciences and policy, is as impressive as the overall rise of nonprofits in Latin America, and research privatization mostly means PRCs. With few major exceptions to date (although more are developing), private universities mean privatized teaching, not research.

PRCs present just the opposite balance. If for nothing but their proliferation and number, we would be compelled to study them.

We naturally ask why PRCs arise. As a corollary, we wonder what their creation tells us about the problems of other research structures. Logically, too, when we see institutions that are already numerous and still proliferating, we are compelled to learn what they do, how they do it, and how well they do it. Natural interest in these matters is enhanced here by the nature of PRCs as nonprofit organizations forming and building part of a wider privatization and affecting all sectors.

International Philanthropy

PRCs also claim the attention of those interested in nonprofit sectors or Latin American development because of their connection to international philanthropy.[12] PRCs write a remarkable chapter in international philanthropy's history.[13] This is so despite the retreat from the massive assistance efforts of the postwar decades, which include unprecedented efforts to export progress through university development.

This study compares international philanthropy's earlier effort regarding universities to its more contemporary effort regarding PRCs.[14] For introductory purposes, however, I mention a few intriguing ways that philanthropy for PRCs differs from earlier higher education efforts and many other instances of international assistance: assistance comes mostly from private donors (foundations), goes mostly to nonprofits, often accounts for the bulk of the recipients' income, and is usually viewed as successful.

This study considers the following conflicting claims raised about international philanthropy (Friedman 1980):

—It promotes innovation and progress; or it acts in safe, unimaginative ways.

—It cooperates with recipients, facilitating their agenda; or it imposes its own agenda.

—It acts apolitically, or positively, for pluralism; or it acts for a conservative status quo.

—It acts independently; or it acts with big government.

—It uses private power for public good; or it perverts the public mission.

Of course, similar debates rage in regard to domestic philanthropy as well.[15] Parallels emerge between domestic and foreign roles of big foundations (Arnove 1980b), especially in how these foundations were pivotal in developing U.S. social and exact sciences and how they sometimes chose freestanding research institutes over universities (Kohler 1991: 10).

In sum, PRCs are pertinent to our knowledge of philanthropy and to the debate about its desirability. Although chapter 4 deals most directly with the financial dimension, all chapters are about nonprofit organizations that are largely creatures of international philanthropy.

THE RESEARCH WORLD

The significance of PRCs also stems from a record of success in a major endeavor—research—where Latin America lags badly. A thematic question in the study of science is why and how research takes root, but in less developed countries attention focuses on its inability to take root or to account for more than a small fraction of the world's science and technological production (Pyenson 1978: 92; N. Stepan 1976; Vessuri 1983: 38).[16]

Ensuing sections highlight Latin America's lack of development in research generally, the PRC breakthrough, inadequacies in the literature on higher education and research, and an international overview of the institutional setting for research.

Latin American Underdevelopment

In research, Latin America has not broken to the fore of even the Third World. Ritualistic references to Mayan astronomy or Argentine Nobel prizes in physics and biochemistry (IDB 1985: 7) are more pathetic than positive, more defensive than proud. Latin America ranks just slightly ahead of Africa and behind all other regions in share of GNP devoted to research and development; perhaps only Cuba and Costa Rica get beyond 0.5 percent, versus more than 2 percent for most developed countries, followed by South Korea and other rapid modernizers (Vessuri 1986: 20–21; Arregui and Torero (1991: 41–42, 83–88). Decades of concern and international assistance allowed Latin America to improve its global standing in terms of expenditures and numbers of trained personnel in R&D.[17] But in 1980 the region claimed only 1.8 percent of the world's R&D expenditures, 1.3 percent of the scientific authors in international journals, even fewer of their citations, and fewer than 2.5 percent of the researchers, while it had 5 percent of the world's economic production and 8 percent of its population (Sagasti et al. 1984: 1167; Brunner 1991b: 151).

The economic crises of the 1980s diminished Latin America's financial effort. Its share of total R&D expenditures fell to less than 1 percent. Additionally, with the exception of Brazil, trailed by Mexico and Venezuela, the region's lagging nations have not closed ground on the region's leaders, despite the latter's stagnation. Chile laments its dashed expectations over recent decades but remains a regional leader; Argentine stagnation and turmoil over a longer period is notorious and yet, with Chile, Argentina retains a notable per capita advantage over even Brazil and Mexico on standard scientific indexes (Fuenzalida 1987: 119; Brunner 1988a: 101; Brunner 1991b: 123–32; Larraín 1985: 157).

Before the 1950s, sustained, planned, and institutionalized research programs were rare. Foreign-assisted modernization efforts helped but have had more success in creating researchers than research structures. Universities have mostly failed to integrate research within their teaching faculties, while research centers within universities show patterns of both success and failure (Sagasti 1979; Levy forthcoming). Probably fewer than thirty of the roughly seven hundred of Latin American universities have serious research functions that go beyond ad hoc efforts by individuals. The difficulty in institutionalizing university research is critical in appreciating the contribution of PRCs in the social area.

It might appear, however, that PRCs are just a dot on the Latin American research map. Some 60 percent of Latin America's R&D, measured in financial terms, takes place in government structures, with 25 percent in universities, and probably much of the rest in private enterprise (Vessuri 1986: 21). Colombian data (also for 1978), show that about 75 percent of research is done in government centers (mostly agricultural research) and universities (mostly medicine) (IDB data; Franco and Tunnerman 1978: 323–27). In sum, government and universities are the two major homes for R&D, while the third sector occupies only isolated niches in the key research fields of natural science, medicine, and agriculture.[18]

The PRC Breakthrough

Yet if one also regards social science and policy research as major research areas, we must balance the measures just cited on gross research efforts with other measures and factors. R&D figures may exclude "soft" research areas. Further, social research has much greater weight in numbers of scholars than in expenditures. And indexes based on publication in international journals are less inclusive, and less meaningful, in these research fields than in those less affected by national and local context. Nor is the hierarchy as great; the assumption that the best scientific articles by Third World researchers will be published in First World journals should not be carried into social fields. Moreover, the nature of the subject matter yields much more varied and subjective criteria about what is better research. Gross data typically invoked to show Latin America's backwardness in research are misleading for social science and policy.

Another perspective is that even the R&D figures underscore the need to explore extrauniversity research. As chapter 2 alerts us, some "government" research centers (GRCs) are relatively autonomous and resemble PRCs in significant ways. A similar point emerges for URCs (university research centers).

Latin Americanists are aware of the multiplication of social research at least in their countries of specialization.[19] Within many subject areas, one struggles to keep up with the increased flow through proliferating journals, books, and working papers, both domestic and international. Much of the boom relates to PRCs, home to so many of the best trained and most prolific social researchers. Peruvianists will immediately recognize the imprint of the IEP; Chileanists, that of CIEPLAN; and others, of CPES (Paraguay), the CEDES (Argentina), IUPERJ (Brazil), and El Colegio de México (Mexico). The list extends easily; those concerned with particular disciplines or problems, from economics to demography to women to labor to environment to public opinion polling to service delivery, will recognize the importance of various PRCs in various nations.

PRCs lead. PRCs are often the most productive and prestigious social science structures and—because their output achieves high quality, relevance, consultancies, and contacts—have the most influence on policy. Many assume a leadership role that intellectuals and students have traditionally played in Latin America: a claim on national consciousness and identity. Social commentary in Latin America has heretofore rarely sought an academic niche isolated from political and social life, as commonly found with U.S. social science (Camp 1985). PRCs are today's engaged institutions par excellence. They write a new chapter in the history of Latin American intellectual life. Beyond all this, PRCs account for an impressive share of the region's respectable graduate education in the social fields.

To assert that Latin American PRCs lead along these dimensions is not to assert that they do in each nation, much less in every pertinent respect. But leadership goes beyond the Southern Cone cases that most Latin Americanists might expect. Without claiming that any four-part categorization could achieve the accuracy of a more complex one, or that the following formulation is superior to any conceivable alternative, I offer this tentative division of countries regarding social research.

1. *Nations where the research is plentiful and mostly, sometimes almost exclusively, packed into PRCs.* The clearest cases are Chile and Argentina. Uruguay may fit if "plentiful" is adjusted for national size. Peru fits, though much of the research is not academically oriented. Peruvian PRCs have proliferated incredibly. Some say almost every active Peruvian social researcher is linked to a PRC; others say public universities still produce if we credit the different theoretical and methodological approaches found there.

2. *Nations where the research is more limited yet has grown impressively and, again, is largely packed into PRCs.* This category includes Paraguay, Bolivia, Central America outside Costa Rica, and possibly both the Dominican Republic and Haiti. Whereas Paraguay's PRC supremacy used to rest on one PRC—the CPES—these nations now generally boast multiple PRCs of note.

3. *Nations where both PRCs and universities contribute a major share of the research.* Brazil, Mexico, Costa Rica, and on a less impressive scale Colombia and Ecuador fit here.[20] In Brazil and Mexico, universities lead by number of personnel, but leadership shifts toward PRCs when the criteria accentuate qualitative rather than quantitative dimensions.

4. *Nations where PRCs clearly have less weight than universities.* Leaving aside Cuba, which has no PRCs (but some interesting public research centers), Venezuela is the only sure case.[21] And Venezuela, along with Mexico, Brazil, Colombia, and many smaller nations, exemplifies the growing importance of URCs, which not only capture our attention through comparisons with PRCs but may mark an evolution toward a greater role for PRCs.[22]

This overview sustains an assertion that PRCs, leaders in Latin American social research, now compose a formidable subsector of higher education. PRCs form a vital part of the diversification that has characterized Latin American higher education since the 1960s. No longer does Latin American higher education take place in only a national university or a set of public universities; it includes private, technical, regional, and other institutions. And just as university does not cover all higher education, it certainly does not cover all research.[23]

Despite such turns away from the university, the study of research in non-university settings remains scant even in the industrialized world (Clark 1993c; Gellert, Leitner, and Schramm 1990). A four-volume encyclopedia on higher education worldwide includes no chapter on research centers or the institutional setting of research (Clark and Neave 1992). This lack of work on research structures is part of a wider inadequacy in the higher education literature, on structures other than traditional public universities. Both institutional diversification and inadequate study of it are common in most of the world. Higher education increasingly means more than "university," but the literature is slow to reflect that.

Like other research centers, PRCs should be considered part of higher education.[24] The lacuna is at least as large there as for any other major part of higher education; few works on it exist outside the United States, and only one Latin American book stands out as an exception (Brunner and Barrios 1987), followed by a fine CLACSO (1991) survey and analysis of its own constituent centers, and only a few national studies. Other than those used for the conceptual framework, few secondary sources exist for the present study; instead, the researcher must turn to archives, evaluations by donors, documents and self-descriptions at individual institutions, and interviews. Fortunately, this can be done in a way that relates PRCs to other research institutions, thus providing a broad, though obviously not comprehensive, vision beyond PRCs.[25]

Reasons for the lack of work on PRCs include the recency of their huge growth coupled with the general lack of analytical work on higher education. Another factor is the image of heroic PRCs upholding freedom against tyranny; to an extent, mere existence has marked success, and analysis, especially critical analysis, might seem pointless, petty, or regressive.[26] Perhaps, too, researchers at PRCs are reluctant to analyze their own institutions, which serve them well. In any event, these researchers work within funders' "programs" or projects, and research on research is not a designated priority. By contrast, study of grassroots organizations is a funding priority, contributing to a growth of literature on these nonprofit neighbors that far outstrips research on PRCs.[27] Notwithstanding this growth, the general lack of work on the third sector outside the United States has been another reason for the lack of work on PRCs.

Whatever the explanations, the inadequate analysis of Latin America's PRCs means inadequate appreciation of their weight and spread. For example, the proliferation and importance of PRCs outside the Southern Cone is only sporadically recognized. Similarly, inadequate analysis means inadequate appreciation of the diverse and astonishing achievements of these organizations. Given their international prestige, however, inadequate attention also means inadequate appreciation of their problems and limitations.

Far from dismissing the rest of Latin American higher education, a study of PRCs offers a fresh perspective on it. Despite some losses to PRCs, universities retain major political, social, and economic roles, including heavy representation within its 7 million students of the privileged classes, the training and recruiting of its countries' leaders, contributions to social and political legitimacy, safeguards for freedom, and forums for protest. Yet even the public university, easily the most studied component of higher education, has been the subject of woefully little analytical work given its importance and given the literature on other social and political institutions. Even though a growing core of Latin American scholars is producing more research, very few foreign scholars make the study of Latin American higher education a major pursuit, and books with ample empirical bases and regional scope are scarce (Courard 1993; Levy 1986).

This is not the place for a fuller literature review, nor does this study concentrate inclusively on higher education.[28] Still, analysis of why PRCs grow tells us much about university performance—its failure to meet expectations but also its paradoxical successes, such as producing social scientists who wind up at PRCs. More generally, comparisons with PRCs highlight by contrast major features of university life, including funding and governance, and major features of university social science, including its academic and political orientations. In particular, comparison with PRCs informs us about a vital but barely explored feature of the region's universities, their URCs. The present study should, therefore, help to fill a void, moving us a step closer to informed views of the Latin American university and research landscape. Those views could assume extra importance as policy-making agencies, domestic and foreign, contemplate change.[29]

International Patterns and Issues

This study also contributes to the literature on comparative higher education by exploring the fundamental question of research's institutional setting. What follows here, to provide context, is an international overview of where research is housed and where PRCs exist.

Presumptions of a strong, natural affinity between research and universities base themselves excessively and stereotypically on U.S. experience. Some affinity does exist in the modern university, but it is neither overwhelming nor inevitable (Clark 1993b; Wittrock 1985: 13–18). On the contrary, multiplying nonuniversity research centers leave teaching aside, and the trend will likely continue, especially as governments seek to cut costs through direct, competitive funding of their research needs, uncomplicated by teaching and other university activities; at the same time, critics point to the dangers of the trend toward research centers (Clark 1993a; Neave 1993: 160). In any case, the centers clearly constitute an important part of the enormous institutional fragmentation associated with an era of both mass and specialized higher education.

Nor is the presumption of a university research setting historically sound. University control over advanced knowledge has been much less common than university control over certification of general knowledge (Geiger 1992; Ben-David 1977). Centuries ago, leading universities at Paris, Oxford, and Cambridge resisted a research mission. At other times, they were not given the option. By the twentieth century all advanced countries had centrally financed, specialized research institutes in fields considered crucial to national development (Schwartzman 1984: 202; Ben-David 1971: 173).

Latin America's own research roots are not firmly in the university. On the contrary, attempts by domestic reformers and foreign donors to place research squarely within the university confronted an alien history. Observatories, museums, health organizations, and the like—not universities—provided the major homes for the arrival of scientific research via European immigrants decades earlier, though URCs also arose; and most intellectual influence on social policy came from *pensadores* (thinkers) outside the university (Schwartzman 1985: 104; Balán 1982: 220). Contemporary data showing just 25 percent of R&D in universities contradict myth and hope, not history.

Regarding contemporary reality in other regions, most of continental Europe, led by France, houses research mainly outside the university. The university concentrates on professional training and certification. When French university professors do research it is usually outside their institution, with separate government funding. French research takes place chiefly in the CNRS, formed in 1939 from the centralization of specialized institutes, not from either usurpation of university research or the undirected pluralist proliferation that characterizes Latin America. By midcentury many smaller centers developed outside the CNRS, with public financing. France exemplifies Europe's slow acceptance, and weak implementation, of the research-teaching ideal. Despite some overlap in personnel and functions and despite much criticism, institutional separation is more extreme in France than any other developed nation (Neave 1993; Fox 1990: 95–98; Ben-David 1977: 17, 40, 107). The Soviet Academy of Sciences is another example of the pattern's wide dissemination in Europe.[30]

Even the German university-research nexus hardly matches conventional impressions, which stem from Germany's pioneering role in creating the research university early in the nineteenth century. Wilhelm von Humboldt inspired the University of Berlin with the idea of tying research and teaching together and imbuing students with the research ideal. By the end of the century, the university was the main home for research and the model for many in Europe and beyond (Ben-David 1977: 62). Before long, however, professional training gained enough political strength to vie with research for the university's mission. That strength increased with the "massification" of the 1960s, when attempts to create protected research universities fizzled. Earlier, university rigidity in not accommodating new fields and nonchaired professors had stimulated the creation of extrauniversity research centers, led by the Max Planck Institute (Mommsen 1987; Ben-David 1971: 132–33). Nonprofit institutions are growing with the aid of government money and university problems; they constitute one of the four research sectors. Even in mainstream fields—history is one—an increasing number of professors do extrauniversity research at least part-time. The locus of German research today arguably lies outside the university (Beyerchen 1990; Gellert 1993).

Elsewhere in Europe there are some think tanks, such as the Netherlands Scientific Council for Government Policy. Often these are publicly funded, sometimes they are linked to political parties, sometimes they are international in composition, as with the European Centre for Policy Studies. And formerly communist nations have moved to a variety of research institutions.[31]

U.S. universities replaced German ones as the recognized world leaders in research. Their ascension owed much to an ingenious adaptation of the German model. Pivotal was the construction of a potent and secure graduate level tied to research yet politically viable by virtue of its fit alongside a general undergraduate level. Graduate studies have their own identity, legitimacy, and control over access and curriculum. By contrast, European graduate education is both weak and hardly distinguishable from the undergraduate level, while Japanese graduate education is more formal than strong (Rhoades 1991; Clark 1993a). Further, the professions do not dominate university units as they do in Europe, and U.S. interinstitutional diversity allows some universities to develop elite or specialized research missions while most institutions concentrate on teaching. Extrauniversity research is proportionally smaller in the United States than in Europe, claiming no major area of its own (Ben-David 1971: 147), whereas universities set the general research course.

But university dominance must be qualified even in U.S. research. It holds for basic research but not for overall R&D, where industry does the bulk. Even for basic research, the university lead was not secure until the 1920s and now holds only in comparison to any single other institutional type rather than to all others combined (Gumport 1993: 243–44; Geiger 1986).

Although the U.S. research university emerged soon after the Civil War, the early twentieth century saw the creation of many PRCs, including what Karl and Katz (1981: 245) call "universities without students." The Rockefeller Institute for Medical Research, the Carnegie Institute of Washington, and the Russell Sage Foundation were early leaders. Industrial laboratories, including those at GE, ATT, and Dupont, were also prominent. In 1927 the Brookings Institution was formed from preexisting groups to bring research knowledge to policymaking. By the 1950s, policy advice from think tanks was institutionalized. This was followed by a proliferation of these groups: two-thirds of the roughly 100 think tanks based in Washington D.C. have been established since 1970 (J. Smith 1991: 214). Along with such liberal and centrist think tanks as the Urban Institute and RAND have come such conservative ones as the AEI, the Heritage Foundation, the Hoover Institution, and Cato and Manhattan Institutes. Hundreds of think tanks have been identified. Additionally, both GRCs and for-profit research groups limit university dominance. Universities have responded by creating a variety of URCs.[32]

In Asia, Japan stands out since World War II for the preeminent research role has been played by for-profit enterprises, although universities also play a role—and there is some interest in PRCS (Bartholomew 1990; Smith pc). China's emulation of the Soviet system, featuring large institutes doing most of the nation's research and none of its teaching, has not precluded the creation of more autonomous, government-funded centers outside the ministries, such as the Development Research Center. Since the late 1970s, China's modernization policies have included support for research universities. South Korea, Taiwan, Singapore, and Malaysia rely heavily on GRCS and URCS (Altbach i). Malaysia's single important PRC, the ISIS, was created by the government in 1984 to supply policy advice.

India is a leader not only in Asia's research overall but also in its variety of research sites (Geithner i). Prior to the twentieth century the Indian university lacked a research tradition, and civil servants accounted for most of the social research (Datta 1989: 78–79). Newly independent India quickly turned to national laboratories instead of to universities, and these laboratories have generated most of India's research. Later, the Ford Foundation aided in the creation of management institutes. Since late 1970s, PRCS have proliferated, sometimes established by former government officials. They have attracted philanthropic funding along with funding from national and state governments (Eisemon i-1; Eisemon 1981: 169–74).

Universities are comparatively central to research in Africa. But again, little research was done in the colonial era, and at independence universities were looked to mainly for career training. The centrality of university research is fading in Nigeria, Kenya, and other African nations, although another trend is toward URCS with their own libraries and laboratories (Eisemon 1981: 182; Court 1991: 333). As in Asia, an ever-expanding range of research centers includes governmental, parastatal, international industry, and national and local NGOS, all competing for funds (Coombe 1991: 40–42). Government hires university social scientists, who are civil servants in any case. But the collapse of public bureaucracies and universities, joined by the World Bank's and AID's support for private sector development, is promoting international organizations, consulting centers, and quasi-research NGOS, including some social science training. Most of these lack notable or stable research programs and are borderline PRCS. The Nigerian Institute of Social and Economic Research connects to some of these PRCS, and University of Ibadan social scientists staff consultancy firms. Stronger examples of PRCS are the African Centre for Technology Studies in Kenya, the Centre for Basic Research in Uganda, and SAPES in Zimbabwe. As the

Nigerian case suggests, serious prospects exist for PRC expansion in Africa, especially given the World Bank's interest in new ways to structure research (Eisemon i-2; Court pc; Gerhart pc).

The international perspective thus shows the Latin American research structure as fitting a norm in that it bypasses the university. The university is only one historic and contemporary option as a research locus, and never attains a monopoly. Recent trends show an increasing number of research homes both within and outside the university. No settled view emerges of what is the best mix, let alone the best institution—quite the opposite. Nations around the world are dissatisfied with the way extant structures perform; or they see new research needs requiring new institutional homes. The proper institutional setting for research is a contemporary policy question of great importance. PRCs are an increasing part of the answer, especially for social research and especially for Latin America. The assumption must be discarded that the existence of think tanks or PRCs depends "quite heavily on unique attributes of the American political system . . . and social system . . . not to be found in other countries" (Weaver 1989: 577).

2 Mapping the Center and Periphery

The universe of PRCs, like that of other nonprofits, is varied and complex. To map it requires an analysis of PRCs alongside related institutions, which lends perspective on PRCs. Comparisons between PRCs and other organizations therefore appear throughout the book. As a first step, reference to other organizations is essential for defining PRCs.

No clear-cut line defines the universe of PRCs.[1] The goal here is not to dichotomize between PRCs and other institutions; it is to understand the PRCs' domain, including the mix surrounding it.

Many organizations not treated as PRCs share some of their characteristics. These organizations include nonprofits that are not research oriented and research centers that are public or for-profit.[2] Then too, variation exists among PRCs; to call an organization a PRC is not to assume it is identical to other PRCs. Nevertheless, certain factors fix the center of gravity of PRCs. Beyond that, reasonableness and explicitness are the guiding principles by which institutions are labeled PRCs. If one acknowledges complexity and ambiguity, noting where the periphery lies and where debatable contours emerge, there is nothing wrong with concentrating on selected components of a center or even with analyzing centers that others might reasonably exclude from the PRC universe. On the contrary, there is much right with such an approach: we gain perspective on criteria and, more importantly, on organizations kindred to PRCs. Indeed, areas of overlap and interaction between the third sector and each of the other two sectors, as well as between PRCs and other nonprofits, are illuminated. We map the terrain to gain a realistic, broad, and useful view of these centers and their pertinent periphery.

The term *periphery* is especially apt for its double meaning: (1) the outer reaches of a phenomenon, in contrast to its core, and (2) the surrounding space beyond the strict limits of the phenomenon. Institutions on the first periphery are PRCs, whereas institutions on the second are not, but that line is not always clear or vital. The same holds for the line between "classic" PRCs at the core and PRCs on the first periphery. But no confusion arises between the core and the second periphery, where fundamental differences always appear.

CRITERIA

Structural Identity: Separateness

PRCs are freestanding. They are not part of other organizations. They are not part of governments or universities or other private organizations. They may be linked to such entities but only if they enjoy their own separate, juridical identity.

Networks of PRCs challenge but do not necessarily negate separateness. If we temporarily leave aside international networks, Chile's Academy of Christian Humanism was the most prominent network. But research was done by affiliated PRCs under the AHC aegis rather than by the AHC per se. The AHC itself was not a PRC so much as an umbrella for PRCs. At the peak of its protective role under military government in the 1970s and 1980s, before it became a teaching university separate from most research units, the AHC had institutional agreements with two international networks, covered six research programs, and sheltered many otherwise separate PRCs.[3]

More often, PRCs are identifiable single entities, even when they subsume particular "areas," "programs," or "centers" or when they are criticized by evaluators as "holding companies." El Colegio de México is the main multi-unit PRC examined here. Without its less weighty programs, it comprises seven centers: African and Asian affairs, demography and urban development, economics, history, international relations, literature and linguistics, and sociology. Argentina's Di Tella Institute (ITDT 1990: 6) has both an economics and a social center as well as an associated education center; the Bariloche Foundation has departments. Even esteemed units are usually less well known than the PRC that houses them, as with CPDOC at Brazil's Getú-lio Vargas Foundation. Colombia's CINDE and CCRP, Peru's GRADE, and Venezuela's IESA like Cato and Brookings in the United States, further show that most PRCs are identified integrally much more than by their component units.

Major questions about PRCs' structural identity turn more on relations beyond the individual center than by those contained within it. Consider private entities that create and maintain their own research centers, a situation paralleled when the government or the university is the larger entity. Centers physically located inside the entity are not PRCs because they are not freestanding. Yet the difference may be slight between these centers and those PRCs that work for the entity while holding a separate juridical status.[4] The larger private entities include political parties, unions, businesses, and religious, professional, and social movement or advocacy organizations—or associations of groups of any of the above.

In Colombia, for example, political parties draw on their own PRCs; and PRCs specializing in coffee, sugar, or cement work closely with the businesses that fund them. Other Colombian businesses use internal research units (Aldana i). CINEP is linked to Colombia's Jesuits, as CERPE, CIDE, and CEAS are to Venezuela's, Chile's, and Brazil's Jesuits. The Xavier educational center was a similar center in the Dominican Republic, whereas that nation's CEPAE is linked to the Council of Ecumenical Churches, which has Canadian and U.S. counterparts (Sánchez M. i-1). CIEF, which is tied to Uruguay's church, does research on topics such as the family. Thus we already see ample overlap and interaction between PRCs and other non-profits as well as for-profits.

The size of Mexico's PRC sector depends partly on the liberalness of definition regarding the separateness of centers—how far out we go on the periphery. The possibilities include the research center of Mexico's major labor union, Jesuit and Dominican think tanks, and centers linked to the main political party (PRI) and businesses. The party has a research arm at the national level and one in each state, but these arms do little research— rather, they publicize and organize seminars and consultations (Bailey 1988: 95–96). And they lack autonomy. Calling this kind of party organ a PRC (as in Brazil) seems more of a stretch than it does in Colombia. Also, private status is dubious in connection with what has functionally been a government party.

Mexican businesses have long had units for data collection, description, and simple analysis. Most of these units occur at the level of economic group or of peak association, which represents many enterprises; COPARMEX for example, has its own Institute of Strategic Studies, and the CCE has its own CEESP. CEESP supplies legislative analyses, statistical compendiums, market surveys, and reports on such issues as the North American Free Trade Agreement; these are used and cited beyond the business sector. Counterparts exist in some states. Moreover, CEESP's research has become more sophisticated and has branched out to include economics and even sociology. But the CCE business entity controls CEESP's research agenda (Estévez i-1; Shafer 1973).[5] Activity tilted closer to PRC criteria when the National Bank of Mexico helped create IBAFIN as a nonprofit center for research and training in finance, banking, and socioeconomic issues; when IBAFIN closed in 1984, its assets were transferred to CIDAC, which is definitely a PRC.

Business-related research centers are growing in other Latin American countries as well, because of political, economic, and higher education trends.[6] These centers merit increased attention; but insofar as most are not truly freestanding, this study includes them only marginally, for comparative purposes. Much the same holds for consulting centers. They raise definitional issues regarding task, but they also raise doubts about their separateness. Thus they fall outside the core of PRCs to the extent that they (1) merely respond to dictated assignments and (2) do so through confidential, subscription, or other private communication to bosses or clients rather than through the open dissemination of findings that is expected in academic research. But even core PRCs engage in consulting, so that the lines are fuzzy, a reflection of the increasing connections between nonprofit and for-profit sectors.

Nor is the separateness of center from university always easy to judge. The Laboratory of Social Science is formally part of Venezuela's national university, but it functions autonomously, with external funds. Even closer to PRCs are research centers that are private by virtue of location inside a private university. Although they are not PRCs—because they are not freestanding—some nonetheless have only weak links to their university. Some indeed form and operate largely to emulate PRCs' successes. CAIE is officially part of Mexico's leading economics university, ITAM, yet functions with considerable autonomy. CISEPA functions inside Peru's Catholic university but receives no money from it (Spalding 1991: 60). Colombia and Argentina offer further examples of research centers that combine a presence on campus (including the sharing of professors) with considerable autonomy in finances, governance, and identity.

Other university centers like those at the Dominican Republic's Pedro Henríquez Ureña Universidad, are so directly tied to their wider institution that people identify activities more with the institution than with the center. This is the typical U.S. pattern as well, though examples of greater separateness also exist (e.g., the National Opinion Research Center at the University of Chicago). Sometimes complications, such as those faced by Mexico's CAIE (Estévez i-1), lead to formal separation. This was the fate of Georgetown University's Center for Strategic and International Studies. Stanford University furnishes two prominent examples, the Hoover Institution and the Stanford Research Institute.[7]

Structural Identity: Private Versus Public

Structurally freestanding, PRCs must also be juridically private. They are legally constituted as private organizations, generally *asociaciones civiles* or *fundaciones.* This definition could be tautological for PRCs; the point is that private legal status is a condition for inclusion as a PRC.

Sectoral definition with identified boundaries is a major concern in the nonprofit literature, and empirical studies repeatedly reveal sectoral overlap and fuzziness (Powell 1987). Considerable ambiguity surrounds the functional privateness of many juridically private organizations worldwide, including educational ones. This privateness, in higher education and elsewhere, is most commonly and fruitfully determined by finances, followed by governance (Levy 1979). According to these criteria, PRCs will prove to be quite private. Whereas many legally private institutions rely heavily on steady government finance, most PRCs rely heavily on private sources, and most of their public money comes from contracted services rather than subsidies. Privateness also appears in governance, where the privateness of nonprofits is again often in doubt. PRCs usually have ample autonomy from government control.[8]

In any case, research centers that are both freestanding and juridically private count here as PRCs, with the actual degree of privateness a matter of empirical determination.[9] To handle the "private" criterion differently would invite an unmanageable mess, whereas this way allows a clear designation of what is and what is not a PRC while still leaving open, beyond the definition of PRC, a determination of core versus peripheral privateness.

Despite both the juridical and behavioral privateness of PRCs, I shy away from the term *independent,* used commonly in Chile and beyond, because PRCs interact intensively with others and because most are utterly *de*pendent on external sources for income.[10] In the jargon of organizational sociology, PRCs would be private institutions, usually specialist, with narrow niches, and adjusting through both choice and accommodation to the demands and opportunities of their environment, while change comes largely through the creation of new institutions (Hannan and Freeman 1977).

By stressing nonprofit status—which fits the reality of the great majority of PRCs—we do not exclude for-profit centers if they are separate from larger for-profit organizations and if they focus on research as a core activity. In practice, few centers meet these criteria. But as is recurrently a problem in the identification of nonprofit organizations, a center may be commercial in nature and yet avoid the distribution of profits by redeploying or otherwise consuming earnings. Also common among nonprofits generally and PRCs specifically (Orlans 1972) is the co-existence of profit-making activities alongside nonprofit activities. PRCs may legitimately pursue and then reroute commercial income to their research activities. But nonprofit centers created by for-profit firms—less to do research than to make money—fall into more dubious terrain, as with Peruvian centers created to lure international philanthropy. Those centers fail to meet our definitional criteria on task.

Task

Task is as important as structural identity in identifying PRCs: PRCs are research organizations. The term PRC excludes academic organizations geared to associational activities, discussion, or coordination more than to research. Ford-funded examples include Brazilian associations in science, social science, and population studies and the Center for Mexican Writers, once a favored Rockefeller recipient; the Venezuelan Association for Scientific Advancement, a nonprofit created in 1950, has been a major forum for scientific discussion and promotion (Vessuri 1984: 201), as has Peru's Permanent Seminar on Agrarian Research.

Above all, I exclude institutions where teaching is the main work. Most higher education organizations in Latin America and elsewhere, especially private ones, do not do much research; they primarily teach undergraduates—students at the first postsecondary level. This holds true for public technical institutions, as well, such as Mexico's IPN. These institutions may do much of the research in their fields, but that research remains subordinated to teaching.

As research organizations, PRCs emphasize investigation and writing. Additionally, the investigation and writing should have some academic flavor. For example, the research agenda must not be dictated solely by external nonacademic interests, and dissemination must not be restricted to bosses or clients. But most PRCs do not do research exclusively, nor is all their research academic. Matters of degree, then, are critical. It is difficult to establish a line regarding academic flavor: only in classic PRCs is this flavor unsullied or at least dominant. It is easier to insist that a PRC make research at least as integral as any other activity; in centers with more than two activities, research may be the single most important undertaking even if it does not account for the bulk of its work. In polling centers, like Gallup-Argentina or CEOP in Mexico, it is not enough that their data be used in research elsewhere if the centers themselves do not incorporate research (with some academic flavor) as a major task.

The determination of how much a center devotes itself to research is not always clear. For one thing, lines between individuals and their institutions are sometimes fuzzy, especially when dealing with a major figure; Venezuela's free-market-oriented CEDICE, associated with the Chamber of Commerce as well as the Metropolitan University, is not much of a PRC beyond the influential and respected work of economist Emeterio Gómez. For another, many centers exaggerate their research activity. Most of all, several tasks undertaken by centers blend in with research.

Rather than occupying ourselves with defining one center in and another out according to their relative emphasis on academically oriented research, let us proceed with the idea that the more a center does this sort of work, the more it fits the study. I deal marginally with many organizations that are weak on this criterion and concentrate on those that are strong on it. Moreover, when dealing with centers that handle multiple tasks, my focus is on the research aspects.

Just as no academic flavor need permeate all activities, research need not be basic. In fact, PRCs do more policy research than basic research, a key to their importance beyond their own walls. Many employees are "social analysts" (Brunner and Barrios 1987: 182) more than academic social scientists. Many PRCs are think tanks; by a broad definition of think tank, most are just that. On the other hand, though many think tanks are PRCs, others are not private, not freestanding, and not engaged in their own research.

Where think tanks do an adequate amount of research, their applied orientation may again raise questions about whether the freestanding criteria applies to behavioral as well as juridical status. Links to particular political parties vary, as they do in the United States. Some borderline PRCs risk subordinating research to policy and politics, whereas the research weight of an El Colegio or most well-known U.S. think tanks is unassailable. In between, Chile's CED has been a surer PRC than the CPU for Christian Democracy or than the CEP on the liberal right (Godoy i). Once more, the effort to define PRCs shows how they link up beyond the nonprofit sector, this time toward the public sector.

Regarding academic field of research, the definition of task is inclusive. PRCs may deal with any field or combination of fields. Still, observed concentrations give a better sense of the subject matter: (1) Research clusters around the social sciences, especially sociology and economics. (2) This, however, usually means applied work in a variety of social fields more than basic disciplinary research. (3) PRCs increasingly move beyond social concerns to topics such as technological adaptation and the environment. (4) Most PRCs specialize; chapter 7 considers the limitations where pluralism in the nonprofit sector builds from the narrow niches of component organizations.

Chilean data—the most comprehensive for any nation's PRCs—show sociologists as easily the most numerous of the disciplinary researchers, followed by economists and specialists in education. But the nature of PRC work tends to blur training background, rather than maintaining disciplinary boundaries the way universities do (Lladser 1987; Garretón 1981: 66–75), so specialties range from conventional social sciences to social activism. Outside Chile, the two leading disciplines also appear to be sociology and economics, but with economics lacking the solid university home it has in Chile and with centers featuring contract research.[11] A Paraguayan survey shows that PRC tasks include social studies on youth, culture, women, needy children, special education, human rights, and judicial assistance, with little academic social science (CIRD 1990; Cerna pc).

Political studies at PRCs are usually political sociology, political economy, or above all, policy analysis, but a more identifiable political science focus has also emerged, as work on voting behavior shows. And three key reasons for the preponderance of sociology and economics over political science are receding: (1) the limits that regimes set for study and, relatedly, for action by social groups that might use the research, (2) the view that economics basically determines politics or that institutions (from parties to legislatures to elections) are marginal to Latin American policymaking, (3) a lack of scholars, as disciplines developed at different paces in Latin America, with political science trailing, partly as a result of donors' priorities.

PRCs also include anthropologists, historians, philosophers, lawyers, and other professionals; yet these researchers routinely turn their attention to PRC projects outside the core areas of their training. Thus, although historians may trace the evolution of current issues, PRCs with serious history programs are relatively scarce; Uruguay's CINVE and Peru's Bartolomé in Cusco (CBC) are among the notable exceptions. So are PRCs in anthropology, like Chile's CAPIDE. Humanities is especially rare. Also in Chile, CENECA is the main exception; and philosophy became part of the PRC scene after the military takeover in 1973 (Jaksić 1989: 11). The unusually broad El Colegio de México has both a humanities and a history center. The lack of emphasis on most of these disciplines relates to their continuance within the university but also to the PRC premium on direct contributions to development. Centers linked to larger private entities predictably emphasize policy work following the entity's main concern: business-related centers focus on economics and finance, union and social movement centers focus on socioeconomic matters, and partisan centers focus on politics. Among PRCs with large graduate programs, business and management are important fields.

An exception is Chile's CECI, a natural science center and a core PRC (Teitelboim i; Hidalgo i). It boasts four research areas, especially biophysics. Colombia is exceptional for the major presence of PRCs in science, alongside only a comparatively modest presence in social policy.[12] Brazil and Argentina established some early PRCs in science, which then met different fates; and CLAF is a regional nonprofit that has offered graduate studies in physics (Schwartzman 1991: 203; Vessuri 1986: 11).

But most PRCs that include natural science do not concentrate on it. Chile's ICAL works in biology but emphasizes social studies. Argentina's Bariloche Foundation concentrates on natural science in a few units, while most units do social research. More common is some mix of personnel within a given center or project, typically to attack a social problem with an interdisciplinary approach. Colombia's CCRP incorporates the biophysics of reproduction with population studies. Environmental study is a rising concern; CIPMA is a Chilean leader. "Appropriate technology" centers are likewise ascendant: CATER in Ecuador, CEMAT in Guatemala, and CETAL and TEKHNE in Chile employ engineers to study how people can construct solutions to their problems; and the Chile Foundation explores how to adapt advanced technology to humble settings (Baquedano 1989; Muga i). Ecuador's CIUDAD (N.d.) and ALAHUA employ architects in research, technical assistance, training, and diffusion in urban settings. Chile's GIA, GEA, and AGRARIA, like Peru's FDN, are counterparts in agrarian technology. Other PRCs, some for-profit, concentrate on industrial research.

Health-related foundations also run the gamut between the PRC core and periphery. Some specialize in the study of disease, as Venezuela's Luis Roche Foundation did in its day (Vessuri 1984: 203). Biological research at CIDEIM in Cali, Colombia, attacks tropical diseases. Some centers mix clinical medical practice with research. Argentina lists twenty-nine such medical "foundations," such as the Favaloro Foundation for Medical Research and Teaching and the Albert Einstein medical center, CIMAE, which claims twenty-five researchers (FJMA 1980: 266–67). Venezuela's AVEDIS and Trinidad medical centers show how prestigious professionals can mix clinical practice with continuing education, consulting for public policy, and applied and basic scientific research that does not require large laboratories (Pérez i). More commonly, physicians and medical researchers not in PRCs work with PRCs interested in health policy, as at Chile's CPU.

RESEARCH, PLUS

Because PRCs generally mix research with other activities, we must consider those activities to appreciate PRCs' range and importance. The main activities are graduate education, consulting, and social action.[13] To some extent, of course, the mixing of tasks goes against the notion of specialist institutions.

Graduate Education and Consulting

Chapters 6 and 7 analyze the teaching done at PRCs, but one must first consider how to judge whether institutions that teach are PRCs. Without attempting to dictate a firm line, I simultaneously exclude institutions focusing on undergraduate education and include institutions providing graduate teaching, which is more naturally linked with research. It would be arbitrary to exclude centers where research is at least a co-equal activity with teaching (which holds for probably no Latin American institution with many undergraduates).

This book makes only passing references to institutions where the primary emphasis is on teaching and is closely tied to practical training, even if they require a four-year degree for entrance. Examples include some major recipients of international philanthropy.[14] The agriculturally based CATIE in Costa Rica is one. So are several centers focusing on business and administration, an increasingly robust and competitive area of study. Panama's IPDE lacks a strong research effort. More prominent is Colombia's School of Business Administration, but even there graduate education occurs along with undergraduate education.

Because it lacks undergraduates, INCAE would more plausibly qualify as a PRC. Located in Nicaragua and Costa Rica, with Ecuador now "incorporated," INCAE was created in 1964 by Central American business, AID, and the Harvard Business School. It has added economic and political analysis and policy studies to ongoing activities that mix research and graduate teaching. Still, INCAE is a borderline PRC because research remains limited compared to master's degree studies, short-term training, and perhaps consultations (INCAE N.d.: 1–2).

Other business schools fit better as PRCs, though they are not drastically different from INCAE (Anderson 1987). Brazil's Getúlio Vargas Foundation, in São Paulo and Rio, carries out significant research. Venezuela's IESA combines graduate studies, short courses, and extensive consulting with research on economics, management, society, and development (Dent 1990b: 410; Kelly de Escobar i). At El Colegio de México, graduate education truly mixes with research in many fields. Indeed, research predominates. An increasingly important Mexican counterpart is CIDE, along with the leading provincial *colegios*. Other nations lack counterparts, which may not be surprising for small nations like the Dominican Republic; but even Argentina has only limited counterparts.

Although classic depictions of research associate it most closely with teaching, the complementary tasks most extensively and integrally linked to research in PRCs are consulting and social action *(promoción)*. Much of the consulting and social action amounts to political lobbying. Consulting and social action overlap when centers receive payments from third parties, or directly from popular groups, for *promoción*. These activities bring PRCs into cooperation for social action with the rest of the third sector as well as the public sector and with the for-profit sector for other consultancies.

The growth of consulting centers gives organizational form and direction to what has long been done ad hoc by individuals. Furthermore, consulting has increased with the rise of information needs, international philanthropy, and privatization. Most PRCs are now partly consulting firms. New centers account for much; older centers have moved in this direction; and many classic PRCs, among them Mexico's CEE, have long done consulting. According to the criteria established above, however, pure consulting firms are dubious as PRCs. Except for CIEA and the Economic and Development Foundation, the Dominican Republic's consulting centers exist basically for their direct clients and are known by few others. In between come many that publicly downplay their consultancies and exaggerate their research (though Bolivia's CINCO has stressed the former). Most of the fast-growing institutes dedicated to public opinion polling or other surveying are marginal to this study, as are consulting centers (e.g., Costa Rica's CINDE) that facilitate contacts between donors and recipients or that promote research more than they do it. But many bonafide PRCs, including Colombia's SER and FEDESARROLLO, also facilitate these contacts.

Mexico again illustrates the entrepreneurial flavor of many centers, mostly not PRCs and definitely not central to this study. The nation is well represented in the World Association for Public Opinion Research by both freestanding private centers and centers tied to larger private and public organizations (Basáñez i). In addition, financially oriented consulting firms are very important in Mexico City and Monterrey, less so in the more traditional business environment of Guadalajara. For example, the IME sells information on government legislation, especially regarding changes connected to the nation's move toward free market development. The center develops an analytical index and publishes a monthly journal. Yet the audience is limited to subscribing businesses: the center's own advertising stresses the provision of solicited information within days and describes its main task as "research at the service of business" (IME 1991). Other Mexican consulting centers provide an array of services in social, educational, communications, and technical fields (de Ibarrola pc-1).

Social Action

Like consulting, social action, or *promoción*, weaves PRCs through all three sectors. Both activities, sometimes intertwined, show PRCs building interactions among overlapping sectors and even stitching the sectors together. In social action, however, a clear ranking of the sectors appears: the intersection is least with the for-profit sector, ample with the public sector, and most extensive within the nonprofit sector. After all, social action encompasses the bulk of the organized third sector.

Promoción includes molding public opinion, professional lobbying, advising, training, project formation, information gathering and dissemination, and evaluations. Most beneficiaries are underprivileged and grassroots or community organizations (Navarro, 1994), though others include middle-class advocacy groups and governmental or international agencies.

If the research component is too limited, the organizations are not PRCs. This holds for many grassroots nonprofits dedicated to charity or empowerment, even if they perforce must gather and use some information. Costa Rica's Association of New Alchemists has just one researcher on its thirteen-member staff (Carroll 1992: 212–13). Closer to PRCs are many *promoción* centers that do some descriptive studies, as in Ecuador. And many social action centers do enough research—in order to guide that action—to qualify as PRCs. Bolivia's DESEC shows a now typical mix: active in *promoción*, especially in peasant affairs, housing, and forestry, it also does research on socioeconomic issues in rural Bolivia and combines all this with preparation of projects and seminars, training, and service (DESEC 1990).

It is not just a matter of doing research on the one hand and social action on the other. Much research is "action research" or "committed research." NGOs may outweigh "independent research centers" in some nations in their total number of social scientists (Calderón and Provoste 1990: V–9). But the relation of the research and social action tasks is mutually reinforcing more than mutually exclusive. If the number of PRCs is exaggerated by counting all PRCs that also do *promoción*, it is understated by not counting social action centers that increasingly have research components.

The blurred borders between PRCs and social action centers can be further appreciated within nations. One approach is to review Ford Foundation recipients in several large nations. While Ford is the chief funder of Latin America's PRCs, "education and culture" is but one of its seven program areas. Recipients getting grants under the categories of human rights and social justice, governance and public policy, population, international affairs, urban poverty, and rural poverty and resources may or may not do major research, but at least in the funder's eye, this research is at the service of other concerns.[15]

Most Ford recipients in Brazil have been action oriented more than research oriented. A partial list includes the Center for the Defense of Women's Rights, the Brazilian Association for Video in Popular Movements, the Brazilian Interdisciplinary Aids Association, the Association for Community Cooperation in Disadvantaged Areas of Salvador, and some church organizations such as Caritas. On the research end (Schwartzman pc-3) are IUPERJ, IDESP, Social Science Research Associates, CEBRAP, the Carlos Chagas Foundation, ECIEL, the Getúlio Vargas Foundation, and the Institute for the Study of Religion. Ford's listing of Mexican PRCs, encompassing the Barros Sierra Foundation, the CEE, and El Colegio de México plus some provincial *colegios,* is also shorter than its listing of social action centers. The Center for Development Assistance has received aid for work on nutrition; Education and Development of the West has received funds for action research on rural development in Jalisco; and the Center of Research and Rural Training has received funds for applications and evaluations of methods of peasant training (FF archives, computer printout). Beyond Ford's list are places like CEESTEM, which uses interviews and data in its social action projects. Although Mexico has lagged behind many Central and South American nations in *promoción,* socioeconomic crisis, coupled with diminished state subsidies and a new attitude of nonreliance on the state, has led to changes (de Ibarrola pc-1; Foweraker and Craig 1990).

Even in Chile, where the academic component is unusually strong, social action is part of the typical task for Ford's recipients. CIDE's research staff meets routinely with field staff to work in community education, and the Center for Women's Studies works directly to help the nation's peasant women. PET aims to strengthen the labor movement and help poor people forced out of jobs. It operates through its fourteen full-time researchers but also through training, advice, and extension just as many centers not targeted by Ford show strong professional and academic participation in applied research (Klenner and Vega 1989). Social action nonprofits are also engaged in tasks not requiring much research.[16] Perhaps only ten Chilean centers of any size make research paramount over action, the same number estimated earlier for Buenos Aires's academically respectable PRCs (Brunner 1990a; Balán 1982: 237).

At the IEP in Peru, research has been the overwhelming mission, but most of Peru's centers show a different mix (Cotler, Grompone, and Rospigliosi 1988). Many formed at the end of the 1970s, drawing on both leftist activists and technical specialists who had worked for the military government. Social scientists are prominent at many centers dealing with community development, popular participation, and education. But countering that trend is the conservative Summer Institute of Linguistics, a church-related organization that has done some serious linguistic research yet mostly produces bible translations and its own brand of social action (Walker i). Some centers do diagnoses only, while the Center of Participatory Studies is an ideological lobby. Even the better known centers have only small research staffs; probably only two or three centers more than ten years old would qualify as mostly research centers (Spalding 1991: 26–27). GRADE shows that the proportion of research can grow, however. While it remains a consulting firm that evaluates social projects, especially international ones, it also qualifies as a strong research center. Some members favor the academic trend, others oppose it, and some want a mix like that at Colombia's FEDESARROLLO (Arregui i).

FEDESARROLLO, in fact, shows that top Colombian PRCs do considerable applied research or extension. Further examples include CINEP and the National Forum of Colombia, which concentrate less on research than on advice to urban groups and other grassroots nonprofits. CINDE combines research with service, dissemination of information, and consultancies for international organizations, including the OAS, UNICEF, UNESCO, and the UNDP. FUNDAEC offers training along with research in the use of appropriate technologies. FESCOL finances socioeconomic research and helps present ideas to the government (B. Smith 1990: 312–13).

Other countries do less social action through nonprofit centers. Like Argentina, Venezuela is an example, despite exceptions like CISOR, a PRC eventually absorbed into a social action nonprofit; an increase in social action has been recently promoted through international assistance and government contracts (Vessuri i).[17] Whatever the trend, the research-social action mix is a salient characteristic of Latin America's PRCs and of its nonprofit sector generally.

OTHER RESEARCH CENTERS

Just as PRCs are not limited to research, so research centers are not limited to PRCs. Instead, PRCs are best seen as part of a mosaic of research structures. Many university and government centers undertake tasks that match the definitional criteria for PRCs and do so with a functional autonomy that bolsters the parallel. The same holds for many international research centers; beyond that, some research centers are simultaneously international and private.

University Research Centers (URCs)

The lines separating PRCs and university research centers are usually clear: URCs are not freestanding, and most are not private. Even so, URCs are in many ways halfway between mainstream university faculties and PRCs. URCs commonly emerge to give research a chance it does not otherwise have in the university.[18]

Mexico's UNAM has perhaps the most formidable of Latin America's many URC networks. The science part of the network includes fifteen institutes, eight centers, and three programs, in addition to laboratories and observatories. The humanities–social science part includes eight institutes and five centers (de la Fuente i; H. Muñoz i; UNAM 1988). The engineering institute was formed within UNAM, incorporating previously external units. UNAM's "centers" tend to be smaller but can grow into "institutes," or they may split off from them. All these units together (more from the science side) account for about 10 percent of the academic personnel (Reséndiz i; Suárez 1984: 29). The University of Costa Rica shows the URC pattern within a much smaller institution (Garita pc). Beyond such "national" institutions, URCs now exist in many other public and private universities. Three Mexican public examples are the Institute of Paper, Wood, and Cellulose at the University of Guadalajara, the Center of History and Social Research of the Autonomous University of Puebla, and the Center of Social Research at the University of Colima.

Compared to PRCs, URCs concentrate more on basic research. Yet URCs show more entrepreneurial zeal than do the traditional faculties. This is expected at private university URCs and is confirmed by those at the Dominican Republic's Catholic university, but even public university URCs now see a need and opportunity for effort. A weightier distinction between URC and PRC tasks concerns teaching. URCs do much more. University modernization programs frequently emphasized the creation of graduate education units combined with research. An important case was the University of Chile's ESCOLATINA, promoted by the Rockefeller Foundation and others as an economics center for Latin America (Coleman and Court 1992). These

URCs would be the counterparts to PRCs that combine research with graduate education.

Field of study is another area in which URCs and PRCs tend to differ. URCs concentrate much less in the social area, or in any single area. For example, at the Dominican Republic's national university, CIBIMA concentrates on marine biology while CERESD does social research. The natural sciences stand out at URCs because PRCs are generally inactive there. The cost is prohibitive. In addition, politics does not so readily push science out of universities. The URC lead in other fields is smaller but notable. Engineering and architecture are examples even in nations where PRCs are strong overall (Scherz i). Humanities, including history, is also more common at URCs, as for example the Center of Applied Linguistics at Haiti's National University. And even in social science, individual URCs generally cover more disciplines than their more specialist PRC counterparts.

Government Research Centers (GRCs)

Fields of study also tend to differ between PRCs and GRCs, the latter also known as government institutes, laboratories, observatories, and museums. GRCs include social science, especially if one so labels studies in education, but social science accounts for a minority of the research. GRCs usually emphasize applied science or technology, with agriculture and medicine prominently included (Roper and Silva 1983), fields where universities and businesses do too little research and where most PRCs do not operate.

Mexican GRCs do substantial work on energy, engineering, telecommunications, health studies, and the like (Fajnzylber 1987: 301; de Ibarrola pc-2). Alongside the technical institutions, which mostly teach, are networks of technical research institutes focusing on industrial and agricultural matters. International parallels exist: Malaysia has a rubber institute and also an economics institute; France has atomic energy, agricultural, and other national research institutes (R. Fox 1990: 99). These sorts of institutes have been prevalent in the large Latin American countries since the 1950s and reached smaller nations by the 1970s (Cano Gallego 1981: 28). Aided by research technology and expertise from international organizations, including the UNDP and the FAO, Chile developed twelve institutes—in fish development, metallurgy, agriculture, forestry, and so forth (Lavados i-2). Argentina exemplifies how fields of interest may involve the military, as with the navy's nuclear energy center, where achievement and continuity contrast with the otherwise turbulent context of Argentine research. Much Argentine scientific research takes place in large GRCS (Adler 1987). Fields of study like these explain why GRCS have larger research budgets than universities, even when universities have more researchers.

Most major differences between GRCS and PRCS relate to ownership. GRCS depend mostly on direct government funding and enjoy less autonomy. Definitionally, GRCS are obviously not private, and most are not freestanding.[19] Nonetheless, GRCS vary in their degree of contrast or similarity to PRCS. Physical location itself varies, with substantive consequences. Research centers proliferate within, or are linked with, specific ministries. But many are tucked into decentralized public agencies or parastatals that have grown alongside traditional ministries in recent decades (Segal 1985: 197). The petroleum agencies of Latin American's two largest producers, Venezuela and Mexico, have their own research centers.

The substantial autonomy at Venezuela's research centers suggests a continuum of GRCS, culminating in *public research centers*. Public by juridical identity, these centers are relatively freestanding and academically autonomous. The terminology highlights their symmetry with PRCS. Apart from the definitional division by juridical (public) status, two differences separate most public research centers from most PRCS: a reliance on government subsidies and a concentration on other than social studies. Large graduate programs may be a third difference. Yet public research centers are close enough academic kin to PRCS that they are often mistaken for them, just as PRCS receiving public funds are often mistaken for juridically public centers.

One of Latin America's leading public research centers, and also one of its leading science centers, is Venezuela's IVIC. Like the private IESA, and unlike any other nonuniversity institutions in the country, it grants its own graduate degrees. It autonomously defines its own research agenda and functions like a PRC (Vessuri 1984: 231), though its personnel interact with the national university. Also in Venezuelan science and graduate education is IDEA; cut out of IVIC, it was a public foundation (IDEA 1989) until its 1994 incorporation into the Simón Bolívar Universidad.

The concept of public research centers may even fit some of Cuba's many GRCS, from the Center of Research on the International Economy (something of an official think tank) to CEA, possibly the nation's most academically respected social research center, to the newer CEAP. Revolutionary Nicaragua also created public research centers, CIDCA among them.

Mexico stands out for public research centers in social research, another reason that a study of PRCs and their periperhy has greater relevance for Mexico than first appears. The kinship between public research centers and PRCs is especially strong because Mexico's leading PRCs—El Colegio de México, the regional *colegios,* and CIDE—are publicly funded, and teach. They are thus similar in some respects to the public CIESAS, which is tied to the venerable National Institute of Anthropology and History, which has established regional centers. CIESAS, a Ford Foundation recipient, has just 22 undergraduates, compared to 2,364 at the "national school" linked to the same institute; its 30 graduate students are equally split between the master's and doctoral programs. More like a typical Latin American PRC is CIESAS-Occidente in Guadalajara, which is marked by a substantial full-time staff and a lack of degree programs (ANUIES 1989; Wessman i). As indicated below, FLACSO could be added to the list of Mexican public research centers in the social realm.

Other Mexican public research centers concentrate in agriculture or the hard sciences. Overshadowing all in agriculture is the College of Postgraduates, henceforth referred to as Chapingo (for its location). This study refers to Chapingo more than any other single GRC. Chapingo has formal links to the agriculture ministry but is a research and graduate center with relative autonomy. It teaches nearly 500 graduate students, almost all at the master's degree level.

In science, with oceanography leading the way, CICESE in Baja California has approximately a hundred graduate students, almost as many full-time professors, and no undergraduates. National institutes include one each in astrophysics, optics, and electronics, all with graduate programs. But overshadowing all science centers is CINVESTAV. Created in 1960 for science research and graduate education (though it also has social departments tied mostly to education), CINVESTAV teaches some 650 students, 125 doctoral and the rest master's; 68 more, all master's, study in programs outside Mexico City (ANUIES 1989). Anticipated as a wing of the IPN, to which a legal knot remains, CINVESTAV has developed under revised decrees as an autonomous, decentralized public entity. It receives funds directly from the education ministry and allocates them as it sees fit, allowing for salaries higher than at the IPN. CINVESTAV also grants its own degrees and appoints, evaluates, and promotes its own professors. It is correctly perceived as its own academic institution (de Ibarrola pc-2, pc-3).[20]

Considering GRCs overall, the Dominican Republic approaches an extreme of low activity. Its GRCs are negligible, allowing for exceptions in agriculture (Sánchez M. i-2; Dore i-2). Some fear a Peruvian echo: several Peruvian GRCs created in the years of reformist military rule, 1968–1975, have disappeared, and privatization threatens the rest (Cotler pc). But the World Bank (1985) found 934 researchers and well over a thousand other professionals in science and technology working for Peru's ministries in eighty-five laboratories, forty-four field experiment stations or pilot plants, and forty-five other installations. It also found many GRCs to be semiautonomous and decried the lack of government coordination.

Bolivia has since 1984 created two GRCs to address the problem of otherwise limited social research needed by government policymakers. Alongside a counterpart in economics, UDAPSO employs about fifteen researchers on socioeconomic matters. It is deeply integrated into the network of ministries and has little autonomy over agenda-setting; reflecting the government's weakness, however, funding has come almost fully from international sources.

Brazil stands at the extreme of high GRC activity. São Paulo epitomizes the importance at the state level, as shown by the Butantan Institute and the Institute of Technological Research (both tied to the Ministry of Science and Technology) as well as the Biological Institute and the Agronomy Institute of Campinas. The Oswaldo Cruz Institute is a venerable biomedical GRC, municipal but tied to the health ministry. The national network is varied, led by GRCs like the Brazilian Center for Physics Research. Some museums do contract research. The network is strong in social research as well (Schwartzman pc-2; Schwartzman 1992). Among the best known institutions are the IPEA, which is linked to the economics ministry, and the IBGE. The IBGE, employing 11,000 full-time workers, was initially tied to the planning and economics ministry but then achieved status as a public foundation with its own juridical identity and some administrative and financial autonomy; it is an indirect part of the federal government.

International Research Centers (IRCs)

An additional home for research—the international research center, or IRC—finds its strongest representation in agriculture, which weighs so much within overall research expenditures. Granted, IRCs sit alongside other structures even in agriculture. PRCs do pursue agricultural economics, agricultural sociology, and various approaches to raising peasant consciousness, participation, and living standards, but their work is limited. GRCs form another piece of the puzzle. Universities participate both through faculties of agronomy and economics and through URCs; special agricultural institutions of higher education, concentrating on teaching, are prominent as well. Led by Rockefeller, foundations have supported each of these options. But the IRC, heavily dependent on international assistance, occupies a special place in agriculture.

CIMMYT has played a pioneering role in research on corn, wheat, barley, and other crops in Mexico and beyond. Additional IRCs follow the model, including CIAT in Colombia, which is based on joint efforts by the government, Rockefeller, and Ford. With roughly 100 scientists and 1,200 support staff, CIAT concentrates on spreading technology about tropical food production and quality.[21] The CIP, which focused on potato research, illustrates how host nations provide personnel and research emphases though senior researchers tend to come from the advanced nations. Violence by the Shining Path forced the transfer of many functions from Peru to Ecuador. CATIE covers Central American nations and the Dominican Republic for advanced training and research. The international research network in agriculture, formalized with the 1971 creation of CGIAR, extends beyond Latin America to the Philippines, India, Kenya, Nigeria, Liberia, Ethiopia, Syria, Italy, the Netherlands, and the United States. Agricultural IRCs remain financial priorities of foundations, AID, and others (Cassen 1986: 119). They enjoy—or suffer from, or both—some insulation from national research environments (Segal 1986a: 104); they also stimulate those environments, as with CIMMYT for Chapingo in Mexico.

Other than agriculture, IRCs tend to be in the social fields. Because of their special importance, CLACSO and FLACSO are introduced separately below. Those listed here are a sampling to help us appreciate the busy international institutional scene that echoes many of the dimensions already discussed for PRCs. Thus, training courses commonly exist alongside core research activities, yet few IRCs offer formal degree programs, and some centers promote or coordinate research more than they do it themselves. Moreover, IRCs vary as to private-public status. Like public research centers, many public IRCs approximate PRCs in their academic autonomy.

Unlike any GRCs or URCs, however, some IRCs are PRCs. Among the many IRCs that are intergovernmental, including several of the agricultural ones cited above, some have legal nonprofit status in their own nations (Brunner and Barrios 1987: 91). In Central America, CATIE is both intergovernmental and a nonprofit civil association, as is IICA, which is dependent on the OAS; INCAITI, on the other hand, is a public IRC (Vessuri 1986: 11; CSUCA 1989: 191–230).[22]

Several international associations have universities as members. Their goals feature university improvement, sometimes regarding research and including the promotion of research projects about universities. But most of them probably do not themselves do enough research to count as IRCs. Headquartered in Chile, CINDA runs programs and consultancies to modernize university management and pedagogy and to tie universities to industrial and local development (Lavados i-1). Launched with twelve universities as members, the Ajijic center performs some similar functions but is linked more to a single university, Mexico's Autonomous University of Guadalajara, which also has a strong presence in organizations that promote international contacts by leading educators (García Guadilla 1989: 122–23). Other networks include UDUAL, which covers Latin America, and CSUCA, which covers only Central America. CSUCA had grand designs for a regional coordination of Central America's public universities before it evolved into something of a regional research center; it now tries both to do research and to promote research at its seven member campuses.

Where international networks comprise mostly research centers rather than universities, the networks themselves still promote or coordinate research more than they do it. At FLACSO, constituent centers are, or approximate, PRCs. CLACSO incorporates university units as well as freestanding centers. CRIES tries to coordinate the best Central American PRCs while also publishing work itself (Fernández 1989: 28). ECIEL's focus was empirical economic studies (F. Herrera 1985: 318–21); RIAL's was international relations. SELA formed in 1975 to promote common positions among Latin American nations in international forums, and CEMLA formed in 1952 to serve central banks—two further examples of intergovernmental agencies with independent international legal status (SELA 1990: 2, 20).

The more the regional centers do research, the more they fall into the category of IRC. PISPAL, which has likenesses elsewhere in the Third World, draws support from Ford, Rockefeller, the IDRC, and the U.N. for its social science research on population control (Harkavy and Diescho 1988: 1–2). CET is a single-site regional center specializing in trade, transnationals, and technological applications. Some PRCs and IRCs rotate headquarters; ILET's began in Mexico in 1975 but shifted to Chile in 1983 and later added an Argentine site.[23]

IRCS or networks of IRCS may also be part of broader international organizations that are not primarily educational institutions, let alone research institutions. Centers tied to international companies might be cited, Bayer in Argentina for one, but with doubts about the weight of academic research as well as about separateness. More important here are centers linked to the large intergovernmental organizations (e.g., WHO), perhaps with cooperation from the host government. The intergovernmental organizations are homes, as well as financial sources, for IRCS.

UN agencies are the major examples.[24] CREFAL, which represents fifteen Latin American nations, is tied to UNESCO as well as to the OAS and the Mexican government, but it boasts academic autonomy and its own juridical status. In higher education studies, with its main center in Venezuela, CRESALC is also tied to UNESCO, again with some academic autonomy, though the primacy of coordination over research probably leaves CRESALC just outside the IRC category. RIDALC, which is linked to the UNDP, promotes interchanges. CEPAL, established in 1947, is especially important. It subsumes several IRCS and highlights both the intergovernmental status of many IRCS and the favored status of Santiago. Note, as examples, CELADE in demography and ILPES and CLADES in socioeconomic planning. Some IRCS that are not exclusively Latin American also have their regional headquarters in Santiago. One is the ILO, with its headquarters in Geneva and centers in several Latin American nations, such as CINTEFOR (1977) in Uruguay and PREALC in Santiago. For Central America, Costa Rica is the key host nation, as CSUCA, ICAP, and CATIE show.

TOTALS AND SPECIAL CASES

Totals

As this study focuses regionally, it obviously forgoes some advantages associated with intensive case studies. No presumption is made here that either approach is inherently better. The value of a broad, initial sweep in identifying patterns, variations, dynamics, issues, trends, and so forth must sooner or later be complemented by in-depth investigations of single nations and small groups of centers. Toward the other extreme, future work should include more standard surveying of PRCs throughout the region. This study is neither comprehensive nor the last word in what to examine.[25]

At least for now, it is more tempting than informative to state a total number for PRCs. Similar statements have been made for the far more studied U.S. panorama (Weaver 1989: 563). Obstacles to confident estimates are the variety there is in definition, in labeling, and in what merits coverage as well as the lack of official compilations or prior scholarly attention. These obstacles are not unusual for nonprofit or other private organizations, especially when they are small, multitudinous, rapidly evolving, unaccredited, and barely regulated. A minor adjustment in criteria or date can produce very different totals. Nonetheless, for those interested and for whatever it may be worth, some estimates follow.

Most regional tallies of research centers are ad hoc, or they focus on a particular subject area and thereby exclude many PRCs and include many centers that are not PRCs (e.g., CRESALC 1984; Dent 1990b). CLACSO's survey is the best for social science but, as shown just below, is inadequate for PRCs. Within Central America and the Caribbean, CRIES lists forty-eight member centers in its network on social and economic research, excluding nine "regional" ones that include South America and fifteen collaborative centers outside Latin America (Norori pc; CRIES 1991). But the list encompasses GRCs, URCs, an entire university, and various other associations. ASIES counts twenty-nine "private research centers" in Guatemala alone, if one excludes eight URCs, though ASIES acknowledges that some of the twenty-nine are "mixed," and the count excludes certain centers found in other surveys (Zelaya pc; Dent 1990b: 403–04).

The closest we get to comprehensive, consistent information is in the Southern Cone, but skepticism makes sense even there. A conservative total comes from an insistence that an academic focus be unadulterated or at least that participatory research be combined with and subordinated to it (Brunner and Barrios 1987: 193–94). For the mid-1980s, Chile, Argentina, Brazil, and Uruguay together would then have about 60 "independent academic centers," with 500 to 700 researchers, about half of them in Chile. Brazil's fewer PRCs represent a minority of the nation's social scientists, whereas Uruguay's represent nearly the totality. Numbers can go much higher by less stringent criteria, however. Argentina's total PRCs might be put at 30 or 70 or, less persuasively, many more.[26] A Uruguayan survey finds 112 NGOs doing research as a primary or secondary activity in 1991, 17 in the "social science" category; for 1990, 92 NGOs include 30 in the "study and research" category and many more in "applied research" (Barreiro and Cruz 1991; Barreiro and Cruz 1990; Cruz pc-1, pc-2).

Even the single most studied nation shows variable numbers. Chilean experts recognize that this variability stems largely from ambiguous reality. The most extensive survey finds some forty-nine PRCs with 664 professionals, perhaps more than half of whom claim to be full-time researchers. These 1987 figures considerably exceed those of a few years before and yet fall considerably short of those soon to follow. A good guess for 1990 was that nearly 900 people devoted most of their time to research, supported by numerous helpers (Lladser 1987: 11, 20; Lladser i-1).[27]

Difficulty in counting applies to the rest of South America as well. Spalding (1991) presents an extensive though not exhaustive listing of Peruvian centers considered for possible SAREC support, but many are mostly for *promoción*. A Paraguayan survey identifies 131 NGOs, but few do serious research even as a supplementary activity; instead, most do consultancies, training, project execution, *promoción*, and data gathering (CIRD 1990; Cerna pc). A reasonable listing focusing on social science in Bogotá approaches twenty PRCs, but beyond FEDESARROLLO, SER, and CINEP, solid PRCs are few, unless we reach outside the social fields (M. Serrano pc-2; Aldana pc-1). Finally, though Venezuela is so atypical that some of its higher education experts would not commonly cite any PRCs, my definition encompasses several.[28]

Whatever one makes of figures like these, numerous PRCs are spread across Latin America; this study combines broader strokes with some concentration on cases. That concentration means, first, some nations more than others. Within the category of Latin America, which excludes the Anglophone Caribbean, Haiti is barely included. The nations explored most are Chile, Argentina, and Mexico. The first two epitomize those where PRCs dominate in social research and where macropolitical instability and repression have been major factors. Mexico represents a different landscape, shaped much less by macropolitcal tragedy; there are few classic PRCs, yet the research center panorama is rich with other PRCs and kindred institutions. Ample field research in these nations has oriented my general thinking about Latin America's PRCs, but further field research, including site visits, was done in five other nations, and written and interview material has come from almost all nations.

Four special cases, repeatedly referred to throughout the volume, require a brief introduction here. Two are Latin America's leading international networks composed largely of PRCs. The third is the leading national network of PRCs. And the fourth is probably Latin America's most important single freestanding social research center.

CLACSO—Latin American Social Science Council—is a private nonprofit organization located in Buenos Aires. CLACSO has consultative status with UNESCO and encompasses nineteen nations, though its greatest weight is in the Southern Cone. It is a confederation that does not itself do much research but covers roughly 120 affiliated social science research centers with some 5,000 people (Ansaldi and Calderón 1989: 51–57). CLACSO was formed in 1967 by Latin American research centers and by social science luminaries Orlando Fals Borda, Gino Germani, Felipe Herrera, Helio Jaguaribe, Raúl Prebisch, and Víctor Urquidi. Its purpose, pursued through interchanges, advice, forums, and assistance, is to promote research, graduate education, and cooperation in social science. It is, in fact, Latin America's main organization for so doing.[29]

CLACSO is important here for the window it offers on its member centers. A key is its own surveys, which testify to some research function for CLACSO itself. The surveys show a proliferation of centers over recent decades: most have been created since 1971. CLACSO also helps determine if centers are PRCs because it excludes centers where research is not a major task (CLACSO 1991; CLACSO and OECD 1984). But CLACSO goes beyond PRCs on structural criteria: it is not limited to freestanding or private centers. It includes as members some units within PRCs, as seen with El Colegio's centers. It also includes university faculties and URCs, many from Brazil and Mexico. As of 1970 more than half the member centers were from universities, whereas fewer than a third were "autonomous" centers, public or private; by 1988 the figures basically reversed, largely due to the growth of PRCs. Still, because PRCs are usually much smaller than university centers, the latter weigh heavily in CLACSO's totals. And while CLACSO includes much beyond PRCs, it is not inclusive for any type of research institution, including PRCs. All this makes it hard to draw conclusions on PRCs from aggregate CLACSO data.[30] Fortunately, the data sometimes allow disaggregation by institutional type. I draw on the CLACSO self-study (CLACSO 1991; Calderón and Provoste 1990; Calderón and Provoste 1989; Ansaldi and Calderón 1989) with an eye for comparisons involving PRCs and for broad tendencies that would be sharper at PRCs alone.

FLACSO—Latin American Faculty of Social Science—was created in 1957 as a regional intergovernmental institution, with the help of the Chilean government, UNESCO, and the OAS. Its overall governing structure includes a high council, a directive committee, and a secretary-general (Ianni 1967; FLACSO N.d.: 7–9). But FLACSO has taken different courses in different nations. Chile's FLACSO came close to formal PRC status in 1979 due to the nation's hostile dictatorship, whereas renewed democracy reinstated the standard intergovernmental status. At the other extreme, FLACSO-Mexico has relied on public funds and is labeled public (ANUIES 1989: 24). This book refers more to FLACSO-Chile than to FLACSO-Mexico; FLACSOs in Argentina, Guatemala, and Costa Rica have more of the PRC feel. Nonetheless, academic autonomy must be balanced against intergovernmental status, authority, and representation on councils. Private or public appearance then may depend on funding, usually nongovernmental except for teaching programs. In sum, FLACSO adds to the PRC universe, varying between the core and the peripheries.

Headquarters for the nine-branch FLACSO shifted from Chile to Costa Rica in 1973. Costa Rica's branch illustrates how FLACSO's units can be autonomous, with their own boards and pursuits (Araya i-1). "Centers" are formally the top tier in FLACSO's network, in that they engage in research, graduate education, and technical assistance. Mexico and Ecuador have centers. "Programs" are similar but smaller. Argentina, Bolivia, Brazil, Chile, Costa Rica, Cuba, and Guatemala have programs. "Projects" are specific, time-bound undertakings (FLACSO N.d.: 11–13, 25). The Dominican Republic has only a project and thus lacks its own office and mostly channels money to researchers at leading centers outside of FLACSO. But substantial variation exists even within categories. Chile's program is, for example, much more significant than Brazil's.

FLACSO's network is of course much smaller than CLACSO's, but its academic focus and quality ensure its importance. Like CLACSO, FLACSO's research is mostly the sum of its centers' activities.

FLACSO-Chile, like ILET, links international to national networks; special agreements tied these centers to the largest national umbrella for PRCs, the Academy of Christian Humanism. The AHC's research projects brought in over forty Ford Foundation grants from 1977 to 1987, without counting nonresearch grants. After initial years with only individual projects on a rather ad hoc basis, the AHC built true research programs by the late 1970s (Fruhling 1985: 96). Prior to the 1990s, when the AHC's protection against regime repression would no longer be required and important associated units would leave the fold, and therefore in terms of this book's material, the AHC encompassed six prestigious "research programs": CERC on various contemporary issues, GIA and GEA in agriculture, PIIE in education, PET on labor economics, and a human rights program. Thus the AHC figures prominently in this work, even though, as with CLACSO, I usually deal with its constituent centers. These eight (six "programs" plus FLACSO and ILET) join CIEPLAN, SUR, CIDE, CIPMA, CENECA, ILADES, CLEPI and others to compose the heart of Chile's unmatched PRC sector. Additionally, many of the PRCs outside the AHC have interacted with the AHC, and some overlap has existed in administrative leadership.

El Colegio de México is the most significant single-site institution. It is atypical, however, in certain respects, which deters ample reference on many topics, including PRC growth, and demands a rationale for its prominence elsewhere.

For one thing, El Colegio is unusual for its deep involvement in graduate education. But my definition embraces centers that combine graduate education and research. Indeed, El Colegio is considered here partly in order to explore this subset of research centers, encompassing the likes of Brazil's Getúlio Vargas Foundation, Venezuela's IESA, and FLACSO. As the graduate-research form of PRC may well blossom in Latin America in coming years, it is worth remembering that El Colegio offered no graduate programs in its first two decades (Harrison n.d.: 6). Within Mexico itself a strong match with El Colegio is CIDE, which was created in the early 1970s; though CIDE faltered early on, it has now assumed research and policy importance.[31]

More controversially, however, El Colegio is unusual for being public in several senses, a fact that may make the PRC designation jarring. Indeed, many Mexicans and others familiar with the institution assume it is juridically public. Government subsidy accounts for most of its income. But El Colegio shows many key characteristics found at other leading PRCs that are privately funded; in any case, public funding is a reality, internationally, at many nonprofit organizations. It is also a trend for Latin America's PRCs, though El Colegio's direct subsidy through a budget line remains special. Public funding is especially common for PRCs engaged heavily in graduate education and both training and consultancies for government. A further sense of public status stems from the government's hand in creating El

Colegio and in some matters of its present governance, such as appointment of its president. Yet other juridically private institutions have such involvement; regarding creation, some were once public, and U.S. private think tanks such as RAND and the Urban Institute were created largely by the national government.

All in all, El Colegio's atypicality in graduate education, finance, source of creation, and governance is only partial and does not argue for exclusion. Moreover, El Colegio's importance to understanding freestanding social research centers (for example, the limited breadth of their research) does not depend on its privateness. Most basic to considering El Colegio as a PRC, however, is its juridical status; even this is debated, but there is reason to choose private over public in this respect.[32] Using other definitional criteria, one may well label El Colegio public, but here that would defy the policy of labeling centers by their legal identification and then empirically exploring degrees of functional privateness and publicness. The main arguments regarding juridical status, as well as related matters of privateness and publicness, hold for CIDE and the provincial *colegios* as well.[33]

Further reasons for analyzing El Colegio are multiple:

1. The institution is unrivaled among Latin America's freestanding social research centers for its historic trajectory over a half century.

2. It is similarly unmatched in research scope combined with quality.

3. It has had a major impact on other academic institutions both within and beyond Mexico, including CLACSO.

4. As think tanks proliferate in Latin America, El Colegio may be seen more as a trailblazer than an oddity.

5. The impact in Mexico is especially direct on CIDE and a network of provincial colegios that, together, show that El Colegio's profile in teaching, finance, and governance is not unique among Mexico's PRCS.

6. As its nation's preeminent freestanding social research center, El Colegio facilitates our inclusion of Latin America's second largest nation and promotes an understanding of such centers in nations not commonly associated with PRCS—but where economic and cultural openings present prospects for growth in conventional PRCS (Rubio pc-1).

7. Fruitful comparisons are possible with Mexico's national university, UNAM—the largest university in Latin America and one of the largest in the world—particularly with its extensive URCS.

8. El Colegio also forges a bridge to juridically public research centers that encompass graduate education and otherwise display many traits like

those at some prominent PRCs; Chapingo is the main case but CINVESTAV and others exist within Mexico alone and carry the analysis of research settings beyond the social fields.[34]

El Colegio warrants consideration because of its significance, not its typicality. However atypically, it lies technically within our PRC definition and illuminates important dynamics of research centers.

BEYOND THE UNIVERSITY

This mapping of the center and the periphery provides a preliminary overview. It should also help illuminate key features of the variegated terrain covered in the rest of the book.

In terms of sectors, initial observations have been consistent with mainstream literature about the third sector. Mostly, that sector is neither indistinguishable nor easily, neatly, or totally distinguishable from the other two sectors. PRCs share many features with institutions in the for-profit and public sectors; juridically private centers often display substantial publicness while juridically public centers display privateness. Even where PRCs do not find likenesses in other sectors, they still interact vigorously with those sectors, often weaving sectors together.

Similarly, in terms of research structures, PRCs show distinctions and commonalities in comparison with other institutions. Such comparisons also appear between PRCs and many nonprofit organizations that do not produce much research.

At the core of the PRC universe lie classic PRCs that are rather easily recognized: they are juridically private, unquestionably freestanding, and devoted mostly to research, much of which is manifestly academic. Lying nearby, on a periphery still inside boundaries for PRCs, are centers that are not inherently less or more important. Some have strong ties to another organization within the nonprofit sector or in the for-profit or public sectors. Almost all mix other activities with research. Except probably for graduate education, these activities cast some doubt on the research component of such PRCs, even while they complement it.

Farther along are institutions that do not meet all definitional criteria for PRCs. Yet, as they meet some, they resemble PRCs in key respects. This periphery includes centers tied to universities, governments, and certain international networks. It expands the analysis of research settings and higher education and facilitates comparisons to PRCs throughout the study.

Other characteristics do not definitionally separate PRCs from other institutions. Those already identified include size, field of research, and international status. Those that are thematic to the ensuing chapters are growth, finances, politics, and academic performance.

3 Growth

Public Failure and Beyond

Several factors impel us to study the growth of PRCs. The simplist is to discover why and how important institutions arise and expand. Interest is especially keen when growth is rapid. Moreover, the growth relates to phenomena transcending PRCs alone. One phenomenon is the failure of mainstream institutions—the university, most heavily, and government, most broadly. Another phenomenon is Latin American development overall, including privatization, democratization, internationalization, and social differentiation.

Most thematic to this study, PRCs' growth is integral to the spectacular nonprofit privatization that undermines predominant two-sector models of development, including the centrality of the public sector in social areas. As established in the first chapter, this privatization goes beyond the transformation of public into private institutions. It encompasses a variety of changes that increase the proportion of activity handled in juridically private sectors (or even increase the proportion of functional privateness in all sectors). This proportional shift occurs through the creation of new nonprofit institutions and the expansion of existing ones, both fueled in part by flight from the public sector.

A detailed analysis of PRC growth provides insight into the nonprofit privatization generally. The connection is especially compelling because most PRCs are more than research organizations: they overlap with other nonprofits in social service delivery, grassroots activity, human rights and other advocacy concerns, consulting, and training. Like much of the third sector they help build, PRCs show how visions of grand state-led development give ground to belief in direct action through small, private nonprofit institutions (Fruhling 1987: 124).

54

This chapter identifies and analyzes three major determinants of growth in PRCs. The first deals with macropolitics, according special attention to the role of regimes. The second shows how PRC growth stems from the university's problems. Whereas these first two parts emphasize mostly "push" factors, the third emphasizes "pull" factors, including development trends and the supply of financial and human resources.

Each of the three parts considers the appropriateness of the theory of public sector failure. This theory—henceforth called public failure, for short—broadly parallels the better-known theory of market failure, which explains governmental assumption of tasks by the lack of profit possibilities for potential private providers of collective goods. Public failure theory suggests that the government decision-making process fixes service for its citizens at the level desired by the median voter—or at least by a political voting process. That service therefore inclines away from the options favored by minorities, whether in terms of quality, culture, values, or other preferences, and pushes these dissatisfied minorities toward an alternative sector (Weisbrod 1988; Douglas 1987). That sector may be for-profit but, given the lack of profit potential in many of the activities in question, it is often nonprofit.[1]

Public failure is one of the two leading theories of nonprofit growth. Contract failure, emphasizing trust in nonprofits where purchasers lack information on which to judge for-profits, is most prominent when the nonprofit expansion appears to result mainly from rejection of the for-profit sector (Hansmann 1986a). But public failure is most prominent when the rejected sector is the public sector, a strong tendency for Latin American nonprofits, as it is for European nonprofits. For institutionalized research, the public propensity has been clear. By perception at least, PRC growth definitely represents a rejection of the public sector.

But public failure theory may not be the only explanation. Although this chapter is a rare effort to assess that theory in a detailed context, it makes the theory central only where the facts of nonprofit growth warrant.

MACROPOLITICS: THE ROLE OF REGIMES

State Repression

The most visible, immediate cause of the rapid spread of PRCs is repressive military regimes, which force a massive migration of social researchers from the public sector to the nonprofit sector.

A wave of military takeovers started in Brazil in 1964, followed by Argentina in 1966, and gained full force in Chile and Uruguay in 1973, rejoined by Argentina in 1976 (Collier 1979). Along with more ambiguous or transient cases in other Latin American nations, military rule covered the great majority of the region until the 1980s. Traditional dictatorships had usually set more limited agendas aimed at blocking leftist threats. In higher education, they coupled repression with some tolerance for the university as an opposition center. But the new authoritarianism sought to root out deepseated problems and build a new order through long-term rule. In the university world, the change brought an unprecedented assault, particularly in the social sciences (Levy 1981). Professors were pushed out. Major fields of study were terminated. Social science required a new home for survival.

The new authoritarianism's impact on the university-to-PRC transition did not come all at once. Although the initial impact was huge, reverberations continued for years. Several military regimes renewed hard-line action a few years after their first assault slowed: Chile in 1976 and Argentina and Brazil at the close of the 1960s. This sometimes forced centrists to follow PRC paths already traveled by those on the left. Many scholars who had tried to hold on in the universities succumbed eventually to political pressure or political-economic pressure. After all, most of these regimes cut social welfare expenditures, with universities often especially hard hit. And the economic crunch combined with an academic crunch. Prior strides in adding facilities and full-time faculty were undone. As programs were abolished and so many lines of thought prohibited, social scientists had little to cling to in their universities. So even those like the Catholic University of Chile economists who left peacefully and voluntarily to found CIEPLAN did so chiefly as a result of the regime's policies (O. Muñoz i).

While free market economics was given special university status and some nonideological social science offshoots were tolerated, most social studies were either banished or cast adrift. GRCs assumed some research burden, but social fields were not their main concern, nor could one expect inclusiveness regarding subject matter or personnel; funding allocated to Argentina's multitudinous new centers by the science and technology council bore out the restrictiveness (Vessuri 1986: 15; Cano 1985: 109). Instead, PRCs would be the main new homes for social research.

Comparisons within the Southern Cone confirm the finding that state repression spurred growth. Chile's coup brought a big wave of PRCs. Within a couple of years, the AHC opened, protecting individuals and then shielding and developing programs (Livingston i-2; Fruhling 1985: 60). Tiny Uruguay's group of PRCS also stems in large part from its 1973 coup, with less prior development. CINVE broke off from the national university's economics institute in 1973; CIESU, which had formed a little earlier, grew when university sociologists joined it in 1975. With CIEDUR, they would form the core of Uruguay's academic social science (Spalding, Stallings, and Weeks 1990: 102–11).[2]

Argentina, in contrast, had already experienced repeated repressive rule. From 1945 to 1955, Peronism forced refugees from the public sector to flee into various private organizations, though science and architecture loomed larger than fields like sociology at that stage. With democratization, many returned to the university only to be shaken by the 1966 coup, which brought the birth of PRCS as well as private universities. CICSO formed with the exodus of six UBA sociology professors. Repression also bolstered the established centers, like IDES and Di Tella. In the nation that led Latin America in social science research, PRCS led the nation, at least outside IRCS and economics (Harrison, Burnett, and Waggoner 1967: 21–26; Balán N.d.). Further boosts came with Argentina's hosting of newly formed CLACSO and the FLACSO teaching program, which had to leave Chile after 1973. But then the Peronist mania preceding the 1976 coup, and the coup itself, sent a new wave of refugees staggering to the already large assemblage of PRCS (Brunner and Barrios 1987: 126–29).

Yet Argentina, Uruguay, and Chile hold much in common compared to Brazil in the relationship between regimes and PRC formation. Brazil's repression naturally led to some PRC formation; CEBRAP's birth in 1969 from repression at the nation's leading university, the USP, is a prime example. However, Brunner and Barrios (ibid., 119–20) report that 87 percent of social science projects remained in the universities near the end of the authoritarian period. Some PRCS, such as IUPERJ, germinated more from the pursuit of intellectual and academic professionalism. Nor did the 1976 migration from USP to form CEDEC stem directly from military rule (Schwartzman pc-4; Rodrigues 1982: 17). Most tellingly, many fewer PRCS sprouted than in Chile and Argentina, as Brazil's military presided over a great development of university social science. Explanations lie in the far lesser development of the social sciences at the time of the coup, meaning a lesser threat perceived by the regime, and in the generally milder degree of repression outside two exceptional periods.[3] From 1972 through 1980, 53 percent of Ford's money to Brazil went to public universities, with 25 percent to "private organizations" and only 3 percent to "research centers," versus an Argentine breakdown of 0 percent, 80 percent, and 17 percent, respectively (Moller and Flores 1985: 60–68).

Repression has also produced important PRC advances in other nations. Central America's development is more recent and limited than its Southern Cone counterpart (Vega 1989: 38; Lungo i), but regime and overall violence brought major expansion in the 1970s and 1980s. Threats to a newly created social science promoted especially Guatemalan and Salvadorean PRCs, which later welcomed returning exiles. Central America also illustrates, however, the sad regional reality of continued government and extra-governmental repression under formally democratic regimes. PRCs there must still protect social research from attack.[4] The regional CRIES includes anonymous members fearing for their safety, and tragedies at El Salvador's CINAS, for example, illustrate why.

Bolivia is perhaps South America's closest counterpart to Central America's pattern of creation amid repression and instability. Paraguay under Stroessner, in contrast, is the continent's example of creation amid rather stable repression; social research would have to take place in PRCs (Calderón and Provoste 1989: 73). But the main example of stable authoritarianism in Latin America is Mexico. There, a major regime impact has been to thwart the growth at least of the classic PRCs. The regime has been mild enough to allow social research development primarily in the university (Ruiz Massieu 1987: 45), albeit increasingly in URCs. Also, a cloying authoritarianism helped make both criticism of government policy and openness to international assistance "anti-Mexican" and risky. Unlike other Latin American nations, Mexico has developed its PRCs more in partnership with government than in opposition to it.

Overall, the powerful nonprofit growth produced by Latin America's authoritarian rule strengthens basic public failure theory. Two points, in conclusion, underscore this strengthening.

First, like market failure, public failure routinely refers to the failure of one sector to undertake a given task. The usage makes sense when that sector's activity was a strong or reasonable expectation. Yet the usage is more persuasive when it concerns a real shift of activity, people, and resources from the public sector to a private sector. Empirical documentation of such shifts is sparse in the nonprofit literature, where the theory rests mostly on economic modeling.[5] But the shifts are probably common in the spread of Latin American and European nonprofits. Clearly, Latin America's repressive regimes have pushed a good deal of social research out of the public sector into the nonprofit sector.

Second, the growth analyzed to this point undermines the democratic-majoritarian assumption routinely invoked by economists, above all—but by others, as well. O'Neill (1989: 16) sees nonprofit development where unprofitable activities have "insufficient popular appeal." Douglas (1987: 46–48) explains the growth of diverse nonprofits within pluralist democracies, arguing that democratic government must leave the insufficiently popular to nonprofit action and that nonprofits are among the first casualties of totalitarian regimes.

In fact, however, the majority of the world's regimes have been neither democratic nor totalitarian but authoritarian. These regimes often can pursue unpopular policies in the public sector and reduce its size. They bypass or even repress many preferences and needs of the majority. This creates a great potential demand for nonprofits, in some ways greater than in representative democracy. And authoritarian regimes, unlike totalitarian ones, generally allow private institutions with some autonomy to remain as long as they do not directly threaten the regime's existence (Linz 1975). Nor, for that matter, should we assume that democratic government is so responsive that it tries to deal equally with all its citizens. Even if it tried, and succeeded, an accurate model of pluralist bargaining and coalitions would show some minority preferences included and some majority preferences excluded in public sector policies.[6] The "median voter" concept seems awkward at best. It did not guide our analysis of PRC growth in response to repression. Instead, when any nontotalitarian government produces any good or service, which will not satisfy all, it may open the way for distinctive alternatives in the third sector.

State Weakness

Just as PRCs grow from repression by strong governments, so they grow from inactivity by weak governments. This, then, is a second form of public failure that counts as government failure.

Failure in the sense of a shift from one sector to another is palpable where government discontinues a role it discharged in the past or comes to perform the role poorly. But state weakness also manifests itself in "failure" to undertake roles. This is a failure to engage rather than a failure in engagement. It is less tangible. Whether to count this as failure depends in part on expectations about sectoral responsibilities. It probably makes sense to highlight public failure for the growth of Latin American and European nonprofits but not for the growth of U.S. nonprofits. In the United States, propensities and expectations are stronger for private action, so one tends to explain public sector involvement by invoking theories of market failure or "voluntary failure" (Salamon 1987: 109–13). An alternative approach is simply to note that a new or expanded activity enters a given sector, without charging the other sectors with failure.

State weakness is notorious in Latin America. Authoritarian regimes paper over this underdevelopment. Strong as they may be in repressing opposition, they often prove feeble in pursuing socioeconomic development. Some shroud abdication of responsibility in antistatist principles. What concerns us more in this section, however, are regimes that do not hide their development policy weaknesses with repressive strength.

Here too, many (postauthoritarian) regimes have taken a neoliberal road including an ideological defense of the limited state. In those cases, PRCs become part of a mainstream political-economic trend. Governments become unable or unwilling to spend money for the studies and services expected of them. Sometimes they do not pay enough to retain top research talent. In short, political and economic factors contribute to a shrinking state. Throughout Latin America, the idea of the state as the central, vital social engineer has suffered a severe setback. The region fits a worldwide disillusionment with public enterprises, which were created largely in response to problems within the central bureaucracy (Heath 1990). PRC expansion into the void resulting from state shrinkage in research and social service is a form of privatization. It corresponds to other nonprofit expansion in response to the frustrations of state-centered development.

Social researchers in many nations give up on public bureaucracies, which were major employment centers for them. Many migrate from the bureaucracy directly to PRCs, as well as to IRCs and the for-profit sector. In Central America, as economic crisis and neoliberal beliefs mean less money and opportunity to pursue development projects within government, once idealistic social scientists try their luck in PRCs instead (Vega 1989: 40). This exodus is the flip side of the state giving up on its own bureaucracies.

Young democracies, including redemocratized ones, sometimes cannot assemble the tools that PRCs have: talent, expertise, experience, and networks that reach not only the needy but also other research users and international philanthropy. Thus the Uruguayan government repeatedly contracted with PRCs to do their analyses. Other governments never had much capacity. CEDOH was created by professionals and scholars to help fill a void in basic information on Honduras. In Paraguay, money from AID, the Panamerican Health Office, and German sources has gone to a PRC for a national survey on population and health, covering such issues as fecundity and mortality (CEPEP 1991; Melián pc). Elsewhere, gripping illustrations of bureaucratic failure occur where the state's abilities visibly disintegrate, as we now see for Peru and the Dominican Republic.

The decline of the Peruvian state was dramatic. It resulted from involuntary failure more than from neoliberal choice and led to significant for-profit and nonprofit privatization in many fields (Webb 1991; M. Smith 1992; Spalding 1991: 20–24). In research, the state's collapse opened the door for PRCs to proliferate in the 1980s. Compared to other nations, the initial flood of social scientists went more into government than the university (Cueto i-1). The subsequent rise of PRCs is therefore part of the general rise of Peruvian nonprofits as alternatives to the faltering government. The 1977 shift to CEDEP of academics previously involved in the National System for Support of Social Mobilization, SINAMOS, is an example. Such PRCs attract international contracts to perform public tasks. While Peruvians debate whether their government is basically incapable or uninterested in doing more (Arregui i), international donors would not entrust their contributions to a government ridden by strikes and uncertainties. Thus, the labor ministry surveyed market conditions less than it once had and authorized foreign-funded national surveys in its name, as by the Institute of Informal Sector Development with UNDP funds (Post i).

The Dominican Republic's Ministry of Planning was once the government's principal ministry, with a substantial research capability (Sánchez M. i-2). Its leading works were rich in detail and useful for social scientists as well as policymakers. But the ministry came to do less and less, and the national statistics office hardly functioned. Previously regular annual publications were published five years late. Prestigious former officials created their own PRCs when the ministry could no longer hire that caliber of talent. In 1985 the Center on Population and Family drew on foreign funds to do a large study of basic demographic trends.

Typical weaknesses fall short of complete collapse, however. The state does not itself do the research or the share of research once expected of it. This is found in developed countries as well. U.S. think tanks are partial alternatives to bureaucracy. Then too, it is natural to use PRCs that already function well—like ASIES for its regular diagnoses of Guatemala's socioeconomic situation. The preexisting nonprofit expands partly because it is already there. In any case, delegation to PRCs does not always betray severe weakness. Indeed, state-PRC cooperation is compatible with healthy government. It contrasts with the extreme where government loses the capacity to finance research, set an agenda, or utilize the findings. Nevertheless, many situations short of the extreme still uphold state weakness as an important factor in the surge of PRCs.[7]

Positive Macropolitical Factors

Under civilian regimes state weakness becomes more significant than state repression in explaining PRC growth. But so do positive macropolitical factors. In reality, the weakness and positive factors frequently blend. Most of the region's democracies simultaneously, if gropingly, seek political-economic privatization and social development. Unable or at least disinclined to do the social development work itself, government turns toward nonprofits. The flavor becomes one of intersectoral partnership more than a simple replacement of public by private—much less the opposition of government and nonprofits.

Public failure theory must yield ground where positive macropolitical factors promote nonprofits. The theory suffers from zero-sum assumptions about privatization. Salamon (1989a: 3–9, 1990) shows how U.S. nonprofits grow when an expanded welfare state finances new tasks that it does not directly administer. The state helps provide what it does not directly produce (Jänicke 1990: 33). Public failure theory does not address nonprofit expansion in partnership with government. My findings take the point beyond what Salamon (1990: 222, 230–31) associates with the "peculiar" U.S. evolution. These findings also support comparativists who argue that states and societies sometimes expand simultaneously; but whereas they emphasize the paradoxical strengthening of antagonistic actors (Evans, Rueschemeyer, and Skocpol 1985a: 352–55), our evidence shows true collaboration.

An international dimension of positive macropolitics arises when governments support the creation of PRCs aimed partly at rescuing scholars from foreign nations. El Colegio de México is a treasured Latin American example. The Mexican government helped found the institution to attract

Spanish scholars fleeing civil war. Thirty years later, the government bolstered El Colegio and created CIDE, both of which became homes for South American scholars fleeing military repression and austerity. Similarly, the Ecuadorian government helped bring FLACSO north after the organization's troubles in Argentina (Cosse i). In fact, these cases also involved intranational factors, and most government aid for the creation of PRCs is fully an intranational matter.[8]

Even leftist regimes may set favorable circumstances for nonprofit private institutions like PRCs. They naturally enlarge their own public institutions, including public research centers. But where leftist regimes do not dominate their society or even their own government apparatus, as in Velasco's Peru and Allende's Chile, they also turn to sympathetic PRCs. At the same time, their lack of total control (with the exception of Cuba) allows the opposition to form its own PRCs. Nicaragua is the most recent and extreme case to date, probably reflecting the regionally increased importance of PRCs by 1979: Sandinistas relied heavily on supportive PRCs, such as INIES, as well as on public centers. A social science association, ANICS, reached back to Somoza's days, but PRCs proliferated under the leftist regime. The nation had twelve major nonuniversity centers along with minor ones, and the government made little effort to bolster the university. Nor did the opposition stand by passively. Political parties formed their own centers, mixing training, organization, and proselytizing with research (Fernández 1989: 28, 74–75; Vega 1989: 40).

Yet democracy is the form of government that best works with PRCs. The two ensuing chapters, on finances and politics, amply confirm that. In evolutionary terms, the PRC-government partnership is most exciting where democracies take advantage of, and then further promote, the PRC infrastructure developed in response to authoritarianism. Like other nonprofit organizations, PRCs outlive the repression that once made them grow (B. Smith 1990: 237).

In fact, prior to democratic government, redemocratizing evolution toward the new regimes promotes nonprofit growth. The fading power or declining repressiveness of military regimes opens space for PRCs. This includes PRCs related to political parties. Brazil's political opening spawned new activity at PRCs (Rodrigues 1982). Much more room for research, communication, and criticism emerged in Argentina after the PRCs lowered their profile in the late 1970s. In Chile, when authority to allow new institutions passed from the interior ministry to the justice ministry, dissident

PRCS could operate more easily and broadly (Lladser i-1; Lladser 1986). Various groups built PRCS to prepare for their role under civilian rule. Exiles could return to ILET or, in 1984, to CECI in the sciences, just as Central American exiles would return home to centers like CSUCA. Some PRCS encountered government officials committed to moderation and a respectable transition process.

However much political opening propels PRCS, the actual ascension of democracy intensifies the process. Offsetting the diminished need for PRCS where the state assumes educational and other socioeconomic responsibilities is the increased demand for PRCS working in partnership with government. Accompanying this is a greater freedom for PRCS and associated nonprofits. The third sector has expanded greatly in Brazil since the 1980s and in Argentina since 1983; Uruguay also shows nonprofits waxing under democracy, though Chile shows some decline as the state reassumes certain responsibilities (A. Thompson 1992; Cruz pc-2). The great majority of Guatemala's PRCS, which mix research with public policy advice and promoción, have arisen since 1985 (Alvarez pc-1). Both the late authoritarian and early democratic surges parallel the nonprofit blossoming in Eastern Europe, where entrenched interests also still block needed university reform (Siegal and Yancey 1992).

Whereas some political actors hold the statist view that nonprofits are suitable alternatives only when government abdicates its responsibilities, others either always believed in nonprofits or came to do so during the dark days (Furhling 1985). The new democracies need the PRCS for research, information, ties to grassroots and international organizations, budget relief, rapid responsiveness, and so forth. They use PRCS in order to be active. For example, the Uruguayan government consults CERES about its own options for action. Moreover, many government officials maintain relations with PRCS where they once worked. And while some social researchers give up on the bureaucracy, others try to serve it from their bases at PRCS.

The positive regime effect holds where democracy first appears as well as where redemocratization is happening. PRCS and other nonprofits sprouted after the downfall of Trujillo in the Dominican Republic in 1961. Stroessner's fall in Paraguay brought a boom in PRCS dealing with economics, international relations, the environment, and popular groups, as universities failed to respond to the fresh demand for research (Moreno pc).

Long-standing democracies logically show sustained, less sudden amplification. In Colombian, FEDESARROLLO was created in 1968 to tie together government, business, and university, especially in social research; CCRP followed in 1973, with government and for-profit groups cooperating to do research, training, and extension in demographics; and CRESET formed in 1984 for economic research on developing countries, especially in Latin America. In Costa Rica, CIAPA opened in 1975 to diagnose, analyze, and propose policies regarding socioeconomic and political problems in Central America and is already surrounded by younger centers. (Fischel i-1). Indeed, social democracy appears to be a type of government generally compatible with nonprofit sectors (DiMaggio and Anheier 1990). PRCS originated in Latin America prior to its descent into military rule; Chile in the 1960s and Argentina in the 1950s were the leaders.

And positive macropolitical dynamics clearly go beyond the governmental side. Political parties, advocacy groups, religious organizations, and businesses are among the nongovernmental political actors that forward their interests by creating PRCS. Some cannot function under authoritarian rule. Others gain latitude under democracy. Moreover, the ascendant form of democracy, emphasizing pluralism, decentralization, and a restricted state, seems especially conducive to such organizational activity.

Nonprofit growth transcends any single regime or political context. Authoritarian repression is a major cause of PRC proliferation but so is the termination of that repression—as well the free flow of democratic forces. PRCS grow under diverse, even almost opposite, macropolitical conditions: both state repression and state weakness tend to support public failure theory, but positive macropolitical conditions do not.[9]

UNIVERSITY FAILURE

Public failure is relevant beyond the macropolitical arena. The woes of the public university lead to considerable expansion of PRCS. The evidence that follows basically confirms public failure theory. But the evidence also broadens the theory, which in a sense modifies it.

Confirmation comes, as it did regarding state repression, from the real shift out of the public sector into the nonprofit sector. More than before, it becomes clear that the failure need not be objective. Making explicit what seems implicit in public failure theory (or what, alternatively, would constitute a modest broadening of the theory), perception of failure is sufficient to account for changes in behavior.

The concept of public failure is substantially broadened by moving from the macropolitical to the university arena. The theoretical literature usually refers to "government" failure to explain nonprofit growth; and even where it refers to the public sector, it focuses on government policy (Rose-Ackerman 1986: 4–5, 19–54; Douglas 1987: 48–50; Weisbrod 1988: 16–23). An extension to a more general "public" failure notion allows for situations in which the status of the government as a whole is not critical. Government may indeed function rather well, but particular public institutions, perhaps not administered directly by government, do not function well. Problems in the public university—funded by government yet often autonomously administered—fit this picture.

Disillusionment

Universities were to spearhead the grand postwar development, which was thought to depend on rapidly discovered, transmitted, and applied knowledge. Alongside ambitious efforts by governments and their universities came unprecedented international philanthropy. But by the mid-1970s the golden era of optimistic effort had ended. Of what remained for higher education, universities held a diminished share. Domestic governments became disillusioned with their universities. But it is useful to focus on foreign donors because their voluntary status leaves them great latitude to allow their funds to underwrite their beliefs. Those foreign agencies that did maintain a presence turned increasingly to other institutions, such as national science and technology councils. Foundations and European governments looked increasingly to PRCs. These agencies exaggerated the failure of university assistance and were explicit about their shift to alternative institutions. The Ford Foundation's 1975 Annual Report (43–44) notes that its efforts in education and social science for development had to switch from universities to PRCs in several nations. Whatever role military government played in some of these nations, philanthropy skirted universities elsewhere as well.[10]

I do not minimize the role of state repression or weakness by analyzing university failures or by identifying failures born or sustained mainly within the university itself. Moreover, the documentation of how university failures caused PRCs to form in nonauthoritarian settings helps us appreciate that university failures also existed under authoritarian regimes and were not fully caused by those regimes.

The analysis focuses on recent decades, when discernible public university crises appeared and the great regional burst of PRCs occurred. But precedents exist, including democratic situations where the clear rationale for PRC creation was to escape university problems, as with Argentina's Di Tella in 1958. In Venezuela in the 1950s, private, government, and foreign agencies pursued science research in the Luis Roche Foundation, a PRC. This center yielded in 1958 to IVIC, a public research center. The initial cause was repression by the Pérez Jiménez dictatorship, but national university politicization then became more important and continued to be as university scientists fled to IVIC between 1969 and 1971 (Fuenzalida 1987: 119–20; Vessuri 1984: 203–16). Mexico's big research push in the 1930s into institutions other than universities coincided with the near collapse of the national university. The government worked with the Rockefeller Foundation, which departed from its international tendency to support agricultural universities by turning instead to special international institutes (Fosdick 1952: 184–86; Levy 1980: 26–27). El Colegio soon followed in social research.

From University to PRC

The exodus from university to PRC was most visibly gripping when repression blanketed the Southern Cone. But developments there stimulated parallels throughout Latin America. Scholars fled northward, often into new or expanding PRCs. Those who had been at PRCs back home were direct transmitters of ideas regarding structures and procedures not previously contemplated in their new nations. Also powerful, however, was a more diffuse demonstration effect. Scholars, donors, and others could see how PRCs functioned in the Southern Cone. The notion of a demonstration effect makes particular sense because the nations that led the way in PRCs were those with the most advanced social science communities. The same nations also provided leadership for IRCs, which also served the flow of the new ideas. Yet demonstration effects depended on the existence of powerful factors throughout the region that made people seek alternatives to university-based research. Growth could be spurred from the outside but required strong domestic pressures. By the 1980s the pathways from PRCs to universities were ubiquitous.[11]

Central America's PRC growth traces partly to regime repression, but it accelerated under more benign regimes.[12] Honduras's establishment of a PRC monopoly on social research occurred despite a lower level of repression than that suffered in Guatemala and El Salvador (Fernández 1989: 63, 72). Another revealing feature of Central America's institutional shift, replicating a pattern seen earlier in other nations, is that so many of the PRC leaders are former leaders of university reform movements. They had championed not only political reforms but also academic reforms. Many of these people wound up in PRCs after finally giving up on their universities, perhaps after passing through, and also giving up on, government ministries. Especially poignant is CSUCA's shift from idealistic leader of Central American university regional integration to mostly a research center (Vega 1989: 38; Lungo i; Cox i). Meanwhile, Costa Rica helps prove the Central American rule by exception. Its ability to sustain a comparatively good public university restrains the proliferation of PRCs.

Colombia and Peru are two Andean examples of growth not stemming from authoritarian rule or regime change. By the mid-1960s, their public universities suffered dreadfully from the troubles afflicting most of the region: a poorly prepared student body, limited staff development and resources, outdated curriculum, difficulty establishing research structures, declining average academic quality and prestige, credentialism, diminished job prospects for graduates, disruptive politicization, and tremendous resistance to fundamental reform.

Public universities have therefore yielded substantial ground to private universities in Colombia and Peru (Levy 1986)—so one result of public failure has been privatization within the university sphere. Yet most of the private universities suffer for academic deficiencies as horrible as those in the public universities, and PRCs extend the privatization to tasks where even top private universities rarely compensate for lost hope at the public universities. In Peru, Colombia, and beyond, most elite private universities concentrate more on commercially oriented studies than social sciences. And few do research. Outside its Catholic university, Peru boasts almost no exceptions unless we include the contract research at institutions like the Universidad del Pacífico. Bolivia's single notable exception concerns its Catholic university in some economic and social areas. But even these universities frequently must look to URCs to bypass their faculties in the search for funds.

Several factors slow the traffic from university to PRC in Colombia. One is that the macropolitical problem has been not military government but extreme violence and terror: threatened social scientists who cannot find safety in internal exile at PRCs have to leave the country altogether. Another factor is that Colombia was a strong national center of university reform; also, it had a favored status as a recipient of assistance and, consequently, developed fine universities. Led by the Valle and Antioquia universities on the public side and Los Andes and the Javeriana on the private side, Colombia maintained several good university social studies programs. The National University recovered some ground by the 1980s under a vigorous rector. Although frustrations—topped off by death threats—brought his resignation, administrative and academic reform went forward. Still, economic crisis and political violence wore down Colombia's leading universities in the 1980s. The shifting of foundation grants from the National University to public and private university alternatives and then, increasingly, to PRCs such as CINEP and FEDESARROLLO fits a broader Latin American pattern (Lavados i-1). Given all the restraining factors in Colombia, the spread of PRCs there is evidence of the strong regional forces at work.

Peru had fewer braking forces. Its sad university trajectory did not allow many exceptions. PRCs proliferated more extensively. The IEP was created in 1964 by philosophers, historians, anthropologists, engineers, and others chagrined by the university's incapacity for academic reflection and study of national realities (Cotler i). Although it repeatedly floundered, the IEP eventually assumed perhaps the leading spot in Peruvian social science, as no solid public university path emerged through the years. Within a year of the IEP's birth, DESCO appeared. Then, in the late 1970s, social scientists who had worked for the reformist Velasco government left for the academic world. They greatly favored PRCs over universities, and by the early 1980s more than fifty centers sought international academic assistance (Myers 1983: 508; Marrou i). That figure grew by the decade's end. Created in 1980 for academic and applied social research, GRADE would by 1990 already be a senior member of the PRC sector (GRADE 1990: 7).

Bolivia further shows how PRCs emerge largely in response to weakness at the university. Bolivia's public universities suffer from degrees of politicization, lax standards, poor instruction, low retention rates, and other inefficiencies that stand out even by the continent's standards. They do almost no research. A diverse panoply of PRCs has evolved. Whereas CINCO closed shop and CERES suffered from personality clashes and fragile funding, and retreated from basic research, centers like CEBEM arose. The range extends from consultancy, women's, and environmental centers on the PRC periphery to PRCS like THOA, CIPCA, and CEDLA, which engage in more basic and historical analysis. All these private centers join a limited number of GRCS and URCS that serve policymakers in socioeconomic fields.

Chapingo is an especially important example of how public research centers also arose as research alternatives to universities. Its roots reach to the famous Rockefeller–Mexican government research initiative in CIMMYT, itself partly a reaction to UNAM's inattention to agricultural educational needs and agricultural economics (Jiménez, Fernández, and Galindo 1978: 18–38; FF #65288). By the early 1960s the government and international philanthropy made a huge effort to build a complete agricultural university, blending research and training along with extension. From the United States they borrowed such features as an integrated campus, a board of trustees, and a full-time staff. But academic political strife was endemic, and the research mission was never adequately safeguarded (Alcalde i; Jiménez i; Díaz i). Research was separated out into Chapingo.

Among PRCS, Mexico's El Colegio is a solid counterpart that combines social science and humanities research with graduate education. From early on, the Rockefeller Foundation helped Alfonso Reyes and Daniel Cosío Villegas act on their conviction that UNAM had too many other missions to put research, objectivity, and academic excellence at the top (Lida 1988: 140–44; El Colegio 1987b: 7–14; Urquidi i-1). El Colegio originally received UNAM's backing, even while it provoked its jealously, because it promised to avoid duplicating tasks. Provincial *colegios* have likewise struggled not to challenge their state universities too much and yet to offer a research alternative to them.

Failed Tasks

Public university failures include a mix of things done poorly and things not done much at all, despite reforms aimed at incorporating them; private universities make fewer relevant efforts. Research is the crucial example relevant to PRCS. It is integral to the mission that Latin American public universities have claimed for themselves, especially since the 1950s. And research was one of the highest priorities of international philanthropy for universities. Following the U.S. model, the goal was to institutionalize research in the universities, linking it integrally with teaching.

The results have disappointed both at established universities trying to reform with heavy foreign assistance, like Colombia's National University, and at universities initially established on a research-teaching model, like Mexico's Autonomous Metropolitan University. Nor is a strong positive trend in place. After military regimes undermined research, redemocratization has not brought automatic reversal. University renaissance is more about liberties and rising enrollments, the latter contributing to a massification that makes research tougher. Uruguay's public university grew 61 percent from 1984 to 1988 (Labadie and Filardo 1989: 7), still short of the Argentine explosion.

Among the reasons for university research failure are traditionalism, the opposition of those incapable of performing research, noncompetitive appointments, rewards inferior to those for university administration and especially for nonuniversity employment, and insufficient ties to industry (Vessuri 1986: 6). Let us focus on two principal concerns: (1) the juxtaposition of research and teaching and (2) politics.

Latin American universities are generally unable to blend teaching and research. Teaching remains the priority. More accurately, professional training remains the priority. Although dominance by the traditional giants of law, medicine, and engineering has dissipated, the premium remains on obtaining credentials and jobs. Those pursuing professional training have difficulty setting aside time and resources for research. The predominant teaching style—lectures without class participation, interaction, or individual reading and study—is antithetical to research development. Instructors are still mostly part-time, many being engaged primarily in professional practice. Yet many full-time professors also do little research.

Some universities have vice rectorates of research, who help to protect research's place, but research is not usually central to university budgets and is vulnerable when cuts come. Latin American graduate education is still mostly geared to specialization and is not tied to research. There is some truth in Atcon's (1966) description of teaching as a virus that has spread to all other university activities. No wide national support has developed for research, and funding is limited. If research succeeds, it does so in protected niches.

Public university politics cripples research in many interrelated ways, most of which fall heaviest on the social science area. Already noted are the politicization brought by regime repression and the relegation of research to a place behind professional training on the university's agenda.[13] Two further types of university politics should be added.

The first is the strong pull toward standardization. As argued for Mexico (Fuentes, Gil, and Kent 1990), a great contradiction arises because only a few professors do research well, while others insist on equal pay, resources, and privileges. In the university's politics, it is risky to say no to the others. Thus the research effort is either spread ridiculously thin or abandoned. Argentina's twenty-nine public universities, despite all their real differences and need for greater differences, are equal under the law, with standard hiring, salary, and other policies that make it very difficult to protect research within the university (Balán 1990).[14]

The second additional aspect of university politics that undermines research is interest group activism, of which student politics is but the best known. In the United States, just a spurt of such activism led many to see think tanks as alternatives to politicized and antigovernment universities (Orland 1972: 141). Think tank–government interactions in democratic Latin America could well increase if student activism increases. Moreover, Latin American activism often matches political party or other national cleavage because of the university's political importance in terms of numbers of middle-class students, the training of national leaders, and the formation of ideology. Such cleavage stimulated the creation of Chilean PRCs as early as the 1960s (Orellana R. 1986: 230); and it is why El Colegio sees UNAM's politics as inescapable. Though PRCs spring up in reaction to cleavage at private universities, as at Colombia's Andes and SER, reactions to stronger public university activism are much more common. And though student activism at public universities peaked in the late 1960s and early 1970s, it remains decisive in resisting academic rigor.[15] Furthermore, worker unionization and representation on decision-making bodies also frustrates serious social science researchers. Critics find Argentine university research crippled by rampant internal democracy, which leads to excessive uncertainties and a responsiveness to nonacademic pressure; such changes at redemocratization led many disgruntled researchers to give up on tiresome university politics (Balán 1990; Cavarozzi i). Authoritarian regime notwithstanding, Brazilian workers and professors captured public universities to such an extent in the 1970s as to stimulate a vigorous creation of both PRCs and special research institutes in technical and agricultural fields. Refugee researchers complained that the public universities had expanded unduly, despite the regime's policy of funneling most enrollments into private institutions. The Brazilian case is especially interesting because it shows the problems of university research even in the nation with probably the greatest breakthroughs in such research (Schwartzman and Castro 1986; Miceli i; Schwartzman pc-1).

These political problems are circular. Campus groups close the university, making wary governments and foreign donors diminish their contributions; frustrated university scholars look elsewhere, as do those who have finished graduate school abroad; disgusted governments and donors cut even more, contributing to further disorder and fewer opportunities; and so forth. The result: many of the best prepared students exit to the less disrupted private universities, and many of the best social scientists exit to PRCS.

Additionally, because research is not the only mission of PRCs, and because most of its research is not pure research, the tasks coupled with the research are also relevant. Many public universities manage these poorly, though again the record is not so positive for universities in most other regions either. The bridges between knowledge and society or development are weak.[16] This holds for extension service, particularly to marginal groups. It also holds for contracted service or research. Where public university employees engage, they usually do so as private consultants, for the university usually lacks both a base and rewards for contract research, and there is the danger that projects will be gobbled up by the university's basic structures (Drysdale i).

URCs: Inadequate Alternatives

The failure to establish research within faculties has led universities to build research centers outside the faculties. Our main interest in these URCs lies in their relation to PRCs. In sectoral terms, URCs are a splendid example of addressing public sector failures through reform in the public sector. In many instances, the failure of such reform reinforces privatization. Analysis of URCs is also important because URCs themselves constitute a major, barely studied, aspect of Latin American (and other) efforts to institutionalize research. Although some URCs work tolerably and some work well, their record is insufficient to reverse an overall sense of university failure in research. The creation of URCs more commonly parallels than usurps the creation of PRCs; or it is a step toward that creation. We first consider URCs as alternatives to the university mainstream and then their inadequacies in performance.

Alternatives to the Mainstream

URCs arise much less than PRCs from macropolitical failures. Especially in public universities, URCs are not safe from state repression or financial limits. Argentine military rule pushed sociology out of the UBA's Instituto Germani; PRCs like the Di Tella provided a safety net. URCs are typically too integral to the wider institution to provide sanctuary for beleaguered scholars. Sometimes, though, even authoritarian governments treat URCs as less politically sensitive or radical than the faculties. More benign governments are more likely to value URCs as worthwhile research alternatives to faculties, perhaps as privileged pockets, sustainable amid the austerity the wider institution endures.

The preference is clearer for international philanthropy, however. Freer than domestic government to pick and choose within the university, international donors disproportionally favor URCs over university faculties. Critics denounce foreign assistance for not trying to establish research and new disciplines within existing faculties, but where assistance tried, it often ran into problems or was made unwelcome (Fuenzalida 1982: 135; Fuenzalida 1983). The formation of URCs was often a tacit admission that such efforts had fallen short.

URCs were already abundant before PRCs surged. The University of San Carlos's Institute of Economic and Social Research emerged in 1958 to systematically study Guatemalan social reality and, along with GRCs, was accorded "great autonomy" (Vega 1989: 21, 38). CENDES, in 1960, took on development studies at Venezuela's national university. UNAM's chemistry institute in the 1940s, the UCH's economics institute in the 1950s, along with counterparts in Chilean sociology, are other prominent examples. Among the forerunners, peaking in 1913, was the physics institute at Argentina's Universidad de La Plata.

Contemporary examples abound. UNAM's network of URCs may be regarded as both elitist and inescapable if the university is to do significant research; in Mexico's provincial universities as well, URCs blossom because they are less vulnerable to the disabling politics of the mainstream (Lomnitz i-1; Beltrán i). Panama's national university has institutes in national studies, geological sciences, criminology, and other fields. Facilitated by a university law in the 1970s, URCs proliferate in reaction to the multiple problems of Venezuela's public universities. Colombia's IEPRI sees its creation as recognition that the national university would otherwise lose its role as the critical conscious of the nation (García Guadilla pc; IEPRI 1990: 9). Most generally, URCs emerge because universities fail to fulfill the dream, pioneered at places like Chile's University of Concepción, to bring research into teaching departments (Stitchkin i; González i).

Data juxtaposing URCs and PRCs give less concrete, yet nonetheless suggestive, evidence that URCs are alternatives to the university mainstream. If PRCs are also alternatives to that mainstream, then it is interesting that URCs are more prevalent where PRCs are less prevalent.[17] PRCs are most widespread in Argentina, Chile, and Peru, nations in which URCs are not so formidable. URCs weigh in more in Mexico and Venezuela, where PRCs are fewer. The juxtaposition harks back to the observations that PRCs advance during military rule and that URCs are infeasible alternatives in that circumstance. The CLACSO data further suggest that PRCs dominate among constituent centers in Argentina, Chile, Uruguay, Bolivia, and Paraguay, with a lesser presence in Colombia, Costa Rica, Ecuador, and Puerto Rico (though also Brazil), followed by Mexico and Venezuela.

But this juxtaposition also suggests movement over time from URC to PRC, notwithstanding longitudinal overlap. Recall the evolution, between 1970 and 1990, of CLACSO's centers from mostly URCs to mostly PRCs. And those data understate the overall trend insofar as CLACSO leaves aside many recent PRCs where academics mixes with other missions. Because of reservations about such inferences from the regional data, however, I turn to concrete cases for evidence that URCs are inadequate to forestall PRCs' growth.

Inadequacies in Performance

Whatever their founders' intentions, URCs do not obviate the need for PRCs. Direct evidence for the inadequacy of URCs comes where the university-to-PRC migration is in fact a URC-to-PRC migration. One such migration occurs when URCs splinter. Factions may form PRCs, as when Chilean scholars squared off over Marxism in the late 1960s and early 1970s; or factions may join existing PRCs as with Uruguay's CIESU and Chile's CIPMA (Orellana R. 1986: 230; E. Fox 1980: 21, 72). The most dramatic shift, however, is the near total transformation of URCs into PRCs. Both PIIE in education and CIEPLAN in economics from the Catholic University of Chile, as well as CEUR in regional and urban studies from Argentina's UBA, exemplify the wholesale transplantation of organizations from within to outside universities (Lladser i-2). State repression required PRCs rather than URCs. The Dominican Republic shows that other centers move out because of perceived university failures more than from macropolitics.[18] This follows a U.S. pattern witnessed at universities like Columbia and Stanford (Orlans 1972: 43, 143).

Even where growth in PRCs does not result so directly from failures at URCs, that growth is commonly an indication of those failures. The perceived failure of Puerto Rican URCs to do publicly oriented studies contributed greatly to PRC growth in the 1970s and 1980s (Quintero N.d.: 41).

Incontrovertibly, PRCs do much of what URCs set out to do. We need, therefore, to outline the problems encountered by URCs.

Brazil's URCs suffer from many of the usual difficulties. Although some were hurt by repression, their problems more often resulted from university enrollments, opposition to Americanization, resistance to intrauniversity stratification (including the university administration's reluctance to allow outside money to flow directly to centers rather than through administration), and both their and the government's inclination to distribute resources according to political criteria, such as regional equity, more than academic performance (Schwartzman 1984).

URCs lie in a politically vulnerable position within the university. Faculties and sometimes administration undermine them in particular ways, even while URCs also suffer from universitywide problems.[19] University faculties derive strength from their entrenched positions within traditionally decentralized universities. Above all, they hold a monopoly on teaching, including professional training and concomitant ties to powerful professional associations beyond the universities. They usually resist attempts to create anything that smacks of an alternative or privileged pocket within the university.

Pressure for standardization undermine URCs' typical quest for distinctiveness, as seen in UNAM's union-sustained requirement of uniform wages. Where standardization wobbles, however, jealousy and conflict threaten URCs, as at Colombia's National University. Or anxious faculties may block establishment of URCs in the first place, as with proposals for political science and European studies centers at Argentina's UBA (M. Serrano i; Catterberg i; Cano i). The pioneering introduction of institutionalized research into Chile's UCH in the 1950s and 1960s met resistance less from the weak faculties with little research pretensions of their own than from the powerful faculties (Fuenzalida 1984). Where URCs nonetheless emerge, compromises are required.[20] A principal one involves the absence of postgraduate education, which is allocated instead to the faculties.[21]

Donors have shared the frustration over faculty-imposed restrictions on URCs. For Ford, cases include UNAM's biomedical institute, which was afflicted by university red tape, and the Center for Legal Assistance at Chile's Catholic university, which was hounded by the law faculty in the early 1970s (FF #73538, Nina Manitzas to Peter Bell, Sept. 21, 1973; Cuneo i; Figueroa i). The Rockefeller Foundation also repeatedly found its work with URCs undermined by resentment in the faculties—the Federal University of Bahia, Brazil, being a good example (Coleman and Court 1992). A top unit such as the endocrinological laboratory at Chile's Catholic university, which has received generous assistance from Rockefeller, Kellogg, the IDRC, AID, the U.S. Air Force, and European donors, charged reverse discrimination by its university administration, which had concluded that other units needed its help more (Croxatto i).[22]

Virtually every UCR-faculty relation presents problems. At Argentina's UBA, almost every URC is tied to a specific faculty, which controls it (Mollis pc-1). Although the University of Costa Rica's URCs are structurally more separate from the faculties, faculties still can control resource distribution (Garita i; Estrada i). The university has specialized "centers," despite faculty opposition, largely because "institutes" have failed to achieve sufficient autonomy (Macaya i; Fischel i-2). Chile's national university shows how institutes suffer from dependence on faculties or even are absorbed by them (Harrison, N.d.: 14; Coleman and Court 1992: 107). On the other hand, UNAM's "centers," which escape some of the constant conflicts characterizing faculty-institute relations, are rather marginalized and are widely seen as separate fiefdoms. An AID-supported effort at Bolivia's Universidad Mayor de San Andrés placed a public administration unit outside the mainstream structure—and then saw it suffer from a lack of university support. Similar problems confronted an AID-supported textile institute at Peru's National Engineering University (Adams and Cumberland 1960: 201, 170–76).[23] Additionally, the strength that comes from direct dependency on the rectorate, rather than on faculties, can lead to resentment within the university.[24] All these examples speak to the difficulties of public sector reform within universities.

Of course, URC-faculty friction does not necessarily doom URCS. Brazil's USP houses important centers like the one on violence—even while the role of a new network of URCS lacks definition and struggles over things like libraries and space (NUPES 1990: 1–5). The Universidad Simón Bolívar boasts institutes linked to Venezuelan industry. Overall university quality is one of the key factors that affect which Latin American URCS perform well.

Another factor is field of study. URCS may achieve more success outside social studies, the terrain in which most PRCS take root. This was the case for some of the first URCS: Argentina's UBA and La Plata offered enclaves for foreign scientists early in the century, and UNAM's institutes date to 1929, well before the great acceleration of URCS starting in 1974 (Vessuri 1986: 12; Fortes and Lomnitz 1991). Today, UNAM's hard sciences stand out for their achievements, whereas the UBA in several fields shows the difficulty of creating special structures within traditional universities.

Thus far, the discussion has centered on public URCS. The fundamental reason that private universities do not thwart PRC growth is that few private universities do research (Levy 1986: 287, 259–74). Panama's private university does not do research, leaving social research to the PRCS; the same is true of the Universidad Francisco Marroquín and Guatemalan PRCS and of Paraguay's Catholic university versus CPES and BASE-IS (Fernández 1989: 99–100; Palau pc). Argentina also fits here. Additionally, private universities did not produce more URCS because they presented fewer problems that would compel a flight from their mainstream.

That said, private URCS are increasing as part of the broader flowering of private universities.[25] Each of the top few Dominican private universities uses URCS (Silié pc). Indeed, PRCS are models that private universities (and now some public ones too) try to follow in their URCS. The idea is to build strength, prestige, and resources. In Peru, Pacífico and Catholic universities award incentives to encourage faculty members in URCS to seek grants (Walker i), a process paralleled at Mexico's ITAM. Top Venezuelan private universities also have URCS that do social research, particularly contract research, and therefore are partial alternatives to PRCS.

Private URCS encounter fewer institutional pressures for standardization. Examples include the Center for Social Research at Peru's Pontifical Catholic University, where some but not all members belong to a faculty, and a computer-oriented research institute at Mexico's Technological Institute of Monterrey. But private URCS do not escape all problems found at public URCS. Colombia's Andes has created centers partly to gain salary flexibility, which in turn is resented outside the centers. The AID-assisted Center of Social Science at Paraguay's Catholic university soon found itself in conflict with the university over its commitment to research vis-à-vis teaching (AID #5260095). And we have also seen instances where URC personnel or entire private URCs shift to PRCs.

To conclude, URCs are reactions to failures in the university mainstream and serve as alternatives to PRCs—often the main alternative within universities and the public sector. However, their success is too limited to block the proliferation of PRCs.

PULL FACTORS

To this point, the discussion has highlighted push factors in explaining the growth of PRCs. State repression, state weakness, and public university failures push—even force—researchers and related actors to seek an alternative. Only the discussion of positive macropolitics has involved mostly pull factors. The rest of the chapter redresses that imbalance.

If "failure" is defined as anything a sector does not do, the concept may become loose or trivial. No public or private sector handles all tasks, certainly not to everyone's satisfaction. Or the concept becomes circular: any activity located in one sector may be attributed to its absence elsewhere. A focus on empirical shifts from one sector to another helps avoid such pitfalls. But "failure" is too loosely applied where, like market failure theory, public failure theory turns attention away from positive factors. Rather than pointing always to one sector's failure, we must also consider forces that attract people to another sector. Unlike public failure theorists, I allow that the nonprofit sector can be the first choice (Salamon 1990: 230); in this sense, the *third sector* label may be infelicitous. Also, as public failure theory ignores pull factors, it is weak on why one sector serves where another did not. No zero-sum rule guarantees that what one sector does not do another will (Badelt 1990; Anheier and Seibel 1990a: 381).[26] Emphasis on the public sector's failure to satisfy extant demand underplays the positive side of why the nonprofit sector grows.

The ensuing two sections on pull factors treat (1) heightened demand for tasks that PRCs do well and (2) the supply side, which allows PRCs to make a positive response to demand. "Pull" thus means a positive force. The potency of push factors declines once two legitimate forms are functioning—once nonprofits exist alongside public institutions. Established forms grow partly because they are already there, for reasons not terribly different from those allowing other forms to grow. Push factors are more powerful in explaining most of the creation and early expansion of PRCs, but successfully functioning PRCs then become attractive to many who can choose between them and universities. The rising importance of pull factors applies to researchers, donors, contractors, clients, foreign colleagues, and domestic political groups. A crucial policy question is thereby raised concerning the degree to which PRCs are institutions of necessity, deserving of support, or institutions of choice, deserving of more circumspect scrutiny.

Heightened Demand

Democratization and privatization have unleashed multiplying demands for information and research.[27] (The analysis of positive macropolitics dealt mostly with democratization.) Privatization includes both for-profit and nonprofit organizations. Both types, as they gather steam, have increased the demand due to changing power relations, competition, and technologies. Another part of the story is the subjective appreciation of the importance of information and research. For example, Mexican business increasingly regards research as a necessity rather than a luxury (Zaid pc). At times, disdain for empirical information yields to exaggerated belief in the policy guidance it can supply.

Consulting centers, whether nonprofit or for-profit, are products of the heightened demand that is connected to overall privatization. They have proliferated in much of Latin America, Asia, and elsewhere. In some cases, their founders first unsuccessfully explored setting up shop as URCs. Peruvian peripheral PRCs do marketing and public opinion studies, which are published in high-cost, subscription-only, periodicals; their success encourages classic PRCs to compete in the new market for quick policy information (Cotler pc). Venezuelan centers, likewise, have gained domestic prestige; they constitute part of a wider privatization, which includes IESA's ascension to the policy pinnacle.

The proliferation of social action PRCs is also pertinent. It is valid to cite government failure, through both repression and weakness, but it is also valid to cite the rising demand for the research in question. This demand comes largely from the enormous expansion of other nonprofits, as well as from social movements, throughout Latin America. In addition, international donors, with their focus on the poor, NGOS, and social movements, contribute to rising demand. So do new democratic governments. Consequently, the number of social action PRCS increases fast, and the amount of social action work done by preexisting PRCS swells; this twin evolution toward the social action side is evident in nations like Bolivia and Uruguay (Contreras i; Chaparro i). Uruguay's CIEDUR (N.d.: 6–8) typifies PRCS that have moved from an academic genesis to a mix of academics and social action. At an extreme, some centers exchange academics for social action. Among the religious centers in this category are Brazil's CEAS and the Dominican Republic's CEPAE. Whereas many classic PRCS premiered in the 1960s, among them Paraguay's CPES, Peru's IEP, and Brazil's IUPERJ, many new centers have less academic leanings. The Peruvian case suggests that, where social action centers add research, this odyssey too results largely from a heightened demand for research as well as from the realization that research guides good action. Overall, a booming nonprofit sector greatly increases the demand for nonprofit research centers engaged in relevant activities.

Demand for research contributes to PRC growth—in absolute though not proportional terms—even where the demand does not favor any particular sector; again, not all growth requires distinctive explanation as long as two or three sectors already exist. But several dynamics give PRCS, as nonprofits, some natural advantages.[28] All these dynamics can somehow be stuffed into public failure concepts—whenever the public sector does not win, it has in a sense failed—but only by moving the conceptual emphasis away from the empirical one. Where a new PRC arises, we could as easily refer to a failure of the rest of the nonprofit sector as to public failure. More prudently, we should affirm that PRCS are often more suitable than university or government research alternatives. Government itself may seek an outside view that its agencies cannot provide, a common rationale for U.S. government contracts to think tanks. URCS may reasonably take a more theoretical approach than clients want. All this relates to PRCS' responsiveness and to familiar claims about the flexibility of existing nonprofit organizations or the rapid appearance of new ones where opportunity calls.[29]

Serious normative and policy issues present themselves. Not all expansion in response to demand, especially such specialized demand, is desirable, or appropriate, for every type of institution. These issues are held for the final chapter. The point here is that only a loose concept of public failure explains nonprofit growth regarding tasks the public sector rejects or tasks that simply flow more readily into the private nonprofit sector.[30] Nonprofits are frequently institutions of first, rather than second, choice And demand intensifies in areas where PRCs are the first choice.

The Supply Side

Heightened demand for nonprofits remains inadequate to explain non-profit growth unless supply is also available. PRCs need researchers and funds. And supply has its own dynamics. It does not automatically or passively follow demand. If demand is a necessary factor, it remains an insufficient one. Yet public failure theory, like market failure theory, often ignores supply (Young 1983; DiMaggio and Anheier 1990: 140–41).

Where supply simply cuts loose from prior attachments to public institutions, the public failure concept is pertinent if one can account for why the suppliers are willing to turn to nonprofits. Some of this occurred with donors' disenchantment with universities worldwide (World Bank 1980). But PRCs also attract fresh supply. This reinforces a sense of nonprofits as first-choice organizations.[31] Indeed, as supply is not merely a response to demand, a new and diverse supply of funding opportunities promotes PRC proliferation. Agile nonprofit entrepreneurs scurry to open PRCs geared to whatever funders are anxious to support at the moment. The IDB's interest in such areas as the environment, for example, encourages PRCs to work in that field.[32] After the discussion here of supply's role in PRC growth, ensuing chapters deal further with supply.[33]

As commonly happens with the nonprofit sector, religious organizations helped lead the way for PRCs. Jesuits created, staffed, and financed many early centers. Chilean examples, between 1963 and 1966, include INPROA in agrarian reform, ILADES in various socioeconomic areas, and CIDE in education; the Catholic church created CIDE to help with its religious schools. Foreign churches, especially European, also played a role. Despite liberation theology and other religious influence on the grassroots components of PRCs, however, PRCs increasingly draw on secular supply. Their supply is more secular than the private university's, which has also evolved toward the secular from the religious.

Funds

That financial supply is a variable, rather than a given, should be clear when the supplier is a voluntary actor. Leaving funding details aside here, the point is that almost all funders of PRCs act by choice. No guaranteed flow of resources stems from law, political obligation, or tradition, making this funding unlike that for public universities. Nations, sectors, and institutions with similar needs to those of major recipients may receive nothing.[34] Under even the direst conditions of flight from military repression, or of donor despair with universities, the philanthropic contribution to PRCs was not inevitable. Ford's funds were necessary to widespread PRC creation, but this creation was not a given, not even a conscious design. A diluted parallel holds for the IDRC's ongoing assistance to Argentina and Chile, and a powerful parallel holds for the foundation money that allowed the rise and "privatization of the social sciences" in Central America (Puryear 1983: 7; Tillett 1980: 68; Fernández 1989: 27–28). The point also holds for individual PRCs in more tranquil times: they require but do not automatically receive grants; Ford's grant to Colombia's FES in 1964 was at least as much a matter of the foundation's will as of PRC need.

Because donors and paying clients are actors with choice, the importance of PRCs' attractive features is again apparent. Donors came to prefer the nonprofit sector for crucial aspects of development assistance.[35] Consider one idea much discussed in theories on nonprofit growth: trust.[36] The idea usually refers to a mistrust of for-profit agencies, but it works here for mistrust of government. Donors involved in Central America chose PRCs to steer clear of government corruption and repression; SAREC believes that funding through government, which it uses for natural sciences, is inappropriate in the social sciences because of distorting political influences (Vega 1989: 41; Spalding, Stallings, and Weeks 1990: 20).

To fuse analytical categories together in real situations is to see how financial supply works with, not instead of, push factors. Donors did not act in a vacuum. It often took a lot for them and others to abandon great hopes in the mainstream of higher education. They facilitated more than engineered the sojourn from university to PRC. As in Colombia in the 1970s, foundations saw themselves accompanying professors who had decided to migrate (Himes i). Public university failure and international philanthropy went hand in hand.[37]

Producing the Human Resources

Of course, finance is useless without the other crucial supply: human resources. This is one reason that many U.S. think tanks locate near university campuses (Orlans 1972: 43). A huge university success paradoxically provides a supply of researchers for PRCs: university development in the postwar period produced a critical mass of social scientists. Many received scholarships for graduate study abroad. New disciplines, subdisciplines, and methodologies emerged. So did a strong belief in both basic and usable research. In most nations, these changes occurred kaleidoscopically, while critics derided the trends as imperialistic, shortsighted, or otherwise doomed to failure. When macropolitical or university failures befell nation after nation there were already social scientists, and budding social scientists, and social science infrastructures to come to the rescue. There was an eagerness to build more. When the scourge of authoritarian rule passed, it was clear that even its most vicious attacks had not wiped out a belief in social research but had, instead, forced internal and external exile. Existing PRCs expanded, new PRCs arose, and much was saved. Exiles returning from abroad swelled the ranks at PRCs.[38]

The supply of researchers was largest, and earliest, in precisely those nations that would lead the PRC ascent—Chile and Argentina. The high incidence of PRC founders and heads who had been foundation scholarship holders is striking. Almost all nations followed. Whereas Chile produced these researchers with its university modernization of the 1950s and 1960s, Brazil did more in the 1960s and 1970s, and its increased supply of sociologists, anthropologists, and political scientists staffed PRCs; Peru's rapid production of intellectuals by the 1970s likewise contributed (Rodrigues 1982: 19; Cueto i-2). Although most intellectuals have belonged to the political left or center, the eventual formation of more conservative think tanks depended on the prior appearance of conservative intellectuals.

As with the supply of funds, the supply of human resources interacts with push factors. The supply is "loose" and therefore available to new PRCs partly because public failure closes doors on what had been the largest opportunities; yet push factors without a large human resource supply could not lead to massive PRC growth. It follows that just a modest push can yield strong effects if the supply is large. Also as with funds, the supply of human resources is not automatically destined for one sector or another or one institution or another, so much depends on the pull of the nonprofits and the choice of individuals.

The Researchers Choose

The question of whether researchers enter PRCs because viable public options are absent or because PRCs are more attractive is tricky. The answer is clear only at the extremes. The situation where repression purges scholars has been well publicized: PRCs become the only option for the continuance of social research in the country. Less recognized about PRCs, but obvious in developed nations and increasingly pertinent in Latin America, is the other extreme.[39] Individuals leave institutions at which decent careers are possible in order to establish or join PRCs. Their motivations include a desire to earn more, to achieve fame, to increase productivity, to contribute more, to specialize, to work more comfortably, or to work with greater autonomy. The existence of a financial incentive contrasts with the common finding that nonprofit institutions must attract people willing to endure financial sacrifice.

Sometimes already famous figures, well established at PRCs, decide to establish their own, smaller PRCs.[40] Many PRCs form when some inside a PRC choose to break away. Examples include a bifurcation of Paraguay's BASE-IS; the IDESP break from CEBRAP in Brazil; the break of CEDES, CEUR, CISEA, and others from Argentina's Di Tella (Tillett 1980: 16); the break of Argentina's CET from ILET; that of Nicaragua's INIES from CRIES; that of a women's center from Chile's AHC; and that of GRECMU from CIESU in Uruguay. Although reasons range across most of those responsible for PRC creation in general, here the notions of choice and pull loom large in terms of comparative, specialist advantage for the new PRC and personal advantage for the individuals. One could call this PRC, or nonprofit, failure; my preference is to emphasize that researchers, like donors, choose. Public failure theory too easily bypasses the issue of choice (Badelt 1990: 61).

For social researchers, the PRC is increasingly an option alongside business, government, or emigration, all of which become attractive inversely to university attractiveness. Consider the course taken by scholars in the Dominican Republic who serve their government, witness its decline, and then establish PRCs such as the CIEA, despite offers from universities (Dore i-2). Writing about those headed for PRCs from universities, Tedesco and Blumenthal (1986: 21) cite a "growing disenchantment with teaching." Many researchers who were pushed out of universities can now return but prefer not to. At top Chilean PRCs like CECI and CIEPLAN, and at counterparts in Argentina and elsewhere, researchers cite such factors as university bureaucracy (Latorre i; O. Muñoz i; Krotsch i). Many academics who were resigned to being unable to live a middle-class life on a university salary do comparatively well at PRCs.

The tug of pull factors on the human resource supply is apparent and perhaps special for certain types of PRCs, including many on the periphery. The consulting center is one. Mexican and Venezuelan economists in those centers could get university or government jobs.[41] Another is the PRC built around a particular political party and formed to hire former officials. Right after the Sandinista electoral loss in 1990, officials, including university rectors, made PRCs one of their options. Peru's *apristas* have done the same. So have Venezuelan public servants; political leaders can establish their own center, "starting at the top" rather than entering a university at the bottom (García Guadilla i).

Mostly, however, Venezuela is an exception that highlights the rule that PRCs gather force through attractiveness. Venezuelan PRCs have a limited hold on social research. Broader privatization brings heightened demand; but that is recent and still yields peripheral, rather than classic, PRCs. One explanation for the lack of Venezuelan PRCs lies in the absence of military rule since 1958. Yet PRCs proliferate under civilian rule elsewhere, and most of Venezuela's public universities suffer from politicization and mismanagement, which have spurred the expansion of URCs. The uniquely attractive rewards that university professors receive across the board are therefore crucial.[42] Their average monthly salary is reportedly almost triple that of government professionals and exceeds that of government ministers. Professors may receive sixteen-month salaries, year-long sabbaticals every seven years, housing assistance, full pay at retirement, and death insurance payable to children up to age twenty-one—all for working largely union-set hours (O. Albornoz 1979; O. Albornoz 1993; Naim 1992: 47; Grannel i; Ettedgui de Betancourt i). The government's Ayacucho foundation and science and technology councils award extra funding for both continued education and research projects. Venezuela leads Latin America in the availability of full-time jobs within the professoriate. Even as they join consulting centers, many researchers retain a major share of their university positions (Vessuri i; García Guadilla i). Critics point out that excessive benefits for limited performance hurt the university and the nation, but if the university has failed the nation, it has not, at least in a pecuniary way, failed its academic staff.

Competition underscores how pull factors determine where the human resource supply goes to work. Elite private universities—hardly images of failing institutions—increasingly try to match the pull forces exerted by competitors on academics who are free to choose.[43] Since 1982, Mexico's ITAM, Ibero, and Monterrey Tec have all created URCs to attract talented young scholars uninterested in the traditional private university teaching job, offering them research and consulting opportunities. But the URCs then must struggle to hold on to such talent, which soon finds more attractive opportunities in separate centers, nonprofit and public, and in the business world (Estévez i-1). INTEC's CEDE in the Dominican Republic was established for several of the university's eminent figures, but they eventually preferred the greater autonomy conferred by PRCs.

In sum, not only magnitude but also choice of destination are impressive aspects of supply, for both financial and human resources. PRCs do well partly because supply enlarged, partly because they made themselves attractive. Of course, the growth and direction of supply evolved through intense interaction with heightened demand, however much we analytically distinguish supply and demand. Neither nonprofit growth generally nor PRC growth specifically can be understood by either supply or demand alone.

CONCLUSION

Similarly, PRC and nonprofit growth results from both push factors and pull factors. These factors interact, though the relative weight of push versus pull differs identifiably by macropolitcal situation, university performance, type of PRC, and so forth.

Macropolitical differences show that the balance between push and pull also evolves over time. The most obvious evidence comes as PRCs proliferate where military regimes give way to democracies.[44] The change in regime weakens push factors, though they remain due to austerity, university failure, and other difficulties. Meanwhile, democratization, privatization, and internationalization bolster the pull factors of both demand and supply, which are crucial to continued PRC expansion.

The importance of pull factors exposes weaknesses in public failure theory. The theory can be applied, somehow, to nearly all aspects of private growth—but only by stretching reality and terminology. It is marginal where nonprofits grow more from relatively nondistinctive causes, partnership with government, heightened demand, and choice in the provision and destination of supply. Exclusive reference to public failure would underestimate the expanse, significance, and attractiveness of PRCs and other nonprofits. Increasingly, PRCs are academic, political, and economic institutions of choice that fit the dominant development model more than they escape from it.

On the other hand, public failure theory proves crucial to much privatization and pertinent to still more.[45] It is particularly strong where we find evidence of tangible failure, that is, actual migration from one sector to another. This has allowed a dynamic, analytical approach, following change over time and thus avoiding the often static as well as vague sense of public failure theory based on economic modeling. Furthermore, I have found it logical and appropriate to opt for a broad application of public failure theory with regard to perception of public failure and to the failure of the public sector to act. These represent something less than the empirical migration out of the public into the nonprofit sector based on the former's objective failures, yet there is still a sense that people turn to the nonprofit sector after finding the public sector wanting. But in two other respects my broad use of public failure goes beyond extant theory: beyond government to other public institutions and beyond democratic to authoritarian contexts.

Accordingly, a reformulation makes public failure theory more useful in understanding the nonprofit blossoming epitomized by PRCs. Even the reformulation has its limitations, however. For one thing, it is too multifaceted to carry the presumed cogency of extant theory. Worse, even the broadened formulation does not guide analysis of the positive factors in nonprofit growth.

A suitable conclusion, therefore, emphasizes the diverse roots of nonprofit growth. Demand encompasses new and rising demand as well as previously unmet demand. Supply includes financial and human resources. Public failure refers to a lack of quality or distinctiveness or fit or quantity. It refers to governments, university faculties, and URCs. And it refers to a variety of tasks headed by research while not limited to it. Macropolitical factors include the political-economic and the ideological, the shrinking states and the growing states, authoritarian regimes and democratic regimes. Economic contexts of expansion and austerity both stimulate PRC growth.

Even similar PRCs grow in different ways under different circumstances. Furthermore, PRCs do not constitute a simple, single phenomenon. Like the factors responsible for their growth, PRCs are complex and variable. Fortunately, the concepts and categories developed here help effect more than a morass of raw data or a gross simplification of it. They yield different explanations, different mixes of factors, as reality dictates. And they do so in a way that goes further than a list of factors and a claim that most cases somehow fit the list. They allow us to take actual cases and show empirically, with conceptual interpretation, how and why privatization occurs where and when it does. Strong patterns and tendencies emerge.[46] Privatization's ubiquity, as well as its complexity and variability, thus becomes analytically manageable.

More than any other region, Latin America has experienced a combination of factors that, together, produce a leading private, nonprofit role in social research. Appreciating how this large nonprofit sector has come to be, we now explore how it functions. Patterns of growth illuminate patterns in finances, politics, and academic performance. Already, however, the inadequacy of dual-sector development models is evident. A third sector arises from failures in the public sector and from increased demand and supply emanating in all three sectors.

4 Finances

Philanthropy, Diversification, and Control

The supply of sufficient, stable income is a central challenge for nonprofit organizations. Such supply facilitates growth or effective maintenance and performance. Its absence means trouble.

The question of finances assumes special significance for nonprofit organizations because they stake special claims to autonomy and cherish autonomy as an end in itself and as a means of achieving flexibility, effectiveness, and other performance criteria. A core claim of diverse resource dependency theories—that the amount and type of funding, like other resources from the environment, shapes recipient organizations—is therefore of particular concern for nonprofits (Powell and Friedkin 1987: 182). Indeed, finance is the main reason scholars cast a skeptical eye when boosters claim that nonprofits constitute the independent sector.

Additional significance for the autonomy of nonprofits—or of research, or of Latin American development generally—arises because of the atypical and potentially dangerous origin of PRCs' income in Latin America. To appreciate this atypicality, we might consider nonprofits' funding elsewhere as well as the common funding of higher education.

One of the two major funding sources for U.S. nonprofits is fees paid by clients or members. These exceed philanthropic contributions; furthermore, contributions by individuals exceed contributions by foundations and corporations (O'Neill 1989: 9–11). The other major source of income for U.S. nonprofits is government. Contrary to popular impression, government has long funded nonprofits, boosting more than displacing them (Salamon 1987: 100–110). Contracting out government work to both nonprofits and for-profits is an increasingly important form of privatization, wherein government retains the responsibility for providing, but not administering, services (Gormley 1991a: 4–5; Hammack and Young 1993; Kramer 1981). In Western Europe and the Third World, government financing is even more salient, inasmuch as fees and domestic philanthropy are less common. Studies of nonprofits in international perspective properly highlight government funding (James 1989: 139–285).

Government has also provided the bulk of foreign assistance to developing nations, whether that assistance is funneled through the donors' public agencies or through nonprofit agencies of the giving nations (B. Smith 1990: 6). For universities, most foreign assistance has been public money, with the IDB easily leading the way in Latin America. And of course most funding for Latin America's universities, research, and intellectual life in general has come from domestic government (Camp 1985); this is the usual pattern worldwide.

The financing of Latin American PRCs breaks with these patterns. First, their income has come mostly from foundations. Judged by source as well as purpose, this is philanthropy. Second, their funds are largely derived from foreign sources. Such dependence obviously does not exist in developed nations for either higher education or nonprofits; among developing nations, it is associated much more with African than Latin American educational institutions.

Within Latin America's third sector, PRCs are neither ordinary nor deviant; that is, the sector has drawn substantially on foreign funds but usually not as much as PRCs have.[1] Concern over an organization's financial dependency naturally becomes even greater when the donor is foreign; thus, control is a major topic in the assistance literature (Cassen 1986; Roett 1972), though calls for a study of assistance to Latin America's research centers hitherto remained unanswered (King 1981: 249).

Putting together these two unusual features of PRCs' income—the dominance of foreign and private funds—this study enlarges a still small literature dealing with nonprofit dependence on international philanthropy (Anheier 1989; B. Smith 1990). In their formative years, PRCs represented an extreme of such dependence; they have become more typical as they have attracted some domestic funding, largely public.

This chapter considers PRCs' major and minor income sources.[2] It distinguishes between sources for individual centers and those for the aggregate sector, identifying and analyzing tendencies for certain types of PRCs. The second half of the chapter concentrates on the tricky issue of control versus autonomy.[3] There, the inquiry narrows from all income sources to only international philanthropy. Reasons for this narrowing include the prominence of these funds overall, the even greater dominance of foreign funds once we exclude contract work (which does not raise the same issues about autonomy and control), and the special concerns about dependence on foreign sources. Also, the growth of other funding sources is too recent to allow a comparable assessment; the analysis of philanthropy should provide a context and tools for that assessment in the future. Evidence mocks any simple hypothesis that "he who pays the piper calls the tune," and instead reveals patterns of both control by donors and freedom for recipients.

INCOME SOURCES

Dependence on International Philanthropy

PRCs have relied overwhelmingly on international finance, which often carries extra weight as hard currency or as a nurturing resource at a PRC's precarious birth—both parallels with grassroots nonprofits (Carroll 1992: 153). That degree of foreign support has surpassed any assistance category labeled "supplemental" (White 1974). It thus differs from funding in even the heyday of university assistance—the 1960s and the first half of the 1970s—as well as from previous and subsequent university assistance. Pivotal as it might be, foreign money has never constituted the bulk of university income in Latin America, rarely more than a significant minority, and that usually for only a few years.

Those nations in which social research occurs mostly in PRCs are those nations in which the research is mostly foreign funded. Corroboration comes from the CLACSO survey, despite its inclusion of many URCs financed mostly by their own universities: foreign sources account for more than three-fourths of the total in ten of seventeen countries (Bolivia, Peru, Chile, Ecuador, Paraguay, Uruguay, Guatemala, Honduras, Nicaragua, and the Dominican Republic), followed by Costa Rica, Argentina, and Colombia; that leaves only Mexico, Venezuela, Brazil, and Cuba less than one-fourth dependent (Calderón and Provoste 1990: VI-16). All forty agencies listed as financiers for Peru's DESCO (1990: 43–44) during its first twenty-five years were foreign.[4]

Foundations

Furthermore, where PRCs are most prominent, the foreign funding has generally come from foundations. Chile has probably been the leading recipient of Ford Foundation, IDRC, and SSRC funding; perhaps 90 percent of Bolivian PRCs have depended almost entirely on international philanthropy (Puryear 1994; Gamarra 1990: 201).[5] In nations where PRCs and universities produce the social research, most PRCs have depended on foreign philanthropy. There, however, the dependency usually falls short of the extreme seen elsewhere. From its 1976 inception, CEDEC has received funds from decentralized Brazilian agencies and from the state of São Paulo (CEDEC N.d.: 1, 10); the situation is similar for IUPERJ, among others (ibid., 1, 10); IUPERJ 1991: 2). Yet both those classic PRCs illustrate that, regardless of nation, PRCs that best fit definitional criteria on academic research have relied on international philanthropy.

The connection between foundations and PRCs epitomizes the tendency of private donors to give to private organizations. Here the connection goes far beyond the foundations' disproportional giving to Latin America's private over public universities. It contrasts with the tendency of most public foreign assistance to go to public institutions and, to press further, with the stronger tendency of domestic government money to go to public institutions. Foundations need not consciously seek a more pro-private course than other givers do. Rather, they appear naturally suited to work with these small, specialized, private institutions. It is a mutual match. Foundations have seen PRCs as the best alternatives to further their purposes, as outlined in the previous chapter.

U.S. foundations head the list of donors. This is true for the best-documented South American PRCs. It is also true for Central American PRCs (Vega 1989: 38). Among U.S. foundations, Ford is number one, easily. Its support has been important to Mexico's El Colegio and CEE, to Chile's CIDE and FLACSO, and to Argentina's CEDES, CEUR, and Di Tella—indeed, to almost all the important and some of the not-so-important PRCs in the region. Even In Brazil, where most of Ford's money went to universities, PRCs had more of the social science funds; the Getúlio Vargas Foundation, the Carlos Chagas Foundation, CEBRAP, CEDEC, and IUPERJ were favorites, and Ford often accounted for impressive shares of their total income.[6] In Peru, where European donors are prominent, Ford has given for decades to the IEP and, more recently, to the Peruvian Center for International Studies, GRADE, DESCO, and the Bartolomé Center in Cusco. If Ford, AID, and the IAF are the three main U.S. sources for Peruvian NGOs (Andean Report 1992: 33), Ford's supremacy rises the closer one gets to the PRC core. Ford also balances Europe's strong presence in the Dominican Republic, giving to centers such as FLACSO, Fondo (Foundation for the Advancement of the Social Sciences), and CIPAF (FF printout; Dore i–1). But Ford has never been the lone U.S. foundation in the region. With Rockefeller retreating over time, Tinker, MacArthur, Hewlitt, Heinz, and others have entered. Most of the foundations specialize more than Ford. Kellogg is a key foundation for health research; Hewlett gave at least its first million dollars solely to Mexico.

The privateness of assistance to PRCs is underscored by the separateness of U.S. foundations from government. One might have guessed otherwise. Just as Nielsen (1972: 388) states that the big foundations often cooperate with their own governments, so others argue that those same foundations, when operating internationally, cooperate with both their own governments and host governments (Arnove 1980b; Berman 1983). PRCs provide supportive examples, but three points run counter to that literature. First, the partnership is positive cooperation more than negative foreign influence. Second, at least U.S. foundations have usually acted apart from either government in funding PRCs. And third, during periods of military rule, foundations have funded PRCs that were in opposition to their own governments.

Less Private Sources

Moving beyond U.S. foundations, we better appreciate the extensiveness of the foundation-PRC nexus, but also that it is not always fully private. Since the 1960s, developed nations have put public money in the hands of their own nation's private assistance agencies (B. Smith 1990; Siegal and Yancey 1992: 49). In Western Europe, these include foundations. PRCs then benefit from various configurations of West European donors (Brunner i–1), ranging from freestanding foundations, as in Holland, to more pronounced government roles, as in Spain, Italy, and France, to blurrier foundation-government mixes, as in Sweden and Norway. Much of German public money is funneled through three private foundations—Friedrich Ebert, Konrad Adenauer, and Friedrich Nauman—each linked to a political party; the Adenauer Foundation explicitly favors nonprofits over public organizations. Canada's IDRC, which concentrates on the Southern Cone, is a public agency dependent on the Parliament but not administered by government, though recent changes throw its autonomy into question (IDRC 1986: annex 2; Tillett 1980: 34).

From the U.S. government, AID is probably the leading contributor. It is dominant in funding Honduran social science (Vega 1989: 46). It also contributes to neoliberal think tanks, including Hernando de Soto's ILD in Peru. The U.S. government does not fund foundations operating abroad, though it does fund some foreign NGOs (B. Smith 1983: 80–105), and it funds public and private U.S. universities that contribute to PRCs in indirect ways, such as tuition assistance for graduate study by junior researchers who work at PRCs. The main U.S. government-foundation hybrid is the IAF, a government corporation created in 1969 and operating much like a nonprofit, with private as well as public funds and a private board appointed by the president. The IAF assists peripheral PRCs involved with social action and assists classic PRCs doing research for self-help organizations. It is one of the two leading government donors to CLACSO centers; the other is Sweden's SAREC, established in 1976. If one still considers the IDRC governmental, it would lead the group. In any case, the IDRC and SAREC trail only Ford as funders of CLACSO institutions—and of its PRCs in particular (Calderón and Provoste 1990: VII-11).

A different ideological look springs from agencies like the National Endowment for Democracy, which joins AID in promoting private sector action. How far conservative U.S. foundations will go in funding like-minded PRCs abroad as they have done at home is uncertain (Zald and McCarthy 1987: 114). Liberal international groups (Resource Center 1990) and many Latin American intellectuals in conventional PRCs suspect a major and rising role for conservative U.S. PRC think tanks headed by Heritage and the AEI, along with the German Nauman Foundation. Garretón (1981: 90) reports AEI help for Chile's CEP. The ICEG, headquartered in Panama and dedicated to market-oriented human resource development, is another supplier, operating with money from AID, corporations, and foundations.[7] Also important, on the public side of international assistance, are multilateral organizations, led by the IDB, the OAS, and UN agencies. Only a small, often unspecified, portion of their higher education funding goes to PRCs.[8] The IDB, for example, relies on public agencies as it directs its work mainly to agriculture, science, and technology (Segal 1986b: 155).

Moreover, multilateral funds to PRCs come more through contract research than philanthropy for recipient-proposed projects. But the line is often fuzzy, and project support rises. In the 1990s the IDB created a fund for research in applied economics, which has primarily benefited PRCs. And where multilaterals give for social research, PRCs and related organizations are major recipients. They handle the research or organizational and administrative aspects of undertakings in the donors' priority areas. With its $850 million in loans related to the environment in 1991, and with additional projects under consideration that could amount to $7 billion in new investment, the IDB works with nonprofits for information, consultation, and implementation (IDB 1992). Like foundation money, bank money often goes to centers that lie on the border between PRCs and social service nonprofits.

Multilaterals are the main financiers of Paraguay's third sector (Duarte 1991: 19).[9] Multilaterals also fund IRCs, including some that are PRCs. CINDA receives the majority of its income from the IDB, the UNDP, and others, complemented by domestic consultancies and dues from constituent institutions (Lavados i–1). Paraguay's CEPEP is another center tied to an international network, but it exemplifies those IRCs that receive funds from their parent institutions (in this case it is the International Federation of Family Planning; Melián pc.) The UN is, of course, the most important parent institution. CELADE (1990) draws mostly on UN sources, which also support IRCs outside the UN network; UNESCO is a major source for FLACSO (N.d.: 23–24). Additionally, many IRCs have drawn on several multilaterals, as with ECIEL and the IDB, the OAS, and the UNDP (F. Herrera 1985: 321), or CEMLA and the IDB, the IMF, and the OAS (SELA 1990: 21). Thus, IRCs like CEMLA and RIAL draw on both multilateral and foundation support.

But foreign public funding of PRCs is often complicated. The need to work through host governments was a special obstacle for both multilateral and bilateral agencies when authoritarian regimes held sway.[10] Even in nonauthoritarian times, the IDB and the World Bank find difficulties. One problem is host governments' disinclination to guarantee loans to private institutions, whereas foundations have more flexibility to work directly with these institutions. Another is legal impediments (as in Peru) to the receipt of extra compensation for those who also work in the public sector. Nonetheless, multilateral funding is an important PRC source under democracies.

Trends

The evolving profile of foreign donors sketched to this point results in part from the introduction of some new donors but more from the redirection of older ones. Many donors have given to PRCs even as they have reduced funding for broad university development and URCs.[11] The crucial difference between foundations and other donors is that the former give mostly to research centers—adding significantly to PRCs while maintaining assistance for GRCs, URCs, and IRCs—whereas other donors give mostly to much larger, public recipients. A cataloguing of Rockefeller and Ford grants from 1972 to 1980 shows the foundations giving more to Latin America's research centers than to its universities.[12]

Even when foundations have turned to PRCs, however, they have not turned exclusively there. Just as PRCs do not depend totally on foundations for their foreign money, so foundations give to other research institutions. But no other research institution relies mostly on foundations. Beyond the URCs and IRCs already mentioned, a special word should be said about agricultural IRCs, which draw great amounts from foreign foundations, surpassing any PRC. Between 1966 and 1983 the Ford Foundation gave more than $14 million to CIMMYT, including money for its core budget. Ford's main PRC in all Latin America, El Colegio, received less than $5 million between 1963 and 1987. In fact, CIMMYT received the majority of Ford's total funding to Mexico in the 1970s, though "to Mexico" is deceiving, since the center is international (FF archives computer printout; FF #69128, #65132). But agricultural IRCs draw most of their funds from multilateral and binational agencies (IDB 1986; FF #67204). Between 1974 and 1988, the IDB targeted more than $100 million to CIAT in Colombia, CIMMYT in Mexico, and the Potato Center in Peru; and AID continues to outdistance the Mexican government in annual giving to CIMMYT. Indeed, some international philanthropy goes to agricultural ministries.

Having identified related phenomena, I need to reiterate the strong link between private philanthropy and private recipients.[13] As we turn to indigenous sources of research support, we will see that the PRC income profile is increasingly complex.[14] But as we also see how other research institutions rely mostly on indigenous and public sources, the PRC connection with international philanthropy continues to impress. PRCs represent a unique nonprofit privatization in research funding.

International philanthropy has been so important that any decline brings justifiable fear and tangible problems to PRCs. One aspect is that European, especially German, donors now turn to the east more than to the south, a turn that could affect all Latin Americaa nations. Those depending heavily on Europe are most vulnerable. Peru, for example, despite Ford and IDRC support, has drawn heavily on Dutch sources, followed by German ones

(Walker i); partly in response to that danger, SAREC commenced activities in the 1990s. The Dominican Republic illustrates early erosion: the Ebert Foundation closed its office and left only a few programs running (Dore i–2). Ecuador's CEPLAES has likewise been forced to tilt further away from research and toward social action. In Argentina, the decline of international philanthropy has led a few places to close, while more prestigious places like CISEA, EURAL, and CEUR have had to cut back (A. Thompson 1994: 32). Central American PRCs lobby donors not to retreat, arguing that the underlying problems of violence and poverty persist just as the chance to address them improves with greater peace and democracy (CRIES 1991: 6).

Public Domestic Sources

The threat posed by declining international philanthropy, aggravated by shaky exchange rates, tells as much about the fragility of PRCs as about the crucial contribution that international philanthropy has made. For PRCs and other nonprofits to weather the threat, they need new funding. They need domestic sources. Starting with public sources, the analysis draws contrasts to funding for other research centers and then identifies the conditions most associated with government funding of PRCs.

Contrasts to Other Research Centers
The affinity between foreign philanthropy and PRCs is underscored by the contrasting income profile for most other Latin American research centers, for whom the government is usually the overwhelming source of financial supply—or at least a major source. And those government funds generally come through direct subsidy.

Most nonuniversity scientific and technological research takes place in GRCs; private industry does little. The finest GRCs, Mexico's Institute for Electrical Research and Center for Research in Applied Chemistry among them, often enjoy major collaboration with foreign actors. In fact, foreign money exceeds domestic money for some research.[15] But the domestic money comes mostly from government. The rule is the same for GRCs that are public research centers. Other research occurs in public university faculties, also funded by government. Private university faculties do little research.

URCs are intermediate cases. Compared to university faculties, they receive funding from diversified government sources outside the central ministerial budget, notably from national science and technology councils. Brazilian sources include municipal governments. And URCs receive proportionally much more than faculties from foreign philanthropy. Indeed, the URC share from foreign philanthropy is rising (Calderón and Provoste 1990: II-19).

Even early on, a good deal of assistance to universities was aimed less at undergraduate than at graduate education and research, which often meant URCs. An example was Ford's grant in reproductive biology to UNAM's Biomedical Institute, one-half for innovative research, one-fourth for scholarships, and the rest for travel, libraries, etcetera (FF #71099). Laboratories were major recipients, as Rockefeller and Kellogg support at the Catholic University of Chile attests. In nations that welcomed large assistance, social science URCs also made the list, as with the University of Chile's graduate economics (FF #61372) and the Institute of Rural Economics at Brazil's University of Minas Gerais. Other examples, such as NUPES at Brazil's USP, illustrate the continued importance of foreign assistance and a common mix: project funds and other pivotal, supplementary funds come largely from international philanthropy, while the university provides the URC its own infrastructural resources, including secretarial, communications, and computer facilities (NUPES 1990: 1–4).[16]

Colombian URCs also garner diverse income. IEPRI (1990: 12–13) at the National University draws constantly from the university while adding, within its first three years of operation, funds from the government's science and technology council, the Ford Foundation, and Colombian foundations such as FESCOL. At the Universidad de Los Andes in 1989–1990, CEDE drew on quite an array of funders for its economics research.[17] Still, the main source for most URCs is government subsidy filtered through the universities' administrations. An example is the Center for Social Research at the University of Puerto Rico, though Rockefeller and other foundation money contributed one-sixth of its income in its early years (Quintero N.d.: 32). Moreover, the foreign percentage of URC income has usually declined with the general decline of foreign assistance to universities since the mid-1970s. Even before that, URCs depending mostly on foreign aid, such as the educational research institute of the Catholic University of Chile, were exceptional. The same university's economics center drew heavily on the university's budget, while as a separate PRC, CIEPLAN, it would soon depend on external help. In Mexico, UNAM's biomedical institute drew 75 percent of its 1975 income from the university, plus other money from government, despite OAS, IDRC, and Ford help. And UNAM's social science URCs have until recently mostly emulated faculties in rejecting foreign donors at least as much as potential donors have rejected them (FF #71099; Lomnitz i–1).[18]

The data strengthen, by comparison, the association of foreign foundations and PRCs. URCs lie between PRCs and university faculties—but closer to the latter. Unlike PRCs, they count mostly on public money; also unlike PRCs, they count mostly on domestic money. The domestic, public financial profile is obviously even more characteristic of GRCs. Domestic money is not absent from PRCs, however. Nor is public money. As they move more into the political-economic mainstream, PRCs are becoming less striking financially for what they are missing and more striking for their plurality of funders, both public and private.[19]

The domestic income of PRCs is mainly public. This obviously limits privateness, but it echoes the common U.S. and European policy of government financing for domestic nonprofit organizations. Public finance for nonprofit organizations is a major development for Latin American higher education and politics. It can be understood, for the PRCs, in terms of the tasks they pursue, the types of government that are supportive, and the form that this financing takes.

Task

For decades, PRCs combining graduate teaching with research have counted mostly on domestic public funds. El Colegio de México and Brazil's Getúlio Vargas Foundation lead the list for Latin America.[20]

CIDE, IMES, and the provincial colegios also fit the Mexican list. Indeed, government is so central in Mexico that little latitude has existed for PRCs without public money. Government subsidies usually cover regular salaries, though foreign money can be indispensable for significant research endeavors. This again shows the proximity between Mexico's private and public research centers. Among the latter, CINVESTAV has attracted international philanthropy, especially within some units, while receiving most funds directly from the education ministry. Chapingo also required a large initial foreign contribution; Plan Chapingo in the 1960s received large support from four donors: AID and the IDB for physical infrastructure and academic departments, and the Rockefeller and Ford Foundations for scholarships, technical assistance, and services (IDB Project; FF #65288). But the Mexican government quickly became the main financier. International assistance now accounts for a small share of expenses, though it remains critical to the institution's excellence (Alcalde i; Jiménez i). The contrast between CIMMYT's and Chapingo's financing relates to a government commitment to fund its own institutions as opposed to international ones.[21] Also, Mexico's public and private research centers both are prededents that suggest that expansion of teaching at PRCs elsewhere in Latin America could well bring expanded subsidies. Funding for special programs to train government personnel is already widespread.

Compared to teaching, applied research is a less reliable but increasingly relevant task for attracting government money. It is also a much more common activity. Actually, some of the less common applied activities are the most attractive. Science PRCs are natural recipients of funds from science and technology councils. Colombia's CIB is a good example; and Argentina's CIMAE gets much of its money this way, including funds from the national and Buenos Aires provincial councils (FJMA 1980: 31). The Argentine government likewise funds an assortment of foundations that do medical research as well as the Bariloche Foundation for scientific research. PRCs that link social and nonsocial research and those that do research in appropriate technology have gained importance.

But most PRC research remains in social areas, and so it is crucial that here, too, funded applied work has increased. The rise of PRCs involved in social action is pertinent. As in Uruguay, PRC work in applied social tasks draws largely on national sources, including government, while more basic social science research does not. No dichotomy exists, however. SAREC funds CIEDUR's technical assistance for popular organizations and all major Uruguayan PRCs do both applied and basic research (Chaparro i; Cosse pc). Moreover, democratization has increased government contracting in much of Latin America, including contracts with peripheral PRCs engaged in consulting as well as social action.[22]

Regime

In discussing type of government, one must differentiate among authoritarian regimes. Cuba's communist, antiprivate system ruled out the very existence of PRCs. Repressive military regimes have funded private centers only in exceptional circumstances. Even IRCs linked to intergovernmental accords have struggled under these regimes. FLACSO-Chile lost its government income, and FLACSO-Argentina received a minority of its income from government (as compared to one-half for Ecuador's and nine-tenths for Mexico's FLACSO branches).[23] IRCs more confidently count on funds from host governments where democracy either reappears, as with FLACSO-Chile, or remains in place, as perhaps with CRESALC in Venezuela.

Mexico is the main case of civilian authoritarian rule, though several Nicaraguan PRCS received funds from the Sandinista government (Fernández 1989: 28). The Mexican regime has long been El Colegio's, CIDE's and FLACSO-Mexico's major funder. Outside those teaching centers, recipients have included the CEE and the Lucas Alamán Foundation; the Barros Sierra Foundation is a leading example of PRCS favored by recent modernization policies (Rubio pc-1; Basáñez i).

Democracy, however, is the politics most conducive to domestic funding of PRCS and other nonprofits. Sometimes funding emerges in the waning years of authoritarian rule, during transition. Debatable evidence appears in contemporary Mexico, while firm if limited evidence appeared in Chile. The most important case was Brazil; two reasons were its prolonged transition period and the absence of the widespread government hostility to social science manifested in neighboring republics.

Evidence that PRCS then get increased funds with establishment of democratic rule comes from every pertinent nation. Officials who themselves were previously at the PRCS routinely purchase PRC services. Brazil's CEBRAP illustrates how funding initiated before full democratic takeover greatly increases after it, and how state as well as federal sources are important: in São Paulo, state money for PRCS matches federal money (Miceli, 1990). The 1983 Alfonsín government immediately became a financial source for FLACSO and other Argentine PRCS disposed to undertake surveys and other solicited activities; the Bariloche Foundation, which lost its government funding after the 1976 coup, soon drew 25 percent of its income from the democratic government. Argentina also shows the importance of a democratic government's facilitation of access by PRCS to public foreign assistance (Cosse i; Cavarozzi i). In Uruguay, too, renewed democracy has brought significant government funding for such PRCS as CIESU and CIE-DUR. Paraguay's CDE is a further case where international money was joined by government money upon democratization; it benefited from the 1989 creation of DIBEN, an office to aid NGOS (Moreno pc). DESCO is but one Peruvian PRC that receives government contracts for matters ranging from education to judicial reform, though government's decline in the 1980s pushed PRCS like DESCO, CEDEP, CEPES, and even some labeled leftist to seek increased funds from the World Bank, the IDB, and AID (DESCO 1990; Andean Report 1992: 32). Within older democracies, Colombia's FEDESAR-

ROLLO and CCRP are solid examples of PRCs receiving government con-tracts.[24]

Support from friendly governments is clearly a boon for PRCs. Yet the picture is not all positive. At a broad level, social organizations and move-ments that forge their myths in adversity may face new problems when the environment is more accepting. Dangers to autonomy, or privateness, are real. Additionally, domestic funding may free foreign donors from their sense of responsibility, especially as competing claims are so pressing. In Chile and other nations, the prospect sends a chill through the NGO sector (Downs and Solimano 1989: 205–08). Yet state support may remain a shaky alternative.

Form

Government finance takes a different form depending on whether the recipient is a PRC or a public organization. Whereas the latter depends overwhelmingly on annual subsidies, usually from the education ministry, the PRC usually receives government money less regularly and less directly. Only PRCs with major teaching programs function on annual government subsidies, and even these, like the Getúlio Vargas, also receive some money through special government funding (Cunha pc). The difference between special funds and annual subsidies helps to maintain a private-public dis-tinction, as special funds allow PRCs to maintain a market-orientation and probably greater autonomy than would direct subsidization. If direct subsi-dization is consistent with corporatism, government funding of PRCs is often consistent with pluralism.[25]

One indirect form of government assistance comes in tax exemptions, as at Venezuela's IESA. Another comes where salaries are paid at public institutions, mostly universities, to people who also work in PRCs. This parallels public subsidization of private universities. Where universities are weak, the PRC-university arrangement usually involves only part-time uni-versity teaching and salaries. But in Brazil, where many public universities are strong, subsidization of PRCs is also strong; some of the researchers at PRCs draw full university salaries. A different parallel emerges with the government bureaucracy. In Guatemala, Honduras, Costa Rica, and Pan-ama many who work in public administration also work part-time in PRCs (Vega 1989: 39). Public employment in Latin America need not constitute sole employment.

Additionally, decentralization of national government funding for higher education translates into diversification of institutional recipients. This trend corresponds to the European evolution away from centralized higher education finance and structure. Like URCs, PRCs are recipients. National science and technology councils channel money to PRCs where central bureaucracy would not. Council money has been important to Brazilian PRCs, though FINEP has turned away from "soft" areas (Schwartzman pc-4). It has also been important to Argentine PRCs, just as it supports social research outside the PRCs in Costa Rica, Colombia, and Venezuela (Calderón and Provoste 1990: VI-7). Social action PRCs and even classic PRCs doing research on social problems benefit where governments seek to attack poverty through partnership with nonprofits. Chile's Fund for Social Solidarity and Investment is an example (Loveman 1991: 11). Less common is money targeted at a specific project or undertaking, such as the education journal published at Mexico's CEE.

Councils and other decentralized public agencies increasingly offer merit pay to individuals as well to support their specific research projects. Uncertainties abound, however. Ecuador has yet to make the move. The Peruvian council helped in the 1980s, then slipped. Moreover, inflation erodes the value of the funds. And the funds often benefit principally science or technology, as in Uruguay and Argentina. The Argentine case also shows how policy may or may not direct funds outside the university: initial funds were aimed at university professors, but the 1966 and 1976 coups reversed this direction; redemocratization brought a return to the university, but it was brief (M. Albornoz 1992: 326–27).

Nevertheless, several nations have helped support and retain both senior and promising scholars. Mexico's SNI is a leading example, and Venezuela's Program for the Promotion of Researchers shows significant similarities (Medina 1992). As of 1991, SNI reached 6,442 researchers, 40 percent in junior or candidate status, with a total budget of $40 million, which allowed more than $1,000 per month at the top (Malo 1992: 344–45). Inclusion in the program is for three to four years, with review for renewal. UNAM has the most recipients, disproportionally from its URCs, but public research centers like CINVESTAV and Chapingo rank much higher by the percentage of their staffs, as El Colegio does in the social area.[26] Brazil's supplemental grants, likewise, have major impacts on those both in the university and outside it (Miceli i). Councils also contract with PRCs to do needed research or organizational tasks to prepare larger projects targeted at universities or noneducational institutions.[27]

For all the complex arrangements, however, the one crucial link between the form of government assistance and the PRC's task is that the money is usually earmarked for a particular project. This holds for projects proposed by PRCS or their researchers and for contracts assigned by government to willing PRCS.

Several factors limit the public side of domestic finance. Prior practice works against rapid change. Government financing of research centers remains greater for GRCS and URCS, as the major source for each, than for PRCS. Public institutions lobby against the privatization implied in helping PRCS at public expense: Mexican state universities object to government assistance for the provincial colegios, and Peru's unions object to contracting out social work projects to PRCS.[28] From the other end of the political spectrum, neoliberal governments may leave their tasks to privately funded nonprofits, as they often do with grassroots organizations (Carroll 1992: 170). Thus, government disposition to help PRCS, even friendly PRCS, is not a given; in times of economic difficulty, disposition to such help may be especially limited, much to the chagrin of those who expected more from ex-colleagues now in high places.

All this leaves government as the main domestic source because of its sharp increase and because promise and recent change more than sustained contributions characterize the alternative sources that are so important to U.S. research. The trend, however, is toward greater domestication and diversification of PRC income, which makes the privatization of PRCS' domestic financial base a reality. Three sources of private funds are marketed research, self-finance, and indigenous philanthropy.

Marketed Research

Marketed research provides evidence of overlap and interaction between the nonprofit and for-profit sectors. Peripheral PRCS with for-profit characteristics form to conduct and sell research—for example, those that survey public opinion or do political polling. Other PRCS form in collaboration with the private organizations that fund them; their "market" is relatively fixed. Many centers rely on one patron organization. A Mexican example is the CEESP, funded by its powerful business association. Among the nonprofit patrons are unions, political parties, and especially churches. Thus CINEP counts on Colombia's Jesuits; on the other hand, Peru's Bartolomé in Cusco looks well beyond the Dominican order (Cotler pc).

Intersectoral blurring may occur within PRCs, as well. For-profit activity may increase in PRCs that are themselves legitimately nonprofit. It is common for education and other nonprofit organizations around the world to engage in profit-making activities to pay for their other activities (Skloot 1987: 387; James 1989: 291). Mixing of this kind is natural where PRCs combine research and other activities. Venezuela's Trinidad medical center generates about 85 percent of its income from clinical practice, which then subsidizes its research; Mexico's Barros Sierra has one branch that sells services and another that does research; Colombia's FEDESARROLLO uses the "extra funds" it generates to finance projects, publishing, and seminars (Pérez i; Rubio pc-1; Escobar pc-3). Cross subsidization may disappear only at extremes: pure consultancy firms are common, but these are not PRCs, whereas PRCs wholly committed to pure research that generates no immediate income are rare.

Mainstream PRCs from Argentina to the Dominican Republic (Silié 1988: 125) have made great progress in generating income through the sale of research. In so doing, they have made a breakthrough—laudable, lamentable, or both—in the history of Latin American research. On the foreign side, contracts with multilateral agencies, governments, and foundations have increased. On the domestic side, however, contracts have predominated over grants. Domestic contractors spring from all three sectors in an open market situation. Among the nonprofits, the church leads (Vega 1989: 42), though lay social action groups are also prominent. Such market activity links social research to both human needs in the nonprofit sector and economic production in the for-profit sector—to a degree surpassing what the region's universities have ever accomplished. Nor does increased government contracting undermine the market; on the contrary, the state becomes more a market player and less a direct producer or subsidizer.

In addition to contracting, some PRCs garner significant income from sales of their publications. At the top might be ideological centers, followed by other think tanks, and solid academic centers. Argentina's rightist Center for Studies on Liberty got 53 percent of its income from sales; conversely, the Center of Research and Social Action garnered only 3 percent (FJMA 1980: 28–29, data for 1978). Even classic PRCs sell their journals, books, and perhaps working papers. The best, like their leading URC counterparts, sell internationally as well, gladly accepting hard foreign currency. Peru's IEP derives about 20 percent of its income from such sales.

Naturally, selling in the marketplace is a form of dependency. It is not terribly restrictive for individuals and PRCs hawking work integrally related to their main research pursuits, but it causes major problems when PRCs feel pressured to focus on contracts and sales rather than on basic research. In the early 1990s, for example, the economic group at Argentina's CEDES relied on contracts and sales for probably 90 percent of its income (Balán i–2). Pushed far enough, marketing may convert classic PRCs into peripheral PRCs. For better or worse, PRCs change the basic contours of autonomy and accountability in Latin American social research. They trade dependence on a central subsidy for dependence on clients and the competitive market-place, a shift integrally connected to the region's new political-economic model and intersectoral activities.

Self-financing

To reduce the dangers in such dependencies, nonprofit organizations may increase self-financing. Only three of CLACSO's centers garner a major-ity of their income from self-financing (Calderón and Provoste 1990: II-15), though CLACSO usually excludes PRCs most reliant on market sales. More typical of successful self-financed PRCs is Brazil's CEBRAP, where self-financing accounts for 10 percent of income.

Tuition does not provide much help for PRCs. Either no income or mar-ginal income through fees for nondegree courses is the rule. Some degree-granting PRCs, including El Colegio, follow the traditional public university antipathy to tuition rather than the private university reliance on it. More-over, graduate education and research are funded only in small part by tuition, even in U.S. private universities.[29] Business schools that do ample research probably impose the most substantial tuition among Latin Ameri-ca's PRCs.

Endowments seem ideal for nonprofit higher education institutions (Hansmann 1986b), but they have little tradition in the region. No PRC approaches the Brookings Institution, which draws one-fourth of its large income from its endowment, or the Hoover Institution, with an endow-ment exceeding $125 million (J. Smith 1991: 272, 280), not to mention the endowments of top U.S. universities. Nevertheless, PRCs—along with inter-national philanthropy—have pioneered in this area within the Latin Ameri-can context.

The Ford Foundation has made several efforts to establish endowments to provide a sustaining income that would diminish the need for external assistance (Moock 1980). Classic PRCs that have received at least a half million dollars in endowments include Brazil's CEBRAP (1975), Chile's CIEPLAN (1987), and Peru's IEP (early 1990s); more modest grants for classic PRCs in education include Mexico's CEE and Chile's CIDE (FF archives, computer printout; Muñoz Izquierdo i; Gatti and Chateau 1988: 40). Argentina's Di Tella Institute and Mexico's El Colegio were other early recipients. As of the late 1970s, Di Tella still received substantial income from investments (FJMA 1980: 81), but the institute's decline poisoned the overall atmosphere and the endowment was not well handled. At El Colegio, Ford gave a $2 million initial boost. Mexico's economic deterioration reduced that considerably, though the institution made an effort to rebuild, and the government helped with a fiftieth anniversary present (FF #68229; Urquidi i–1; Székely i).

Another novel Mexican example goes beyond Ford: CIDAC is that rare PRC with an endowment formed indigenously. After both business and government contributed in the late 1970's, the bank denationalization led to the closing of IBAFIN in 1984, and assets were used to help form CIDAC (Rubio pc-2). Outside Mexico, SAREC-funded PRCs have requested their funder to help establish endowments (Spalding, Taylor, and Vilas 1985: I-3). The endowment idea may gain potency as a natural link, during privatization, of a vibrant nonprofit sector and a potentially more involved for-profit sector.

Indigenous Philanthropy

Voluntary giving is another aspect of privatization that shows more promise than presence, domestically. For the Third World (other than India) and Eastern Europe, it is a rare source for nonprofits generally and for research nonprofits in particular (Eisemon and Kourouma 1991; Siegal and Yancey 1992: 33–34). Corporate philanthropy is one option. Of some twenty-five SAREC-funded PRCs, only Chile's CIPMA gets significant corporate money—and that is from foreign businesses concerned about the environment (Spalding, Stallings, and Weeks 1990: 16, 80). But involvement by domestic corporations are rising. National affiliates of international companies, such as Nestles—Colombia, may help import the custom. Some national money goes to the decreasingly rare PRCs on the political right. Chile's CEP and Argentina's Mediterranean Foundation receive mostly domestic corporate funds—once reportedly 86 percent of income for the latter (Godoy i; FJMA 1980: 171).[30] Some Argentine businesses give to a variety of PRCs to ensure good will and contacts regardless of which party is in power. In Mexico and elsewhere, corporations turn to research centers for reliable data and analysis, whether those centers are closely allied institutionally with the corporations, are truly separate, or are URCs. The Peruvian case shows that PRCs must compete with elite private universities for the still modest corporate donations to higher education.

Foundations give more than corporations. Here too, however, Latin America has little tradition. The links between PRCs and foundations remain overwhelmingly international. The growth of Latin American foundations merits attention yet receives almost none (Stromberg 1968; A. Thompson 1992). These foundations emerged with industrialization and prosperity, broadly following the U.S. pattern of the first half of this century (Odendahl 1989: 160). Early Venezuelan examples include the Luis Roche, 1942; the powerful Eugenio Mendoza, 1951; and others based on oil revenues, such as the Creole, 1956 (Spear 1972: 31–35). The downturn in oil revenues in the 1980s epitomized a general downturn for the region, which hurt philanthropy. Colombian wealth has likewise led to such major foundations as the Carvajal, established in the 1960s, and the FES. Colombia in fact boasts what is for Latin America an exceptional philanthropic tradition, backed by supportive tax policies (B. Smith 1990: 261). Relative prosperity also promoted the growth of Brazilian foundations; CEBRAP reports that 40 percent of its income comes from domestic foundations, including local ones.

Latin American foundations also grow from contact with international foundations; some foundations are direct national extensions of other nations' foundations. In Colombia, FESCOL is linked to Germany's Friedrich Ebert Foundation, and the Santillana is an extension of Spain's Santillana. Contacts with U.S. foundations help spread the ideology of private, pluralist activity and business responsibility. Alongside its Brazilian and Argentine counterparts in the multinational Lampadia Foundation, Chile's Andes Foundation, created in 1985 by prospering business leaders, looks like a classic U.S. foundation operating in a market economy.

That said, limits on the foundations' role abound. Many "foundations" do not fit the conventional idea of private donor organizations targeting private wealth to recipients.[31] They are not "independent foundations" (Ylvisaker 1987: 361; Odendahl 1989: 159). Instead, the term foundation generally designates little more than nonprofit. The designation is used partly to help attract money (as in Costa Rica; Araya i–1). Most foundations are recipients more than sources of philanthropy. Or they are transmitters; Paraguayan foundations that give have first received from elsewhere (Cerna pc). All this helps explain how a nation like Argentina, with little prosperity for decades and with a statist tradition, had more than 800 foundations in 1982.[32] Argentine foundations arise mostly to raise money, and Brazilian foundations, such as the Esperança, and most otherwise varied Chilean foundations are also receivers (A. Thompson 1992; Larraín i).[33]

An additional deviation, common in Latin American higher education, is the foundation with a one-to-one relationship with its university. They are thus like fund-raising boards more than separate foundations choosing various recipients.[34] Business groups create a parent foundation, or patronato, which then creates the university or guarantees its solvency. This is common at private universities, including Venezuela's Andrés Bello and Metropolitana, Argentina's Notorial and Belgrano, and Mexico's Technological Institute of Monterrey and Autonomous University of Guadalajara (Levy 1986: 130).[35] Argentina's Di Tella brings the form to PRCs; and Venezuela's IESA, in 1987, added its foundation.

Moreover, some foundations are basically PRCs. These include Brazil's Carlos Chagas and Getúlio Vargas; Colombia's FEDESARROLLO, CRESET, and Foundation for Permanent Education; Mexico's Barros Sierra; and the Dominican Republic's Fondo. More common are foundations that are partly PRCs or peripheral PRCs. Paraguay has five or six of these; Colombia's Santillana, formed in 1989, anticipated the addition of its own researchers (Bejarano pc); and the important Carvajal mixes research with its other emphases. PRC foundations are thus at least partial counterparts to those U.S. "operating foundations" devoted largely to in-house activities, including research (Ylvisaker 1987: 361; Orlans 1972: 3, 39). The Twentieth Century Fund and the Institute for Advanced Study are examples.

Where Latin American foundations truly give to separate recipients, PRCs are not usually major targets. Of the Venezuelan foundations cited, for example, the Mendoza gives priority to agriculture and child care and the Creole to education at lower levels. Colombia's Eduardo Carranza and Chile's Beethoven support individual artists and cultural events, whereas the Ricardo Galindo Quelquejeu provides food for Panama's poor. The Carvajal, set up to aid Colombia's poor, concentrates on technical assistance and training for tiny businesses; many of the nation's foundations emphasize construction and recreation (Aldana pc-2; B. Smith 1990: 253,

262). Even Colombia's FES, created in 1964 with help from Rockefeller and Ford to aid the Universidad del Valle, among others, now covers four different fields, stressing aid to the poor; research is just one priority within the education field.[36]

While the Argentine survey shows more than half the reporting foundations identifying education as their priority, this rarely means donations to higher education. And beyond direct support for foundations' own universities, higher education means mostly scholarships, sometimes for conferences. It does not mean support for institutions per se. Mexico's Lucas Alamán, Venezuela's John Boulton, Argentina's Aragón, and Brazil's Atlantic for Education, Arts, and Science are examples. Venezuela's Gran Mariscal de Ayacucho is easily the giant, though it is largely a government agency notwithstanding its 1975 shift to foundation status for the purposes of attracting more private money and gaining flexibility and autonomy (March 1982: 6). The Lampadia, which in 1989 donated $8.5 million from its separate branches in three nations, emphasizes scholarships through merit review procedures resembling those found at prestigious U.S. foundations (Christian 1990).

The extent to which scholarships and other research assistance benefit PRCS is unknown. A prospering foundation world could potentially mark an important break with Latin American tradition, which would benefit the equally innovative world of PRCS. Like all sources other than direct subsidy, foundations may particularly help PRC personnel.[37] They could therefore enlarge the gap in rewards between PRCS and universities.[38]

Summarizing

In sum, private domestic funding commands much more attention now than it did in the 1970s, mostly because of the rapid rise of marketed research but also because of other breakthroughs against tradition. Private domestic income usually trails domestic public funding and, especially, international private funding, and it is limited and unstable compared to the private financing of U.S. social research, especially at think tanks. Nonetheless, such funding constitutes a significant privatization in the context of Latin American history. A new breed of private nonprofit institution, often quite entrepreneurial, receives funds from a fresh variety of private sources, both nonprofit and for-profit. With democratization, however, PRCS also pioneer in nonprofit receipt of public funds, so the privatization in question is not a simple growth of private over public—especially as private foreign philanthropy declines. Financial diversification beyond international philanthropy has involved powerful new interactions among sectors.

Following Salamon (1987: 104), I categorize PRCs according to their primary source of funds: private giving, fees, or government.[39] Unlike most U.S. nonprofits, Latin America's PRCs depend overwhelmingly on private giving, which is mainly from foundations, especially foreign foundations. Fees virtually never dominate. Income generated by research and service activities composes most private domestic income. Also growing fast, often from near zero, is government funding—usually indirect and decentralized, rather than from ministerial subsidies. A few PRCs have long been dependent on government money, typically PRCs involved in graduate education, but many PRCs are diversifying their income and many new PRCs attract diverse funding from the outset.[40]

CONTROL VERSUS AUTONOMY

The dependence of PRCs on foreign funding is continually bemoaned, even in the largest nations (Comissão Nacional 1985: 79). On the other hand, neither the degree nor the deleterious effects of control are simply proportional to the percentage of funds coming from abroad. Control is especially difficult to gauge when dealing with the voluntary financing of specialized private organizations. There is more mutual matching than classic power of "A" forcing "B" to do something "B" does not want to do. Yet only a blurry line separates free choice in mutual matching from inducements that lead "B" to want to do things that would not otherwise be priorities. The relative autonomy of PRCs is tricky to assess. Nevertheless, key points and patterns can be discovered. We look first at factors limiting PRCs' autonomy and then at factors sustaining it.

This analysis concentrates on the impact of international philanthropy, the main funder for PRCs. Comparisons are drawn with funding from domestic government; as that funding increases, it will require more scrutiny.

Selectivity as a Control Mechanism

Intense donor selectivity, characteristic of international philanthropy to nonprofits, implies donor control, when what matters to donors are the particular characteristics of the PRC or even the particular characteristics of the PRC's proposed project. Not to suit the donor is to jeopardize the financial lifeline. In Latin America, such selectivity exceeds, in certain ways, the level reached in foreign assistance to universities in the 1960s, which was also selective compared to financing by the domestic government (Levy 1991). Donors then often based their decisions on nationwide factors, related to macropolitics or the overall higher education system. Colombia, Chile, Central America, and Brazil were targets more than were Mexico, Argentina, Uruguay, and Venezuela. In contrast, national variables rarely affect donor assistance to PRCs except as they reflect themselves inside individual PRCs. To be sure, the heavy assistance to PRCs in Chile, Argentina, Mexico, and Brazil stems partly from such broad factors as the nations' size, the early development of the social sciences, and for the first two nations, the extended period in which university alternatives were absent. But attractive PRCs receive donors' assistance regardless of nation.

And attractive PRCs have arisen in each nation (outside Cuba), even those where social science overall is weak. Thus, SAREC has given to El Salvador's CINAS, to FLACSO-Guatemala, and to regional centers in Central America, to CERES and CEBEM in Bolivia, and to CPES and BASE-IS in Paraguay. Ford has given to some of these and to centers like CELA in Panama, CEPLAES in Ecuador, and the Haitian Center for Social Science Research. Smaller donors also have given to PRCs in these nations, such as Adenauer to Guatemala's ASIES (Fernández 1989: 40). By comparison, Ford has never or rarely given to universities in Paraguay, Panama, Ecuador, Haiti, or Uruguay. The experience of Mexico, of pre-1966 Argentina, and of nations where universities sometimes receive funds further demonstrates that PRCs receive donations even during periods when their nations' university faculties are off limits for assistance.

In one sense, foreign assistance appears less selective regarding PRCs than regarding universities: probably most PRCs receive funds, if we strictly identify PRCs with basic research, whereas only a small percentage of universities are ever favored.[41] Of course, many PRCs do not continue to receive funds as they once did or as their programs require, which helps explain PRCs' precarious financial shape. Rather than disproving selectivity, this rather widespread funding of PRCs has underscored their attractiveness in terms of size, focus, and academic, social, and political performance. It is difficult to establish an academically oriented PRC without foreign philanthropy. In any case, even donors that give to a large number of centers usually give to only a minority of the potential pool, especially if we include peripheral PRCs and concentrate on only one time period.

An analysis of selectivity must distinguish between sector and institution, which most accounts do not do. Only an occasional analysis explicitly focuses on pluralism at the institutional level (E. Fox 1980: 11). Others deal explicitly or implicitly with the sectoral side yet deliver general statements about the pluralism of donors that PRCs enjoy.

The sanguine view makes sense for the sector, since selectivity is lessened as multiple donors step aboard. Such pluralism is common for systems composed of a multiplicity of specialized private institutions. Paraguay's two-hundred-plus NGOs, for example, have drawn from twenty-two international agencies; Chilean PRCs have drawn from fifteen major donors and numerous others (Duarte 1991: 9; Brunner 1990c: 7). Even the Dominican Republic, one of the two nations with the least funding diversity in CLACSO, has received funding from Ebert, Ford, Adenauer, the IDRC, AID, and others. CLACSO's centers, overall, have attracted more than a hundred international sources (Calderón and Provoste 1990: VII-1, 12).

At first glance, the diversity might not look much different for individual institutions. Many PRCs have many funders, and few depend exclusively on any one over time (Fruhling 1985: 68). In the late 1980s, Argentina's EURAL (N.d.: 5) counted on Ford, MacArthur, Tinker, and Ebert, along with UN agencies, foreign embassies, and domestic sources. The nation's FLACSO received funding from the IDRC, Rockefeller, Tinker, MacArthur, and Volkswagen, along with domestic funding (Mollis pc-3). Over a ten-year period, Uruguay's CIEDUR (N.d.: 5) attracted European Catholic organizations, CLACSO, the IDRC, NOVIB, SAREC, UN agencies, Ford, Ebert, and others. Chile's CIDE had over ninety funders, while its educational counterpart in Mexico, CEE, enjoyed the "economic collaboration" of some 508 organizations and 638 individuals in its first decade (Gatti and Chateau 1988: 39; CEE 1974: 83–98).

Colombia's FEDESARROLLO shows the variety possible where domestic public and private sources are both active. Its 1989 income came from foreign donors and contractors, 38 percent; the Colombian government, 21 percent; Colombian private sources, 18 percent; publications, 11 percent; conferences, 8 percent; and endowment, 4 percent (Escobar pc-1). Funding variety is also enhanced as PRCs assume tasks beyond research alone.

Usually, however, pluralism diminishes and selectivity increases for the individual PRC. The tie between a foreign donor and its typical recipient is tight. Examples abound among Latin America's PRCs, as they do among individual nonprofits elsewhere. Guatemala's ASIES depends heavily on Adenaur, and Argentina's CICSO and Uruguay's GRECMU depend heavily on SAREC. A second look at the Dominican case shows that Ebert and Adenauer have selected their own targets. Furthermore, particular donors are attached to particular PRCS within umbrella networks. To note simply the funding of the AHC by Ford, the IAF, the IDRC, and several European governments is to risk leaving a misleading impression of pluralism for Chilean PRCS (Lladser 1988a: 5).

Although a PRC may attract different donors over time, it tends to have few at a given time, despite some foundation preference for joint ventures. Impressive ten-year lists shrink greatly when attention focuses on any given year. For example, Ford was dominant at the Dominican Republic's Fondo until around 1980 (Dore i–2). And new PRCS often become viable with major early support from a single principal donor, as with Uruguay's CINVE and Ford in the mid-1970s (Spalding, Taylor, and Vilas 1985: II-27).

Additionally, though there may be several donors, one is often pivotal. CEE's helpful hundreds should not obscure the decisive leadership position of Ford—which has been crucial even for such major PRCS as Peru's IEP, where the IDRC, CIDA, Tinker, and Volkswagen have also contributed (Spalding 1991: 79; Cotler pc). Likewise, Ebert has been crucial for ILDIS, while another prominent Ecuadorean PRC relies on Germany's Christian Democratic foundations (Carvajal i).

Sometimes, particular donors give to particular activities or projects or people within PRCS. Peru's GRADE has been funded by Canada's IDRC and CIDA, as well as Ford, Tinker, several UN agencies, the IDB, Ebert, and others (Arregui i; Cotler i), but it has largely depended on the IDRC for macroeconomics and agricultural policy research, on Tinker for dissemination, on Ford for international relations research, and on the IDB for special small studies. Specific projects at the Dominican Republic's CIEA in 1989 and 1990 have relied on either AID or the IDRC (CIEA 1991: 15). The tendency arises even at leading PRCS. Brazil's CEBRAP (N.d.) stakes a legitimate claim that its autonomy is fostered by plural donors, but each of its fourteen major 1991 projects had a predominant or exclusive funder, whether Ford, NOVIB, or another. And FLACSOS offer parallels, as in Argentina's four programs.

Other Control Mechanisms

Donors can control the PRCS they link up to by (1) denying money for certain proposals or setting the dollar amount, (2) making short-term

grants, (3) restricting within-program activities, and (4) insisting on immediate relevance.

Denial and Levels

Donors need not fund a proposal unless they want to, whether "they" is
the home office or, as commonly with Ford, relatively autonomous field
offices. Data are too sparse to show acceptance/rejection ratios, but proposals do get rejected. More often, a knowledge of donors' priorities prevents
PRCS from soliciting money for projects that would be denied. Also obvious
is donor control over how much is given for approved purposes and projects. Any reading of grant files shows that requests are routinely scaled back.
El Colegio's million-dollar proposal for 1968–1972 elicited Ford's promise
of $650,000 and an actual grant of $780,000 (FF #68229, with 1970 and 1972
supplements). Given that supplicants learn to "ask high" but also that they
request sums based on informal word from prospective donors, there is no
easy gauge of control by amount granted.

The authority both to deny funding and to fix the amount of funding
relate to the relatively tight match of donor and institution. For one thing,
as most PRCS lack a steady institutional budget of their own, they are, financially, whatever funders choose to finance. This differs from common
foreign assistance patterns, including much to Latin American universities,
where it is difficult to assess donors' impact because funds may substitute
for funds that the domestic government would have provided or because
funds tied to a specific purpose free general institutional funds for other
purposes (Cassen 1986: 21; White 1974: 95–96). Shaped so much by donors,
some PRCS lack permanent, institutional commitments (CINDA 1987b: 11).
PRCS tied to single donors are especially vulnerable when it comes to denial
or cuts, since they lack alternatives. An alternative is to build pluralism by
shopping a proposal to several prospective agencies.

More subtle is the way donor plurality translates into donor control. A
donor that is one of many need not feel ultimate responsibility for a recipient. The strongest contrast lies with a government's responsibility to a public university that it alone finances: tradition clearly identifies obligation.
While a sole voluntary donor has the authority to do what it wants, it
must balance that off against a perception—the recipient's, society's, or its
own—of its commitment (Levy 1980: 101). This is a major qualification to
mainstream pluralist and nonprofit thought about how multiple funding

sources promote institutional autonomy (Powell and Friedkin 1987: 182; Kramer 1981: 129).

Short-term

A logical counterpart to the voluntary nature of funding is its short duration. Most grants for PRCs cover only a couple of years; many are for less, few are for more. Rarely is renewal a safe presumption. Just as universities may bolster their autonomy when they secure subsidies for multiyear periods, so PRCs' dependence on continual requests is a limitation. If the basic granting process allows the funder to reject or modify the proposal, a repetition of the process increases funders' control.

Recipients complain of *cortoplacismo*, or "short-termism." The academic consequences are several: endeavors that smack of contract research rather than basic research, and limitations on what problems are addressed, on research methods, and on the theory used. Also, recipients must produce concrete results quickly, and they must show "success" to justify the next grant application. Even the best researchers at classic PRCs yearn for donor faith in longer, more academically ambitious projects, after repeated, successful, short-term compliance (Brunner i-2).

Furthermore, "success" may lead to organizational fragmentation, given an absence of larger undertakings. A relation between short-term funding and fragmentation is common (Kramer 1981: 156–57, 170). Scholars at PRCs note the replacement of a beneficent government by "private" procedures, including "permanent competition" and evaluation (Calderón and Provoste 1990: VII-14). PRCs below the pinnacle live an especially shaky existence. Mexico's ILET and CLEE are examples.

Exceptions to *cortoplacismo* do not go far. Funding for projects almost never exceeds the short term. Funding for programs provides more opportunity for PRCs to pursue a line of research, but institutional grants would be a stronger answer to *cortoplacismo*. They are rare indeed from domestic sources. As we have seen, the major source of domestic funding is the project contract, while only those few centers with major graduate education count on subsidies. Brazil comes closest to providing leadership regarding PRC funding; for organizations and individuals, respectively, CNPQ and FINEP fund quality regardless of private-public or university-PRC label (Machado de Sousa i). IUPERJ (1991: 41–42) draws significant domestic institutional support.

Ford, the IDRC, and SAREC are three sources of institutional support. The

Ford Foundation was crucial to the establishment of many PRCs. But most of the foundation's support for PRCs has been project support, especially since the late 1970s. The IDRC's board approved institutional support in 1981, which nine centers then received, but just a few years later redemocratization in Argentina and Uruguay brought a consideration of termination (IDRC 1986: 1–2, 6–7). SAREC, the major donor committed to philanthropy through institutional support, has also considered termination. Some grateful observers deem SAREC unique, the only European donor to care about the centers per se (Calderón and Provoste 1990: VII-4, 7–13). Its policy receives credit for promoting quality, theory, and the development of true research directions (Reveló and Tironi 1988: 24; Gatti and Chateau 1988: 53–56). Above all, it receives credit for promoting trust and cordiality as it protects PRCs' autonomy. This has applied even to otherwise vulnerable institutions, such as Bolivia's CINCO.

By comparison, the typical lack of institutional support is detrimental to quality research. Whereas SAREC funds centers in three-year cycles, the average terms funded by others in the same centers could be half that; SAREC's untied support then winds up covering some infrastructure and, therefore, subsidizing projects sponsored by other donors. The common short-term pattern in PRC funding leads to an excessive emphasis on safety and to the appearance of accountability, at the expense of reasonable risk and substantive accomplishment—a parallel to the effects where representatives face electorates too frequently. A more proximate parallel is to Latin America's grassroots nonprofits, "virtually all" of whose funds are external and "noncontinuous" (Carroll 1992: 169).

PRCs can be so project dependent that they become little more than holding companies for funded projects and their researchers, which undermines structural identity and pushes PRCs from the core to the periphery. Bolivia's CEBEM, for example, has only a minimal ability to provide infrastructure and salaries. And critics charge that even academic leaders such as Peru's IEP are institutional fronts through which researchers seek funds, with the result that IEP's economists fare much better than its historians. The process is circular, as ad hoc project funding undercuts institutional cohesiveness. A partial alternative, as at Chile's AHC, is to charge institutional overhead. PRC "stars" nourish their organizations (Brunner and Barrios 1987: 110), and some PRCs keep funding from undermining institutional coherence.[42]

Such efforts and exceptions go against the general tendency, however.[43]

PRCS receive most of their money through projects, and these projects are short term. Institutional funding comes from few donors and goes to few PRCS.

Program

A related political-academic consequence is as crucial as short-term funding: a PRC must work within the donor's program priorities. Voluntary funding is often very specific. In the jargon of foreign assistance literature, most funds for PRCS are "project" funds rather than "program" or "sector" funds, which allow recipients more leeway (CEDE 1977: 67–68). To be more precise, funding is usually for specific projects within a program priority of the donor.

The salience of funding inside programs, joined with the fractionalizing effects of *cortoplacismo,* corroborates the dependency critique that donors undermine the coherence of Third World institutions (Nagel and Snyder 1989: 13). Peruvian PRCS, for example, too often become incoherent as they try to include whatever donors might want; they find it hard to retain people between projects (Spalding 1991: 96–100). On the other hand, another organizational tendency of PRCS is reinforced: "an irresistible tendency towards specialization" emerges as PRCS compete for narrowly defined grants (Brunner and Barrios 1987: 240).

But the main point about dependency is donors' control through restrictiveness. What is not on the program's agenda is often out of bounds. This goes beyond the restrictiveness associated with foreign assistance to university faculties; that assistance has generally promoted basic disciplinary development and innovative fields of study over traditional professional training. Thus economics, sociology, natural sciences, and demography were favored, with certain methodologies, over mainstream law and medicine. Philanthropy to PRCS is much more targeted by task.

Program restrictiveness is not unusual for foundations. Even those most committed to academic development—Ford, Rockefeller, and SAREC—usually insist that proposals be "within program." European private foundations and governments concentrate still more on individual projects of special interest to them (Spalding, Taylor, and Vilas 1985: I-4), as do newer U.S. foundations. Grants for PRCS, generally soft money not sunk into fixed salaries, are especially suited to a foundation ideal of focusing on carefully selected activities. For Ford's funding in Central America, for example, that means research on human rights, women, and the debt; vaunted foundation flexibility comes into play with quick approval, not inclusionary subject matter (Lungo i). Although it is exceptional for the latitude it allows in other respects, SAREC is not exceptional here.[44]

Tight program control is lamented even by those recipients who discredit most charges of donor political control. Nor is program control denied by donors. On the contrary, they speak readily of it, if not quite in those exact terms, sometimes venting frustrations about PRCs' unresponsiveness. Why, asked Ford's head in Mexico, do Mexican academics in social and agricultural science centers not pay more attention to foundation priorities concerning poverty and policy (Cox i)? Contrary to polemics, donors are not out to control academics per se; instead, in the abstract at least, donors sincerely believe in both academic freedom and national sovereignty. SAREC declares enhanced national sovereignty as a funding goal. Increasingly, however, donor priorities are not solely academic. Increasingly, donors look to academic nonprofit organizations to fit in with the proliferating network of social service nonprofits. They look to PRCs to help with particular practical problems or concerns, from providing better nutrition for schoolchildren to promoting equality for rural women. In broad terms, these are steps in the long path away from large grants for university development to much more specialized funding for particular programs. Whereas earlier grants aimed at institutional development, present ones make institutions secondary.

This sort of control over the research agenda leads to poor scholarly results (see chapter 7). Among these, and consistent with resource dependence theory, are waves of "in" subjects spawning clone programs. A sense of isomorphism emerges as PRCs assume similar characteristics in their common pursuit of the golden goose.[45] PRC leaders hear from counterparts in other PRCs about what donors like now. "Oh, you got funds for that? We'll try" (Fruhling i). Donors then seem to fund what PRCs ask for, but this mutual matching is asymmetrical. The same charge was leveled against philanthropy for universities—that universities went where the money was (Cepeda 1978: 496–98). But the concern is graver for organizations that rely more on international philanthropy.

"In" topics for the funding of research have included human rights (or topics as specific as quantitative analyses of human rights violations), public opinion, political violence, indigenous populations, and mass communications. It is revealing how rapidly Latin America skipped from almost no international relations or women's studies research to vast networks of such research. A Peruvian international studies center was developed in 1984 largely because Ford stood ready to provide a quick grant. Chile's formidable AHC network had no women's studies until Ford started promoting the topic; Ford and Ebert played major roles in encouraging the development of CIPAF and other women's centers in the Dominican Republic (Lladser i–3; Sánchez i–2). However, the vagaries of funding can also mean that "in" topics are sometimes quickly "out."

Another perversion results where donors facilely push their regional fads in inappropriate nations, funding topics like community development where there are no adequately trained researchers (Lomnitz i–2). Funding where critical masses are absent contributes to hyperproliferation of tiny PRCs. And donors push their *de moda* issues in nations where other issues of equal or greater importance consequently suffer, as when Chilean PRCs investigate ethnic minorities and malnutrition without looking at problems of transportation and pollution (Fruhling i; Lladser i–2).

Most "in" topics are, of course, neither alien nor unimportant. Valid priorities figure in their selection. Only some are leading social science topics in the donor nations, and many support innovative activities (CINDA 1986: 15)—though an insistence on regionwide emulation could undercut the claim. Thus accusations of an imposed agenda of esoteric or First World concerns are false. Yet there remains the matter of donors' affecting priorities in what to study and, through short-term funding, how to study it. For sustained work on historical, philosophical, or humanistic themes, funding is scarce indeed (Brunner i–2). Within Chile's almost totally foreign-funded PRC sector, a historian researching the nineteenth century guessed she was alone in working on such an "esoteric" concern (S. Serrano i). A year later, she was working at least part-time for the government.

Relevance

Ironic inversions of classic dependency therefore emerge: donors do not serve to isolate centers on the global research periphery. Quite the contrary, they play a huge role in stimulating unprecedented horizontal cooperation among these centers. They also stimulate the integration of their work into mainstream international academic work, albeit with limitations (Altbach 1987). Further, far from pushing Third World researchers toward esoteric, theoretical, discipline-based, methodologically sophisticated treatments of issues of concern principally to advanced scientists, foundations push practical, problem-oriented, rapid research into issues very much affecting the everyday lives of Latin America's own population, especially the disadvantaged.

Because chapter 6 elaborates on the relevance of such research, the discussion here relates only to funders' roles in encouraging relevance. This encouragement is especially powerful where contract research predominates, which is increasingly often. But the trend toward relevance also shows up as donors shift priorities. The IDRC and Ford, for example, now emphasize application. Bilateral sources, multilaterals, church organizations, and European secular organizations have always had this emphasis; consequently, despite their shifting priorities, foundations remain the chief sponsors of basic research.[46] Evidence suggests that funders tilt a PRC's balance between applied and basic research, promote a greater applied effort when a URC transforms itself into a PRC, and push an entire nation's PRCs toward community action and away from the academic preferences of these centers. Examples include Chile's PIIE, the Dominican Republic's CEDE, and Brazil's PRCs (Tillett 1980: 27; Sánchez M. i–1; Schwartzman i–1). Paradoxically, then, the pressure is not toward, but away from, the First World's academic mainstream. The sacrifice is of academic excellence and disciplinary development in the pursuit of immediate relevance.

Funding tied to programs, waves, and immediate relevance undercuts foundation claims about flexibility. More to the point here, it undercuts recipients' claims of—or yearnings for—basic nonprofit rationales, including experimentation, innovation, diversity, and autonomy.

Many of these considerations regarding PRC dependence on funders are familiar in the U.S. social research system (Orlans 1972; J. Smith 1991: 116) but in much diluted form. The voluntary features, whether related to private or federal government money, are superimposed on an infrastructure based on such relative certainties as annual government subsidization and fixed or rising university salaries and facilities (Geiger 1989). Among Latin America's PRCs, the voluntary features are the system. No grant or contract, no income. This great reliance on voluntary action by funders leads to a good deal of rather involuntary behavior by recipients.

Lack of Control

Factors already identified that point to a lack of donor control of PRCs include the plurality of funders for the PRC system, the multiplicity of recipients for each major donor, the impressive array of donors for some individual PRCs, the lack of disabling donor agendas, and variation among donors. But we need more evidence to understand why many heads of PRCs say they enjoy an autonomy that donors do not, or cannot, subvert (Fruhling 1985: 58, 43). The ensuing analysis covers: (1) variation among donors; (2) PRC autonomy over execution of the research; (3) the El Colegio case; (4) fresh perspectives on stable funding; (5) comparisons with government funding.

Variation Among Donors

More variation exists among donors than yet noted. For example, where program dependency leads to waves of research of a certain kind, flexibility in administration of programs leads to distinct orientations according to the country studied, as seen in funded studies on social movements in Latin America (Stavenhagen i). And some PRCs build creditable program continuity and organizational coherence. Additionally, PRCs and scholars with more credentials earn greater trust and leeway and also have more funding prospects. Thus, Chile's CECI can truly decide what scientific research to do and can reject intrusive donors. Size can also be a factor, especially at PRCs that encompass distinct units. On the other end, Rockefeller and Ford earned reputations for allowing autonomy, "and never saying don't do this" (Ojeda i). Newer donors are sometimes unfavorably compared to these traditional giants (Urquidi i–1). In recent years, SAREC's institutional funding epitomizes leeway.

These facts weaken at least two stereotypes about control. First, foundations do not automatically operate on a power-maximization model. On the contrary, Ford and others insist that the universities and PRCs they fund diversify income to protect both their autonomy and that of the donors, who would otherwise carry too much obligation. The IDRC's policy is that it should carry no more than a third of any recipient's budget (Moock 1980: 19; Magat 1979; 51–52; IDRC 1986: 2). Second, there is no grand plan of philanthropic control. The lack of coordination among donors, noted in other areas of foreign assistance including university development, is pronounced in funding for PRCs. This enhances PRC ability to solicit in a truly pluralist field.

Additionally, donors' purposes vary from each other and over time. Their initial thrusts under authoritarian rule were aimed more at protecting scholars and scholarship than at shaping them. Funding for study abroad illustrates the point. Earlier than that, as seen at El Colegio and the Di Tella Institute, much foundation money went for institution building or disciplinary development, including even history and the humanities. Thus, the Ford of yesterday allowed more leeway than the Ford of today, though Ford today still allows more than MacArthur does. Testimony abounds even for small centers like Mexico's CEE. But funding still sometimes allows for institutional strength and coherence. Aside from institutional support per se, there is support for research programs and projects that fall into viable program and institutional categories. CICSO's work on Argentine class structure and social conflict is one example (CICSO 1990: 8).[47]

PRC Autonomy Over Execution

Whatever the variability in the factors just noted, no major evidence surfaces of donors telling PRCs what to do within projects once they are funded. Donors allow autonomy over how to conduct research and what conclusions to reach.[48] This lack of control relates mostly to a matching between donor and PRC, but it holds where donors support a plurality of politically divergent PRCs. Where donors fund work critical of what they stand for (Ianni 1967: 206–07), detractors speak vaguely of the coopting skills of philanthropic capitalism (Berman 1983). A milder but pertinent criticism of foundations is that they generally push their preferred type of research organization (Arnove 1980a: 314–15); yet they work with PRCs, which differ greatly from donors' ideals about blending research and teaching. And philanthropy for PRCs engenders less criticism than other philanthropy in higher education. Many critics of earlier U.S. government support for Latin American social science regard the foundation-PRC relation as healthy (Portes 1975: 131–39).

Fungibility is one factor that promotes autonomy once funds are received. PRCs may have less room for maneuver than their larger, less coherent university counterparts, but they have some. Funds spent for a priority that is shared by the donor and the PRC free the PRC to spend other money on its own priority. That is legitimate.

Less legitimate autonomy comes when funds are used for unsolicited purposes. A siphoning of funds from nonprofits occurs when individuals wear different hats (Siegal and Yancey 1992: 45; Hammack and Young 1993). Grants to one of the institutions they are associated with may sustain them at another of their institutions. Vega (1989: 3) finds, for example, that distribution of Central American funds has bolstered personal profit or security.

Sometimes this means sectoral blurring, as for-profits use funds ostensibly given to nonprofits. That was the complaint registered by Ecuadoran non-profits against prospective World Bank aid to the Forestar Foundation, which was linked to the timber industry's deforestation plans. Sometimes the shifting of resources involves partisan ends, especially when individuals work for both PRCs and political parties. A printing press or almost any other physical asset bought under a grant may be used for both PRCs and related party activity. Examples include CEDE and Communist Party activity in the Dominican Republic and numerous parties in Peru, Chile, and elsewhere.[49] Such *uso combinado* appears much more common than a blatant, wholesale diversion of funds.

Audits are common, but they are usually not substantive. A greater restraint on illegitimate shifting of funds is that many PRCs believe in themselves, their sacred duty, and their accountability; PRCs may be among Peru's less corrupt institutions (Walker i). Accountability between donor and PRC comes much more through the marketplace and decisions on what to fund than through direct control over the use of grants.

El Colegio de México

Because of its unmatched status as a long-standing recipient of foundation assistance—and as the social research center of unmatched academic scope and achievement in the history of the region—El Colegio merits special attention here. The case provides insight into autonomy—without, however, suggesting that this autonomy is typical.[50] Research in the Ford Foundation archives (FF #73874, #63276, #68229) coupled with interviews at El Colegio, including but not limited to the directors of all seven centers, and with former foundation officers, yields the following account that shows the restrained hand of Rockefeller and then Ford during the periods when each, successively, was the main philanthropic agency; with most indications of influence come more impressive indications of limited control.

The foundations repeatedly conducted reviews and wrote detailed reports of their grants to El Colegio, and they likewise required written reviews by the institution itself. They linked the evaluation process to recurrent grant making. In some cases, they granted funds for only parts of the proposed project. Moreover, the foundations advised; assertions that they were mere facilitators, not presuming to offer strong suggestions or criticisms (Urquidi i–2), appear exaggerated. For example, Ford's Kalman Silvert (memo to William Carmichael, Mar. 28, 1972, FF #68229) judged that the institution's critical capacities, along with basic research and training, were too subordinated to eager responsiveness to government wishes.

The foundation also called for more core curriculum and an expansion of higher degree programs (Kalman Silvert memo to Calvin Blair, Oct. 31, 1969, FF #68229). Ford also sometimes influenced the direction and pace of change. It could not be otherwise when crucial support was needed to forge new directions; this had also been true in the early years of Rockefeller's support of the study of history (Ortoll pc). A key factor was the match between the focused PRC and the donor. At El Colegio, as at public universities more than at small PRCs, foundations also affected the balance of power when the institution lacked consensus. If El Colegio did nothing against its will, it did do some things it would not otherwise have done, because of internal opposition or insufficient interest. It also did some things it would not have done until later on or that it would have done only on a smaller scale.

Weighing against all these elements of influence, often outweighing them, are many other considerations. To begin with, El Colegio's funding requests were often granted. Moreover, these usually involved broad disciplinary or programmatic ends rather than specific research projects. Most critical statements by the donors came rather in the style of U.S. accrediting agencies reviewing institutions at home when the issue is not approval but the ongoing search for improvement (e.g., Peter Bell, Alejandro Foxley, and Nina Manitzas, final external evaluation of El Colegio, June 11–15, 1984, FF #73874). The picture is one of partners working together much more than one actor controlling the other. The foundations treated their donee with appreciation and respect.[51] When the institution felt that donors were too critical or directive, it protested strongly. It treated advice more as observations than as suggestions (Harrison i–1). For example, El Colegio continually refused to start doctoral programs before it felt ready. It disregarded enough advice that a frustrated Silvert (memo to William Carmichael, Mar. 28, 1972, FF #68229) complained that the institution's president always resisted and that too little attention was given to the foundation's professional judgment. President Urquidi likewise spurned Rockefeller ideas he opposed (Black i). El Colegio went along mostly when convinced by reason, not force.

From Daniel Cosío Villegas in the 1940s to Víctor Urquidi into the 1980s, El Colegio's leaders were a match for the foundations in a double sense. First, they were proud, strong institutional representatives, matches for any potential challenge from funders. Second, they were well matched in ideas and strategies with their foundation counterparts. They shared a common vision and approach. Given that coincidence, and the hierarchical governance of El Colegio itself, foundations could place great trust in these leaders. Generally, as with grassroots nonprofits (Carroll 1992: 152), matched funder and recipient makes for relatively little criticism by the former of the latter.

The El Colegio case raises concerns about contrasts with certain contemporary patterns involving PRCs, such as the emphasis on specific research projects. But it undermines notions about inevitable dependency in donor-PRC relations. Further, in showing what was characteristic, it provides insights into persisting if weakened patterns in relations, including the greater emphasis on trust than on pressure.

Stable Funding

Another pattern found at El Colegio also holds implications beyond the case: funding for PRCs is more stable than the short-term granting process suggests. *Cortoplacismo* should be assessed alongside less obvious realities of financial continuity.

Continuity then brings us back to mutual matching and mutual dependency. A donor needs recipients to convert its goals into reality. This need relates to the distinction between projects and programs. As projects come and go, funders show a commitment to further projects within the same program area. The CLACSO survey (Calderón and Provoste 1989: 77) even suggests that, while URCs, mostly government funded, enjoy more stability in personnel, PRCs enjoy more stable funding for research. Stability is a multifaceted concept. Then too, some PRCs count on one fairly steady provider while coping with volatility among others. In Chile, Ford for FLACSO and Adenauer for the CPU are examples.

A companion to stability by a given funder operates when existing grants give PRCs leverage for attracting grants from other sources. Even where it is more a matter of one donor following another than of any direct link, initial funding often provides the wherewithal to build a record, which then brings further aid. And there too, donors achieve a prime goal of voluntary giving: seed money leads to activities that continue after the money is spent. This, much more than ongoing dependency, is a foundation ideal. To see it attained only when ensuing income comes from domestic rather than other foreign sources is to take a legitimate but restricted evolutionary view.

El Colegio shows that donors may make a decisive impact before cutting back their funding. The consensus of those long active at El Colegio credits the indispensable role first of Rockefeller and then of Ford, back when the financial base was otherwise fragile (Segovia i; Urquidi i–1; Ojeda i). Rockefeller support allowed initiatives to move the institution from ad hoc individual research to organized research programs and training (Harrison N.d.: 7–15). What Rockefeller did early on for linguistics, literature, and history Ford did in the 1960s for social science. Though foreign assistance comprised only about 15 percent of the budget by the 1960s, it was funneled into cutting edge activities and helped build the base to attract other funds, mostly government funds; all the capital funds for 1962–1964 came from Rockefeller and Ford (FF #68229). Likewise, foundation money allowed the institution to send people abroad, which was crucial to both personal and institutional development. The two foundations also arranged special meetings to prompt other external agencies to contribute, as the IDRC, the UN, and others did in 1971. But their main contribution lay in recurrent funding that helped establish an institution that would attract enlightened, ongoing government support.

Rarely, however, does government step in to replace steady foundation funding for PRCs, unless the PRC is prominent in graduate education. It steps in more often following assistance to universities, including URCs. Examples include UNAM's science after Ford left (FF #67281) and UBA's Institute of Physiology (Nobel Prize winner Bernardo Houssay's institute) after Rockefeller left. These examples also illustrate the greater frequency of government (and multinational agency) follow-up in the sciences. Other forms of financial follow-up are necessary in the social sciences.[52]

Realizing this, foundations have relaxed the fund-and-run strategy they tried for university assistance. Whereas universities often had to pledge to assume all costs by a proximate date, or all costs except for scholarships (Coleman and Court 1992), foundations now often try to secure other international assistance for PRCs. And of course PRCs themselves work hard to maintain the supply line, preferably with plural donors. Evaluations suggest that Ford's grants to the AHC, 1968–1973, though never accounting for more than 25 percent of the budget, provided the required resources to entice UN and other funds (FF #68796). Often, as at El Colegio, Rockefeller was the pioneer that others followed.

But even where early philanthropy does not inspire subsequent philanthropy, a kind of stability may emerge. Stability based on the long-term, fixed commitment of one main funder is not required in plural, voluntary, nonprofit sectors. It is natural that funders come and go, and this should not be seen as thoroughly disruptive. Indeed, healthy stability for voluntary sectors composed of specialized, nonprofit organizations may include the death of individual institutions, along with the birth of others. The common reality is less drastic for PRCs. So one can take in stride that CECI started in 1984 with major funding from Tinker, soon drew on MacArthur and Chilean government agencies, and then drew mostly on the NIH (Teitelboim i). The instability of individual donors seems still less menacing in the frequent pattern where one or two dominant donors yield to a greater plurality of donors, as when AID and Ford yielded to the IDRC and several European agencies in educational research centers (Myers 1981: 82). FLACSO-Chile used considerable ingenuity to survive penury when it depended heavily on Ford in the 1970s and then built a stronger diversity of funders (UNDP, SAREC, NOVIB, etc.) in the 1980s (Nina Manitzas, memo to William Saint, Feb. 28, 1983, FF #68796).

All in all, a core dependency idea—that foundations make Third World PRCs reliant on them only to abandon them—does not capture the complex reality, despite the fact that Latin American PRCs were much more dependent than their university counterparts on foreign aid, more dependent than African universities for that matter (Nagel and Snyder 1989: 13). One should be very wary of cries dependency that arise both when donors fund and run and when they stay for long periods. Whether funding results in dependency rests crucially on which gauge of autonomy is used.

Both individual PRCs and systems of PRCs evolve. Income profiles that change should not be dismissed as unstable. In Peru, for example, in spite of volatility in their financial sources, a surprising number of PRCs have managed to accumulate substantial funds, often more than a million dollars a year, including some institutional funds (Spalding 1991: 29). Further beyond polemics: dependency itself changes over time. PRCs do not rely on funders for merely more and more of the same. It is a matter of judgment as to whether new forms of funding result in an intensification, a relaxation, a worsening—or a maturation—of dependency.[53] PRCs often use international philanthropy to enhance the extent and quality of their activity.

An interchange at the Rockefeller Foundation in 1965 captures this notion of maturing financial dependency. The "brass" made its familiar complaint about how its target institutions were not self-sufficient (not achieving "sustainable development," in today's lingo) after years of assistance. A program officer then asked which educational institution in the world pressured them most for continued support. The answer was Harvard University (Black i).

Comparisons with Government Funding

Assessments of control by philanthropic donors should include comparisons with the main alternative funder, domestic government. As noted, government is the main funder of research throughout the modern world, including Latin America. The evidence allows no grand conclusion about the general consequences of the two forms of finance on autonomy, partly because the funding circumstances are dissimilar, but it does suggest that government has not been a preferable alternative for PRCS to date.

Regarding stability, where government provides basic subsidies to PRCS, some funding continuity is almost assured. The case of FLACSO-Chile shows that cessation is possible, but it is rare. In this sense, government funding is much more stable than philanthropy. The crucial rebuttal is that government rarely provides the sort of subsidization of PRCS.[54] Like foundation giving, government giving is often for projects and without long-term commitments. More than foundation giving, it comes through contracts instead of grants. This difference means either that the two financial sources are not comparable or that government giving is somewhat less attuned to academic autonomy.

Most evidence on government research funding comes from URCS and GRCS; it is merely suggestive regarding PRCS. We have already seen how government funding of URCS may lead foundation funding of PRCS regarding stability for personnel but trail it regarding stability for research projects. Naturally, some URCS enjoy more enviable positions within their institutions than other URCS and, therefore, do better than them. UASD's CERESD in the Dominican Republic is an example. Moreover, many URCS can at least count on infrastructure and support services, which do not depend too heavily on what the next project brings. That stability is especially appealing when PRCS hit hard times: in the early 1990s, while the Brazilian government kept paying scholars in public institutions, leading PRCS lost people completely or partially to second jobs (Schwartzman i-3). On the other hand, government funding cuts can be drastic. The director of UNAM's prestigious Institute of Cellular Physiology complained of a 1986 budget half the real size of the 1980 budget, so that each year his people did not know where they would be next year (Meneses 1987).

Regarding the selection process and autonomy once funds are given, a comparison with government funding further buttresses the finding that philanthropy allows relative autonomy. An important if obvious point is that foundations have funded and trusted PRCs that are critical of their domestic governments.[55] Beyond that, foundations generally rely more than governments on academic criteria. They also use political criteria, as reflected in the ideological matching of particular donors and PRCs and in the emphasis on programs deemed socially important. But many grant seekers note the foundations' greater emphasis on evaluations, peer reviews, and competitive academic processes as compared to government tendencies toward favoritism or quotas (Teitelboim i). Where governments try to promote academic criteria, they come under more direct pressures to do the contrary. Additionally, universities lobby against competitive, "discriminatory," allocation policies.

Argentina shows politicization with the funding brought by democratization. Government personnel favored their own think tanks. After the Alfonsín government blessed places like FLACSO, the Menem government then switched course. The Di Tella Institute and the especially favored Mediterranean Foundation received help from their former leaders in the cabinet. The Mediterranean had good researchers, though without international academic prestige, but less bona fide PRCs also got funds. Meanwhile, although CEDES's team won open IDB competitions, it could not get World Bank money funneled through the government. SAREC agreed not to funnel its social science funds, like its natural science funds, through the government.[56]

The Argentine example also shows the widespread tendency for government to become a funder of PRCs. This leads to some likenesses with private donors, but the example also shows the danger of funding instability insofar as governments change course more often than foundations. Moreover, governments have trouble forging goals and policies as focused as those of foundations. It is hard for governments to achieve the complementary relationship that nonprofit donors often have with their PRCs. Most government higher education finance involves substantial conflict and either control, resistance to control, or both. The situation, common at universities, changes only some at URCs and PRCs, more at GRCs.[57] Conflict and control assume less centrality in relationships between voluntary donors and universities, especially private universities.[58] And complementarity is strongest between voluntary donors and PRCs. Insightful observers at foundations are aware of the essential point: a grant to a university often leads eventually to a difficult choice between abandoning the grant's goals and struggling to preserve them by exerting more control than they or the recipients generally want; grants to PRCs run more smoothly (Wolf i; Harrison i–2).[59]

The mutual matching of philanthropic donor and PRC follows pluralist, market dynamics. PRCs are often escapes from wider, centralized, political contexts.[60] As long as PRCs connect with sympathic funding partners, they can thrive in niches that are rather isolated from the bulk of the system. Chapters 5 and 7 show how PRCs typically assume strict political and academic profiles, with limited internal diversity. This facilitates matching with donors based more on choice, agreement, and trust than on control. Dependency loses its core meaning when funders and recipients are so closely matched. One may say the same about autonomy, or one may interpret matching as consistent with recipients' relative autonomy.[61]

CONCLUSION

The evidence adds up to a qualified success for PRCs. Like many nonprofits—but more than most—PRCs have depended heavily, often exclusively, on private, foreign donors. These donors have been accompanied by other international agencies but especially by domestic ones. Plural private sources, along with decentralized government funding, bring a fresh, market dynamic to higher education. They make for important new interrelationships among nonprofit, for-profit, and public sectors. Both the market sense and the intersectoral ties put PRCs at the core of basic trends in the wider political economy.

This is not to conclude that PRCs or most other nonprofits are financially robust. Diversification ensures neither stability nor strength. Many PRCs are chronically very weak financially. Even most leading PRCs live a somewhat fragile financial existence. They must continually scrounge for money in an uncertain environment. A shift in interest rates, in inflation, in the politics of faraway or nearby places, can spell crisis. Indeed, a PRC's fate turns largely on how it manages under those sorts of trying circumstances.

But the support of substantial international philanthropy, followed by a much more varied financial base, marks a major feat in meeting central nonprofit challenges regarding income acquisition. The acquisition of the original base and the transformation toward a mixed base when international donors retreat are remarkable twin achievements. Chilean PRCs exemplify them both, however alarming the sudden decline of international philanthropy is in the 1990s (Raczynski, Vergara, and Vergara 1994). Some individual PRCs elsewhere also do remarkably well: the Bartolomé center reportedly has more funds than its local government in Cusco, Peru (M. Smith 1992: 38). Others' income may be simultaneously inadequate yet impressive, given the political and economic circumstances. Certainly in the early 1970s, but later too, the financial viability of PRCs was in doubt (Tillett 1980: 62); and this doubt was based on expectations of levels of activity at PRCs, and therefore of required budgets that have been greatly exceeded now that PRCs have procured the funds for massive expansion.

The financial supply takes identifiable tolls on PRCs' autonomy. Until recently, international philanthropy lay at the heart of such concerns. Increasingly, however, it will be necessary to monitor the complex private and public sources that finance PRCs and that tilt the balance from grant to contract. As seen so prevalently in U.S. intersectoral relations, funds from public and for-profit sectors present challenges to nonprofits' autonomy but also present opportunities for collaboration. In any case, the diversification of funding, including the ability to sell services and products, diminishes dependency on international philanthropy and, as such, marks an important change for PRCs.

Whatever the limits on autonomy, they have not prevented success in performance. An extraordinary and still evolving breed of nonprofit organization is able to make impressive social, political, and academic contributions. The single greatest impact of PRCs' finance is disarmingly simple. It enables these nonprofit organizations to do their work.

5 Politics

The Two Faces of Pluralism

PRCs and politics are inseparable. This is already clear from considerations about PRCs' policy orientations, autonomy, growth, and relationships to donors. Whereas international dynamics dominated in the discussion of financial politics, domestic dynamics dominate in this chapter's more elaborate analysis of politics.

Four issues crucial to the politics of the nonprofit sector shape our analysis: (1) how nonprofit organizations sustain liberty and autonomy when their surrounding environment thwarts both; (2) the contribution of nonprofits to freedom beyond their own institutional borders; (3) how pluralism may be limited within nonprofit organizations that, together, comprise pluralist sectors; and (4) the internal governance of nonprofit institutions. Such political concerns are not studied enough in the literature on nonprofits—though haughty claims by nonprofit organizations abound, and each of the four concerns is integral to notions of pluralist democracy.[1] The first two issues compose the macropolitics half of the chapter and the last two issues the micropolitics half.

FREEDOM

Freedom is thematic to this entire chapter. But because the second half analyzes the limits on freedom within PRCs, the heading here refers to the wide freedom exercised by PRCs and also to their great contribution to freedom beyond their own institutional boundaries. Thus the first two sections here correspond to the first two issues for the chapter: the provision of sanctuary within an environment of limited freedom and the contribution to democratization beyond the PRC, whether to help a nation become democratic or to help a democracy to strengthen and extend freedom. A third section, on political moderation, gives special attention to a key facet of the democratization.

In sectoral terms, PRCs build a vital nonprofit alternative to an authoritarian public sector. They provide some strength for a weakened society facing a repressive state. But PRCs also play a major role in generating fresh, democratic ties between the public and nonprofit sectors and, thus, between the state and society.

Sanctuary

The very genesis of many PRCs calls attention to their role in protecting personal and academic freedom. This protection is the best known political fact about PRCs, requiring little proof here. But it requires elaboration and analysis, including a survey of its scope, its limitations, and its intensity. For one thing, this protective sanctuary—by which we understand space for dissent as well as simply survival—has been crucial to the PRCs' other, subsequent political contributions, whose importance reaches to the heart of national politics. Another reason for analysis is that some vital aspects of sanctuary are less known, such as the protection of academic freedom from university politicization. This section considers difficulties, triumphs, comparisons to other research institutions, and explanations. In a sense, however, it is fully about triumphs, as it portrays significant sanctuary, despite the difficulties and the lack of comparative and historic parallels.

Difficulties
Sanctuaries cannot just be assumed wherever repression makes them desirable. For one thing, demand does not guarantee supply. Additionally, totalitarianism is antithetical to sanctuary, to opposition, and even to detached neutrality, all of which most authoritarian regimes tolerate (Linz 1975). No sanctuary through PRCs was possible in Cuba for nonrevolutionaries forced out of the universities.[2]

Nor do established PRCs always survive as sanctuaries. The Argentine case shows that PRCs sometimes fail to protect freedom; several PRCs that functioned under earlier authoritarian governments found that the 1976 military incarnation made sanctuary impossible. Social science at the Bariloche Foundation was hit hard and was scaled back. Even in the early 1970s' interlude between periods of military rule, general political disorder and violence made PRCs risky places; FLACSO activities that were transferred to Argentina after the Chilean coup of 1973 failed to take root; in 1976, they migrated to Mexico.

Earlier still, disappointment visited one of Argentina's and Latin America's most promising PRCs, destroying a leading unit. The Di Tella Institute's music conservatory had been built carefully, selectively. Noting the lack of a top conservatory in Latin America despite the presence of the requisite talent, the Rockefeller Foundation, after rejecting the Mexican and Chilean governments' excessively political initiatives, teamed up with the academic and administrative leadership at Di Tella. The result was an early and striking PRC success, boasting excellent students from the region, Argentine creativity, professional development in the arts, and eminent guest teachers, including Paul Hindemith and Aaron Copland. Di Tella's health was mixed in ensuing years; with the 1966 coup, it failed: military rulers found creativity dangerous, opera incestuous. The conservatory closed. In fact, fear as much as visible repression crippled the conservatory and the institute. Concern about offending the military or the Peronists led to weak policies, including the hiring of undistinguished people (Harrison i–1; Cavarozzi i).

Where precarious survival dictates caution, alongside externally imposed restrictions, PRCs may supply only partial sanctuary. This is common for nonprofits in authoritarian Third World situations.[3] As seen in Argentina, violent environments present special problems. Central America's CINAS operated in exile in Mexico; with regional peace agreements, it attempted a return to its El Salvador headquarters, but individuals found it necessary to desist from certain activities or to leave, and in 1989 the director was assassinated in Guatemala (Spalding, Stallings, and Weeks 1990: 62). Nor is everyone allowed into the sanctuaries. Uncertainty sometimes makes emigration the only prudent course. Social scientists high on the enemy list may flee or suffer even worse fates. Nonprofit sanctuaries may prove, simultaneously, especially important to some leftists, given their lack of acceptable alternatives, and inaccessible to other leftists.

Further limits concern contact with wider audiences or groups. Sanctuaries are sometimes cordoned off severely, a restrictiveness that contributes to a lack of communication among PRCs themselves, as in Chile in the mid-

1970s and especially in Argentina in the late 1970s. There were corresponding restrictions on access to the media, public seminars, and the like, not to mention contact with many organizations, including political parties, associated with civil society. Given the uncertain boundaries, self-censorship on matters like dissemination was widespread (Balán i–1). In Chile, the church's shield was not thick enough to prevent the closing of the AHC's journal *Análisis*. And several governments have blocked PRCs specializing in education studies from pursuing projects in schools.

The major restriction on PRCs' audience is the lack of teaching. Most authoritarian regimes prohibit PRCs from granting either undergraduate or graduate degrees. Creative ad hoc teaching arrangements are not a satisfactory substitute. Although other reasons for limited teaching appear in civilian settings, regime repression makes limits common and severe.[4]

Triumphs

Analysis of the difficulties for sanctuaries under authoritarian rule shows a premier triumph for PRCs: establishment and maintenance of sanctuaries under duress. Beyond that, the breadth and impact of sanctuary prove impressive.

The rescue operations managed at PRCs have been noble and historic. International philanthropy has previously saved scholars and helped them into academic institutions, including both universities and centers like Princeton's Institute for Advanced Studies. The Rockefeller Foundation's rescue of European scholars from the Nazis stands out in this respect. But those rescues required emigration. In other cases, foundations have reacted to danger by themselves pulling out of the affected nation; thus, Rockefeller left the Sudan when diplomatic relations with the United States broke in the 1960s (Black i). In contrast, Latin America's PRCs, teamed with Ford and other pioneering foundations, have provided sanctuary within scholars' own nations. Philanthropy and African PRCs have also teamed up, but much less often (Coombe 1991: 41).

Because of PRCs, people survived who might not have otherwise, certainly not within their own country. Many continued to do social research, while others entered the field, both of which would have been impossible without the PRCs. Social scientists and social science could have disappeared from the Southern Cone without the PRCs and their philanthropic supporters. Much the same might be said of Central America and places like CSUCA. Also, PRCs in one nation repeatedly protected academics purged by other nations in the region: Argentina for Brazil, then Chile for Argentina, then Brazil for both others, Mexico for all three, and so forth.

Some depictions of the phenomenon exaggerate because they do not appreciate how PRCs have historically picked up the slack for other institutions. Timerman (1987: 125) sums up the wondrous freedom maintained by PRCs in several nations with his reflections on Chile: "It is the first time that people within a ferocious Latin American dictatorship have had the intellectual energy to reflect upon themselves from within their country." But in fact, the lack of precedent depends on one's interpretation of "ferocious." While exile was common under earlier dictatorships, and was facilitated by acceptance of individuals into brother nations, universities were also sanctuaries for dissidents who could remain within their nations. In certain respects, then, PRCs have become the islands of political space that universities once were. Additionally, PRCs partly substitute for other nonprofit organizations that provided sanctuary under prior authoritarian regimes—labor unions, professional *colegios*, and political parties.

That substitution is itself a major triumph. PRCs uphold an honorable tradition when other nonprofits are too heavily repressed to do so. The point is most important in relation to universities, because modern authoritarian regimes, which reached their zenith in the 1970s, tended to repress the public university much more than earlier authoritarian regimes had done (Levy 1981). Private universities have sometimes become creditable nonprofit alternatives—partial sanctuaries. PRCs have easily surpassed them, however, and are thus the major sanctuary within higher education. They join the church in several nations as society's leading institutional sanctuaries—twin towers of nonprofit hope. So PRCs do not just substitute for other institutions; they assume leadership under more trying, repressive conditions.

PRCs further promote sanctuary by helping other nonprofit organizations that offer safe haven. The mutually supportive PRC-church relation is especially noteworthy. Additionally, PRCs help establish and energize grassroots organizations that offer free space. PRCs also provide space for forums, meeting places, and publication outlets. Sanctuary under authoritarian regimes goes beyond protecting endangered scholars and scholarship. Once again, PRCs help build the broader third sector.

The free space at PRCs is also impressive for its vitality. The research topics are proof. There is no retreat to neutral, arcane, or remote issues, no escape into methodological exercises. A leading subject in the years right after military takeovers was the breakdown of democracy, followed by topics such as strategies for redemocratization. The bulk of socioeconomic research addressed issues of rising inequities and progressive alternatives to regime policies. Sanctuaries from repression, PRCS often engaged the principal political issues emanating from repression.

In sum, PRCS contribute impressively to sanctuary under authoritarian rule. They do so by their own vibrant presence, by picking up the slack for other nonprofits, and by supporting others. The third sector's contribution to freedom through sanctuary under authoritarian rule is a historic triumph, and the PRC is a sectoral leader.

PRCS also offer sanctuary under civilian regimes. Although less heroic or essential, this sanctuary is increasingly important. PRCS contribute additional free space within an academic world that has its own free space but that also has restrictions. For nations like the Dominican Republic, PRCS open up space that is simultaneously free and truly academic.

In reality, the settings cannot be neatly divided into groupings that do or do not require sanctuary for social research. Instability and uncertainty in Central America have presaged dilemmas later faced in redemocratizing settings such as the Argentine. Guatemalan scholars returning from exile found PRCS to be places to renew their vocation and their ties to their nation while avoiding the Universidad de San Carlos for its political-economic problems and the risk that university affiliation would carry in case of renewed military rule (Vega 1989: 39). Sanctuary from university difficulties is a growing political role of PRCS.

PRCS also serve as safety nets for scholars tied to a particular political party or an administration that loses power. PRCS then become sites for developing critiques, alternatives, or more basic academic work while individuals hope for a return to power. This is something of a Brookings think tank model. Sandinista social scientists flocked to URCS and PRCS following the electoral victory of Nicaragua's center-right. Elsewhere in Central America similar patterns loom as party members settle into their own PRCS. Christian democracy and social democracy fit the pattern in Guatemala and Costa Rica.[5]

Other Research Centers

Another way to appreciate the extent of free space at PRCS is to contrast it to the fate of academic freedom elsewhere. When university faculties no longer supply sanctuary, URCS add little. Even in the exact sciences and the professions, repressive regimes have directly or indirectly purged some dissidents and deprived others of the minimal resources and atmosphere required for practice. Like university faculties, URCs are of course much freer under democratic than under authoritarian governments. Researchers enjoy about as much freedom from government as their peers in PRCs except for their ultimate dependence on government funds, and URC autonomy is restricted more by the university than by the government.

If sanctuary from government seems incongruous for GRCs, remember that public research centers are a subcategory of GRC defined largely by substantial academic freedom. Even for GRCs more generally, disabling restrictiveness is not a given. High-quality academic personnel expect latitude for open investigation. In addition, there is some government recognition of the need to satisfy those expectations in order to attract and retain top people. Consequently, heavy-handed interference is newsworthy, as when geologists at Mexico's Institute of Electrical Research ran into trouble in the 1980s for expressing reservations about security at the Laguna Verde nuclear power plant.

Furthermore, GRCs may offer relative sanctuary from instability across administrations, if not regimes, and from politicization within administrations. Some scholars point to Argentina's Atomic Energy Commission as one case, though others point to detentions there; and there is no doubt about the ill fate of other Argentine GRCs and of Brazilian efforts in physics (Adler 1987; Tillett 1980: 15). Even apart from instances like these, agenda setting is naturally much more controlled at GRCs than at PRCs. Also, Venezuela and Chile before its coup show how conflicting pulls of political parties threaten sanctuary at GRCs. Overall, GRCs present a mixed picture regarding researchers' freedom. But they offer little alternative to the sanctuary afforded by PRCs in the politically sensitive area of social research during difficult times.[6]

Explanations

Finally, why have repressive regimes allowed PRCs to be unique sanctuaries of freedom? Why, for example, was perhaps only one Chilean PRC, VECTOR (Puryear 1994), hit by major violence? A similar question could be asked regarding many of Latin America's social service nonprofits.[7] No fully convincing explanation exists, and it might well have been otherwise. But pieces of the answer exist. Courage is one. At least four other pieces merit attention.

First is the limited PRC contact with larger groups. In fact, this point raises the larger point that PRCs, like other nonprofits—indeed like any opposition under authoritarian rule—can be tolerated as long as they do not pose a serious threat to the regime's existence. This is at once a crucial point and an easily exaggerated one, given how much PRCs have challenged regimes and even weakened them. Still, the small, specialized nature of PRCs allows room for freedoms that would seem too challenging if allowed at large teaching institutions.

A second factor concerns regimes' reluctance to intensify the alienation of powerful antagonists. Chief among these antagonists are the church, domestic groups holding moderate political positions, and international opinion. Church protection, epitomized by the AHC umbrella in Chile, is formidable when regimes are sensitive to the church itself (national and Vatican) and to its domestic and international influence. Among directly involved international actors, donors are important. They furnish international attention, legitimacy, and support that raise the cost of repression by regimes. Consider this contrast: most donor assistance to universities, whether by public or private agencies, was provided in close conjunction with host governments; most ensuing donor assistance to PRCs, predominantly by private agencies, was provided in at least indirect opposition to government. In addition, PRCs serve an array of international organizations. Their internationalism brings protection.[8]

A third reason for tolerance is PRCs' policy contributions. Along with other nonprofits, PRCs perform services that may make it easier for repressive regimes to cut public sector funds and to allow these regimes to pass on to others' the responsibility for public welfare. Additionally, governments sometimes avail themselves of policy advice from PRCs, notwithstanding the antagonism. CIDE's impact on Chile's educational planning and teaching environment, for instance, continued after 1973 (Reveló and Tironi 1988: 19).

Finally, fourth, genuine divisions within governments contribute to leeway. Until 1979, Chile honored intergovernmental commitments to finance FLACSO, though it also engaged in its repression. The government was split on the financing point, with some concerned not to arouse UNESCO, to which FLACSO was affiliated. Similarly, the Peruvian regime acted with more than one mind-set, especially over time. In 1973, in response to critical publications, there was a threat to close the IEP or to imprison members. The IEP therefore vegetated for a while. But at other times those in the ruling military who sought to preserve a progressive image held sway. Power was widely fractured among ministries where the IEP had friends as well as enemies (Cotler i).

Democratization

Sanctuary itself provides some democratic space, but PRCs go further. They promote broader democratization, beyond the PRCs' own organizational boundaries. Democratization, here, means both the extension of democratic practices under basically democratic or authoritarian regimes (called "liberalization" by some) and the transformation from authoritarian to democratic regimes. This section on how PRCs promote democratization dovetails with the section in chapter 3 on how democratization promotes PRC growth. It looks at the role of PRCs in democratic transition and consolidation, their relations with democratic government, and political recruitment.

Transition and Consolidation

Without explicitly citing PRCs, the literature on the change to democratic regimes highlights factors where PRCs in fact play a major role: the utilization of available free space, pragmatism, moderation, leadership skills, the reconciliation among political elites, and research findings that lead to success on key policy issues and that thereby forestall populist or military reactions (Malloy 1987: 236–39; O'Donnell, Schmitter, and Whitehead 1986). Works emphasizing democratic consolidation refer to elite consensus on rules, interactions among elites, the moderation of ideology, a diminished intensity and expression of conflict, and the increased value placed on democracy as an end in itself (Higley and Gunther 1992).

PRCs are leaders in acting in democratizing ways within authoritarian contexts. As noted above, PRCs are not snug, disengaged sanctuaries. From their institutional base, they launch activities that reach far. They criticize and document public sector repression and regressive socioeconomic policy. They contribute to a policy dialogue and form a key part of a third-sector network of dissent and alternative proposals. They are linked, for example, with human rights organizations, political parties, and other opposition groups, including traditional associations respected in the political mainstream, such as the Brazilian Bar Association (Fruhling 1985: 2, 64–66).

Chile's AHC provided information that the church used for its critical pronouncements. Like Uruguay's CINVE in national planning (E. Fox 1980: 26), the AHC sometimes contributed to as much of a shadow cabinet as could be managed under authoritarian rule. PRCS thus played a role in delegitimizing military rule. And the vigor of their dissent normally increased as regimes weakened, as in Argentina in the early 1980s—after years of caution by PRCS.

Many PRCS then played visible roles in the actual transition process, a nonprofit contribution to an emerging public sector. Chilean PRCS, especially, assumed pragmatic leadership in reconciling elites, in the building of the victorious opposition coalition through reconciliation, and in the coalition's negotiations with the departing government. By the mid-1980s, foreign funders clung less to a nonpolitical posture and saw support for PRCS as support for transition. The CED, FLACSO, CERC, SUR, and ILET were crucial in providing forums, polling data, and other policy analysis for the democrats moving from opposition to rule (Puryear 1994). Uruguayan PRCS played a lesser but still important role in providing technical advice to parties and social organizations; and Argentine PRCS analyzed specific issues (Cosse pc; A. Thompson 1994: 30). And the democratizing role went beyond the Southern Cone. Ford's grants to Guatemala were used to expand political space and make debate more plural; both there and in Paraguay, Peru, and Bolivia, as well as at South America's better-known PRCS, democratization became the leading political topic (Cox i; Spalding, Stallings, and Weeks 1990: 97–101, 129). Here was information, pragmatic information, presented on the key policy question of how to effect transition.

PRCS do not stop aiding democratization once democratic governments emerge. Democratization is not a one-stroke process. Nor is the existence of democracy best treated as a simple dichotomy. Even where citizens freely select their leaders, Latin American democratization requires expanded citizen participation and information. PRCS are active on both counts. The educating, monitoring, and publicizing of public opinion are salient examples; so are national forums, like those run by Guatemala's ASIES. PRCS champion many public interest issues that attract growing citizen participation, such as CIPMA on environmental rights in Chile (CIPMA 1992). Just as PRCS build up a battered civil society under authoritarian regimes, so they build up a still weak civil society under democratic regimes.

Democratization also requires socioeconomic progress, whether that is part of democracy itself or a valued means to make democracy survive.

Without that progress, populism may undermine democracy directly or, by provoking military intervention, indirectly. Intertwined with other non-profits, PRCS assume a major role. They concentrate on socioeconomic questions, combining progressiveness with pragmatism. This thrust arises under democratic as well as authoritarian regimes. Colombian PRCS like FESCOL promote equitable public policy (B. Smith 1990: 244–56). In the 1990s, Eduardo Frei's priority attack on poverty enlisted Chile's PRCS. To take a more controversial case, Peru's powerful ILD pursues democratization through decentralization and deregulation (de Soto 1989: 259; Bromley 1990: 331). PRCS help nongovernment actors like unions or Central America's displaced citizens (Vega 1989: 41).[9] Even PRCS that give advice to government also give to nongovernment groups; Peru's Flora Tristán center does so regarding women's issues.

This commitment to democratic consolidation through expanded participation and equity thus includes criticism of elected regimes. Criticism occurs in probably all nations but is sharpest where the governments are arguably least democratic or where they pursue contentious neoliberal policies. In Central America, CINAS gives voice to the weakened democratic left, and CRIES continually offers alternatives to neoliberal debt and macroeconomic policies, just as CINVE stands against the neoliberalism of government and other PRCS in Uruguay (Spalding, Stallings, and Weeks 1990: 37, 63, 112). One can debate whether government or PRC policies better serve democracy; what is clear is that PRCS' criticisms of government usually promote a valid view and contribute to democratic expression and debate.

Relations with Democratic Government

Notwithstanding their criticism of government, PRCS very much promote democratization in conjunction with government. Chapters 3 and 4 touched on that in showing why democratic governments assist in the founding and financing of some PRCS. The PRC role in democratic consolidation is especially important, given that most Latin American democracies assume power facing serious economic, social, and political problems. CEDES is a good example for the Alfonsín government in Argentina, as are CERES, CIESU, and CIEDUR in Uruguay. CIEDUR (N.d.: 15) stresses how it formed during the nation's worst repression and then found "a new reason for being under democratic rule." Following Peruvian military rule, the Belaúnde and especially García administrations turned to PRCS for programs (M. Smith 1992: 35–36). The provision of policy-relevant research is a major service that PRCs present to governments. It is enhanced by its empirical content, as in work on Brazilian poverty (Miceli i). In other words, PRCs fit the generalization that nonprofits increasingly help formulate policy in cooperation with governments that cannot do so on their own; and they increasingly emulate patterns of cooperation between the third sector and government seen in developed countries (Seibel and Anheier 1990: 16; Salamon 1990).[10]

Such eminently pragmatic activity for democratization destroys simple images of PRCs as dissidents. On the contrary, the PRC analyst is a new incarnation of the Latin American intellectual who attempts to influence policy more than find academic refuge (Camp 1985). Analysts seek influence through government, or as spokespeople for the national conscience, or both. The motto of one prominent PRC is To Think for the Nation (FEDESARROLLO 1990). Most of the think tanks echo that. PRCs thereby partially displace university professors and institutionally unaffiliated intellectuals. Compared to their predecessors, however, their approach is more often pragmatic, is based on applied research, and is shared with policymakers. Several PRCs engage in polling to discover and publicize what the nation itself thinks.

In practice, many PRCs mix cooperation (and contracts) with criticism, as U.S. think tanks do. Paraguay's CDE, created in 1985 to promote democratization, accepts the invitation to help guide decentralized government agencies "to reformulate the whole obsolete framework the country has had" (Moreno pc), but it also produces socioeconomic indexes that are the sole alternatives to official ones.[11] Guatemalan social scientists use PRCs to remain free of government, to work supportively with government, and to negotiate with government. The negotiation includes pressuring to further open up democratic society—a pivotal way in which PRC scholars with international connections bid for a "great, potent, and cumulative impact" (Vega 1989: 43).

Of course, PRC autonomy, criticism, and ties to nongovernmental institutions, including opposition parties, mean choppy relations with some democratic governments. Officials in the Belaúnde administration denounced Peruvian PRCs as fronts for subversive activities. On the other hand, PRCs can serve nondemocratic governments. Streams of policy-relevant research from both El Colegio and the Barros Sierra Foundation to the Mexican government proved that. Demography, economics, municipal administration, and technology are areas in which surveys and consultancies have been prominent. Observers may reasonably disagree on whether service like this has democratizing effects. To take a regime of a different stripe, the Sandinistas received policy assistance from PRCs as well as from public research centers on matters including agrarian development, squatters, and fiscal issues (Fernández 1989: 74–80). But given PRCs' hostility to Latin America's most common type of authoritarian regimes—military ones—service to dictatorships is unusual. Contacts between PRCs and intellectuals of military governments tend to be minimal (Fruhling 1985: 70), at least until a credible transition is under way. Put in more positive terms, PRC-government cooperation blooms in democratic contexts.[12]

Beyond all this, PRCs play a major personnel role for government. One means is the training course, through either direct provision at the PRC or through researchers' assistance in courses offered elsewhere. Mexico and Argentina, respectively, show these two forms with regard to their national foreign services. Mexico may also presage a growing role for PRCs elsewhere in Latin America: the preparation of students for important government jobs. Roughly half the graduates of El Colegio's Center for International Relations assume government jobs, mostly in the foreign relations ministry (Torres i). The centers of demography, economics, and sociology are also major providers.

Political Recruitment

But the most direct personnel role is entry into government. Beyond common part-time consultancies, many individuals move from the nonprofit to the public sector. Here is a payoff not considered by foundations when they began supporting PRCs. According to a high Ford official, the foundation never dreamed it was warehousing and training people for redemocratization (Carmichael i).

The redemocratized administrations in the Southern Cone drew amply from PRCs.[13] In Argentina, CEDES's director became a planning undersecretary, and others moved to the same ministry as well as to positions in economics and as negotiators with the IMF. Former CISEA director Dante Caputo became foreign minister, and a former CEUR director became an undersecretary (IDRC 1986: 4; A. Thompson 1994: 30). FLACSO personnel joined the government in the education area. Social scientists from PRCs similarly entered government in Uruguay. Some researchers at CINVE and CIEDUR became senators (Cosse pc). As was predictable by 1990, the huge

PRC-to-government movement that transformed Chilean politics was epito-mized by the almost automatic ascension of CIEPLAN's head as finance min-ister and a colleague as labor minister.[14] Here FLACSO's contribution cov-ered more areas than in Argentina. Other PRCs provided key people in their special areas, as did PET in planning, labor, and economics and PIIE in education. Within the first half year of democratic rule, probably more than 30 percent of Chile's senior researchers from PRCs had shifted to govern-ment (Brunner 1990c: 7). In the different context of democratic takeover elsewhere, PRCs also provided critical talent, as from the ASIES in Guatemala and CINCO in Bolivia.

The trend deepened as the democratic torch passed beyond the initial postauthoritarian governments. Illustrative was the ascencion to ministerial rank of figures like José Joaquín Brunner, a giant in Chile's PRCs. Most striking was Fernando Henrique Cardoso's election as Brazil's president after service as finance minister—and after an illustrious academic career. He had shifted from university to PRC and was perhaps best known for his articulation of leftist dependency theory.

Recruitment to government jobs brings problems, but these appear con-sistent with democratic process. Again, only Mexico shows a heavy connec-tion to undemocratic government; and again, the ultimate effect on democ-ratization is debatable. Much more commonly and increasingly, PRCs serve a particular democratic government or party. This service lacks the drama of transition periods but is important to democratic consolidation.

Passage to government may mean major academic sacrifice for political ends. Chilean PRCs suffered a blow in 1990, despite their unmatched devel-opment. Intense debates developed within PRCs over their relative commit-ment to scholarly research versus collaboration with government. The de-bate sharpened at places like CIEPLAN when some academics returned from officialdom with the idea that the PRC should consult extensively for parties and the government, while others stressed the center's academic role. The initial Brazilian brain drain jeopardized all good PRCs except a few at the top (Brunner and Barrios 1987: 185, 224), a trend that continued under subsequent administrations. Argentina's Mediterranean Foundation suf-fered academically, though not financially, as researchers formed the bulk of Carlos Menem's economics team headed by the foundation's own Do-mingo Cavallo as minister. Brain drain is especially ominous given that most PRCs are small and fragile. They are more vulnerable than U.S. think tanks, let alone U.S. universities. PRCs would need a more distinctly academic rationale, or myth, to counterbalance the allure of government. At present, PRCs are handy recruiting sites for democratic governments.

The severity of brain drain is partly offset, however, where democratic parties move in and out of power. Argentine PRCs welcomed back colleagues turned out of government by the Radicals' 1989 defeat. On the other hand, the evolution from the first to the second democratic administration in Chile did not involve a change of party. Some researchers simply did not return to their PRCs. Some regained their formal affiliation but spent less time in academic work. Others, however, returned to try to shore up the academic standing of their PRC. FLACSO is an example, after the first government drained it of so much talent; but ILET is an example of centers that faded (Lladser pc-2). Still, the movement between PRC and government is such that replenishment at PRCs depends on bringing in younger talent.

A positive point for democracy where cycling between government and PRCs occurs involves the strength of the opposition. This cycling can enhance the viability of civil society and encourage a responsible, prepared opposition. PRCs allow the opposition to rearm intellectually and politically. Costa Rica has benefited from something along these lines in recent years (Araya i–2). As PRCs serve and staff different administrations within a democratic regime they promote democracy in a way that sustains their contributions to original democratization. It becomes routine for new administrations to employ PRC staff.[15]

PRCs keen to work with government also run the risk of identification with that government. This is a general danger for nonprofits that advise or otherwise cooperate with government. When does government's political use of nonprofits undermine the organizations' integrity? Some consider excessive the Jorge administration's use of the Forum association to rebuild support in the Dominican middle class (Sánchez M. i–3). When does collaboration exclude other, plural views? Some Argentines denounced a FLACSO monopoly on Alfonsín's education policy. Risk involves perceptions as well as reality. IESA's officials complain that Venezuelans fail to distinguish between the PRC and its former members in high government positions. Naturally, too, special risks arise over association with failed or unpopular government policies, as Peru's ILD learned.[16]

In sum, most dangers in the PRC-government recruitment link are not only intrinsic to democracy, the relation mostly supports democracy. Put another way, PRCs help reshape political recruitment in Latin America, and that reshaping is democratic. The starkest contrast lies with recruitment through military training and coups. More gently nudged aside are political parties and universities. In many nations, parties first shared or lost ground to public universities. Then, especially since the 1970s, private universities gained at the expense of their public counterparts. Graduate education abroad also gained rapidly, in turn giving an extra edge to those institutions most able to send people in that direction; elite private universities do well in this respect, but PRCs (followed by URCs) are the domestic institutions most intertwined with foreign graduate study in fields crucial to political recruitment. Mexico is the best-documented case (though atypical regarding democracy) of the rise of public universities and then private universities and foreign education as recruitment channels (Camp 1984; Levy 1986: 114–70). El Colegio and Chapingo lead a group of private and public research centers that must be added to that picture—indeed, that rank as the tightest elite transmission belts.

In fact, the shift in political recruitment on the nonmilitary side comes less from the full substitution of one institution for another than from partial substitutions and—mainly—additions. In Mexico, the party and public universities remain channels for some political positions, while private universities and PRCs assume more prominence in political-technocratic positions. Greater discontinuity in Chilean national politics opened the way for a fuller substitution by PRCs, but that should be temporary. In less volatile times, PRCs will assume their place alongside better-known civilian institutions of training and recruitment; more accurately, they will interact with them. The clear partisan orientation of many PRCs paves the way for PRC-party interaction. The rise of PRCs in political recruitment represents some shift from public to nonprofit sites and some shift among nonprofit sites.

Other than recruitment, the broadest danger that democratization poses for PRCs and other nonprofits is government usurpation of their tasks—or at least co-optation. Offsetting this danger, however, is the rising partnership between public and nonprofit sectors.

Political Moderation

PRC contributions to democratic transition and consolidation owe much to the political moderation that characterizes most centers. Although moderation would therefore fit logically within the section on democratization, it is important and multifaceted enough to warrant its own section here. Given the more leftist background of PRC researchers and of Latin American social science in general, political moderation means a shift. The impact of the shift on the overall political system is visible first in the molding of ideas and then in the contributions to democratic government.

Policy moderation expresses itself in research topics, methodologies, and findings, as analyzed in the next chapter. By the 1980s, a post-Marxist tone was evident in Central America as well as in the Southern Cone, and dependency theory arguably lost influence in Latin America before it did in the United States (Fernández 1989; Brunner and Barrios 1987: 195–96; Packenham 1992). This policy moderation brings praise from some and denunciation from others. Vega (1989: 42) refers to a "refreshing realism," tolerance, and "gradualism" at Central American PRCs. Predictably, scholars at PRCs and a host of "consumers," including democratic governments, largely share this view. It predominates among international agencies and scholars.

A contrary view from inside Latin America appears in the comparison of PRCs and universities that ends this section. Criticism also comes from abroad. SAREC's evaluators (Spalding 1991: 96; Spalding, Taylor, and Vilas 1985: III–5; Spalding, Stallings, and Weeks 1990: 23, 115–20) have criticized PRCs' trendy and exaggerated tendency to dismiss all Marxist study, including lots of macrosociology, or to treat democracy as if it were a state of mind; too much attention goes to public opinion, interest groups, and political parties rather than to issues of domination by the state, the military, and private and public foreign interests. Much more vitriolic is Petras's assessment (1989, 1990).[17] Petras writes in the tradition of C. Wright Mills and others who see intellectuals in institutions as too timid (Zald and Mc-Carthy 1987: 99). He argues that foreign foundations buy off intellectuals at PRCs. These intellectuals live a bourgeois academic life, indulge in detailed analyses of nonrevolutionary matters, bolster hollow democracy, get cozy with government, and generally displace brave "organic intellectuals," who focus on class-based social problems and tie their work to radical politics. Other critics, in milder form, denounce the evolution of IRCs like CEPAL from a critical essayist approach to one of professional and applied social science.

At least criticism, like praise, shows recognition. Too common still is the simple assumption that the politics of Latin American social research is ideologically leftist. Also common are misleading conclusions drawn from scant observation; some write of the domination of leftist orthodoxy through emphases on dependency, authoritarianism, and neo-Marxism (Dent 1990a: 6). The picture of PRCs gets confused further where other nonprofits are mostly on the left (Andean Report 1992: 32).

I analyze several salient aspects of the political moderation of PRCs. These aspects are the move to moderation, the restricted left, the rising right, the technocratic turn, and a comparison to universities.

The Move to Moderation

Chile exemplifies the dominant political moderation of PRC work, as expressed in policy-oriented publications and forums. Concerning national political-economic policy, the tendency is to pursue equity concerns, such as increased wages, educational access, and public housing, but only without jeopardizing crucial macroeconomic indicators. Services must be paid for through production, not debt—or mere faith that public expenditures will ultimately justify themselves in soaring production. CIEPLAN leads the way. Prior to the 1990 change of regime, and the prominence of its members in high government posts, CIEPLAN built and publicized the opposition's caution to the public not to expect rapid or massive government assistance (CIEPLAN N.d.).

Another indicator of political moderation is the acceptance of a broad role for nonprofit organizations, of which, of course, the PRC itself is a prime case. This is a rejection of the leftist rejection of nonprofits as privatization, as weak, unwarranted substitutes for state socioeconomic responsibility. It is also a departure from another prior attitude: indifference.[18] Instead, PRCs work a great deal with nonprofit grassroots organizations, which also reinforce realism about the state's limited capacities and advance trust in pluralist alternatives (Díaz-Albertini 1990; Downs 1989). In other words, PRCs promote the idea of moderate pluralist democracy based less on a comprehensive role for a progressive state and more on a role for diverse social institutions along with the state.

Nonprofit pluralist models usually suppose tolerance for opposing views and organizations. Dialogue and mutual accommodation diminish the priority of defeating the opposition. They thus diminish the intensity and expression of conflict while increasing consensus on rules of democratic process. Chilean PRCs facilitated a crucial reconciliation between the center and the moderate left. Although the effort was weak in the initial years of military rule, when mutual recriminations for the fall of democracy were intense, it gained strength in the 1980s. It encompassed rightists as long as they supported democracy and helped to marginalize the Communist Party. The realization of the need for cooperation then carried over into governance. Chilean PRCs played a pivotal role in democratization from the demise of authoritarian rule on into democratic consolidation.[19] PRCs were not as central outside Chile but played some similar roles.

PRCs were, for one thing, centers for the transformation of the Latin American left. Basic tenets were rethought, and many PRC members rejected or modified their own Marxist beliefs. Chile, Brazil, Argentina, Peru, and other nations experienced a rethinking of leftist political ideology (Brunner i–i; Brunner and Barrios 1987: 195). Leading thinkers took more critical looks at revolutions, command economies, nationalist economics, and undemocratic leftist regimes, while reaching more positive evaluations about evolutionary change, market efficiencies, foreign investment, and Western democracy. Brunner (1988b) finds a major change from beliefs in certainties and encompassing answers to a humble acceptance of uncertainties and the need for policies aimed at modest improvements. Like Guatemala's ASIES, many PRCs proudly claim objective exploration, not ideology, as their guiding light.

The Restricted Left

Most PRCs are not antileftist but are antagonists of the radical left. To take the extreme case, reportedly all Peruvian PRCs fully reject all guerrilla movements (Spalding 1991: 37). Most PRCs lie in or between the moderate left and the center. If political transformation has included some movement from left to center, it has also included movement within the left from an emphasis on theory and revolutionary change to an emphasis on practical change through applied work to help needy populations. With their emphasis on application, social action PRCs open excellent routes for such change (M. Smith 1992: 30), another transformation not equivalent to the abandonment of leftism.

Given fair readings of modern Latin American intellectual history, the scarcity of PRCs identified with traditional Marxism is surprising, especially since the scarcity preceded the accelerated collapse of communism internationally in the late 1980s. In Peru, at least three of the top PRCs—IEP, DESCO, and CEPES—are tied to the left but not to the traditional left; CEDEP is leftist in that its personnel have supported populist-nationalist causes and the radical phase of the last military regime (Cotler pc). Alone on the far left are a few small peripheral PRCs, with dubious status in research, which combine popular cultural studies and more direct action. By and large, the violent Shining Path guerrilla movement preempted space on the radical left and made leftist social scientists vulnerable to both its and the government's wrath. In the Dominican Republic, CEPAE was notable for its links to Camilo Torres groups (Sánchez M. i–3). Among Chile's many PRCs only the Alejandro Lipschutz had a strong Communist Party influence when the party still had significant support within the general population; in environmental policy, the nation's Greens did not find kindred ideological spirits at the far more moderate, technically oriented CIPMA. Sandinista Nicaragua, with the influx of "professional internationalists" intent on advancing the revolution, was exceptional within Central America for its development of PRCs, though El Salvador, too, outstripped Guatemala (Vega 1989: 39; Alvarez pc-3).[20]

Several factors explain the weakness of the Marxist left. The decline of international communism had an accelerating effect, but the transformation mostly preceded the undoing of European communism, the heightened isolation of Cuba, and the Sandinista electoral defeat.[21] Strong contacts with Western Europe and the United States played a major role. Foreign democratic governments, foundations, and universities helped expose many people from PRCs, or destined to work at them, to other academic and political norms. The image of the United States improved markedly. Latin Americans witnessed the moderation of leftist thought in Western Europe, along with the transition to centrist democracy in Spain. This exposure developed through an incredible network of contacts through exile, visits, conferences, consultancies, professional associations, publications, and especially scholarships for advanced study, teaching, and research. The rising norms of empirical research and other "Western" methodologies and focuses for social research fit well with political moderation. Evidence from the third sector thus contradicts the tendency in the literature on democratization to minimize the positive international influence (Lowenthal 1991; but see Remmer 1991: 486).

Other factors crippled radical leftism from the outset. Military governments extended sanctuary only so far. Marxists either could not remain in the country or had to accommodate to antagonism toward them. By the time others were allowed back they had been exposed to transforming international currents or had at least confronted domestic redemocratizing dynamics, which, as in Brazil, had a deradicalizing effect (Brunner and Barrios

1987: 184). On the other hand, in nations spared harsh authoritarian rule, traditional leftists were not forced out of the universities. PRCs tended to attract leading social scientists critical of leftist disorder. Another factor working against radical leftism is funding. Foreign foundations and public agencies are more inclined to fund moderate than radical leftist social scientists. This inclination stems at times from the sober political reality that repressive governments would not otherwise allow a foundation presence in their nations. More generally, it stems from the donors' own political and academic sympathies. Smith finds leftist tendencies among many European donors to Latin America's grassroots nonprofits, but *left* basically means the moderate, liberal, or democratic left—not the revolutionary left (B. Smith 1990: 75–111; Packenham 1973). The lack of funding for the ideological left is clearest with U.S. donors.

The Rising Right

Complementing the transformation of the left is the growth of nonleftist activity. Some PRCs contribute to political moderation by their own muted ideology. Then there is the notable rise of markedly rightist PRCs. Whereas a case for PRCs' political moderation once rested more on the scarcity of ideological centers, now it rests also on the claim that rightist PRCs counterbalance the left and introduce pluralism to the PRC universe.

The historic absence of rightist PRCs fits with my understanding of the interaction between supply and demand in the growth of PRCs. In the beginning, there was no financial supply. Rightist international philanthropy was almost nil. Most U.S. foundations were conservative but were parochially oriented to domestic affairs, whereas the giants engaged in international work were not conservative (Nielsen 1972). Active European foundations were not rightist, either. Within Latin America, tax laws did not award incentives for businesses to contribute. More than that, businesses did not generally value or seek research. This meant limited demand. Authoritarian governments further limited demand and supply for rightist PRCs, especially because they did not drive rightists from the universities. And at a fundamental level, the supply side of personnel was minimal because Latin America lacked a tradition of rightist social science and intellectual activity in the postwar period.

Yet a countertrend has developed for each of these considerations, suggesting new possibilities for rightist PRCs, consistent with the general pull factors in the growth of PRCs. Rightist U.S. think tanks were scarce until the 1960s, with sharp acceleration delayed until the 1970s. The AEI, Heritage, Hoover, Cato, and others arose in reaction to a perceived monopoly by liberal, antibusiness forces, a heightened demand by a growing conservative movement, and a rising belief in the political power of ideological ideas. These centers achieved extraordinary success in finance, media, public opinion, and the presentation of rapid, influential policy ideas (Saloma 1984; J. Smith 1991: 216–23). This development provided an international model, with echoes in Europe and Latin America.

Latin America's human resource supply for rightist PRCs grows from several factors associated with the growth of PRCs in general, including study abroad. Especially relevant, however, is the increased flight from public university politics, usually leftist, rather from than government repression, usually rightist. CIAPA, which draws funds from AID, was formed mostly with professors from the University of Costa Rica. Especially relevant regarding the financial supply as well as the demand for conservative PRCs is the right's new desire for an intellectual presence. Peru's center-right "realized it needed to recapture the intellectual space that had been the virtual monopoly of the leftist intellectuals"; new PRCs, along with non-profits supported by evangelical and other churches, now deny the left a monopoly in the social action area (M. Smith 1992: 47–48). The previous chapter also notes the role of U.S. agencies and think tanks in financing or otherwise promoting pro-market PRCs.

The heightened demand for rightist PRCs thus represents a further internationalization in Latin American social research. It also represents a new role for the nonprofit sector in support of the for-profit sector, through information, analysis, and services, as well as a new role for the for-profit sector in support of the nonprofit sector, through finance and legitimacy. In other words, a rising nonprofit sector connects integrally with the for-profit sector. Indeed the rise of rightist PRCs means increased interconnections among the three sectors, insofar as regimes pursue privatization and a limited state (Chalmers, Campello de Souza, and Borón 1992).

Notwithstanding their recent birth and potential, rightist PRCs are still few if we use as criteria strong ideological orientation, PRC self-designation, and focus on academic research. Ideologically rightist PRCs are more visible and influential in the United States. To the extent that ideology is important in Latin American PRCs, it is more leftist than rightist—but change is unmistakable.

Most of Latin America's ideological PRCs on the right have little academic recognition. In Peru, perhaps only the Center of Studies on Law and Society and a few marginal institutions trying to shape public opinion stand clearly on the right. In Chile's vast network of the 1980s, perhaps only the CEP qualified as rightist and credible; created in 1980, but with no permanent staff, it enshrined University of Chicago economics and conveyed its orientation by making Nobel Prize winner Friedrich Hayek its honorary president (Lladser 1986: 52, 61). A conspicuous sign of change appeared when military rule ended and the defeated rightist candidate for president immediately helped establish the ILD, having learned from antagonists the political value of PRCs. The ILD quickly became a powerful arm of the right, consulting especially for its allies in the legislature.

Some Argentine respondents cited no examples or just one or two in their nation. But a more inclusive listing might encompass centers of limited consequence, such as IDEC, which is closely tied to the rightist Union of the Democratic Center Party, and the Center for Studies on Liberty, which was established to advance the philosophy of liberty in economics, finance, sociology, and law. More important are the following. CEMA, formed with "Chicago boys" to study monetary policy, was that rare PRC that served the military government. FIEL dates back to 1964 and is supported by Argentine wings of multinational business firms. The Foundation of Research for Development also works largely for business. But the greatest public policy impact was made by the Mediterranean Foundation. Founded in 1977 by businessmen for research on national and Latin American economics, the foundation has an affiliated research institute in Córdoba. It gave direction to Menem's neoliberal economic policy (Mollis pc-3; Brunner and Barrios 1987: 129–30; Gibson 1990).

The variation in the size of the Argentine list highlights definitional ambiguity. Aside from doubts about which are truly research centers, much depends on what is rightist. A blur appears beyond the explicit ideological cases. An early probusiness PRC was the Dominican Republic's Fondo. It promoted modernization in the nation's second city, Santiago, and provided an intellectual counterweight to the marked leftism of the main URC, CERESD (Dore i–2). The Center of Economic and Educational Studies is a parallel from Monterrey, Mexico, but is less important.

The Technocratic Turn

The rise of technocratic orientations regarding social research is crucial. Many PRCs champion this revolution. Leftist social scientists commonly label these PRCs rightist.

However, these PRCs pride themselves on the apoliticalness of their work or on their objective approach to political issues, especially compared to the ideological approaches in public universities. They emphasize their application of special, technical skills to research and policy problems. An illustration lies in the comparison CERES draws between itself and Uruguay's University of the Republic. Peru's CEPEI epitomizes the several Peruvian PRCs specializing in international relations. In most cases, it is a matter of degree. Colombia's FEDESARROLLO does much progressive work, yet for its proclaimed objectivity, pragmatism, and work for the government, it earns the rightist label from some who uphold notions of committed research for fundamental structural change. The shifting balance between ideological and technical approaches then affects government policy through flows of both information and personnel. CIEPLAN-Chile and El Colegio de México are two leading examples (examples that show that technical influences are not new—though they have intensified).

Proliferating think tanks and economic consultancy centers fall into either of the two rightist categories (ideological and technocratic) or are a mix of the two. Costa Rica's CIAPA probably mixes the ideological and technocratic (Dent 1990b: 401, 407). Peru's ILD is rightist in its fervent belief in deregulation and free markets, but its championship of "popular" capitalism is harder to tag. De Soto himself, author of *The Other Path*, which has been called the "political manifesto" of Latin American neoconservatives (Durand 1992: 248–49), is a Swiss-trained economist who wants to be known as the sort of European social democrat capitalist who believes that state enterprises can work. Others in the ILD might be identified as conservatives. The ILD has the strength and backing to foster kindred PRCs in Central America (Arregui i; Walker i).

Developments like these render traditional left-right labels less apt. Whether *rightist* is the appropriate political label for most rising think tanks and consultancy centers is debatable. They are more rightist than leftist and more rightist than the earlier, classic PRCs. Yet many could be labeled centrist for their lack of strong or extreme ideology and for their emphasis on practical problems and approaches. However impressive the pluralism of the PRC sector is, the small presence of the ideological right and left limits it. Timerman's (1987: 125) glorification is therefore a little misleading, even for Chile: "There isn't a political tendency or an ideological outlook or a religious or philosophical discipline that is not represented in one of these organizations." PRCs concentrate more in the politically moderate zone.

prcs versus Universities

The PRC moderation expressed in the ascendancy of technocratic orientation, centrism, and nonradical leftism assumes extra significance because of contrasts to university social research. Two qualifications are necessary. One concerns private universities; the other concerns periods where military regimes in Chile, Argentina, Uruguay, and other countries drove most social science out of public universities, leaving behind only neoliberal or technocratic pockets. Consequently, political science, sociology, and especially economics inclined more to the right in Chilean universities than PRCs. It remains to be seen what colorations these nations' universities will ultimately take and whether PRCs will be models for moderation; in the early years of new democracy, Chile's universities were more moderate than its neighbors'.

To date, however, the main comparison has been between PRCs and public universities with established social research records, and these universities have not matched PRCs in leading leftist transformations. To be sure, even the university left has changed some. For example, European leftist diversity enters through the works of Foucault, Tourraine, Giddons, and Habermas (H. Muñoz i). But orientations have not changed nearly as much as in the PRCs. Peru typifies how public university teaching and research remain much more dogmatically Marxist. Mexican critics, likewise, conclude that their public university tends to train Marxists rather than sociologists or economists, Marxists who know *Capital* and little more (Cotler i; Reyna N.d.). Officials in international agencies observe that PRCs provide a more modern and intelligent left with which to negotiate, giving a distinct advantage to nations with major PRCs (Ratinoff i).

URCs hold an intermediate position. This seems logical, given the norms of work and international contacts (see chapter 6). Both of these fall between the norms of university faculty and PRC, though they are closer to the faculty. Even in fields like physics, the contrast between UNAM's leftist faculties and URCs is strong; UNAM's social science URCs are less leftist than their corresponding teaching faculties, with the sole exception of economics; and they publish more, especially by international standards (Schmidt i; Ornelas i). But even at these URCs, the highest academic training comes overwhelmingly from the faculties at UNAM itself, the reverse of the situation at El Colegio, with its preponderance of foreign advanced training (Muñoz and Suárez 1984: 420–21). And while UNAM's social science remains generally leftist, including the URCs outside legal studies (Barquín i), El Colegio's is mixed and rarely beyond the moderate left.

In Guatemala and the Dominican Republic, little social research takes place outside PRCs and URCs. ASIES, Guatemala's leading PRC, is tied to Christian Democracy, or the center-right, though it has added some Social Democrats to its staff. The Institute of Economic and Social Research and the public university's other two major social science URCs are further left, as shown by their staunch and brave criticism of the nation's fraudulent elections and democratic facade from 1972 to 1982 (Alvarez pc-2). In the Dominican Republic, PRCs may be a little more to the left than counterparts elsewhere, but most are to the right of UASD's CERESD, the nation's main URC for over two decades. CERESD is Marxist dominated: most of the staff holding doctorates received them in communist Eastern Europe. Whereas CERESD is home to leading leftist intellectuals, including Gilberto Casa, the nation's top non-Marxist intellectual, Frank Moya Pons, has been a leader at Fondo (a PRC). CERESD emphasizes topics like modes of production, the deleterious effects of multinational corporations, and the degree of capitalism versus feudalism in the nation's economy (Sánchez M. i–1).[22]

Whether the comparison concerns PRCs versus URCs or PRCs versus faculties, the distinction between private university and public university is pivotal. Although private universities do little conventional academic research, they do applied and consultancy research, often through URCs. These orientations suggest obvious likenesses to technocratic PRCs. Where an ideological tone dominates, it is usually rightist. The major exceptions are the good, older Catholic universities engaged in basic research. The Dominican Republic shows the general tendencies: most of its private universities do almost no social research. Even the leading three do little, and most of that is in URCs, with either technocratic or rightist emphases; the one private URC that inclined toward committed leftist research, INTEC's CEDE, could not remain within its university. Mexico's ITAM may presage a role for private URCs along the political lines mapped by PRCs.

The main political gap, therefore, concerns public universities and PRCs. It is further captured by the former's stiff criticism of the latter, part of a broader leftist critique of NGOs.[23] Some UNAM professors call El Colegio's work antirevolutionary, technocratic, foreign oriented—in sum, politically the status quo. In Central America, similar cleavages arise between the University of San Carlos and Guatemalan PRCs, while leftists at the University of Costa Rica condemn research centers, including some URCs, as tools of transnational companies and foreign journals that undermine research aimed at national change (Vega 1989: 43; Paniagua pc). In Brazil, where the bulk of social science remains in the universities with leftist tendencies, common charges against PRCs include conservatism and excessive closeness to the United States (Massi 1989; Miceli 1989a).

PLURALIST RESTRICTIVENESS

The greatest contribution PRCs make to pluralism is to sustain and promote alternatives to government policy. Also decisive is interinstitutional pluralism within the PRC sector, as individual PRCs differ politically from one another. But ignored in the account up to this point—and in standard images of PRCs—is the severe limit on pluralism: internal homogeneity, reinforced by hierarchical governance. Such homogeneity and governance are in fact common for specialized private institutions, including nonprofits. They are neither marginal nor easily modified traits. On the contrary, they may lie at the core of these institutions' identity and mission. They are logical and perhaps necessary counterparts to the celebrated face of interinstitutional pluralism. The very pluralism praised thus far comes in institutional packages that limit pluralism.

Nonpluralist Institutions in Pluralist Sectors

Limited pluralism within recipient centers runs counter to the stated intentions and claims of donors (E. Fox 1980: 7) and of PRCs themselves. Fruhling (1985: 41, 67, 73–74) writes that PRCs need internal pluralism partly because donors demand nonpartisanship; thus, PRCs bring people together. Others suggest that donors should deny funding to centers lacking plural voices (Spalding, Taylor, and Vilas 1985: IV-2). Moreover, claims about pluralism often fail to distinguish between interinstitutional and intrainstitutional dimensions (Spalding, Stallings, and Weeks 1990: 14), leaving the impression that pluralism is more widespread than it is. But the main problem in understanding the lack of pluralism comes more from lack of information than from misleading information. This section explores the typical nonpluralist reality, partial exceptions, and reasons for the typical reality.

The Nonpluralist Reality

Most individual PRCs exclude most political lines found in the PRC sector, which itself excludes some lines found in the wider society. Some PRCs encompass several portions of the political spectrum; more express one basic tendency, sometimes with a loose affiliation to others. Thus, CIEPLAN allows a relative pluralism, as when it added the Christian Democratic left after 1976 and when it accepted young graduates of Catholic University of Chile's "Chicago" economics faculty. But these additions came only after a coherent core had been established, with decision-making control guaranteed (Godoy i).[24] The clarity of this core allows a PRC to have a meaningful identity. This clarity means that the characteristic political moderation of PRCs is not political blandness.

The Chilean case shows that the labels may be more exact than simply *centrist* or *renovating leftist,* let alone *leftist.* The CPU is clearly Christian Democratic; and VECTOR connects to a wing of the Socialist Party.[25] As in the broader Chilean political arena, a secular-religious cleavage cuts across the center-left cleavage to fractionalize further, though some PRCs build across the secular-religious divide. A women's group left the AHC to set up a separate center due to conflict with the church over abortion (Spalding, Taylor, and Vilas 1985: II-11). The AHC-VECTOR cleavage turns on both a center-left and a religious-secular fulcrum; attempts at pluralism smack of tokenism, and the "distinctive coloration" of both is well known in Chile (E. Fox 1980: 70). Even nations with much less PRC development show the contrast between plural sectors and nonplural institutions. Alongside Guatemala's ASIES on the center-right lies AVANCSO on the center-left. Of two Dominican PRCs specializing in women's issues, CIPAF is more to the left and Women in Development is more to the right, with INTEC's URC in between. Few of the nation's PRCs even pretend or aspire to political pluralism (Sánchez M. i–2).

Many peripheral PRCs tied to such external organizations as government agencies, businesses, and nonprofits—especially political parties—have clear political profiles. Sectoral overlap occurs when PRCs are think tanks for parties governing the public sector. The political focus is sharper still where PRCs are connected with one wing of a party.

Colombia exemplifies nations with parties that have long been at the political system's heart. The Institute of Liberal Studies is tied to the official Liberal Party, the Galán Foundation to a faction of that party, the Mariano Ospina Pérez Foundation to the Conservative Party, the Center of Colombian Studies to the Social Conservative Party, and the Center of Social Research and Studies to the Communist Party. PRCs that are not so tied to a party but that have clear political profiles are the CINEP, which is Jesuit and progressive democratic, and FESCOL, which is social democratic (Serrano pc-1, pc-2). Peru's fragmented party system and extensive PRC network is yet another Andean case.[26] Argentine parties have associated "foundations." CELADU is related to Uruguay's National Party; ASIES is related to Guatemala's Christian Democratic Party (Barreiro and Cruz 1990: 55; Fernández 1989: 40). The Brazilian case shows how PRCs relate to parties or specific wings of parties even where party systems are not strong (Rodrigues 1982: 19).

Exceptions

Exceptions merit attention, and partial exceptions are numerous. Some PRCs elevate internal pluralism to principle. Argentina's EURAL and Guatemala's ASIES (N.d.: 1) are examples; and Brazil's CEDEC (N.d.: 1) claims to bring together researchers with opposing positions and party preferences. Researchers at Peru's GRADE differ over such matters as whether to work directly with private enterprises. However, critics dismiss GRADE's pluralist claim as a cover for its rightist and technocratic reality, while GRADE itself wonders if it can maintain pluralism (GRADE 1990: 1; Arregui i). FDN brings together agrarian researchers who pride themselves on subordinating their individual ideologies for the delivery of practical, nonpartisan assistance (Carroll 1992: 200).

Chile's CERC has included the Christian Democrats, independent centrists, and socialists. Mostly, though, CERC must be seen in the context of membership in the AHC confederation, which imposed only minimal affiliation requirements, notably respect for church thought. Early on, when the AHC was tied to the Christian Democrats, it was more limited. The Ford Foundation pushed hard for the inclusion of several projects conducted by leftists, and when the rather leftist FLACSO lost its government subsidization in 1978 it was admitted to the AHC, after tough internal debate at the AHC (Livingston i–1). Pluralism also may appear across centers within individual PRCs. El Colegio's seven constituent centers differ among themselves, whereas they display some distinct political orientations internally. El Colegio further shows that large PRCs tend to be less tightly defined politically.

When researchers from PRCs work together across ideological divides, it is often interinstitutionally. This occurred famously in Chile's period of reconciliation leading to redemocratization. Major actors included FLACSO on the left, CIEPLAN in the center, and the CEP on the right. The CPU substituted as the centrist group when these PRCs accepted Ford and U.S. government funding to work together (though still dividing tasks into three distinct parts) to guide higher education policy for the emerging democracy. Such collaboration epitomizes a nonprofit sector comprising specialized centers that are both interinstitutionally diverse and intrainstitutionally homogeneous.[27]

Finally, though PRCs are not oriented toward internal ideological interaction, many subordinate ideology to the point that researchers with different personal ideologies work together on practical tasks. This point, which is very important for Latin America's nonprofits in general, reinforces earlier observations on the strong pragmatic sense of many PRCs.

Reasons

The typical lack of pluralism within PRCs is not principally the PRCs' fault, if it is a fault at all. Reasons for the lack include a combination of warranted defensive action, logical counterparts to limited academic undertakings (themselves conditioned largely by scarce opportunities), and a natural binding within environments of limited alternatives. The last factor relates back to dependency on foreign donors.

One form of defensive action occurs when highly politicized environments push researchers toward safe, firm allegiances. Peronist outrages in the 1972–1976 period led to an increased identification with the Radical Party by Argentine social scientists. There—and in Uruguay and elsewhere—PRCs would start small, with a priority on solidarity, personal affinity, and lack of conflict, before proceeding to a carefully selected growth (Cavarozzi i; Cosse i). The "nucleus" was to be secure before the "rings" were added (Brunner and Barrios 1987: 105–11). The division of so much of Chilean politics and society along party groupings led to PRCs with party allegiances even before military rule. Identity, then, can be a stance against hostile forces or a way of obtaining rewards. Furthermore, as small size is more easily associated with internal homogeneity, PRCs must remain small for defensive reasons, limiting their range in teaching, extension, and research lest they awaken powerful opposition.

Also explaining the lack of political pluralism within PRCs is academic narrowness (identified in the ensuing chapters). A focus on just one policy area or discipline diminishes the likelihood of the political diversity usually found in university settings. Academic narrowness also precludes the necessity of PRC researchers reaching out to other PRCs and researchers or accommodating their views. PRC researchers usually publish in working papers of their own PRCs. If they published in journals refereed by scholars from centrist, leftist, and rightist PRCs along with scholars from other types of organizations, they might have to meet broader requirements. But when researchers publish outside their PRC, it is often in an ideologically compatible outlet. PRCs are not alone in restrictiveness.[28] But they represent an extreme form—more extreme than they pretend.

The bond among like-minded individuals is understandable in highly factionalized contexts and surely in contexts that are also repressive. Typically, a major figure gets things going and then attracts key followers: only these need "apply." Selection takes place without the formal *concursos,* or competitions traditionally prized at the public university. Where merit is required, as at good PRCs, it must be combined with affinity, including an ability to get along and work together. PRCs are unlike universities, where coverage of a broad range of subjects is a major consideration and people must be recruited to fill designated positions; in that sense, PRCs have greater latitude to choose who they want. PRC involvement in extension and other political activities furthers the need for like-minded associates. And the binding process naturally assumes a two-way dynamic: those who are politically at odds with a PRC's profile do not want to join. Where conflict might arise within PRCs, secession becomes tempting. Conflict resolution may therefore lead to the hyperproliferation (analyzed in chapter 3) more than to intrainstitutional accommodation.

These notions of binding fit mainstream pluralist theory and newer nonprofit theory. Seibel and Anheier (1990: 12–13) describe nonprofits as low in formality and high in solidarity and "acquaintance" networks. The nonprofit form helps the plural sector to handle a variety of interests without rending conflict by allowing them to coalesce in separate institutions (Dahl 1982; Douglas 1987). The governance of the nonprofits, then, logically reflects the organization's will, which may well be a minority in the larger system.[29]

Additionally, tight political profiles are logical, and sometimes required, responses to dependence on foreign donors. Many donors themselves have political agendas, including those tied to international political party movements, especially democratic socialism and Christian democracy. Recipients must fit these agendas. The Ford Foundation once exemplified those with broader agendas, but it has retreated from the emphasis on pluralism that it sought, with little success, in its earlier grants for university development.[30] Today, it pursues a more defined, targeted political agenda and does not press as much for internal pluralism.[31] The idea (Fruhling 1985: 23) that nonprofit recipients must convince donors that they are nonpartisan is exaggerated. As with other claims of nonpoliticalness, this claim is at times itself a political pitch for legitimacy. The truth lies less in the absence of politics than in the absence of political conflict, as donors match up with like-minded recipients rather than with internally divided institutions.[32] Only a distinctive institutional profile allows PRC leaders to state clearly what their group stands for and how it will perform.

That sort of profile is less sensible for a university pursuing multiple purposes across a broad academic range and with an assured annual subsidization by a general provider, typically government. The PRC-university contrast weakens where the fragmentation of Latin American universities has produced rather distinctive profiles according to individual faculty, with a consequent lack of interactive pluralism. URCs in the social sciences are also intermediate cases.[33] The generalization withstands the partial exceptions: PRCs—usually nonprofit specialists—are remarkable for their political homogeneity.

Hierarchical Governance

Hierarchical governance helps guarantee the narrow ideological profiles. A lack of democratic participation appears ironic, given the progressive ideology, as well as the prior involvement, of many PRC leaders in the fight for university democratization. It also appears ironic given the progressive work that many PRCs do. Hierarchy is more popularly associated with conservative nonprofit organizations, including churches and private universities—not to mention for-profit private institutions. PRCs' hierarchical governance is rarely identified, much less analyzed.[34] Like internal homogeneity, hierarchy is usually ignored. PRCs and their funders are rarely forced to deny or defend the hierarchy.

As with internal homogeneity, the main point is not to fault PRCs but to understand their functioning and constraints. This section looks at key elements of hierarchy, PRCs that test the generalization's limits, reasons for the hierarchy, and comparisons to other types of research centers.

Key Elements of Hierarchy

Elections are not the favored form for selecting leaders at PRCS.[35] Sometimes elections are tacked on as a formality, as at Chile's PET. Sometimes they amount to the power holders' informal "election" of someone, without fixed procedure or secret ballot. Beyond that, incumbency is typically long term. Regular election periods are uncommon. So is turnover, unless leaders move on to outside political positions.[36] Alternation is an option, as when the head of one of PET's three programs becomes the head of another. Turnover based on policy change is rare: it could undermine the PRC's defining political identity.

PRC governance is in some ways even stricter than governance at small, nonelite, private colleges and universities, the extreme of restrictive governance profiles previously analyzed for higher education institutions (Levy 1986: 243–51). Governance there includes external boards and owners, along with alumni. Compared to those institutions and to U.S. nonprofits, Latin American PRCS and other nonprofits either are less likely to have external boards or their boards are less intrusive. Among PRCS, external boards are most natural for centers linked to corporate institutions.[37] Most PRCS, instead, concentrate authority in their internal leadership. Even at Venezuela's IESA—with its corporate orientation and a large graduate education that makes it partly resemble a university—the board is relatively inactive while directors (who are professors) largely run the institution (Gómez and Bustillo 1979: 90).

PRC founders, usually academics, are often members of the PRC's chief governing body. An eight-member commission elected yearly by a General Assembly runs Uruguay's CERES (N.d.), but the assembly includes only the founders and members selected by the founders. Such bodies represent internal more than external authority. Compared to most private universities, PRCS' hierarchical governance is more compatible with institutional autonomy and shows an even greater concentration of power.

At the extreme, the "great man" runs "his" center. Authority may assume charismatic dimensions. De Soto at Peru's ILD and Constantino Urgullo at Costa Rica's CIAPA fit this description. Perceptions of excess may hurt the PRC, as with the ILD in the international community by the early 1990s. In any case, a strong identification of a PRC with its leader is common. Examples have included Domingo Rivarola's CPES in Paraguay, Patricio Cariola's CIDE and Alejandro Foxley's CIEPLAN in Chile, Jorge Hardoy's CEUR in Argentina, Luis Paz's FDN in Peru, and Frank Moya Pons's

Fondo in the Dominican Republic. A critical test then becomes whether the PRC accumulates the institutional strength to sustain the loss of its founding figure. In Mexico the tests for Jorge Bustamante's *Colegio* in Tijuana and for Guillermo de la Peña's CIESAS-Occidente have been passed by the CEE and El Colegio. Argentina's CEDES passed the test when Guillermo O'Donnell left. In fact, some of these PRCs had already grown well beyond dependence on the departing founder. This growth sometimes involves rule by a directive council or board.

Related to its undemocratic aspects, hierarchical governance typically means the low representation of certain groups. Younger scholars, including those who have followed the leader but are no longer so young, lack access to power, just as they lack access to resources and international contacts (Coatsworth 1989) and academic visibility. A generation gap could cloud PRCs' political future. Indigenous and Afro-Latin groups might fare better if the hierarchy were less rigid (Spalding, Stallings, and Weeks 1990: 5, 25, 89). Women make progress where national democratization absorbs the PRCs' leaders into government, but they still lag. The CLACSO survey (Calderón and Provoste 1990: III–7) finds women holding 27 percent of the doctorates, 24 percent of the directive posts, and 18 percent of the directorships of its centers; the percentages could well be lower for PRCs alone. The dawn of "great woman" centers will mark both change and continuity.[38]

Testing the Limits

Beyond typical PRCs, consider the mix at the PRCs with less hierarchy. Internationally, the least prestigious higher education institutions, which are often small, tend to have the steepest hierarchies. So it is that Latin America's largest and most celebrated PRCs are less hierarchical than typical PRCs, though they are still more hierarchical than universities. Predictably, the PRCs in question are also unusually pluralist.

El Colegio de México (N.d.: 10–11) has maintained hierarchical governance from its inception in 1940. A board of six people still appoints the president. Firmly holding the reigns for some twenty years, Víctor Urquidi (i–2) looks back on struggles and bargains with the faculty over such matters as the creation of new programs, but some admirers within and beyond the institution remember Urquidi (along with other presidents) as a person "who never listened to anyone" against his own judgment.

El Colegio is also important because the parent PRC has explicitly pushed its hierarchical governance model on *colegio* offspring. The center in Tijuana, one of the two best offspring, is a chip off the old block. It too has a directive council and plenty of presidential power. In fact, President Busta-mante essentially constructed the center's power structure through his major role in selecting the council. The council gives representation to key government agencies, including funders, and to the president of El Colegio. Bustamante has been chief from the outset. Admirers and detractors alike point to a strong hand. Indeed, the fate of *colegios* throughout the republic turns largely on how leaders use the enormous latitude allotted them. The hiring of researchers fits the overall pattern: though many are hired simply for given projects, even full-timers are hired through informal processes and mutual matching. CIDE, too, emulates El Colegio's model, with similar-ities in the governing board, the representation of major public agencies, and a selection process for the presidency (Unger pc).

Further evidence of hierarchy comes from the major domestic network of PRCs, Chile's AHC, at least during its peak strength under military rule. An "external" private actor, the church, was the ultimate authority, and the bishop appointed the institution's head. But much power was concentrated at the peaks of individual centers, thereby approximating the situation at most PRCs. The founders—or others with reputation, contacts, and the abil-ity to attract resources—were key. These people combined scholarship and entrepreneurship; in fact, some relied on assistants for their research while they concentrated on fund-raising, politics, and other pursuits (Fruhling i).

Outside the AHC but at the pinnacle of Chile's PRCs, CIEPLAN reinforces the view that academic prestige, coupled with moderate size and a progres-sive reputation built on sturdy opposition to military rule, is insufficient to discourage hierarchy. Power lies with the eight institutional founders, who govern collegially, meeting on big matters and composing the four-member executive committee (CIEPLAN 1988: 5). CECI is an interesting parallel—same nation, different field. Created by four scientists with a common vi-sion, it grew to more than three times that size while still being run by the four, with no real balloting or pretense at participatory politics (Teitelboim i); here, hierarchy exists even outside social research PRCs that must safe-guard pronounced political profiles.

Some top PRCs show evidence of greater participation.[39] Uruguay's CIE-DUR (N.d.: 2) claims a move beyond its four founders to full rights for its fifteen researchers. FLACSO-Chile, as well as the FLACSO federation in gen-eral, boasts meaningful participation. Chile's SUR allows real electoral turn-over, and Argentina's CEDES concentrates power more in an assembly of fifteen than in the director (Lladser i–1; Balán i–1). Paraguay's CDE elects its leader for one year, with just one reelection permitted (Moreno pc). Brazil's IUPERJ elects its director every two years. Peru's IEP has democratized since 1984 with biannual elections in which junior researchers participate. Similar changes have occurred at other Peruvian PRCs—though not most.

Reasons

Certain reasons for hierarchy stem from factors already discussed. For example, when creating PRCs key figures sometimes draw lessons from the association between participation and academic deterioration at public universities. Another example is the need for careful self-control under authoritarian rule; in that respect, demands for wider participation inside PRCs could grow where democratic environments become secure.

The broadest ongoing reason for hierarchy is that it ensures the clear, nonpluralist profile depicted above as fundamental to how PRCs function. For predictable direction, specialized nonprofits minimize the number of important political actors who could introduce ambiguity. This is especially true where these nonprofits are (like PRCs) fragile. Coherence typically comes from a mix of consensus and hierarchical restrictiveness. Also typical is the choice-voice dynamic: you may choose a PRC if the PRC likewise chooses you, but you join without the right to press for significant change. Like the mutual matching of donor and PRC discussed in the previous chapter, the mutual matching of researcher and PRC diminishes but does not eliminate a sense of control. It is a mistake to dismiss the hierarchy because it is partly informal and accepted in friendly environments (Tillett 1980: 28).

Funders reinforce the logic of hierarchy. The evidence comes mostly from philanthropic donors, but it applies to funding more generally.[40] Donors are reluctant to trust to participatory processes where the resulting directions are uncertain. They therefore entrust funds to like-minded leaders who have their confidence and who have the power to run their institutions.

The decisive role of Rockefeller and then Ford at El Colegio turned fundamentally on this trust. Rockefeller knew that Daniel Cosío Villegas would not tolerate disorder or incompetence; he stated bluntly that student rights were nil (Harrison i–2). To this day, political participation by students is absent despite the importance of graduate education to the institution's academic profile. Also limited are two of the political actors that are increasingly active in Latin American public university governance: unionized faculty and workers. Though even El Colegio has felt worker pressure since the 1980s, the institution's historic practice is to handle most services by subcontracts, avoiding a union presence in governance.

Here too, donors' aspirations or claims to apoliticalness clash with visible political consequences. Just as donors typically support PRCs with clear political profiles, so they support hierarchy at PRCs. In related but friendlier terms, philanthropy promotes "managerial capacity" at PRCs (Calderón and Provoste 1990: I–20).[41] In terms of resource dependency theories, power within organizations tends to flow to those who best handle the environment, including the ability to ensure an inward flow of resources (Hickson et al. 1971). At an extreme, donors turn initially to an individual, who then builds his center, hiring those he wants, and then securing further funds. This was the pattern for Moya Pons and the Ford Foundation in the Dominican Republic (Sánchez M. i–2).[42] Similarly, de Soto (1989: xxiv) recalls how he used his initial funds to write proposals to foundations: "Then once I had obtained funding, I did what I have always considered my strong point: I recruited a magnificent team which today is the . . . [ILD] and contracted excellent advisors."

The hierarchical pattern tends to reinforce itself. Note how nonleaders react to their subordination. Some pursue "the dream of their own center" (Cueto i–1). This is understandable, given their present lack of voice and the potential rewards of leadership elsewhere. It is a dynamic that breeds additional hierarchical PRCs. Most followers remain followers, however. They remain so without turning to protest, despite the undemocratic norms and their own professional immobility. Operating in a rather clientelistic system, they seek benefits from their leaders more than they challenge those leaders, their center, or the basic features of hierarchy. An exception is revealing: in its early years the *colegio* in Tijuana reportedly faced a protest from researchers angered by the center's hierarchy, particularly the decisive hand of the president. The president fired them.[43]

Other Research Centers

Some factors that explain hierarchy at PRCs also operate at other research centers, but I lack the evidence to assess matters of degree or the related question of how much hierarchy is natural to viable research organizations.[44] Hierarchy is no surprise regarding GRCs, or even the sub-category of public research centers. Their institutional hierarchy connects directly with government. They do not match PRCs in administrative autonomy even when they match them in academic autonomy. The Mexican government's role on the boards of El Colegio and CIDE (N.d.: 21) and in selecting the center's head resembles the norms for public research centers elsewhere in Latin America. The government also names the director of FLACSO-Mexico and generally plays a larger role in governance than that seen in FLACSOS elsewhere (Alvarez pc-2). The education ministry selects CINVESTAV's director upon a proposal from CINVESTAV's board, whose president is a ministry subsecretary. Chapingo's director is appointed by the agriculture ministry and Chapingo's board, three of whose five members are government ministers. Chapingo unabashedly rejects participatory norms that scar Mexican agricultural universities (El Colegio de Postgraduados 1985: 12; Jiménez, Fernández, and Galindo 1978: 56–58). Parallels appear at more conventional GRCs, such as the Institute of Electrical Research (Schoijet 1979: 3).

Greater variability exists among URCs. A clear tendency, however, is for less participation than in the teaching faculties. Scholars at Mexico's UNAM centers, even more than at its institutes, lack the representation that faculty professors have on university bodies; the rector appoints both the directors of URCs and the coordinators of the URC networks (Jiménez M. 1982: 104–20). A center may be run hierarchically by a noted champion of university and national democratic participation—Pablo González Casanova being one such head. Another paradox is that UNAM's URCs, especially in the sciences, have produced most of the university's recent rectors, reflecting the elite's positive perception of strong academic centers with hierarchical political order. Additionally, the nation's major technological university illustrates the widespread pattern of the automatic membership of high university administrators on URCs' top governing bodies.[45]

CONCLUSION

Freedom, democracy, and pluralism play out very differently for the PRC in society and the PRC in its internal patterns of governance. The governance of PRCs is itself a worthy political topic and a crucial one for scholars of nonprofit, research, and other higher education institutions, and the topic assumes broader interest for its relation to macropolitics.

Nonprofit organizations that both claim to serve democracy and are internally homogeneous and hierarchical should articulate their rationale.

PRCS usually do not. They more often ignore their undemocratic aspects or emphasize how their individual institution escapes the generalization. Although it is appropriate to establish where institutions are relatively plural or open to democratic participation, it is necessary to acknowledge the general limitations and then to explain and assess them.[46]

One solid nonprofit defense, suitable to PRCS, lies in a distinction between institutions and sectors. The coexistence of multitudinous institutions that are internally homogeneous but different from one another provides pluralist diversity, choice, and freedom. A related pluralist defense involves a means-ends distinction. If internal diversity and participation are ends in themselves, most individual PRCS do not score high on democratic tests. If internal governance is a means toward societal democratization, most PRCS earn very high marks. This classic pluralist formulation has wide relevance for nonprofit sectors and institutions. It rests fundamentally on a belief in pluralist democracy consistent with, indeed sometimes aided by, freedom for internally nonpluralist, nondemocratic institutions.[47]

Of course, the ends do not always justify the means. Some trade-offs involve too high a price on the micropolitical side. Other limitations are matters of expediency more than true trade-offs that promote pluralist democracy on the macropolitical side. Without establishing any definitive line, this chapter has inclined toward acceptance of major trade-offs as valid and even desirable. What is less debatable, yet still important, is that individual PRCS contribute to a democratic pluralism in both their own third sector and in the broad public sector, a democratic pluralism that far surpasses that in their own institutions.

PRCS protect social scientists and social science. They provide sanctuary from brutal governments and, in less repressive contexts, from the debilitating conflicts and other problems of public universities. Further, they extend that sanctuary beyond their formal institutional boundaries. Whether we use a limited or an extensive definition of sanctuary, PRCS surpass other research institutions, including URCS and GRCS, in this realm, often supplanting even the public university as pockets of freedom. Beyond all this, PRCS play vital roles in a nation's broader democratization, roles that range from regime change to democratic consolidation and the strengthening of civil society. A major role involves the transformation of political orientations toward moderate democratic visions. PRCS furnish crucial information, policy advice, and leadership personnel for democratic governments and for the democratic opposition. Here, then, is a rare case in which the initial goals of foreign assistance have been not only met but vastly exceeded.[48] Not rare, however, is the association between nonprofit growth and democratization.[49]

PRCs' continued political importance under vastly changed political systems is a remarkable manifestation of nonprofit agility. By cooperating with government while also expanding the scope of political activity in the nonprofit sector, PRCs help restructure the intersectoral dynamics. They promote the contemporary tendency toward democratic but limited states that work with expanded private sectors. Once crucial sanctuaries from dominant political tendencies, PRCs increasingly live in the political mainstream.

6 Combining Quality and Relevance

The significance of PRCS as political institutions does not preempt their academic essence. PRCS mark a sea change in the region's research, education, social science, and intellectual life. Their academic performance is crucial to a concern with evaluating nonprofit organizations, including their service to public, for-profit, and other nonprofit organizations. The more impressive their academic performance, the greater the importance of PRCS.

Whereas the preceding chapters touch on academic issues, here the text undertakes a systematic assessment of PRCS' academic performance.[1] The profile that emerges parallels our evaluation of PRC politics: an overwhelmingly positive international image sustained hitherto largely by ad hoc contrasts and impressions can now be established and elaborated with considerable evidence. In academics as well as politics, PRCS usually fulfill the missions they undertake, even sometimes surpassing expectations. But, again as with politics—and consistent with our basic notion concerning the performance of specialized private nonprofits—we also find severe limitations.

The length and complexity of the academic evaluation requires a division into two chapters, one on triumphs and the other on weaknesses. The two chapters go hand in hand, however, and the introduction here in the first, like a section on models and the conclusion in the second, serves both. The present chapter considers the graduate education received by the PRCS' researchers, the research output, and the controversial matter of relevance. The success that emerges on all three counts is impressive, extensive, and multifaceted. Some PRCS are truly centers of excellence. It is especially important that positive impressions about PRCS get incorporated into the literature on Third World higher education in general and on its research in particular. That literature is overwhelmingly negative regarding both the quality and relevance of performance (Altbach 1991; Gaillard 1991).

ADVANCED TRAINING

Staff Credentials

PRCS far outdistance their university counterparts in advanced degrees held by staff. The distance increases for degrees from foreign institutions; given the quality of the foreign universities in question, these degrees are typically superior to those available at home.

The gap grows still larger for degrees from U.S. universities. These degrees often mark the greatest rupture with Latin American academic traditions, an abrupt modernization. They commonly mark international preeminence in research and graduate education, at least in empirically oriented fields. Quality is further signaled by the complex and rigorous ordeal of graduate studies, whereas European doctorates seldom require formidable course study. Europe has simply not developed a similar distinction between graduate and undergraduate education (Clark 1993c), though obviously many European degrees equal any in the world.

Chilean PRCS provide the best national data. Before redemocratization, roughly 20 percent of the then more than 500 researchers held or were pursuing doctorates, a percentage at once smaller than at prestigious PRCS and yet much higher than at almost any Latin American university. Foreign universities accounted for most of the highest graduate degrees. The universities of Paris and Louvain topped the list, as Western Europe led the way with over 40 percent of the total. The U.S. contribution of 25 percent was much more dispersed, yet spectacular, with doctorates from Harvard, Berkeley, and Yale heading this list. Communist nations accounted for but one doctorate. Chile itself granted most of the roughly 30 percent from Latin America (Lladser 1986: 9; Lladser 1987: 11–24; Lladser 1988b). As the leading PRC in economics, CIEPLAN (N.d.: 5–7) showed that the Chilean universities still produced in economics and also that U.S. doctorates dominated in that field: for the fifteen permanent and associate researchers, all undergraduate degrees listed were Chilean and all thirteen doctorates held or sought were from U.S. universities. A similarly high degree profile, accentuated by U.S. dominance, is true of Chile's science PRC, the CECI. All thirteen senior and associate researchers hold doctorates, six from Chile; the United States accounts for four of the other seven and apparently provided postdoctoral studies—much more common in the natural than the social sciences—to all thirteen (Teitelboim N.d.: 5).

U.S. universities are important in almost all fields. Guatemala's CIRMA, which specializes in history, archeology, and anthropology, has ten researchers with doctorates, all from the United States and Canada. At Brazil's IUPERJ, which is unusually strong in political science, among other fields, all nineteen researchers boast graduate degrees; thirteen earned their highest degrees in the United States, even though no individual university accounts for more than two, with only one other foreign nation represented (Schwartzman i–1).

But it is in economics and management that U.S. dominance is greatest among social fields. This is relevant for PRC contributions to broader privatization and for the revamping of the state. Of six senior researchers at Uruguay's economically oriented CERES (N.d.: 11), five have doctorates and the other is pursuing it; degree-awarding universities represented are the University of Chicago (with three), the University of California at Los Angeles, the University of Rochester, and the University of Michigan. Of ten permanent researchers at Peru's GRADE, eight have or are getting their highest degree in the United States, and seven of the degrees are doctorates (GRADE 1990: 44). Each of the full, associate, and assistant professors at Central America's INCAE (N.d.) holds a U.S. doctorate or is now earning one. At Argentina's Di Tella Institute, four of the sociological center's five permanent researchers have European doctorates, whereas U.S. universities supplied all five of the doctorates in the economics center (ITDT 1990).

With their large share of the top degree holders, good PRCs succeed where mighty university development projects usually fail—building highly trained, full-time academic staffs. In fact, as we have seen, PRCs play a major role in welcoming university refugees and former scholarship holders returning to their native nations. Whereas the great majority of university professors work outside their institutions, probably most PRC faculty devote most of their time to their centers' activities.[2] Perhaps 70 percent of Chile's PRC staff was full-time in the mid-1980s (Lladser i–1). Of course, the diversity of activities at PRCs means that "full-time" rarely means that research or pure academics can be pursued full-time.

The Mexican Case

The Mexican research centers shed light on the advanced-degree profile beyond classic PRCs. I begin with El Colegio de México, Latin America's single most important PRC. Virtually the entire staff at El Colegio work contractually full-time, notwithstanding heavy consulting, whereas even graduate teaching at UNAM lies mostly in the hands of part-timers (de Ibarrola 1986–1987: 17).

Each of El Colegio's seven centers boasts a high educational degree profile, the highest being in centers that are older and not oriented toward applied social sciences. History requires a doctorate for tenure, and both the linguistics and literary center and the center on Asia and Africa accumulate high doctoral percentages, whereas both international relations and demography have a minority with doctorates (Hernández i; Silva i; Treviño i). On the other hand, applied fields show an especially high percentage of U.S. degrees. Economics leans heavily on the United States, along with England and France, whereas sociology has a varied mix, including Latin America and much of Western Europe. Even if one compares El Colegio's professors to UNAM's profesors with doctorates, El Colegio's have the preponderance of foreign degrees. And even in centers with less academic development, these degrees are from such universities as Harvard and Yale for international relations and Wisconsin, Texas, Chicago, Stanford, and UCLA for economics. As sociology and demography and urban development show, foreign doctorates usually are earned after Mexican master's degrees.

CIDE follows El Colegio's lead. With a vigorous professional development program, CIDE may well push beyond its immediate goal that half its permanent staff hold doctorates or be candidates for one (Unger pc). Because of their unusually large size for PRCs, CIDE and El Colegio alone make for a powerful PRC presence in advanced social science degrees held by Mexicans. And because of their size, their role in graduate teaching, and especially their dependence on public funds and political influence, the two institutions also are close to being public research centers.

Like PRCs, public research centers outdistance Mexico's university faculties in credentials. CINVESTAV probably trails only El Colegio among all Mexican teaching units, including URCs, in the percentage of staff with doctorates; it is a pioneer in the development of full-time positions (Campesino, López-Revilla, and Pérez-Angón 1985: 25; de Ibarrola pc-3). In fact, impressive portraits depict many GRCs that may lack the teaching role of public research centers. About 20 percent of the 500 professionals at the Institute of Electrical Research are in the prestigious National Research System, SNI, and the degree portfolio has long been impressive there and at other national institutes (Schoijet 1979: 3).

Chapingo represents a compelling public research center counterpart to El Colegio. Its 309 professor-researchers hold 749 degrees; more than half the 309 have doctorates—roughly 70 percent from U.S. universities, due to assistance programs, geography, and the development-oriented nature of the fields. The rest of the doctorates are from Western democracies, except for 2 percent from former communist nations.[3] Advanced foreign study has proven essential to Chapingo's growth. In the 1960s, with heavy support from foreign foundations, the IDB, and the Mexican government, Plan Chapingo transformed centers that had had few Ph.D.s and limited full-time staff.

Notwithstanding its foreign assistance, Chapingo also shows degree structures free from undue dependence. The 188 advanced U.S. degrees do not come from a few elite places but from fifty-two universities, mostly land grant, led by Iowa State. Most of all, Mexican training precedes foreign study. It produces 90 percent of the four-year degrees (usually from the local university) and 75 percent of the master's degrees (usually from the Chapingo center).[4] Chapingo's founders and present leaders stress their common roots at the university and their insistence that master's programs steep students in Mexican issues so that their doctoral studies are chosen and molded to address these issues. Visiting terms for professors are purposely limited, and each student has a private council to plan for his or her foreign study. And, however much curriculum initially copied U.S forms, Mexican content and applications have assumed primacy (FF #65288; Jiménez i; Alcalde i). Additionally, the staff at Chapingo's regional centers overwhelmingly hold their highest degree, the master's, from Chapingo itself.

URCs also outdistance university faculties, though they trail private and public research centers.[5] Those returning to UNAM after foreign graduate study gravitate to URCs rather than to faculties. Whereas the journey toward faculty deanships may pass through prestigious professional careers without need of graduate degrees, directorships at URCs usually require advanced academic credentials. At UNAM's URCs, 56 percent of researchers have doctorates, compared to 21 percent of faculty professors; 17 percent of URC researchers, compared to 44 percent of faculty professors, have only a four-year degree. The composition of degrees is higher in the natural sciences than in the social sciences and humanities: at science centers, 70 percent of the more than 800 staff have doctorates and another 25 percent have master's degrees, whereas 40 percent of the top-ranked or "titular" researchers in the latter group lack a doctorate, even though it is a formal requirement (de la Fuente i; Suárez 1984: 57; Muñoz and Suárez 1984: 419, 430). But these differences by field are not overwhelming, and they also exist within the faculties; thus, in the fields of greatest URC-PRC overlap, URCs trail PRCs in degrees earned.

Degrees Granted

The quality of the degree structure also rests on degrees granted. PRCs rarely grant degrees, but those that do often give the best their nation offers in the social fields. PRCs even make a quantitative impact in relative terms, because universities have not made a great deal of progress in graduate education. There were perhaps only 67,000 graduate students in all Latin America in 1980 (Vessuri 1986: 9), with perhaps 100,000 today, though a liberal figure could go higher. Moreover, almost half are in Brazil alone, another fourth in Mexico. Outside these two nations, the numbers are woeful. Yet even those numbers exaggerate the truth, as most students enroll in specialization rather than bona fide courses, and rigorous master's or doctoral course work is rare. If there were a figure for serious graduate work, PRCs would hold an important social science share in several nations.

An evaluation that combines these qualitative and quantitative perspectives becomes policy relevant as nations seek the best way to organize expanding graduate education and as redemocratization opens the option of considering an enlarged teaching role for PRCs as well as kindred public research centers. Again, PRCs add a private nonprofit option to the modernization process. Balán (N.d.: 31–32) writes of Argentina: "The only postgraduate courses of any serious level are those offered by some independent academic centers." CEMA gives the best master's degree in economics (A. Thompson 1994: 27). An interesting development is the opening in the early

1990s of the Di Tella University. Its quality derives from the use of the Di Tella Institute's professors to teach graduate courses (Mollis pc-3).

The majority of Brazil's advanced social science degrees come from universities, but the most prestigious come disproportionally from places like IUPERJ, which attracts about one-third of its incoming class from outside Brazil (Brunner and Barrios 1987: 99; IUPERJ 1991: 7). If Getúlio Vargas has slipped a little, it still earns a high standing. Meanwhile, PRCs in administration flourish elsewhere as well; IESA exemplifies soaring prestige, superior to that of Venezuelan universities.

Returning to Mexican data, one indication of PRC superiority is the high percentage of master's degree students who proceed to foreign doctoral study. More than half the graduates of El Colegio's economics center do so (Roces i). In fact, as noted earlier, El Colegio has resisted urging from donors to replace foreign study with what it feared might be weak academic programs of its own. When leaders saw that the international relations master's program failed to attract students of sufficient quality, they shut the program down.

El Colegio has also had the integrity to spurn tempting business and government entreaties to open four-year programs in business administration and economics, which could be financial and political successes, at the expense of the institution's academic focus (FF #730874; FF #65288; Urquidi i–2).[6] Like CINVESTAV, El Colegio admits fewer than one in four applicants, whereas the two leading private universities with the largest graduate programs admit between 80 percent and nearly 100 percent (García 1990: 130). Evaluations by U.S. Fulbright visiting professors repeatedly include comments on the high caliber of El Colegio's students; one prominent scholar ranked the students in international relations smarter than their Harvard counterparts.

Additionally, scattered evidence suggests that graduates of PRCs acquit themselves well in their studies abroad. This builds PRCs' international prestige. It builds international academic and political-economic contacts. And it yields an ultimate impact at home through productive employment in the public, for-profit, and third sectors.

RESEARCH

Far exceeding the initial goals of protecting social science, PRCs advance research production both quantitatively and qualitatively. The testimony is overwhelming and especially forceful when made in explicit comparison to university research. Domestic testimony can assume a circularity, because to solicit the views of leading figures may be to solicit from staffs at PRCs. But this testimony gibes with the international testimony of individuals, repeated written evaluations and grants, and a vast network of corroborating academic activities. I will also establish that PRCs often emulate norms of work of developed nations.

Nothing that follows should suggest that all PRCs are superior in social research to all or even most universities, nor that my judgment of superiority is fully objective, nor that PRCs considered superior overall are superior in every way. Major variation turns on the gauges and institutions in question. It also depends on nation, which harks back to the national comparisons sketched in the introduction, but here the emphasis is on quality of academic performance.[7]

National Patterns

The superiority of PRCs goes beyond nations in which military regimes assaulted universities. Consider first the Caribbean and Central America.

In the Dominican Republic, PRCs lead in social research, while the public university crumbles and leading private universities usually concentrate on commercial fields (Silié 1988: 125). As political and economic disasters have crippled Central America's public universities and undermined Ford's efforts to help the social sciences, PRCs have assumed the lead by measures of their personnel, production, and international finance. Beyond leadership by replacement, the professional quality of researchers easily outdistances anything that preceded it, and the number of credible publications soars.

Superiority transcends some differences among nations, so that Nicaraguan centers have "the best human resources and materials," while Panamanian PRCs do "the most important social research," with CEASPA followed by CELA and others (Fernández 1989: 28, 77–78, 100–01). CRIES is a network of leading PRCs throughout the region. ASIES, AVANCSO, CIEN, CIRMA, and CISMA have contributed to the Guatemalan panorama. In Costa Rica and El Salvador, the URC and Catholic university, respectively, remain the single social science leaders, but that negates neither PRC gains in the first nation (led by FLACSO, CEPAS, CIAPA, and others) nor their general superiority in the second.

Several South American nations and Mexico show mixed patterns where PRCS score well. In Brazil, university social science grew immensely under military rule and dominates numerically, but PRCS such as IUPERJ, CEBRAP, and CEDEC are leaders in social science production, quality, and innovation, as well as in political and cultural impact (Rodrigues 1982: 20; Brunner and Barrios 1987: 119–20). This is basically the Mexican pattern, though there PRCS pack their strength into fewer institutions led by El Colegio, some provincial colegios, CIDE, CIDAC, CEE, IMES, and the Barros Sierra Foundation.

In Colombia, like Brazil, university social science benefited from laudable domestic efforts backed by favored-nation assistance from international philanthropy and no sustained regime brutality. But economic difficulties have contributed to a university decline, and progress in the social sciences never matched Brazil's. If an advantage exists in the PRCS, led by SER, FEDESARROLLO, and CINEP, it is not overwhelming or clear, especially against such URCS as CEDE at the Andes (Aldana i; Facundo D. i). The situation becomes complex as many fine research centers also operate outside the social sciences. It serves no good purpose here to struggle to identify where research superiority might lie in Colombia. The same might be said of Ecuador on a more modest level; still, PRCS like CIUDAD, CIESE, and CAAP are leaders in their fields (Carvajal i), and ILDIS has been called the best single source for reseach materials in economics, sociology, education, and political science (Dent 1990b: 403). Venezuela also has good PRCS, but they contribute a smaller percentage of total production. IESA is the leader in economics and public policy.

In most of South America, however, the situation approximates the Caribbean and Central American modal pattern: PRCS move beyond sharing the social research pinnacle to capture most of it, sometimes a near monopoly. Argentine, Chilean, Uruguayan, Peruvian, Paraguayan, and Bolivian PRCS have produced the bulk of high-quality social research in their nations since the early 1970s. What little the university faculties have done is generally unimpressive; neither URCS nor public research centers have usually added much, though the future could be rosier. PRCS are leaders by default.

But they are also leaders by much more than default. Like their Caribbean and Central American counterparts, South American PRCS raise the social research pinnacle and broaden its scope. For example, FLACSO-Chile has earned recognition as a trailblazer in sociology, political science, and international relations (Nina Manitzas memo to William Saint, Feb. 28, 1983, FF #68796). But fine centers with less international visibility also earn praise; Argentina's CICSO is just one example, and even tiny Uruguay boasts a list including CERES, CIEDUR, CIESU, CINVE, CLAEH, and GRECMU (Merkx 1979: 229, 233; Cruz pc-2).

PRCS have pioneered to new heights among less developed South American countries, too. CPES is Paraguay's obvious exemplar, while places like CDE make worthwhile contributions. Although no Bolivian center matches Latin Ameica's peak centers, leadership still lies largely with PRCS such as CIPCA and CEDLA, as well as THOA, CERES, and CEBEM; in economics, PRCS share the nation's pinnacle with two public research centers and especially with the Institute of Social and Economic Studies of the main Catholic university (Contreras i). Research in such fields as sociology and history has reached new Peruvian heights at the IEP, Bartolomé, GRADE, and DESCO, among other PRCS, while the San Marcos national university has faded into insignificance in social science since the 1970s (Puryear i; Cotler i; Marrou i).

In the best-known and best-documented national case, two distinctive strands of testimony delivered in the last few years of military rule illustrate the high research standing of Chile's PRCS. From the right, *El Mercurio,* the nation's foremost newspaper, and the government's CONICIT both publicly recognized PRC quality in their reporting and rewarding of activities; from the left, noted critics of foreign assistance joined in the view that the level of social science research had improved in quantitative and qualitative terms during the years of military rule (Lladser 1988a: 10; Fuenzalida 1987: 119). Only in economics (impressively) and history (unimpressively) did universities rival PRCS in social research; they rarely stirred themselves in social science until late in the military period (Brunner 1990c: 6). Chile's leaders in sociology remained FLACSO and SUR, along with several PRCS specializing in an aspect of sociology and, as with CENECA, in cultural studies. In political science, FLACSO shared the pinnacle with CERC and, in international relations, with CIEPLAN, ILET, CLEPI, and others.

Publications

PRCS boast of the quantity of their publications, and the claim is usually justified. It is difficult, however, to know exactly what to make of data showing a CIEDUR, in Uruguay, producing in its first decade, with seven full-time and eleven part-time researchers, five books, sixty "investigations," eighty-one seminar papers, and thirty-seven working papers, averaging respectively 155, 128, 31, and 35 pages (CIEDUR N.d.: 9; Buxedas pc). With

139 institution-based researchers and 164 others regionwide, FLACSO (1990: 10, 17) claims for 1989–1990, 36 books among 233 pieces published. A survey spanning two years of work by forty Chilean PRCs reports 99 books, 35 book chapters, 10 journal articles, 367 working papers, and 154 mimeos; the IEP, with probably Peru's best social science publishing house, has produced almost 200 books in its three decades, some selling nearly 25,000 copies (Lladser 1986: 10; Spalding 1991: 79; Cotler pc).

PRCs churn out a dazzling number of journals. Most produce their own journals, and their best are usually the nation's best in the social area. They provide the most incisive analysis, the most reliable and extensive data, and the greatest policy relevance for interested parties in all three sectors. Some are markedly academic, such as IUPERJ's *Dados*, published regularly in Brazil since 1966, and CPES's *Revista Paraguaya de Sociología*. Illustrative of a list far too long to include here are the following journals from good PRCs: in Peru, *Revista Andina* from Bartolomé and *Socialismo y Participación* from CEDEP; in Chile, *Ambiente y Desarrollo* from CIPMA and *Opciones* from CERC.

PRCs also produce many journals that are weaker in conventional academic terms yet are still different from popular, glossy publications. These contribute objective information, historical contexts for current issues, expression of serious opinions, press summaries, and so forth. They may approximate the *New Republic* more than *Newsweek*. The coyuntura approach—a timely articulation of issues—is increasingly in vogue, as at PET's *Coyuntura Económica* in Chile. Other titles in this genre are *Boletín Informativo* from CEDOH in Honduras, *Informe Laboral* from CDE in Paraguay, and *Momento* from ASIES in Guatemala. Journals like these contribute to pluralism and democracy by disseminating facts and viewpoints. Although they do not match other PRC journals in academic importance, they are important for policymakers in government, business, and nonprofit organizations.

Many PRCs generate policy journals alongside their academic ones. Paraguay's CPES issues *Coyuntura Económica* as a monthly, and Peru's DESCO began *Pretextos* as an alternative to its more academic *¿Qué Hacer?*. Exemplifying a tendency to turn out journals in tandem fields are FEDESARROLLO's *Coyuntura Económica* and *Coyuntura Social* in Colombia. Panama's CELA shows that less famous PRCs also produce multiple journals: *Opinión Pública* and *Premisas* join the more scholarly *Tareas* (Gandásegui pc). Large and diverse PRCs naturally lead in multiple publications. CIDE contributes six journals to the Mexican scene.[8]

A few PRCs hold their own by some prestigious international standards, whatever qualifiers appear later. Using Chilean examples, perhaps the most impressive single case is CECI, with a record of scientific publication per person worthy of the Ivy League, including representation in the world's best journals, for example, *Nuclear Physics,* and a special book series with Plenum. CECI's director, a faculty member at the University of Texas, has been affiliated with Princeton, Harvard, and the NIH. In biophysics, CECI has forwarded and defended a leading theory on muscle contraction (Teitelboim i). More typical, of course, is outstanding production in the social sciences. CIEPLAN has an unsurpassed reputation, with professors who could get jobs "anywhere," sustained by voluminous international citations to their work (Lladser i–3). A more extreme position, a debatable but credible rebuttal to dependency notions about the inequitable international knowledge system, is that PRCs have produced a good deal of the world's recent social science knowledge and theory; when Przeworski (1986: 79–80) cites the contributions of Latin American scholarship, his examples are PRCs.[9]

The leading producer is El Colegio de México. By 1986, its long-standing output included about 750 books and 4,000 academic articles (El Colegio 1987a, 1987b: 26). In that single year, El Colegio's own press turned out some 31 books and 30 journal issues. For an average center such as sociology, with about twenty professors, annual production for 1988 totaled 37 articles, including 13 published abroad, and 5 authored and 3 edited books. For years, El Colegio arguably accounted for almost all of Mexico's serious social research (Tierney i). A Ford Foundation evaluation (e.g., FF #68229; Blair and Silvert 1969) refers to both the high quality of publications and their policy relevance, declaring El Colegio a rare Latin American institution that could achieve standards of international quality. In 1984 an evaluation of Ford's recurrent grants underscored the institution's sustained excellence (Peter Bell, Alejandro Foxley, Nina Manitzas, June 11–15, 1984, FF #73874). El Colegio's performance has been truly remarkable in a nation notoriously lacking in research tradition and culture.

Internationalization

The orientations and norms of work at PRCs conform much more than those at universities to standards in developed nations. More of the staff studies abroad, seeks and gains international recognition, and receives international philanthropy. This is further evidence, albeit debatable, of academic quality. It is also evidence of an internationalization that may be an academic end in and of itself—and that both fits and promotes the broader political and economic internationalization at play across all three sectors throughout Latin America.

Westernization is broader than Americanization, but the latter is ascendant. In the 1960s and early 1970s, Argentine PRCs substantially mixed U.S. empiricism with French structuralism and European neo-Marxism (Merkx 1979: 229), but several factors have weakened European alternatives. First, international philanthropy and contacts have come mostly from the United States. Second, several growing focuses tilt inclinations northward; these include the proliferation of PRCs that are policy and economics oriented and the rise of political science. Third is the centrality of the U.S. model of state-private relations to Latin America's political-economic trends.

PRCs are vital conduits of an Americanization that has had difficulty penetrating universities. Those offering graduate education come closer to U.S. curricula and pedagogical models than universities do. IESA is the main Venezuelan example, and it typifies the widespread emulation of U.S. business schools common among Latin American PRCs that are business schools. But again, El Colegio is the leading Latin American PRC with a major teaching effort.

Compared to U.S. graduate programs, El Colegio uses more tutorials and fewer classroom requirements, so that by the second semester of doctoral studies a student may be guided toward a research project and by the third be completely tied to it. El Colegio also emphasizes structural and historical dimensions more and empirical and methodological sophistication less. Yet El Colegio still comes far closer to U.S. norms in teaching than Mexican universities do. Thus, a UNAM sociology doctorate is an almost exclusively individual pursuit compared to its El Colegio counterpart (de Oliveira i). And greater UNAM-El Colegio differences emerge regarding pedagogy, topics, publications, and international contacts.[10]

But research is the main function in question. Given the general failure to integrate research at universities, PRCs are central to the observation that Americanization has gone much further in penetrating Latin American research than teaching (Padua i). PRCs have promoted a powerful shift away from the European savant or master craftsman tradition (Calderón and Provoste 1990: IV-1; Schwartzman 1984: 219; Balán 1982: 218–21) toward more specialized projects. Empirical research, including quantitative dimensions and a value on objectivity, is a key. Uruguay's CERES prides itself on that orientation. Mexico's CEE is a well-documented case; in education generally, PRC research contrasts with university research, which has a more theoretical-philosophical bent (Muñoz N.d.; Myers 1981: 19). PRCs captured eight of the first thirteen competitive awards granted by the IDB in applied economics in the 1990s, with private universities in second place (Navarro pc). Where research still suffers under the weight of antiempirical traditions, the exceptions tend to be in PRCs. And PRCs like Paraguay's CPES build empirical social science where none previously existed; empirical research is an achievement separating Brazilian PRCs and universities (Balán i; E. Fox 1980: 27; Miceli 1990).[11]

Another mirror of U.S. academic culture is the propensity for proposal writing and the legitimacy accorded to external evaluation, including accountability by quantifiable gauges. PRC emphasis on the quantity of their publications and the importance of their journals is one indication of a U.S.-style standard of evaluation. This relates to a powerful publish-or-perish mentality—not limited to junior staff—where publications are necessary for the next grant. So there are continual evaluations, a practice uncommon in universities outside Brazil, at least until the 1990s. A plausible view is that PRCs introduced evaluation into Latin American higher education and, in doing so, have enhanced their own quality (Calderón and Provoste 1990: I-19).

Certainly, PRCs routinely claim that the evaluation process improves their quality, as Central America's CRIES (1991: 6–7) has regarding NOVIB's and SAREC's evaluations. A more skeptical interpretation is that PRCs play the game of praising and thanking donors who are then more likely to keep donating. In any event, PRC researchers themselves accept numerous consultancies from international donors to evaluate sister PRCs as well as other institutions. These consultancies are a form of international recognition—and a source of income.[12]

Their international work styles and recognition bring PRCs into multiple research networks involving developed nations. This is one of the major findings of the first systematic study of Latin American international scholarly relations in the social sciences; the new modes account for much of an increasingly cited convergence in Latin American and U.S. social science (SSRC 1991; Coatsworth 1989).

Leading figures in several PRCs actually travel more and participate in more international conferences than their U.S. counterparts, partly because they lack major teaching responsibilities, partly because they are fewer and their first-hand knowledge and prestige are in great demand, partly because such contacts are essential to their institutions and to their positions. Other forms of interinstitutional contact are more ongoing in nature. CECI has worked with biophysics groups from Harvard, Brandeis, and Duke and has received more than 150 foreign visitors in its first few years.

PRC contacts and recognition are shown in representation on the board of the most prestigious international journal of the region's affairs, the *Latin American Research Review*. Four of the five members working in Latin American nations (1992) list a PRC affiliation, and the fifth lists an IRC, whereas twenty of the twenty-one U.S. and Canadian institutions listed are universities.[13] Although the most prestigious PRCs have generally the greatest international recognition and contacts, other PRCs also are active. Alongside INCAE, Central American examples include CIAPA and ASIES.[14]

At the same time, PRCs are prominent in networks involving sister republics, or horizontal cooperation. This contrasts with most Latin American nonprofits, which are more locally oriented, although associations like the Chilean Association of Nongovernment Organizations show an attempt to build ties, at least within nations. It also contrasts with the general finding that Latin American research groups operate in isolation from one another (Vessuri 1986: 33). And it contrasts with what most universities manage. Although it rarely includes Third World contact beyond Latin America, horizontal cooperation within the region is a PRC triumph. It cuts against the dependency critique of internationalization.

Reasons for horizontal cooperation among PRCs include the influence of international philanthropy, which promotes and even imposes common agendas, transports ideas, and actively supports such cooperation. Reasons also include the nature of PRCs' work and the efforts PRCs make. Compared to teaching, research more easily binds institutions internationally. Beyond places that are international by charter and structure, such as FLACSO and CLACSO, lie PRCs with common focuses. Population studies and women's studies are leading examples. Sometimes cooperation extends all the way to comparative projects, as with research by CIEPLAN, CEDES, CEBRAP, and CINVE on economic normalization policies in the Southern Cone (E. Fox 1980: 25). Moreover, international topics—those that relate to interactions among nations—are especially conducive to contacts, as seen in research on economic integration, international relations, and migration; thus, Bolivia's CERES has worked with Argentina's CEDES on Bolivian migration. Then, too, nonprofit centers like CINDA specialize in promoting horizontal cooperation. Finally, horizontal and vertical cooperation sometimes combine, as with centers devoted to graduate education and research in business or with centers doing research on higher education itself.[15]

Ironically, international cooperation is more impressive than intranational cooperation among PRCs, which operate within pluralist sectors unguided by a coordinating hand. But there are many intranational instances of voluntary cooperation and donor-induced cooperation, parallel to the World Bank's efforts with grassroots nonprofits. Pushed by the IDRC, Peru's GRADE, IEP, and DESCO have joined with other centers, including URCs at two private universities, in the Consortium of Economic Research; these PRCs also participate in Intercentros, involving some interchange and joint publication among some twenty-six social research centers. Cooperation increased partly as a defensive reaction to the Shining Path (GRADE 1990: 12). ANICS has worked since Somoza's days to overcome excessive specialization and isolation among Nicaragua's centers and has published the *Revista Nicaragüense de Ciencias Sociales* (Fernández 1989: 81). In other cases, fewer PRCs—relative peers—pool their efforts. CEDEC, IUPERJ, CEBRAP, and IDESP do so in Brazil; SER joins FEDESARROLLO in the publication of *Coyuntura Social* in Colombia. Modest steps likes these may be enough for PRCs to lead universities and to offer reasonable hope for further intranational cooperation.

URCs and GRCs

Allowing that our information is not systematic, it appears that both URCs and GRCs generally surpass the university mainstream regarding research quality, depending on the definition of research quality.

The Institute of Economic and Social Research at Guatemala's Universidad de San Carlos, CERESD in the Dominican Republic, CENDES at Venezuela's UCV, CEDE at Colombia's Andes, and IEPRI at Colombia's National University are examples of social science URCs with research reputations outranking that of their universities. An indication of the widespread perception of URCs' research superiority is the heavy resentment felt by faculties. The URC lead is expected, given this analysis of URCs as responses to the mainstream's failures, especially in research. Research is usually the URC's top priority; rarely is it for faculties. However, we must also remember that URCs themselves have had many problems. In Chile, a considerable amount of social science development by URCs was destroyed by the military government. And URCs at Argentina's UBA have languished.

Reputable URCs take their place alongside reputable PRCs in Latin American social research, but they stand out mostly in other fields. In the natural sciences, they lead in some nations, though faculties or GRCs dominate in others.

In Mexico, especially—and especially at UNAM—URCs assume scientific leadership within the university. Many indexes of publication output show URCs at the top, along with GRCs (see the April 1987 issue of *Ciencia y Desarrollo*). In 1987 alone, UNAM's science URCs, with some 400 basic research lines and 819 researchers, produced more than a thousand specialized journal articles, 173 book chapters, 652 conference papers, 476 technical reports, and a few hundred miscellaneous works (de la Fuente i). UNAM's science URCs also impress with their international contacts, including convenios with other nations. Another quantitative indicator is representation in the coveted SNI. As of 1987, UNAM's URCs gained forty of the forty-three slots in astronomy, whereas UNAM's faculties had none. In chemistry and engineering, URCs also overwhelm faculties. The 90 percent part-time teaching corps in the engineering faculty carries certain benefits regarding professional training but weighs heavily against research (Reséndiz i). Exceptions are few: the physics institute does not overshadow the physics faculty, and the medical faculty is productive with no exact institute counterpart (Cano Valle i). Usually, however, faculties do not challenge the productivity data per se. Instead, they challenge their relevance and charge that the roots of the performance gap lie in prejudicial allocation of resources by university, government, and foreign donors. Whether or not allocation is prejudicial, it is markedly unequal: UNAM's URCs enjoy benefits over faculties in research funds, equipment, libraries, and full-time personnel in the fields cited.

In science, URCs often share the research pinnacle with GRCs. Mexican GRCs that meet international academic standards include the institutes of petroleum, atomic energy, nutrition, and forestry-agriculture-fishing (Vielle i; Kent i). Among public research centers, CINVESTAV and Chapingo consistently earn high marks (FF #65288), like CIMMYT among agricultural IRCs and like IVIC in Venezuela. Praise for the research performance of Mexican GRCs is striking, given the low regard for the nation's public sector enterprises overall—which is the rule in most of Latin America outside

Chile (Glade 1991). In Brazil and Mexico, the academic performance of GRCs has been acclaimed, as centers like the Technological Aeronautical Institute have escaped the leveling effects imposed by the education ministry and developed solid leadership (Machado de Sousa i; Schwartzman i–2; Schwartzman 1991: 205).

In fact, it appears that public research centers do well regardless of field, including social research. They may even avoid some of the negative effects of proliferation and application to commercial tasks, which weigh on PRCs.

RELEVANCE

Solid performance on international academic criteria highlighted by degrees held and publications, as well as internationalization or Americanization, leaves doubts about relevance. What of charges that Americanized research by PRCs is either irrelevant or detrimental to domestic development?

In Context

Much of the comparative education literature on the international distribution of knowledge makes charges of irrelevance about research in developing countries—that the agenda is set by others, is alien to local needs, and is elitist (Court 1982: 123). One of Latin America's top students of scientific research (Vessuri 1986: 6) finds corroborating evidence in the fields she explores: research bypasses microbiological and genetic concerns critical to health and agriculture, Argentina lacks research on meat conservation despite its importance to the nation, etcetera. Compared to developed nations, Latin America appears to allocate a smaller percentage of its research budget to applied as opposed to basic research, and little to agriculture, which leads some to conclude that foreign aid for scientific and technological development produced an "almost complete failure" (A. Herrera 1973: 20–22).

Research at PRCs might seem especially vulnerable to dependency charges, as it is so directly tied to international agencies. Much comparative education literature holds that these agencies promote research that is irrelevant to Third World problems and instead serve "Western intellectual imperialism" (Selvaratnam 1988: 59). Also, social research is probably most sensitive to the charge.

In Latin America, irrelevance is perhaps the most common criticism leveled against PRCs' academic performance. But the ensuing subsections present counterevidence that, minimally, is too strong to confirm the general criticism. Beyond that: a fair if not provable interpretation is that a combination of inclinations, opportunities, and constraints pushes PRCs to meet sharp tests of relevance that one can like or not but cannot dismiss.

In fact, we have already adduced considerable evidence of PRC relevance. The previous chapter shows how much, and how influentially, PRCs pursue political themes dealing with human rights and democratization, indeed how they apply research directly to such causes; prior chapters establish the substantial overlap between research and social action. PRCs are largely centers for policy research, whether for the government, the opposition, corporations, grassroots organizations, or international agencies. They supply vital information and advice to public, for-profit, and other nonprofit interests.

The role of international philanthropy in promoting relevance, noted in chapter 4, demands a word here. Earlier efforts with university development already expressed donors' practical, applied goals. Perhaps clearest in health and agriculture, these goals also encompassed the social sciences.[16] Instances where assistance emphasized purer research over applications (Adams and Cumberland 1960: 184–85) stack up against strong inclinations by the IDB, the IDRC, the OAS, and others to emphasize the applied or technical (Vessuri 1986: 32; Stifel, Davidson, and Coleman 1982: xii). Regardless, by the mid-1970s, donors abandoned most efforts at university development. The key to university assistance by AID and the IDB became project relevance to non-higher-education priorities, including local agricultural, industrial, and technological development.

Foundations, too, came to stress relevance. The Rockefeller Foundation, long a champion of basic research and the formation of academic researchers—counting on those strengths to lead to good applied work—pivoted toward a more direct focus on practical application; Ford, starting later, mixed the basic and the applied from the outset (Cueto i–1). So far have donors gone that, as we have seen, leading researchers at PRCs decry how insistence on relevance stymies academic pursuits. Philanthropy's efforts are greatly at odds with any image of the First World trying to influence the Third toward lofty academic pursuits out of touch with pressing human needs. And increased contract work, with both foreign and domestic agencies, means further emphasis on applied research.

Mexican Research Centers

Different types of research centers again broaden the view beyond PRCs and again Mexico provides an ample case highlighted by UNAM, El Colegio, and Chapingo. The applied and practical emphasis of research at most GRCs might be obvious in Mexico and other countries, though the orientations and targeted populations of that relevance are worth study. The general picture for URCs is harder to predict.[17]

Researchers at UNAM's URCs in social science and the humanities like to juxtapose their practical and progressive research pursuits, from esthetics to language to juridical matters, to El Colegio's academic pursuits. This relates to the previous chapter's point about the greater leftism at UNAM than at El Colegio. Common efforts to highlight differences between URCs' research and that of prestigious PRCs are not enough, however, to shield URCs from criticism by faculties within their own universities.

The following sketch of accusation and defense between UNAM's faculties and URCs outside the social area shows some symmetry with the university's criticism of El Colegio in the social area. Detractors argue that the engineering URC should do less pure research and, instead, help more in housing construction; they denounce URCs in physics and astronomy as still less relevant (Esteva i). In fact, the attack comes not only from faculties or "from the left" but also from GRCs. UNAM's science is allegedly deficient in application and in the utilization of equipment (Schoijet 1979).

In response, UNAM's URCs defend their attention to basic research, such as the study of binary stars, and also claim many practical contributions to the lives of Mexicans and other Latin Americans. Their journal, *Ciencia y Desarrollo,* includes a sort of running, annotated list of these contributions. The biomedical institutes reports its findings on enzymes, lactation, hormones, and male contraceptives and their success in shaping the study abroad done by those who then return to the institute (Sarukhán i). The chemistry institute lists its findings on the contamination of Mexico's waters (FF #71099), since clean water is a critical problem for millions of Mexicans. Sometimes the contribution is international in application, as with a breakthrough in Parkinson's disease at the Institute of Cellular Physiology. More common are international contacts that concentrate on matters of special concern close to Mexico. Convenios in progress in 1989 included those on the artificial insemination of tropical cattle, the control of insect plagues, tropical ecosystems, potato fertilization, the construction of prefabricated housing, and the production of a national atlas. A convincing negative case about the relevance of URC research in UNAM and beyond would have to rebut or outweigh examples like these.

Similarly, El Colegio defends itself less by upholding the value of pure research than by highlighting its practical research. That tack has something to do with the Mexican context. Much, however, has to do with the nature of PRCs and their greater emphasis on serving goals valued by others than on serving academic development per se. El Colegio is one of those rare PRCs with a serious claim to broad excellence in academia; if PRCs generally fail to emphasize relevance, one might expect to see such a failure at places where academic considerations could tug in the other direction. El Colegio epitomizes PRCs both lauded and denounced for their elite international status.

El Colegio's relevant studies include those on population and regional development, including guidance in government policy, research on the sociology of development, with emphasis on Mexico and Latin America, and work on policy issues in Mexico's foreign relations, ranging from immigration to trade. Even in its perhaps most academically elite and potentially "irrelevant" center, linguistics and literature, El Colegio can claim development of a Spanish dictionary of Mexico, assistance in teaching Spanish to Indian speakers, and a long list of research projects and consultancies for public school education in language and history (Garza i). Data from centers in more obviously applied areas, such as demography and urban development (James Towbridge memo to William Gamble, July 10, 1970, in FF card catalogue #8779), suggest that Mexican and foreign graduates usually work in their country on topics related to their training. Comparable points are valid for several institutions modeled on El Colegio; regional colegios, for example, make a major contribution to regional historical studies.

Continuing the juxtaposition of El Colegio and Chapingo as parallel private and public research centers, we see relevance and application are major, direct concerns at Chapingo, as well. Chapingo builds upon ongoing work at the CIMMYT IRC in greatly increasing average yields in wheat, corn, and barley in a variety of soils (Lowell Hardin and Norman Collins memo to William Carmichael, June 10, 1976 in FF #67204; Cassen 1986: 185). But alongside these claims lie charges of an inequitable distribution of benefits (Cleaves 1987: 27–28; Friedman 1980: 70), because peasants cannot afford the fertilizers or the grains, and the benefits that accrue to others actually make competition and survival harder for the poor. Infusing social science into the curriculum, partly to face this equity challenge, has been difficult. If market demand is weak, the infusion stalls; if demand is strong, so is the outward flow of personnel, which undermines the center's academics.

Chapingo offers the following defenses: regional centers that specifically address problems of the poor in locales that top private university programs shun; a better record than the local public university in work relevant to the poor; perhaps 30 percent of the professoriate working with small farmers; and students required to take time from their studies to work with peasants (Alcalde i; Jiménez i; Díaz i). Typical Chapingo innovations have improved vegetable nutrition, soil and water conservation, rain use, and seed species. And however much Chapingo has emulated the U.S. curriculum in style, it has substituted Mexican content and developed its own approaches to its own problems (Rebecca Fritz, Feb. 26, 1982, memo, in FF #65288).

Whether or not there is enough or appropriate relevance at Chapingo, at UNAM's URCs, or at El Colegio is uncertain; what is clear is that all three institutions do work that appears to be relevant beyond academia. Among the three of the them, many fields of study are covered.

A Practical, Progressive Focus

In general, Latin America's PRCs concentrate rather progressively on the practical problems confronting their populations. This focus is seen regarding group, geography, and policy.

Group

Relevance need not mean a progressive orientation in terms of affected groups. Besides, judgments about progressiveness are obviously subjective. Rising technocratic, economic consultancy, and neoliberal PRCs are controversial in this regard, as is the increased cooperation by nonprofits with the public and for-profit sectors. Many PRCs have reversed the traditional Latin American dislike by higher education of contacts with industry (Vessuri

1986: 33). The dearth of radical leftist PRCs also violates some notions of progressiveness.

But PRCs mostly do fit the common definition of progressiveness, showing concern for political rights, expanding participation, and socioeconomic equity, and emphasizing the problems of disadvantaged groups. Both classic PRCs and social action PRCs either present (and even implement) alternatives to government policy or promote the progressive aspects of that policy. Moderate leftism and centrism do not mean bourgeois inaction; PRC personnel probably engage in more direct action for social change than their university predecessors and contemporaries who speak in more revolutionary terms. Because the previous chapter analyzes the political contributions of PRCs, most examples here show socioeconomic relevance.

PRCs pay special attention to the poor. Many routinely work with grassroots nonprofits. They do original research or adapt others' research to deal with immediate problems, whether supported by government or not. Ecuadoran examples include CIUDAD's work with the urban poor and CAAP's work on indigenous populations. In Bolivia, CIPCA focuses on the peasantry, while CEDLA focuses on labor. In the Dominican Republic, CIEA concentrates on poverty and social services, and in Guatemala, PRCs work largely on problems related to social ethnicity and human rights (Alvarez pc). In Peru, DESCO (1990: 6–9) helps numerous labor unions, religious grassroots organizations, and youth groups through its work in the informal economy. It also produces the best data on the guerrilla war and, with the IEP, the leading works on the subject. Many PRCs give information and advice to workers. CISMA works in the Guatemalan highlands, CICSO works with Indians in the Chaco, CERES works on Bolivian food production and consumption, and GIA does extension work and puts out publications for Chile's Mapuches. Carroll (1992: 205) credits the FDN with linking Peru's academics to peasants and their problems. This sort of work by PRCs aims at empowering the underprivileged.

Women also receive special attention as a mistreated group in need of study and assistance. The Flora Tristán Peruvian Women's Center, established in 1979, is already one of the oldest and largest, with a formal research program since 1987 (Spalding 1991: 70). The Carlos Chagas Foundation has been a leader and an important Brazilian recipient of Ford funds. Uruguay's GRECMU is another PRC largely but not exclusively dedicated to women's studies. CLACSO's Andean and Southern Cone women's centers prominently include PRCs. SAREC has a major support program for women's studies centers (León and Spalding 1992).

Geography

Most generally, the subjects of study are Latin Americans. PRCs home in on local, national, or inter-American problems. They rarely venture further except to inform one of these three focuses. This finding contradicts the dependency charge that research concentrates on foreign concerns and ignores needs close to home. The geographic locus of PRC research efforts and impacts meets criteria of relevance.

Local issues include day-to-day problems where people live, with attention ranging over agricultural, municipal, environmental, and other matters. CEDOH, CEASPA, FEDESARROLLO, and CIUDAD are Honduran, Panamanian, Colombian, and Ecuadoran examples of the way many PRCs pointedly make the study of their national reality and problems their central task. The six major themes at Peruvian PRCs are popular organizations, economics, regionalization, rural development, violence, and the informal sector (Spalding 1991: 34). CDE's studies establish the monthly cost of living in Greater Asunción for use in worker-employer contract negotiations; similarities characterize Uruguay's CIEDUR and CES. Colombia's CINDE is one of many PRCs that concentrate on studying alternative modes of delivering services to the needy (Arango and Nimnicht 1987). Central America's PRCs deal with vital areas, among them food security, underemployment, refugees, and the psychological effects of war. ASIES deals with peace, justice, human dignity, participation, and rural communities in Guatemala.

Even when PRCs study the past, the focus remains local. CEREP's leadership in undertaking Puerto Rico's first new historiography since the 1970s also illustrates PRC pioneering in fields of local interest where the university curriculum leaves a vacuum. Regional studies at Argentina's Bariloche Foundation provides additional evidence (A. Thompson 1994: 26), just as have the regional historical studies at Mexico's colegios.

Probably all PRCs that concentrate on international relations emphasize issues of special concern to their nation or to their nation's immediate region. CRIES studies international philanthropy directed at Central America, highlighting its nonprofits. Colombian PRCs' study of narcotics trafficking and world economic trends of greatest importance to Colombia, CINVE's studies of Uruguay's trade with its neighbors, and CELA's study of the U.S. invasion of Panama show that even PRCs not primarily devoted to international relations may include them because of their national relevance. The international studies focus of many PRCs, like the internationalized orientations of the PRC sector in general, can be criticized as "denationalization" only by those who fail to recognize the interdependence vital to each nation's own health.

Latin American units within IRCs concentrate on issues affecting their own region or all of Latin America, including employment, rural development, and relations with the United States (CINDA 1986: 18; Araya i–1). CEPAL was explicitly created to study and, thereby, to help resolve economic development problems, and it quickly took significant steps in Chile, Brazil, and Central America, reaching into political economy, agricultural and labor economics, and like fields (Ansaldi and Calderón 1989: 22–38). In Peru, Colombia, Costa Rica, Mexico, and elsewhere, agricultural IRCs concentrate on research for practical use. Much of their work aims at the rural poor, though whom they serve on balance remains a debated matter.

Policy
As they work on issues close to home, PRCs usually show a marked problem-centered approach in their research topics. Many PRCs in fact build their work around a single problem or policy area, as their names or acronyms sometimes indicate. CEE's continual push for greater justice and participation in Mexican educational policy is well documented (Muñoz N.d.). CEPEP in Paraguay and CCRP in Colombia approach population problems with concern for reproductive health, women's dignity, and family welfare.

For most PRCs beyond the social sciences, a practical orientation is a given. CETAL, in Valparaíso, works on energy-saving cooking and the medical uses of local plants, while its Ecuadoran and Guatemalan counterparts study appropriate technologies. Some fields outside conventional social science represent special achievements by PRCs and donors, given the traditional reticence of the Latin American intellectual community. Population research at PRCs and IRCs has a commendable publication record, having attracted good young scholars and having cleverly tied itself to the "structuralist" problems (Harkavy and Diescho 1988: 3–6). PRCs now do widely accepted work in the field in Mexico, Brazil, and other nations. Business administration is also a topic of study, mostly at those centers involved in training. The early success of AID and Ford at Getúlio Vargas in São Paulo shines when seen against the opposition of the left and of economics faculties protecting their privileged legal access to certain jobs (Dole Anderson, AID end-of-tour report, June 1963).

Even fields not normally associated with progressive engagement shape themselves, in PRCs, toward immediacy and, sometimes, equity. Management studies at PRCs often mean public management, as with INCAE's Ford-sponsored work with state-run agricultural enterprises, including work under the Sandinistas. Law studies translate into research on hearings for the poor suffering from environmental abuse or into public interest law (Ford Foundation Annual Report 1975: 46–47). Humanities research shows a concern for common people in its attention to matters like folk music and indigenous language.

Similarly, even PRC research most embedded in the disciplines tends to look at relevant policy issues. Most economics and sociology at PRCs deal with pressing practical problems. PRCs that pioneer in political science focus on democratization, the emergence or reemergence of political parties, public opinion, and so forth. An annotated compendium of the region's noteworthy political science institutions cites PRCs almost exclusively (Dent 1990b: 395–410); included are El Colegio, Argentina's CEDES, Brazil's CEBRAP and IUPERJ, Peru's CEDEP, and FLACSOs in five nations. Peru's IEP has four researchers working on topics such as political parties, legislatures, militaries, and women's rights. CIDE's concerns include the modernization of Mexican municipal management and U.S. business perceptions about Mexico's economic opening.

Another finding that underscores the generality of emphasis on practical problems of local concern is that it characterizes even the academically best PRCs. PRCs are truly relevant to the core. Some trade-offs between academics and practice are inevitable, but many PRCs integrate the two. If they relegate one activity to a lesser role, that activity is most likely academics. Documentation shows that Chilean PRCs give considerable attention to current, real problems (Orellana R. 1986: 227). CEBRAP gives technical assistance to Brazil's popular sectors. In Argentina, CEDES furnishes useful methods and ideas to grassroots nonprofits, and EURAL provides a documentation center for policymakers. DESCO works with Peru's poor. A direct concern for Colombia's underprivileged groups marks FEDESARROLLO's economic research on social indicators and even SER's technocratic contract research. A survey of the directors of CLACSO centers finds application, rather than pure research, their highest priority, notwithstanding CLACSO's inclusion of many university units with less applied orientations (Calderón and Provoste 1990). Throughout the region, from El Colegio in Mexico to CIEPLAN in Chile, the academically most prestigious PRCs are not "above" practical issues.

Thus their focus on policy brings PRCs into extensive interaction with policymakers in all three sectors, a fact that runs counter to the claim that social science rarely gets "used" in policymaking. It instead supports the controversial thesis that Third World social science contributes mightily to public policy (Stifel, Davidson, and Coleman 1982: xv).[18]

In sum, PRCs take Latin America a step closer to an old dream of doing coordinated research on practical problems (N. Stepan 1976; Vega 1989: 38, 47). Compared to the research in developed countries, this research appears to be proportionally more geared to immediate practical problems, less to academic disciplines.[19] The dominant spirit is captured in the motto of Panama's CEASPA (1989: 3): Practice, Theory, Practice. The problem orientation means great emphasis on development issues and ways to improve the quality of life.[20]

Relevance Ascendant

Reject the notion of irrelevance: PRCs rarely engage in esoteric or pure research of no immediate relevance. Evaluated from another angle, that of the relevant social research done in Latin America, PRCs, along with kindred research centers, do the great bulk. The question then becomes whether one approves of such relevance. Put another way, the question might be, Relevance for whom and for what? The evidence cited highlights work aimed at improving democratic participation and socioeconomic justice. But this emphasis must not obscure the considerable and probably increasing energy directed at serving powerful policy interests.

Whatever its progressive mix, PRCs' work is widely used. Produced in the third sector and serving government, for-profit, and other nonprofit organizations, this work weakens dichotomous notions about public and for-profit private sectors; it strengthens notions of three interrelated sectors. PRCs' academic performance is impressive in terms of relevance as well as quantitative and qualitative production. As that performance bolsters PRCs' importance, it helps build nonprofit development more broadly.

7 The Subordination of Scholarship

Nothing that follows negates the evidence from the preceding chapter. To read this chapter apart from the last would give an unbalanced picture.[1] Yet an analysis of PRCs requires a look at their weaknesses as well as their strengths. What the best do not do well is often not done well anywhere, marking a failure for the system. The weaknesses of PRCs have not to date been understood or, for the most part, even identified.[2] If positive performance bolsters importance, we must acknowledge where poorer performance restricts that importance.

PRCs' "failures" derive more from tasks not attempted than from tasks not accomplished; they are less failures than limitations. This concept of limitations within acclaimed nonprofit organizations tends to fit the performance of Latin America's private universities and, arguably, private educational institutions in general (Levy 1987). But it is especially appropriate for PRCs, which are usually small, selective, and homogenous.[3]

Few of the PRCs' academic weaknesses are simply the PRCs' fault. Rather, there are reasons for what PRCs do or do not do, and many of the weaknesses are logical counterparts to the PRCs' successes. They result from a responsiveness to the demands and opportunities of the environment. Many involve policy relevance for sponsors and constituencies in all three sectors. Thus limitations on academic importance are sometimes quite consistent with great importance on social and political dimensions. The subordination of scholarship brings benefits as well as costs.

This chapter divides into parts that largely parallel the last chapter's. The first deals with the typical narrowness of PRCs' undertakings. The second explores the major academic task usually avoided by PRCs: teaching. The third then analyzes how narrowness translates into deficiencies in the research produced. Finally, the evaluation of performance concludes with an analysis of PRCs as models for the broader academic system.

NARROW FOCUS

For all its advantages, nonprofit specialization usually means narrowness. This involves the exclusion of tasks that must be performed somewhere. Indeed, much nonprofit innovation may occur outside the system's mainstream. Typical PRCs specialize in a very restricted range of academic tasks. Breadth is gained sectorally, since individual PRCs specialize in different academic tasks (and it would expand much further if this chapter went beyond academic tasks). But many academic limitations of individual PRCs remain even for the PRC sector. Academic narrowness corresponds to political narrowness for institutions but exceeds it for the sector.

Size

Size usually goes hand in hand with academic specialism. Small size limits the importance of many PRCs that otherwise achieve respectability, such as CERPE in Venezuelan educational studies.

Several factors related to their origin and sustenance explain the small size of most PRCs. Authoritarian regimes would not give sanctuary to institutions with a potential for influence stemming from numbers, and universities would resist the creation of large competitors. Both factors argue against conventional teaching by PRCs to a large student body. Another cause of small size is the need for a coherent profile, with hierarchical governance based more on compatibility than coercion. This need relates to identity, community, recruitment, and both financial and political attractiveness. Thus, small size is not an incidental characteristic; it is integral to PRCs, as it generally is for nonprofit organizations.

Data on size can deceive. Befitting agile private nonprofit institutions operating in fluid markets, there is rapid, continual personnel turnover, including many modifications in individuals' roles. Also, different places use different criteria in deciding who is a PRC researcher. PRCs inflate their size by counting research assistants, personnel contracted for individual projects, part-timers, or other support staff. Fortunately, PRCs often furnish some breakdown. FLACSO (1990: 10; Nd: 13) for all Latin America reports 303 academic personnel or, depending on source, 160 or 139 permanent researchers. Figures for some institutions are as follows: Colombia's SER, three researchers and twenty assistants; Peru's GRADE, ten researchers, seven associates, and twenty-four assistants; Panama's CEASPA, five researchers and thirty assistants; and the Dominican Republic's CIPAF, two researchers and twenty-two assistants (Facundo i; GRADE 1990: 44–45; Leis pc; León and Spalding 1992: 26). Argentina's Bariloche would be tiny except when its "associated groups" bring it to twenty full-time researchers, among a total full-time staff of double that; Chile's CIDE has more than eighty employees but only twenty-one researchers (Gatti and Chateau 1988: 38). Moreover, numbers are high among the "name" places, so ad hoc examples can inflate the data. The more numerous lesser known places are usually small. Some PRCs probably stretch criteria to drive the count high and appear more consequential.

One might think of small PRCs as those with five or fewer full-time researchers, middle-sized PRCs as those with six to fifteen researchers, and large PRCs as those exceeding fifteen (Brunner and Barrios 1987: 113, 90). Most PRCs fit either the first or the second category. Seldom does a PRC in the Southern Cone have thirty professional people even counting assistants and associates. Argentina has numerous PRCs with fewer than ten (Balán N.d.). The major survey of Chile's (then) forty or so PRCs shows a mean of ten permanent researchers (a median of eight), without contracted, invited, and scholarship personnel; one could add roughly three associates and assistants (calculations from Lladser 1986: 11–278). Although CLACSO's survey shows an average size of a little more than twenty researchers in its individual centers, that of course includes centers typically bigger than PRCs.[4]

Nations with the largest PRC sectors have a few large PRCs. Peru's giants are DESCO, with 120 employees; the Flora Tristán women's studies center, with 65 full-timers; the Bartolomé in Cusco; and the ILD, with its 75 full-time employees (Spalding 1991: 16; Bromley 1990: 332). Chile's two main education PRCs are large: the PIIE, claiming 24 full-time researchers, and the CIDE, just cited (CRESALC 1984: 14, 17). Argentina's CICSO has 25 researchers, without counting associated ones; Colombia's FEDESARROLLO has 26 researchers (15 project directors and 11 assistants), and Colombia's CCRP has 25 full-timers (Balvé pc; Escobar pc-3; Rojas pc).

It is possible to identify characteristics associated with exceptional size. A supportive national context includes an ample supply of researchers coupled with the dominance of PRCs in social research. At the institutional level, mixed tasks help, though then one can question how much of the center is really a PRC. Flora Tristán is large because it mixes extension with research. But the most important academic mix is research and formal graduate education. Mexico's CIDE has 107 academic personnel, not counting support and administrative positions. Within Brazil's Getúlio Vargas Foundation, CPDOC alone has 39 researchers (Unger pc; CPDOC 1991: 1). Venezuela's IESA has roughly 40 full-time academics. Another academic characteristic associated with large size is prestige. FLACSO is Chile's largest PRC, and has also had roughly 40 academics, though it is now closer to Brazil's CEBRAP, which has a 25–30 person permanent staff, which is nearly matched by Argentina's CEDES. Brazil's IUPERJ and IDESP each employ around 20 researchers.

Good PRCs can be small, however. The number of full-time or chief researchers in some small PRCs are as follows: Uruguay's CERES, six; Peru's GRADE, eight; Colombia's FES, five; Paraguay's CPES and CEPEP, eight and two, respectively; Panama's CELA, two; the Dominican Republic's CIEA, three. CIDAC, one of Mexico's broadest PRCs without a teaching program, has ten full-time researchers. Chile's CEP has none.

A few comparisons give perspective on small size. Whereas typical U.S. PRCs are also small, most of the prestigious ones are larger than Latin America's. The Heritage Foundation has a staff of 135, Brookings has 40–50 senior researchers, and the Center for Strategic and International Studies has 50 senior staff among its 147 total staff, with many adjuncts (J. Smith 1991: 272–79). In Latin America, PRCs are much smaller than other research centers. CELADE is a modest-sized IRC, with a staff of 22, but CEPAL has more than 500 functionaries (CELADE 1990: 22; Cayuela 1988). Public research centers that teach are especially large. Contrast Venezuela's Luis Roche Foundation, a PRC with 8 researchers among a staff of 35, to its public successor, IVIC, with more than 100 researchers among its 600-plus staff (Vessuri 1984: 203). No Mexican PRC approaches CINVESTAV, with its 306 full-timers (de Ibarrola 1986–87: 17). PRCs are also much smaller than URCs, let alone university faculties.[5]

Fields of Study and Geographical Coverage

Being small, most PRCs concentrate their research in few fields. Many do so even as they engage in broadening social action. Chapter 2 identifies the main disciplines—sociology and economics. It allows, however, that PRC sectors achieve more coverage than do their individual institutions and that even the latter do not typically restrict themselves to just one thing; many mix in some technology or science to enhance their social research, while more blend different social fields together. And renowned PRCs usually work in several fields. In fact, pushing against field specialization are such forces as PRCs' agility, mobile personnel, dependence on short-term financing, the shifting financial opportunities from philanthropic, public, and for-profit sources, and rapid change in the broad political economy.[6]

Nonetheless, the rule deserves more emphasis than the qualifications: most research at PRCs is specialized. Many PRCs are home to a single dominant research field. The field of education, alone, furnishes scores of examples, like Chile's CIDE and PIIE (Schiefelbein 1978). Agriculture and appropriate technology are other such areas. El Colegio's two best offspring, in Michoacán and Tijuana, Baja California, specialize in history and migration. Of Mexico's PRCs without major graduate programs, perhaps only the Barros Sierra Foundation and CIDAC transcend tight field specialization.

PRCs with more than a single major field are usually still limited. FEDE-SARROLLO remains narrow even as it adds the fields of economic history, regional and urban development, and political science to its former concentration on political economy. A PRC may cover many fields over time yet not at one particular time; to associate Peru's IEP with economics, history, sociology, and language does not imply that IEP is that broad. PRCs move much more quickly in and out of fields than universities do. Moreover, small research institutions lacking major teaching responsibilities make little effort to cover the basic subfields of their field. Thus, FEDESARROLLO understandably ignores most areas of political science and even of political economy. A good PRC can restrict its fields of study much more than a good university can. Large PRCs with teaching programs cover more fields than other PRCs but fewer fields than universities.

Sectoral scope offsets only some of the narrowness of individual institutions. Little work emerges outside of social fields or subfields that have been accorded development or policy priority. Little emerges, for example, in history and the humanities. Although a university's failure to cover an area may open opportunities for PRCs, it places no responsibility on them. The lack of the study of economics at Paraguayan universities, for example, did not lead to economics work at the nation's leading PRC, CPES (Spalding, Stallings, and Weeks 1990: 97). Blame normally falls on universities for omissions while PRCs gain praise for whatever fields they do cover.

The geographical scope of PRCs is also limited.[7] PRCs are typically single-site entities. Unlike many universities, they do not have workplaces in different localities. Some IRCs are exceptions, but domestic PRCs are usually single-site entities. And sectoral coverage is also limited. As with size and fields, we identify exceptions and then insist on the main tendency.

The farther PRCs are from the academic core, the more geographically dispersed they may be. Social action is the most powerful force for dispersal and accounts for Peru's probably unmatched reach of PRCs into rural areas and into urban areas other than the capital. Economic consultancy centers also form in urban development poles beyond just the capital; Mexican PRCs have proliferated into Baja California, Chihuahua, and Monterrey. The revolution in computers, electronic mail, facsimile machines, and other technology facilitates dispersion. PRCs in agriculture obviously assume an atypical geographical formation.

Still, the geographic restrictiveness of PRCs is impressive. Only 10 percent of Chile's 40 and, later, 86, PRCs have located outside Santiago (Lladser 1986, 1988b). Although Colombia is known for the comparatively strong development of its secondary cities and their universities, academic PRCs still concentrate in Bogota. However, peripheral PRCs have located in cities like Manizales, which shows how proliferation can counter geographical concentration. In Brazil, the concentration of institutions in Rio is striking. And of twenty-five SAREC-funded PRCs in all of Latin America, only CERES (in Cochabamba, Bolivia) is located outside the capital city (Spalding, Stallings, and Weeks 1990: 54). Thus, much more than its universities, Latin America's PRCs concentrate in the capitals.

El Colegio de México

Whether the issue is size, fields of study, or geographical spread, networks are the exceptions that reinforce the rule about PRCs. FLACSO and CLACSO cover much more ground than do any of their national centers. The same is true for the AHC, compared to Chile's individual centers. But most networks are international; and none, by definition, is a PRC. On the other hand, the acceptance of Di Tella, Bariloche, Getúlio Vargas in Rio, and other multicenter PRCs as single PRCs either exaggerates size and scope or identifies exceptional PRCs.

Here we examine the leading multicenter PRC, El Colegio de México, which is unified by virtue of its financial and governance structures and its single-site location in Mexico City. But its seven centers have somewhat separate educational lives. Their lack of intercommunication is notable (FF #730874). Teaching programs are so compartmentalized that little flexibility exists for professors in one center to teach in another, and less exists for students in one to take courses in another. Research is compartmentalized because subject matter differs among the centers but also because each center has its own prevailing methodologies and approaches. These relate, for example, to the differing weight of U.S. influence; in fact, they mark intracenter divisions as well. Asian and African studies and economics are each internally rather unified on this score, whereas international relations and demography and urban development each confronts some split between U.S. classical economics and European emphases. Older centers, including linguistics and literary studies, claim to have developed their own distinctive, indigenous flavor, to which new members are socialized. Diversity within centers is less than intercenter variation.[8]

The treatment of El Colegio as a single organization, despite its intercenter variation, makes it a compellingly large and broad PRC—and therefore an extreme case in which academic limitations and weaknesses are especially noteworthy. El Colegio towers over other Latin American PRCs in research breadth. Where it is limited, other, more typcial, PRCs are even more limited. Not even Brazil's CEBRAP or Argentina's Di Tella comes close to matching El Colegio's size or weight in social research, not to mention the humanities. Perhaps Brazil's Getúlio Vargas comes closest in weight, especially if we combine its Rio and São Paulo institutions, but it is more concentrated in administration, business, and economics. Yet even as the PRC giant, El Colegio was still too academically small and narrow to merit serious consideration from Rockefeller for its university development program (Black i).

To explore further the academic problems found in PRCs we turn now to teaching and then to research.

TEACHING

Alongside other research centers that offer little teaching and university faculties that do not successfully incorporate social research, PRCs form part of a higher education system that has largely failed to achieve its dreams of combining teaching and research in a common institutional setting. In other fields of study, that separation largely involves GRCs and URCs; in the social sciences, it largely involves PRCs. Logically, then, the ensuing analysis is relevant to other research centers and to the general yearning to find appropriate institutional homes for both teaching and research. What follows does not, however, negate the last chapter's findings on the quality of those PRC graduate programs that do exist.

I examine the limitations on teaching in four sections. These deal with the drawbacks of the divorce between research and teaching, the URCs' role, the PRC subset, represented by El Colegio and FLACSO, and the more typical PRC teaching roles.

The Divorce

Some analysts would raise de facto arrangements to principle. They can cite the ample separation of teaching and research in much of the developed world. For them, the events leading to the divorce in Latin America pertain not only to passing history but also to ongoing problems. Above all, they pertain to teaching. Teaching naturally dominates research, where the two are pushed together, especially because teaching is so professionally oriented in Latin America. Powerful professions exert their influence over curriculum, while students lack interest in activities that do not directly satisfy their job aspirations. Relatedly, university graduate education fails to achieve the autonomy it seeks from undergraduate education. Moreover, the scarcity of top-flight human resources for research may suggest the desirability of getting maximum research from each researcher (Vessuri 1986: 8; Schiefelbein i). Beyond the Latin American experience lie general doubts about the research-teaching marriage, as the two functions emphasize different aspects of knowledge (Ben-David 1977: 102). The most popular charge is that research robs time from teaching.

But an analysis of the actual separation in Latin America suggests grave problems with the model of separation. Without research, students, and most teachers for that matter, lose the benefits of contact with many of the best scholars. This is troubling for undergraduates and devastating for graduate students. It kills the Humboltean ideal of the unity of research, study, and teaching. Thus countries like Argentina where PRCs dominate suffer from a terrible lack of social science graduate activity, compared to a country like Brazil, where PRCs and universities are both powerful.

In turn, research itself suffers. The research community is poorly positioned to sustain itself over time. Bright young people lack research role models and instruction and do not themselves seek to become researchers. Such socialization into the academic profession is a major activity in U.S. graduate studies. If PRCs have protected, and even developed, the social sciences admirably for a generation, how well can they do so across generations? The problem is a mirror image of a more commonly noted problem in building and sustaining research: scholarships abroad help train fine researchers, but the lack of a viable institutional setting for teaching and research at home blocks the development of a self-sustaining system. Furthermore, the applied and programmatic nature of much research at PRCs aggravates the situation, because the vitality of future research depends on disciplinary research and teaching. Like other Latin American nonprofits, but more so, PRCs face a serious generation gap.

Danger threatens even the leading, classic PRCs, a danger only weakly offset by limited teaching activities, in-house training, apprenticeships, and scholarships for study abroad at places like Chile's CIDE and Bolivia's CERES. Peru's GRADE accepts a few university students both for training and for the inexpensive assistance these students offer (Arregui i). The training program at Brazil's CEBRAP accepts only six students annually, and the program at Argentina's CEDES is woefully small (Cavarozzi i). Although two-thirds of CLACSO's centers claim some training of young researchers, only one-third of these programs are formal, and the majority lack money and other basics; of course, the formal programs are usually in centers other than PRCs. CLACSO, for example, recognizes that its scholarship and other efforts for young researchers fall far short of the region's needs (Calderón and Provoste 1990: IV-7–8). Several nations, acknowledging the generational problem, have built special categories, for both young researchers and recent returnees from study abroad, into their national supplemental income funds for researchers.

The Dominican case illustrates the general Latin American problem. Thoughtful higher education experts are preoccupied with the nation's inability to form new social scientists or to hold onto the youngest of those already trained. Behind those more than fifty-five years old is a group between forty and fifty-five years old that was saved from the brain drain by the PRCs, but the next generation is barely visible. Whereas social science once attracted many of the best students doing graduate work abroad, now management, information studies, and finance dominate, as the nation's employment prospects in social research are dim. PRCs are inadequate to block the brain drain (Escala i; de Miguel i; Sánchez M. i-3).

The researchers are themselves handicapped by the divorce between teaching and research. They lack graduate students. This problem is not as severe in the social as in the exact sciences, and PRCs partly compensate by hiring research assistants (whose lack of opportunities for advanced study, combined with the typical PRC hierarchy, again suggests difficulties for the future). Beyond this, the PRCs researchers are often cordoned off in their small programs, with inadequate nourishment from other disciplines. Institutional separation thwarts the campus dream of social sciences interacting with one another and with the humanities, the natural sciences, and the professions.

The absence of teaching also robs researchers of what otherwise would be many natural interactions with one another and robs young researchers of a job market of viable size. Finally, researchers lack clout and protection when they are not tied to a mass student base. Venezuela's IVIC, a public research center, experienced such political weakness when the economy declined in the 1970s and it had to compete with the university for funding. Similarly, Brazil's Oswaldo Cruz Institute suffered from its isolation from mainstream Brazilian higher education and general support (N. Stepan 1976: 127). As in France, antipathies arise between teaching and research institutions. By comparison, the U.S. mode of combining research and teaching pays handsome dividends, as both tuition payers and state governments cross-subsidize research and graduate education when they support undergraduate education.

If a teaching-research link is important, two logical avenues to explore are research in teaching facilities (Levy forthcoming) and teaching in research centers. The first is beyond the scope of this study, except for the discussion in chapter 3 of how the failure of research in university faculties has fueled the growth of URCs and PRCs. I turn, instead, to teaching in the research centers, concentrating on PRCs but with a comparative look at URCs.

University Research Centers

A passing observation on GRCs is that they form a dichotomy: most engage in no teaching, or very little, but a few public research centers can account for an important chunk of a nation's graduate education. Individually, these centers often have larger programs than do the PRCs. CINVESTAV's twenty doctoral and twenty master's programs, for example, are crucial to Mexican scientific development.[9]

As usual, URCs stand between PRCs and university faculties. They teach more than the former and less than the latter. In fact, URCs teach less than their backers once expected. Here, I concentrate again on Mexico, and especially UNAM, which other Mexican public universities emulate.

Some of UNAM's faculties, like some Argentine faculties, have their own research centers, but most research concentrates in URCs not linked to a particular faculty. Supporters properly assert that URCs have protected research from the vagaries of UNAM's faculty politics. But the lack of teaching is striking. URCs give no degrees. Only 7 percent of their researchers teach, and the percentage dips still lower for the leading researchers who hold doctorates, few of whom so much as supervise undergraduate theses. They sometimes find it more rewarding to do their sporadic teaching outside of Mexico, although that may be partly because they are disproportionally foreign-born (Grobet V. and Schlaen 1984: 284; Acosta U. and Alvarado E. 1984: 371). At the IPN, (UNAM's national technical counterpart), the peak network of research centers, CINVESTAV, became so isolated that it is considered more a separate public research center than a URC. CINVESTAV has protected research but has not directly nourished undergraduate education (García i). Over the course of twenty-five years, with a full-time staff now exceeding 300, it has produced only 1,074 graduates; yet these figures exceed UNAM's in the same areas (de Ibarrola 1986–1987: 4, 16–17, 90; de Ibarrola pc-2). Such patterns translate into an inadequate supply of young Mexican researchers.

One might expect faculties to press for URCs to teach undergraduates, whether to improve instructional quality or to distribute teaching responsibilities equitably.[10] But faculties typically protect their claims on the professional program. Combined with URC reticence to get embroiled in mainstream university activity, this protectiveness helps explain the meager undergraduate teaching. At UNAM an "almost total separation" exists between leading research staffs and undergraduates, so that few students are prepared for graduate work (Schoijet 1979: 403).[11] Throughout Latin America, instances of undergraduate teaching, such as courses on Colombian Problems given by members of IEPRI at the nation's largest university, are exceptions; even there, teaching is limited to a mix of ad hoc seminars, pedagogical guidance, and graduate education.[12]

Personnel at URCS are more concerned over their isolation from graduate students. Some reasons are obvious, echoing problems faced by PRCS. They include the need for talented yet inexpensive labor, the probing inquiry of fresh minds, and a flow of young researchers to replace older ones. UNAM typifies the frustration for URCS. Their leaders hoped in vain to control graduate education; the engineering institute admits to "fishing" for students, while recognizing how unattractive their unit is to them (Barnés i; Esteva i). Such institutes grant only "research credits" and experience, not grades, thesis work, or degrees. They attract, with those weak incentives, no more than a few helpers (Nadal i). Somewhat greater involvement in graduate education exists in UNAM's social science/humanities URCS, while contact with undergraduates remains minimal (H. Muñoz i).[13]

Similar frustrations haunt URCS elsewhere. Like UNAM, Costa Rica's main university shows how URC teaching usually falls far short of a center-based instructional program. More common is for personnel to give courses in the faculties, which does not achieve the integration of research and teaching. Where the university tries to integrate more, faculties decry incursions into professional training (Macaya i).

The lack of teaching contributed by URCS provides insight into basic problems of linking research and teaching.[14] That the contribution from URCS so little exceeds what PRCS manage is alarming. PRCS with major teaching programs are few, yet there is less sense of frustration or failure; the little teaching done is usually not seen against a more ambitious goal but as a bonus.

El Colegio de México and FLACSO

Even PRCS that provide courses have major restrictions on teaching. El Colegio's teaching appears extensive compared to other freestanding centers but it remains sparse judged by the size of the institution. With roughly 200 students equally split between the master's and doctoral programs, and many fewer in undergraduate and specialization programs, El Colegio maintains an astounding 2:1 student/professor ratio. CIDE increasingly follows the model, though its roughly 200 students are at the master's level (ANUIES 1989: 116; Unger pc). El Colegio's sociology center has not graduated a student per year over the last fifteen years, though that stems partly from the attractiveness of even its noncredentialed students on the job market.[15] An annual or biannual course is the average teaching load in several centers, and professors can avoid teaching altogether. Most center directors estimate faculty teaching time at roughly 20–30 percent, including tutorial and class-related time. Such minimal teaching contributes to the limited course offerings.

El Colegio's defense of its low teaching load underscores the basic limits of PRCs (El Colegio N.d.: 6). First, El Colegio would have trouble attracting or financing more full-time students with appropriate qualifications. Second, the faculty is financially tempted to do consultancies and to teach outside El Colegio, receiving some pay and avoiding the more rigorous preparations that El Colegio's teaching requires. Third, offering more teaching would engender opposition from the universities and risk inviting typical problems of the public higher education system, including student and worker disorder and related interference by government (Urquidi i–2). Fourth, El Colegio's traditional mission is research excellence, as it models itself more on a PRC like the Brookings Institution than on any university. In other words, teaching is limited by a long-standing, unabashed policy that (1) no teaching should exist until fine research is in place, (2) the 2:1 student/teacher ratio should be maintained, (3) no faculty member should be forced to teach, and (4) such policies should be extended to colegios spinning off in other regions, where current enrollments are low.

FLACSO-Mexico, in contrast, has a teaching focus. Sociology graduates feed into El Colegio's doctoral program; its students complete their studies much more expeditiously than their counterparts at the senior institution (Reyna i). Additionally, FLACSO-Mexico's faculty work with students on research projects. But they are not as productive in research as El Colegio's faculty.

At FLACSO-Argentina, also, teaching impact exceeds research impact. The student/teacher ratio approaches 5:1 (if we count 250 students, rather than just the third or so who are active at any one time). Although graduation rates are low (roughly 70 out of 500 enrollees graduated between the late 1970s and 1990), FLACSO-Argentina—along with IDES and perhaps Di Tella and CEMA—has helped save a social science generation and has provided faculty for universities under redemocratization. It has also provided some young blood for Argentine PRCs. But the openness of FLACSO-Argentina's teaching program has meant that the student body is not academically elite, making the institution unattractive to many top researchers. This, in turn, drives down teaching quality. Few foreigners clamor to study there. In research, FLACSO-Argentina and FLACSO-Mexico are not comparable to FLACSO-Chile or, adjusted for national size, to FLACSO-Costa Rica.

Notwithstanding these programs in Argentina, Mexico, Ecuador, or any other national center, FLACSO's overall teaching is limited. Of thirty-six teaching programs spread over ten nations, FLACSO (1990: 1–10) offers only one doctoral and eleven master's programs, while twenty-four programs are diploma and specialization programs. Besides, no FLACSO center sustains a broad teaching curriculum comparable to a university's (Reyna i).[16]

In conclusion, FLACSO performs major teaching and research functions, but its individual centers distinguish themselves in, at most, one or the other. FLACSO does not integrate its high level research with teaching at any one site.[17]

What Is Taught and What Is Not

Beyond the few PRCs that have major graduate programs are the more common PRCs. The spectrum of their teaching activities runs from no linkage with the university to substantial integration. The ensuing discussion focuses on PRCs' own offerings, free-lance university teaching by PRC researchers, and an integration of personnel or programs between PRCs and universities.[18]

Offerings at PRCs

Unlike FLACSO and El Colegio, most PRCs do not have degree-granting programs. Where PRCs account for a significant share of valuable graduate teaching, it is a share of a small pie.[19] The rule holds even for most of the top PRCs, including Chile's CIEPLAN and Peru's IEP and GRADE. The third sector does not adequately fill the hole left by the public sector.

Teaching usually falls short of formal degree programs. More courses fit under specialization than master's or doctoral rubrics. For example, Argentina's Bariloche gives a three-month specialization course annually. Highlighting extension and policy more than conventional teaching, many PRCs run seminars or conferences open to the general public or to targeted groups ranging from the poor to the decision maker. This is an important service to all three sectors.

FEDESARROLLO runs four such seminars a year, with roughly 150 people attending; not until 1991 did it offer its first classroom seminar, nondegree at that (Escobar pc-3). Many PRC courses are for short-term training or particular skills for nonacademic groups. FLACSO-Costa Rica has performed those services for Central American government officials, as the AHC has for Chileans outside of government. By one count, over one three-year period in the early 1980s, the AHC served more than a thousand students, all in evening courses; by another count, the AHC gave thirty-one extension courses to more than a thousand students in 1983 alone (Lladser 1988a: 9; Fruhling 1985: 61). And these courses covered subject matter that the universities would not touch. Similarly, study circles attracted people to study in informal settings where repressive regimes blocked formal instruction; real courses sometimes followed (Lladser 1986: 12). In other cases, "what universities will not touch" has less to do with authoritarian regimes than with a university disinclination to pursue tasks such as outreach, which then become prominent at PRCs, like Paraguay's BASE-IS (N.d.). CLAEH, for example, has given courses on matters such as the history of the Uruguayan labor movement.

PET's courses for labor leaders further underscore the teaching-service nexus and the role of PRCs in building the third sector. Among other Chilean PRCs offering courses are ILADES, PIIE, and SUR, with a few others giving workshops or other semistructured courses. Such offerings undercut the criticism that PRCs lack scope in their areas of interest.

In a few cases, academic courses enjoy recognition abroad and lead to foreign degrees (e.g., Chile's ILADES, in connection with Belgium's Louvain University or Wales's University of Cardiff), though the PRCs themselves lack degree-granting authority (Brunner 1990c: 4–5). Such private sector access to the quality and legitimacy of European institutions resembles the practice in certain Asian and African universities. What the PRCs themselves typically supply in lieu of degrees are certificates affirming the completion of a year's study and scholarships that facilitate that study (Brunner 1990b).[20] Still, aggregated, all these Chilean teaching activities remain very modest for a network of so many PRCs (Lladser i-3). In 1989, when the AHC started a university, the teaching programs were new. They were neither an outgrowth of the PRCs nor closely integrated with them.

CLACSO's self-survey shows that under one quarter of its institutions give any postgraduate education, and much of that is in Brazil and Mexico. Along with Colombia and Venezuela, these nations—where PRCs do not dominate—account for more than 80 percent of the graduate programs and students (Calderón and Provoste 1990: II-13, V-2). Precious few PRCs

dispense much graduate education, not to mention undergraduate education. That courses are offered outside PRCs by PRC researchers does not
change the fact that they are not offered within. Brunner's (1990c: 6)
gloomy conclusion for Chile is: "There are no real links between research
and teaching at the graduate level."

Like URCs, PRCs will probably attempt to expand their teaching. One
option involves joint ventures among centers. Most of these have been domestic but Bolivian-Ecuadoran agreements add a teaching dimension to the
horizontal cooperation discussed above. Some salient traits of PRCs, notably
smallness, make intercenter cooperation necessary. Other traits, including
common interests and funders, also suggest feasibility. But still others, ranging from instability of staff to inadequate facilities, suggest difficulty (Borón
1990).

Paraguay's CPES and Chile's GIA are among the individual PRCs that seek
to build their own graduate offerings. Expansion may meet opposition,
however. On one side, many researchers prefer escape over opportunity
when it comes to teaching, whether at the university or at their center.
Thus, the Ford Foundation's efforts to get more researchers into Dominican universities ran up against reluctance (Dore i-2).[21] On the other side,
keen to protect their interests and status, universities perceive threats where
teaching occurs outside their institutional domain. In Uruguay, this contributes to the clear subordination of PRCs in teaching. Also, universities may
move into a teaching field that PRCs pioneer, which accounts for how Brazil's Oswaldo Cruz Institute lost its teaching program in microbiology (N.
Stepan 1976: 127–228).

Furthermore, a breakthrough involving more PRCs with large teaching
programs confronts sobering historic and political realities. The leaders in
teaching, most notably El Colegio and Getúlio Vargas, were created before
universities had significant aspirations in graduate education. No Venezuelan PRC has been granted official status as an institute of graduate studies
since IESA in 1976. Instead, the National University Council has slowed the
creation of PRCs and made it difficult for them to establish graduate programs. Only "universities" can grant degrees, and institutions cannot be
universities without operating in at least three fields of study and crossing
other hurdles. IESA's application for graduate status would probably have
been rejected today, as its application to add the field of education was; the
Trinidad medical center has been twice rejected (Piñango i; Gómez and
Bustillo 1979: 899; Pérez i).

Free-lance Arrangements

When researchers from PRCs volunteer to teach at universities on a per course basis, the separation of institutions and tasks shrinks somewhat but not fundamentally. Examples abound, and they come from both more-advanced and less-advanced nations and from nations with different political and university systems. These instances follow a pattern established in European countries, Russia for one, where researchers from academies lecture at universities and there is some inter-institutional access to facilities. Almost all the directors of Germany's Max Planck institutes, along with many researchers at other nonprofits and GRCs, are professors at universities, helping to alleviate rigidity in curriculum (Gellert 1993: 33–34).

Staff members of Panama's CELA, Nicaragua's ANICS, and Bolivia's CERES teach at universities. The practice is common in much of Central America (Fernández 1989: 77), as it is in Uruguay. An Argentine example dating to the early 1960s occurred when researchers, living off salaries from the Di Tella Institute, taught courses at Buenos Aires's universities; today, university teaching helps researchers cover their research expenses at PRCs, such as FLACSO (Harrison, Burnett, and Waggoner 1967: 26; Mollis pc-2). The Peruvian case suggests that, where private elite universities flourish as alternatives to faltering public universities, many members of PRCs teach in the private universities, as with GRADE's members at the Pacífico. This is due to the order, quality, and flexibility of those universities. However, the San Marcos national university and Pontifical Catholic University are major teaching sites for IEP's researchers.

Such uninstitutionalized teaching is as sporadic as it is widespread, however, and varies by time and place. It is not common at most social action PRCs, or at consulting centers. Whereas most of the part-timers at Uruguay's GRECMU teach at the university, four of the five senior researchers do not; only three or four of FEDESARROLLO's twenty-six core researchers and IEP's fifteen core researchers teach at Colombian or Peruvian universities, all as part-timers (León and Spalding 1992: 10; Escobar pc-2; Cotler i). Instead, IEP's contributions to teaching are from seminars for teachers and textbook publication. CIPMA contributes information on the environment to provincial Chilean universities.

The Brazilian case is particularly interesting because, unlike the situation in most of Latin America, the social sciences have greatly advanced in the public universities over the last two decades—and because its PRC-university ties are strong. Brazil may be a model for creative teaching-research connections across the public and nonprofit sectors. Universities beckon PRC personnel to teach, and most accept. PRC directors set examples, as IDESP's Bolivar Lamounier and Sergio Miceli have done. CEDEC's staff of twenty mostly hold affiliations with the USP, and a PRC-university *convenio* facilitates ties, though plans to move onto the USP campus and integrate further have failed (Miceli 1990; CEDEC 1990: 3–4; Schwartzman pc-4). USP and CEBRAP have computer terminal connections. Some university teachers resent the PRC intrusion as well as the perceived status differential and the financial assistance given to the teachers from PRCs. But others, including administrators, welcome the quality and prestige that PRC teachers bring to their universities. The unusual institutional strength of Brazil's public universities also promotes the relationship with PRCs, as a university job market helps those PRCs that grant graduate degrees.

Elsewhere, redemocratization has also brought a flowering at least of part-time, freelance PRC-university arrangements. Not only do prohibitions on arrangements diminish, but some universities look to increase their academic standing and their access to foreign funds through PRCs.[22] In Chile, with the political opening in 1983, this meant increased teaching years before the regime change at decade's end. For example, some researchers in the AHC human rights program taught at the law school of the Universidad Diego Portales (Correa i). In Argentina, as in Uruguay, few people from PRCs taught at universities until the last years of military rule, notwithstanding such exceptions as the Di Tella Institute and the Universidad de Belgrano; but since then, perhaps most have taught, and some have even returned to the university (Brunner and Barrios 1987: 139; CICE 1977; Tedesco i; Balán 1990). EURAL's director, who later assumed a high administrative post at the UBA, insisted that all his researchers teach at universities; innovative provincial universities have welcomed researchers who can teach their professors as well as their students (Borón 1990; Cavarozzi i).[23]

As with direct offerings at PRCs, however, teaching efforts made at the university meet resistance. University faculty may rebuff initiatives. Peruvian professors, earning about one-fifth of what their soliciting counterparts from places like Bartolomé earn, argue against the "invasion" of their institution. They object to the researchers' making extra money, and they fear perceptions of their own academic deficiency. Although some Colombians from PRCs are hired for graduate teaching, deans worry about their own control, and policies of standardization for the academic profession are obstacles to offering the incentives most researchers require (Facundo i).

Additionally, as seen in Argentina, the growth of special government funds allocated competitively puts PRC and university personnel in antagonistic postures, especially where it appears that the former usually win.

Moreover, increased freelance arrangements are but modest changes compared to revival and implementation of the ideal that most researchers should be at the university. Although some have returned, including to URCs, the benchmark Chilean case is sobering for those who cling to that ideal (Raczynski, Vergara, and Vergara 1993; Reilly 1994: 58).

PRC-*University Integration*

Somewhere short of the return of researchers to the university, and yet beyond the ad hoc arrangements that have been typical, lie certain forms of integration between PRC and university. (These forms also meet a mix of resistance and welcome.) In some nations, the PRCs' researchers are also full-time university professors. However, insofar as full-time appointment often means less than real full-time work, that situation is not diametrically different from freelance arrangements.

An untidy spectrum emerges. Argentine professors can hold full-time status at universities and yet not teach at all, restricting their university activities to discussions with other professors and perhaps participation in faculty decision making (Mundet i). More common is a relationship similar to the freelancers' except that the teaching occurs every term and involves more courses. These scholars may do at least as much teaching as the universities' full-timers who are not also at PRCs, but the former spend their nonclassroom time at their PRCs. In a few cases, as in Ecuador, most PRC scholars are full-time university professors and some do research at both institutions (Carvajal i). If an Ecuadoran or Argentine ideal remains the housing of research with teaching in the university, it is now a remote ideal that does not block diverse structural accommodations.

In Brazil, by contrast, careers uniting teaching and research are common in university social science. But that does not preclude university-PRC ties. Many researchers who come to teach receive full university salaries, which are good by the nation's wage standards, notwithstanding their open affiliation with the PRCs, where they spend most of their time (Miceli i). Assured salaries lend security to help offset the usual PRC dependence on project funding. Such arrangements deserve policy consideration as alternatives to the common, fragile, PRC-university ties where researchers earn only a small per-course payment.

Finally, regardless of the extent of such integration of personnel, PRCS and universities can build integrated programs. This integration sometimes evolves from PRC weaknesses. Uruguay's public university never deteriorated as much as Argentina's, and the PRCS' lack of tradition and deep legitimacy means they can be pressured into formal ties with universities (Cosse i; Brunner and Barrios 1987: 188). Elsewhere, research centers operate from more strength. CSUCA, most of whose members do university teaching, joins the UCR for a degree program (Vega 1989: 28), as does CATIE, an IRC. In all Latin America, FLACSO's only doctorate is a cooperative venture with the University of Brasília.[24] Argentina's FLACSO has had programs with universities reaching places like San Luis in the provinces and Uruguay (FLACSO 1987: 13); CELADE, IRC, works with Luján's provincial university for a master's degree in social demography. In Venezuela, cooperation exists between CERPE and the Universidad Católica Andrés Bello and between the Trinidad medical center and the Universidad Metropolitana. Expansion of such graduate agreements is possible, but trends are mixed.[25]

In policy terms, each of the PRC teaching options—from PRC offerings to freelance relationships, to integrative PRC-university relationships—must be considered for possible expansion. Rejectionist forces and the persistent ideal of forcing research into university faculties or departments must be weighed against the contributions of present practices, which could be further promoted by scholars, administrators, governments, international donors, and others.[26] In sectoral terms, each arrangement has been consequential and could become more so. Where PRCS add to their own offerings, they bolster the breadth of nonprofit activity. They also bolster the nonprofit sector through horizontal cooperation, where they join forces with other PRCS and where programmatic—and especially individual interactions—develop between PRCS and private universities. Where teaching connects with public universities, however, PRCS build partnerships across sectors.

RESEARCH

Attention now turns to limitations that hurt the quality of research, with an emphasis on deficiencies in output. Such an understanding is a necessary, albeit partial, corrective to the last chapter and the sanguine image that emerges from valid comparisons with university social science and from the international visibility of the PRCs' leading work. The corrective is especially powerful if it applies to the most sucessful PRCs, which means, here, considerable attention to Chilean PRCs and to the region's leading social research center, El Colegio. Academically peripheral PRCs would score lower than the centers analyzed below, but the conventional criteria of academic quality employed here would be less pertinent to their raison d'etre.

Weaknesses at the Academic Core

No clear line separates weakness in the sense of academic tasks neglected from weakness in the sense of deficiencies in the work actually done. However, the discussion has been moving toward the kind of weaknesses about which a defense of "PRCs just do not do that" is inadequate—at least in terms of how classic PRCs want their academic performance judged.

First, only a minority of PRCs are strong in conventional, international, academic terms. It would be difficult to claim much more than perhaps SER, FEDESARROLLO, and CINEP in Colombia and GRADE, IEP, Bartolomé, and DESCO in Peru. Ten might be the total for Buenos Aires, with few in the rest of Argentina (Balán 1982: 237). Even Chile might not exceed a dozen. This means that before the PRC explosion accompanying redemocratization, perhaps only one-fourth of Chilean PRCs truly achieved academic distinction, and the fraction would soon be halved as peripheral PRCs proliferated (Lladser i-2).

Second, even the PRCs on such lists lack a full commitment to scholarship. This relates to the greater growth of PRCs on the periphery than at the core—to the rapid growth of PRCs in which academics joins with grassroots, political, consulting, and other activities. Many PRCs that are heavily engaged in social action or consulting are weak in basic research.[27] Proliferating NGOs in environmental studies, responding to informational needs linked to particular actions, produce very little research of enduring academic quality (A. Thompson n.d.: 32). Tradeoffs also occur in each nation's top centers. Bartolomé scholars struggle to devote half their time to research amid pressure from international funders and domestic Peruvian groups (Walker i). Redemocratization, ironically, magnifies this problem, as leading figures feel policy responsibility or ambition and cut back on their academic work.

Third, a few key people are responsible for the prestige of several PRCS. Although this is true of many good academic institutions worldwide, it is especially telling at PRCS. Extra-academic criteria of hiring, promotion, association, and hierarchy, all play a part. Just as private, nonprofit sectors are usually judged by their leading institutions, so individual centers are usually judged by their leading figures. For classic PRCS, that means those who appear regularly at international conferences, academic centers, and funding agencies. Combining this point about variation within PRCS with the point about variation in quality across PRCS, then, the number of PRC people producing at good international standards is smaller than most imagine (D'Etigny i). This heterogeneity cuts against the notion of tight, unified organizations yet fits right in with observations about hierarchy, access to international philanthropy, and PRC growth patterns.

To revisit the data on degrees held by PRC researchers (so impressive compared to their university counterparts) is to confirm substantial intra-PRC variability. Even at such an esteemed PRC as Colombia's FEDESAR-ROLLO, nineteen of twenty-six full-timers do not have doctorates; only a master's degree is required, and research assistants need only an undergraduate degree. Less prestigious places, of course, have lower degree profiles.[28] Moreover, the data may suggest an excessively flattering gauge; it lowers if one questions the value of some European doctorates awarded without much structured study, and if all claimed doctorates are really held or simply projected (Lladser i-2).

A fourth point is that research at PRCS rarely attains disciplinary excellence. Dependency criticisms have sometimes contradicted one another regarding disciplinary orientations. One basic argument is that funders and other foreign influences push toward disciplinary concerns and publication in disciplinary journals, while a less frequent criticism is that assistance does not allow disciplinary development (Fuenzalida 1970: 102–07). The less frequent criticism is more apt for PRCS. CLACSO's survey shows more than 70 percent of directors listing a specialized program theme as predominant over any disciplinary focus, and more reported a practical before a pure research orientation (Calderón and Provoste 1990: IV-1–5), and these data of course include many university units. Tabulations based on self-assessments at research centers working on education also show acknowledgment of a lack of basic research.[29] A nation as large as Colombia arguably does almost no academic social science, at least outside economics (Aldana i; Facundo i).

Much depends on definitions, of course. Research centers below the region's pinnacle work with theories, as Paraguay's CDE does in sociology, and many centers use works from the disciplines in their analyses. But if we insist on work that includes a strong basic component or that mainly tries to develop or expand theory, PRCs appear weak. How much PRCs at least use sophisticated and up-to-date theory is itself dubious—or difficult to gauge. In any event, disciplinary weakness accompanies lack of teaching. Brunner, who elsewhere puts the best credible face on the lack of disciplinary focuses (Brunner and Barrios 1987: 90), writes that this is the "major risk" of research dependent on PRCs (Brunner 1991: 152) and that systematic graduate teaching in the social science disciplines is "practically non-existent" in Chile (Brunner 1990c: 6). That economics has worked as a discipline stems from its unique university lodging. In contrast, political science and sociology (the largest discipline in Chilean PRCs) have failed to develop their theoretical cores, despite expanding their good studies in particular areas. Brunner thus sees an asymmetry, as work produced at PRCs serves as case-studies for cutting-edge theoretical work by foreigners (Brunner i-1).

On the other hand, multidisciplinary research is more limited than PRCs claim. Beyond the social sciences, PRCs rarely deal with any disciplines as such. Within the social sciences, they do not usually work to fuse the tenets of two disciplines. As with teaching and fields of study, the key problem is not inattention within any given institution but inattention in almost the entire PRC sector. The picture changes, however, if multidisciplinarity means merely drawing on more than one discipline at a time.

Much also depends on preferences. One need not favor the inward disciplinary orientation dominant in many U.S. university departments and journals. PRCs have good reason to downplay disciplinary work in favor of practical orientations aimed at nonacademic impacts. But it is a matter of balance, and PRCs sacrifice much of the conceptual depth promoted by disciplines at their best.

And weak disciplinary work sometimes relates to a general lack of academic rigor. On several counts where PRCs deserve credit for surpassing levels previously or presently attained elsewhere in Latin America's academic world, notably empirical content and methodology, they also suffer from serious deficiencies. Large undertakings, paradigms, and systematic syntheses guided by theoretical concerns are marginalized (Brunner and Barrios 1987: 207). Generalizations are rare—or, as at many Peruvian centers, they spring from inadequate data (Spalding 1991: 95–96).[30] However understandable or justified the subordination of conventional academic ideals might be, it warrants attention and concern.

Publications

Publications reveal such academic weaknesses. To be sure, the quantity of good work impresses, despite questions about per capita production at even some of the renowned centers. The concern here is with quality. Social science quality has improved in Latin America, and PRCs have played a large role in that. But problems with quality are striking, given the centrality and reputation of PRCs. This is the context in which we find a dearth of formidable academic publications; in the context of the weaknesses characteristic of most Latin American academic institutions, some PRC weaknesses would appear as strengths.

The dearth typically means meager book production. Peru's exceptionally large and influential ILD produced only two bona fide books in a decade (Bromley 1990: 332). Among PRC books, including the more common edited works, grounding in disciplinary literature and development with extensive data are rare indeed. Rare, too, are authored books with major international presses.

Nor do many PRC articles make it to the world's most demanding journals. Chapter 6 provides several positive reasons for such localism, and language is a problem. Other factors are more unflattering. Discursive essays are more common than systematic treatments. Also common are empirical pieces that are neither theoretically well grounded nor methodologically sophisticated and that are far from the international academic frontier. The pieces frequently have an important place, but they do not negate the desirability of more solid academic work. Other work is weak enough to lack value even in a local context. Publications on the environment illustrate both tendencies (A. Thompson N.d.: 32–36).

The paucity of solid academic output is predictably most severe in the least advanced nations. Vega (1989: 19) concludes that Central American social science lacks systemization, empirical and methodological development, and general categories based on data; most work is descriptive, diagnostic, partisan, tentative, or discursive.

A key point is the weak peer review process. This goes hand in hand with the observation that people bind tightly together politically in PRCs and that pluralism is minimal. Consequently, peer review tends to be in-house, informal, unrigorous, and not challenged by sharply different perspectives. None of this conforms to international ideals of review. That some undeserving pieces are published is less important than the failure of deserving ones to be critically improved, broadened, or adequately presented through and to a community of scholars. For PRCs as a sector, fragmentation and inadequate academic integration characterize the process. This argument allows that much work at top PRCs could pass external review and that not all pieces, certainly not all policy pieces or works aimed to help particular groups, should go through academically ideal processes. It allows, further, that alternatives are not simple. Most nations lack a tradition of journals and presses that are independent of their own research institutions. They also lack sufficient markets, especially without students in good university social science courses.[31] FLACSO-Chile, for example, produces mostly in-house, with low rejection rates and variable quality.

Consider the typical publication outlets. Invited book chapters are common, including many written and edited by scholars at a given PRC. Also frequent is the publication of articles in the PRC's own journal or bulletin. PRCs rely on such periodicals. Examples include most of those listed in chapter 6. Astonishing as it seems—especially amid an economic crisis—nearly all respectable Peruvian PRCs had their own publication outlet, dictated partly by a siege mentality and an unwillingness to criticize friends (though some see recent improvement here); perhaps two dozen magazines, produced with no serious outside evaluation, sell to small circles of followers and friends (Spalding 1991: 33).[32] Regarding books, de Soto's famous *The Other Path* (1989: xxiv–xxvi) was based wholly on ILD studies and, like other ILD publications, was reviewed and revised by a fixed group of four ILD leaders.

Perhaps the quintessential PRC outlet is the working paper, with a distribution of a few hundred copies. Many of these papers include either scant citations or terribly dated ones. Others include citations largely limited to the works of colleagues within the same PRC or PRC network. Again, this observation allows that more of value appears than at other Latin American institutions and that the practice is similar to that at top U.S. universities, where scholars churn out working papers without a review process or standards comparable to those at top journals—and where the main purpose is simply to supply information. But flanking these are other working papers that do push the scholarly frontier and by a much higher percentage of refereed journal and book publications.

Also as in U.S. publications, but much more so, policy ends restrict open, objective, disinterested research, targeted at a critical community of scholars. Ideological writing is common at those few PRCs far to the right or left and also at the more numerous partisan and other "committed" think tanks. Argentina's IDEC, which is connected with the rightist political party, publishes such material, including the best-selling *El estado y yo*, which denounces state inefficiency (Gibson 1990: 27). For less ideological work as well, the policy purpose drives publication for special audiences. Party leaders, government policymakers, international agencies, and heads of grassroots nonprofits are all candidates. Beyond in-house publication, dailies and weeklies are common outlets. The point is that the main audience for much writing is nonacademic.

Restrictive academic practices are especially acute for the work—the increasing work—produced on contract. Most such work is not readily available to the general scholarly community. As Vega (1989: 46–47) finds in Central America, PRC researchers write for limited circulation to funders, including confidential circulation. Multiplying data, surveys, and analyses do not cohere or build on themselves. Moreover, the process excludes local social scientists from interpreting the data. It denies them much of what they need to build a scholarly community or to construct their own societal vision.

Variability across PRCs allows for exceptions to these weaknesses in publications but also for the fact that most PRCs function well below the peaks. Moreover, variability multiplies as institutions proliferate, with push and pull factors stretching talent thin and with many new institutions plainly subordinating academic publication to other ends. While some PRCs publish splendidly, despite all the limits, most fall short.[33] Even in Chile, publication concentrates at the top places (Lladser 1986: 10). Variability again also arises intrainstitutionally. The estimable productivity of top PRCs often comes from only a minority of the staff.[34]

El Colegio itself, although unsurpassed in prestige within and beyond Latin America, suffers from many of the reservations about output—and not all the suffering can be blamed on the disabling or dispiriting effects of economic crises. By 1990 these trends, along with the rise of private universities like ITAM and of institutionally unaffiliated talent trained abroad, knocked El Colegio out of its clear preeminent position in certain areas, including economics. Research output varies both among and within El Colegio's centers, more like an average U.S. state university than an elite research institution. Special programs may be particularly suspect, as was the energy program. Many individuals hardly publish. Some centers fail to produce books with theoretical and empirical bases. Though there are proportionally fewer working papers and more journal articles than at most PRCs, many of the journals are El Colegio's own. Institutional policy usually requires submission of books to El Colegio's own press, which rarely publishes works by outsiders. Thus, the institution's impressive output of books and articles, cited in the last chapter, turns out to be based (almost two-thirds and three-quarters, respectively) on publication by El Colegio (1987b: 26). The institution's financial and publicity needs may justify such policies, but they have an insulating effect. Additionally, many at El Colegio publish in semipopular intellectual magazines, such as *Nexos* and *Vuelta*, more than in refereed academic journals. And El Colegio's research, like its teaching, often pursues programmatic application at a cost to disciplinary or other basic academic focuses, which in turn hurts its chances at international publication. This includes even the center on demography and urban development, which is more oriented to U.S. methodologies than most of El Colegio's centers are.

All in all, the publication record of Latin America's PRCs—which reflects so much about their general academic profile—finds an instructive U.S. likeness less with universities, the clear U.S. social research leaders, than with U.S. think tanks. Characteristic of the latter are (1) a focus on problems and policies rather than on the discipline, (2) limited peer review, (3) a prevalence of working papers, op-ed pieces, and in-house journals, like AEI's *Regulation* and the Carnegie Endowment's *Foreign Policy*, (4) writing aimed at the media and policymakers, and (5) a great range in productivity across centers.[35] U.S. disciplinary journals, which are produced and refereed by scholars from institutions unaffiliated with the journals and stress theory and method, do not often find their match in the PRCs. Seen from this perspective, the great deficiency in Latin American social research publication is that, whereas U.S. think tanks produce alongside robust universities, PRC production is much, most, or all of what exists in Latin American nations.[36] This leaves a void in research and intellectual productivity. PRC social research is stronger in policy than in social science.

This negative side of output is mainly unpublicized, though many leading experts on social science production, themselves stars at PRCs, confirm it. The view contradicts at least certain general impressions among Latin Americanists in the developed world and numerous evaluations by donors (Brunner and Barrios 1987: 206–07; Spalding, Taylor, and Vilas 1985: 1-2). The discrepancy has several explanations. Some validity probably lies in charges that, however much top Ford officials have insisted on substantial evaluations (Sutton i), donors are tempted to vindicate their prior efforts or are eager to give their money and that personal empathy can influence external consultants. Another factor is the international underestimation of places like UNAM's social science URCs; although their output is probably inferior to El Colegio's, a credible case can be made that it is different more than inferior.[37] But most overestimation of PRCs comes naturally, from appreciating their accomplishments in comparison to that of other institutions, past and present.

More important than dwelling on discrepancies between image and reality is understanding the research deficiencies themselves. However sensitive the negative side is, fruitful discussion does not attempt to deny it fundamentally. Understanding ultimately involves much less criticism for a failure to accomplish than an appreciation of common limits imposed by PRCs' characteristics.[38]

Economy of scale is a good issue with which to demonstrate how academic deficiencies relate directly to the key characteristics of PRCs. The specialist nature of PRCs, with their narrow financial and human resource bases, means an infrastructure inadequate for many research possibilities. Against the magnitude of this problem, efforts at inter-PRC cooperation, (like Peru's Intercentros) have been inadequate. The same is true of PRC-university cooperation.

Libraries provide an example of economy-of-scale problems. On the positive side, FLACSO, Di Tella, CIESU, and FEDESARROLLO boast among the best social science libraries in Chile, Argentina, Uruguay, and Colombia, respectively. Some broaden their impact by allowing access to outsiders. Within Central America, CRIES is a regional leader for materials on contemporary affairs, and Panama's CELA illustrates how a PRC can provide documentation services for outside students and researchers. Within more specialized areas, PRCs are that much more likely to own the top holdings, as with Chile's CIPMA in environment and GIA in agricultural sociology.

But specialization itself makes PRC libraries inadequate substitutes for good university libraries. Even Di Tella has only some 60,000 volumes, FEDESARROLLO has 26,000, and GIA, 8,000. Brazil's IUPERJ has but 18,000, and Peru's Bartolomé only a little more. Average holdings at CLACSO centers remain below 6,000, and PRCs are among the smaller CLACSO centers (CLACSO and OECD 1984: 3–134). In contrast, holdings at U.S. research universities commonly exceed a million and even several million. PRCs with major graduate studies normally have larger but still limited libraries. Venezuela's IESA has more than 40,000 volumes. At the giant freestanding center of the social research world, El Colegio (400,000 items as of 1986), one sees how the paucity of works on non-Mexican history restricts what scholars can explore and publish. Social scientists even in Chile suffer from an insufficient total number of volumes—that is, great gaps in the overall sector—and from dispersion among the many PRCs within the sector. Thus, the best PRC libraries and sectors suffer from a specialism and dispersion that hurts chances for research that is well based, cumulative, broad, and interactive. The more typical the PRC, the worse all these problems are and the more other problems arise, such as the absence of vital recent works.

In fact, such limiting PRC characteristics as small scale are themselves largely conditioned by the PRC's environment. Although repressive regimes have stimulated the growth of PRCs, they have usually restricted their scope and sometimes, as at Argentina's Bariloche, devastated the most ambitious PRCs. Among other environmental constraints are polarized societies, small educated markets, weak research traditions, languishing academic development at universities, self-interested university political power, and financial penury, in addition to the social and political pull factors that draw people and money elsewhere. The list is powerful.

Commitment to academic research is a good issue with which to summarize such environmental influences. PRCs lack a fuller commitment to academic research partly because they have other valid priorities related to their environments. Social distress cries out for immediate help. So does political repression. Social and political polarization also intensify PRC commitments to help "their" group or organization. Political liberalization as well as both for-profit and nonprofit privatization then expands the possibilities for applied work at PRCs. Then too, any aspiration to do basic work may run up against opposition by universities. Meanwhile, opportunities open outside PRCs for some of their major researchers, who either lessen their academic commitment to the PRCs or leave outright; their replacements rarely achieve equal access to funding (Balán pc).

Other important constraints blocking greater commitment to academic research are economic—and precede the decline of international philanthropy, which is a dangerous aggravation. The absence of an ample market for academic research hurts. Tight funds block economies of scale and large projects. Further, beyond the question of total amount is the question of source. Chapter 4 considers how funding means control—that control adds to the problems considered here, since international agencies usually insist on practical applications.[39] Connected with that is short-term funding. Researchers must show results quickly, thereby denying time to explore, risk new approaches, retool, or ponder and bring to fruition large projects. Hired individuals jump from one topic to another as *cortoplacistas,* leaving few to develop a concern profoundly and systematically.[40] "Long-term" projects at classic PRCs might mean two years, not six or eight. At that, researchers may work simultaneously on several projects. Much work is done by those hired strictly by project, as at CIEA in the Dominican Republic, rather than by fixed personnel (Silié pc). Moreover, patterns of PRC founding and funding alike contribute to the multiplicity of small centers, where top people must devote considerable time to administration and where hiring may obey criteria of organizational coherence rather than straight academic merit.

Funds secured through contracts and through most domestic funding take probably an even greater toll on academic development. PRCs' interactions with for-profit and public funders commonly undercut basic research. With responsibilities for consulting, administration, and direct policy impact, PRC personnel who have no major teaching loads lack the opportunity for long-term academic research.[41] Although this chapter's opening paragraph posits that academic weaknesses mean diminished importance, we have seen that the weaknesses often involve trade-offs with political, economic, and social contributions that enhance PRCs' importance.[42]

MODELS

If PRCs fit the notion of nonprofit, specialist institutions that do particular things better than other institutions but are themselves rather limited, how much do they broaden their impact by serving as models? This question emerges from the contrasting positive and negative performance assessed in the previous and present chapters. It is a key question for such institutions as well as for the foundations and others that support them. The hope is that the nonprofits will "lever" the systems.[43] Although pertinent claims form basic rationales for privatization, the scholarly literature on nonprofits provides no clear answer.[44] We look first at El Colegio and then assess the evidence more generally.

El Colegio de México

If functional breadth, longevity, quality, and size increase the potential impact of a model, then El Colegio's mixed impact is perhaps disappointing. Its laudable contributions in targeted pockets have not led to systemwide transformation.

One consideration is the impact on other Latin American nations from graduate study at El Colegio. The percentage of foreign students in El Colegio's centers has been lower in the large disciplines, such as economics and sociology, compared to particular fields, such as demography and urban development and Asian and African studies. Economics had no foreign students in the late 1980s, when five of demography's eleven doctoral students were from other Latin American nations. More important, the overall number of foreign students has fallen because of declining resources and scholarships; also, regulations forbid preference to foreigners, which undermines plans to use El Colegio as a regional model.[45] On the other hand, foreigners who do study at El Colegio make a big impact back home. A survey done at the international relations center reports that 50 percent went into academia, 30 percent into government, and 10 percent into international agencies, often in high positions (Torres i).

El Colegio has, however, been instrumental in the creation and development of other research centers and networks of centers, including CLACSO and FLACSO. But the main effort to use El Colegio as an explicit model concerns the creation of other *colegios* in Mexico. The government encourages the idea partly to curb the universities. El Colegio prefers not to regionalize itself, fearing dilution of its quality; accordingly, the idea of new *colegios* is attractive. The *colegios* may offer feeder degrees, as with Michoacán's master's degree toward El Colegio's doctorate in history, and they concentrate on local concerns. The *colegios* in Baja California and Michoacán perform well academically. The former is Baja's preeminent PRC; the latter's per capita research production in history and anthropology may exceed El Colegio's own. Both regional centers have benefited from dynamic leaders, Jorge Bustamante in Baja and Luis González González in Michoacán. Other *colegios,* including Jalisco in demography, achieve respectable academic levels (Meyer i; Segovia i).

But scholarship at perhaps six *colegios* (e.g., Bahío) does not remind anyone of El Colegio de México. These *colegios* demonstrate the great difficulty of emulating PRC models. To its credit, El Colegio has realistically appraised the difficulty and has issued a sort of ten commandments about the conditions required for success—most of which are quite hard to meet. They include a strong base of full-time and highly trained researchers before opening teaching programs, a very low student/professor ratio, residence near the institution, and attraction of diverse funders without promising them immediately useful research (El Colegio N.d.).

In practice, regional *colegios* fail to achieve academic distinction to the extent they skirt the commandments. Especially outside of the two best, funding is tight. *Colegios* overpromise on useful policy research. The promise either goes unfulfilled or undercuts academic development. Puebla exemplifies the latter as well as the dangers that instability brings with dependence: a supportive governor's successor proved antagonistic to the *colegio.* Also, state governments push for increased enrollments. On the one hand, then, it is difficult to follow the commandments. On the other, to do so is to be small, which limits El Colegio's force as a model. In fact, politics may require smallness so as not to challenge the state universities too much.[46] At present, most *colegios* offer no teaching and only one or two research specializations. Baja's success and good relations with the local public university relate to its restrictive research emphasizing migration (Beltrán i).

The single most heralded effort to duplicate El Colegio de México's achievements came with the 1974 creation of CIDE in the capital. It quickly illustrated the perils of violating the commandments and confirmed just how precious the achievements of El Colegio have been. CIDE was created, with El Colegio's and (mostly) the federal government's assistance, to be a new center for the production of policy relevant research. From the outset, it promised too much too fast to the government, with which it was probably too cozy, and to students seeking positions of influence. It suffered from worker pressures, ideological politicization, and excessive turnover of academic staff. The shortcut to prominence failed, despite nearly a million dollars from nine Ford grants, 1977–1985. Though CIDE made strides, it lacked academic distinction and was a rather marginal institution. It did not emulate El Colegio. Happily, however, CIDE reversed course. It has built an estimable base of young researchers, gained respect, and substantially expanded the weight of Mexico's PRCs. Sober reflection, intelligent leadership, and the nation's compelling growth of pertinent demand and supply for policy research, analyzed in chapter 3, are all factors. Like the provincial *colegios,* then, CIDE has provided mixed evidence on El Colegio's force as a model (Reyna i; Stavenhagen i; Unger pc; Urquidi i-2).

Top private universities, including the Iberoamericana, Américas, and Anáhuac, have benefited from El Colegio, hiring its graduates and contracting its professors to teach. But most of El Colegio's fields are hardly represented in the private universities, which stress more commercial areas, and in economics, they tend to hire from their own groups (Urquidi i-1). Whereas these private universities proudly cite links to El Colegio, the national university and some other public universities are more reticent. Major units (for example, sociology and economics at UNAM) are jealous of, or terribly different from, El Colegio. Others lag too far behind to utilize El Colegio's personnel or work. But this still leaves room for El Colegio to make contributions, including advice on programs, to certain fields at the best provincial universities. These include demography at Guadalajara, Michoacán, and Nuevo León, economics at Nuevo León and Veracruz, and language at Veracruz and Sonora. Units at UNAM are touched through individuals' impacts. Nonetheless, El Colegio has not shaped the bulk of Mexican higher education in social science (Freeman 1973: 27–31).

Once again using Chapingo as a counterpart to El Colegio, to broaden the exploration to public research centers and to a different field of study, strong symmetry appears. Indeed, Chapingo's very creation was partly to extend the already great contributions that the agricultural IRCs were making to the academic core of universities (Vera i; Mosher 1957: 100–113; Fosdick 1952: 189–90). Abundant examples show the payoff from Chapingo. They include the work of Chapingo's own regional centers and the development of the academic core at Mexican and other Latin American agricultural universities as well as at more comprehensive universities with faculties of agronomy (Coleman and Court 1992). A major factor in Chapingo's influence has been its teaching. A 1975 survey found that 86 percent of the institution's graduates were working in the academic world (Jiménez, Fernández, and Galindo 1978: 62). The great majority of the staff holding advanced degrees at the nearby university studied at Chapingo. And 1,000 of the first 5,000 students at Chapingo were foreign; they have shaped their universities in Colombia, Ecuador, Peru, the Dominican Republic, and elsewhere (Alcalde i; Díaz i). But even if one accepts all these claims, Chapingo and the major agricultural IRCs in Latin America have not brought agricultural higher education, in general, up to acceptable standards (FF #73595; Segal 1986b: 155). On the contrary, the way Chapingo towers over the field suggests the limited impact of Chapingo as a model.

A Mixed Record

Similar patterns of impact and lack of impact turn up beyond Mexico: models are at once significant yet fall well short of exuberant claims for nonprofits. Summative evaluation ultimately depends on expectation. (Policy implications are held for the concluding chapter.)

Many PRCs serve as models for other PRCs and related organizations. Some are instrumental in their creation of others, as with the CPU for RIAL and CINDA. IRCs have a special impact on domestic PRCs where they are located, notably in Chile (Orellana 1986: 229). Top PRCs in one nation are sometimes models for aspiring PRCs elsewhere, the way Chile's CIEPLAN was for Peru's GRADE. And to be a model for PRCs is frequently to be a model for Latin America's leading social research institutions. Nonprofits are important as models for other nonprofits.

But to break out to the wider system, nonprofits usually must be models for public sector institutions as well. PRCs must have a strong effect on universities, most of which have been public. The potential is inspiring, as university reform regains vigor. In nations like Chile, special opportunities arise to salvage positive results from the repression that turned university social science into a vacuum within which one could start anew. Whereas a regional evaluation in 1980 would have been bleak, today a new zest for reform is evident. Latin America's universities, like their counterparts in other regions, take striking initiatives long resisted but now integral to political-economic changes that transcend higher education alone. Concerning only financial sources, a list must include the decentralization of government funding, private contributions, contracts by project, competition, evaluation, and differential access and rewards—all of which follow the PRC lead.

Impacts on universities as they actually are, however, have been spottier. A general conclusion from wide but scattered evidence is the following: PRCS stimulate leading social research at leading universities but they do not fundamentally reshape university research, let alone most other university functions, and they arguably even undermine universities in certain ways. Put another way, PRCS stimulate some of the best, but the overall university picture remains woeful.[47]

Consider FLACSO. It played a crucial early role in training founding members of some national science communities, as most graduates stayed in their field (Nina Manitzas to William Saint, 28 Feb. 1983, FF #68796). Looking mostly at the Southern Cone, many report "great" influence in countries where FLACSO was present (Balán 1982: 17–18). Except for places and periods when universities were heavily repressed, this meant a positive impact on universities. For example, FLACSO contributed to a professionalization of sociology (Briones i). Mexico's FLACSO shows influence in later years on various nations' universities. Between 1976 and 1984 it attracted some 200 students from other Latin American nations, a high percentage of whom completed their degrees and later advanced their nation's research trajectory in sociology (Reyna i).[48] But numerous factors, including multiplying enrollments, overwhelm many potential university gains from PRC models. For one thing, if universities have more full-time professors than before, the proportion of these to the overall teaching staff has not greatly increased. To choose one problem from the PRC side: the absence of extensive graduate education weakens PRCS' ability to plant seeds.[49]

Summing up: small private nonprofit institutions created as alternatives to large, suffering, and mostly public ones fail to serve as models that transform the basic system, yet they do serve as partial models. They contribute to some of the best pockets within that system, encompassing certain fields in innovative universities. This view is more positive than that of small, private voluntary organizations as essentially uninnovative, uninfluential, duplicative, or complementary in relation to the work of larger organizations (Kramer 1981; B. Smith 1985: 107). Following on most of the book's findings, this analysis of models suggests that the innovation, distinctiveness, and superiority of PRCS translate into some important influences on other academic institutions but that they also fail to translate in many fundamental ways.

Additionally, even if one approves what the PRCs themselves do and hopes that universities will emulate them more, some influences are troubling. Because PRCs help leading pockets more than mass cores, they add to stratification. Suffering universities fall in relative terms as they find it harder and harder to attract top people or funds, both of which are attracted toward PRCs. The result then frustrates hopes that elite private nonprofit institutions would be models capable of lifting entire systems.

CONCLUSION

Like other nonprofit, specialist institutions in plural systems, PRCs avoid many tasks that the overall system must perform, usually leaving those responsibilities to the public sector. *System* here may mean the research system or the higher education system; in the latter case, teaching dominates the list of largely avoided activities, and the lack of teaching undermines the research function itself.

Narrowness, specialism, and fragmentation may be more troubling for academic institutions than for many other nonprofits. Indeed, they may well be more troubling for those classic PRCs that truly do research than for peripheral PRCs that concentrate on service. Much depends on one's belief in the liberal notion of academic dialogue, debate, cross-fertilization, communities of diverse scholars, and so forth—as contrasted to the image of research progress through fairly tight groups of individuals. PRCs tend to be academically restrictive—tied to a limited set of purposes or to specific consumers or research more than to an open academic community. The lack of peer review in publications or of publications transcending individual PRCs is indicative of an inwardness that must be weighed against the spectacular outwardness that otherwise characterizes PRCs.

Whether or not PRCs are suitable as research institutions, they clearly are not full substitutes for good universities. With reason, domestic reformers and international philanthropy pursued university development in the postwar period. As those dreams went unrealized, PRCs became both understandable and very useful alternatives. But they are partial alternatives. And as models, they have not led a grand university transformation, at least not yet.

Such academic problems are especially disturbing because, in two fundamental senses, they go beyond weak or average individual freestanding social research centers. First, we have established the problems with strong attention to the academically largest and best centers. These are not, by international standards of scholarship, imposing academic institutions. Nor are they moving in that direction. To invoke the cherished philanthropic motto regarding higher education goals, the peaks are not being made higher—in large part because they are too narrow. Yet these academic peaks obviously tower over most PRCs. The inadequacies of El Colegio, for example, would pale by comparison with those at most PRCs. Second, weaknesses have been established from a sectoral as well as an institutional perspective. The pluralist sector achieves much more academic breadth and strength than typical institutions do, but even the sector overall suffers from severe problems. These include limitations in (1) coverage across and within fields as well as regions, (2) disciplinary and empirical work, (3) large-scale studies and publications, (4) peer review, (5) graduate education linked to research, and (6) the ability to rejuvenate through the training of younger researchers. The weaknesses of individual PRCs find only partial remedies at the sectoral level.

But to reach a conclusion on academic performance overall, the weaknesses must be measured against the strengths. Indeed, many weaknesses simply mark the boundaries of a considerable third-sector success.

PRCs are very good academically in many ways. They often represent the best available options. The quality of academic performance relates strongly to the general dominance of PRCs in many nations. In the majority of nations (Argentina, Bolivia, Chile, Paraguay, Peru, Uruguay, and probably all of Central America and the Latin Caribbean except Costa Rica and Cuba), universities match PRCs in social research quality only sporadically. Elsewhere, comparisons are thornier, but an average advantage in quality goes to the PRCs in the two most important social research communities (Brazil and Mexico).

Even in teaching, the nonprofit sector tends to lead where it is involved. Qualitative indicators include degrees given and degrees held by teachers. Leadership by PRCs in social science often extends to sheer numbers as well, albeit largely by default. For nations like Paraguay and Uruguay, PRCs have been almost the sole producers of the new social scholars. But it is especially in research that quantitative and qualitative strengths outweigh weaknesses. And, as models, PRCs have more positive or limited than negative impacts on other institutions.

From another summative angle, judged by a reasonable checklist for scientific research in developing countries (N. Stepan 1976: 8), the PRCs' performance is fairly impressive. Criteria include contributions to international knowledge and service to local and national needs. At least considering the plurality of PRCs, as opposed to individual PRCs, there is a comparative diversity of staff and activities and probably stable institutional shelter. Also, seen against the available alternatives and in the otherwise difficult contexts for research typically plaguing Latin America, PRCs do well in the recruitment and absorption of human resources. Further, PRCs often do well even on matters like number of publications, from which this checklist excuses developing countries.

PRCs, especially when joined by related IRCs, URCs, and GRCs, can take much credit for a salient contrast in the progress of Latin American higher education over recent decades: research has come farther than teaching.[50] In fact, whether teaching has improved is debatable, depending on varied gauges, while research has undeniably advanced far, with valid debate concentrating on matters of degree and emphasis. Overall, the third sector's research performance is both mixed and impressive.

8 Conclusion

Thematic depictions of PRCs have sustained themselves across the evolving foci of individual chapters. PRCs are nonprofit organizations within pluralist private sectors. They have gained considerable political, social, economic, and of course academic importance. In so doing, they have joined a historic nonprofit privatization; indeed, they have often led or otherwise helped build this privatization. For all their contributions to the third sector, however, PRCs have also made significant impacts on the for-profit and, especially, public sectors. PRCs are integral to fresh intersectoral interactions.

The effort to understand PRCs has added, perforce, to our knowledge of nonprofit activity, privatization, state-society relation, international philanthropy, the research function, and comparative higher education, all overlapping with Latin American studies. This final chapter refrains from a straight summary of the findings from prior chapters. But it provides some recapitulation as it first evaluates PRCs in conceptual terms, as nonprofits, and then considers their contributions to pluralist privatization.

AN EVALUATION

The analysis of PRCs has continually yielded evaluative information. Pertinent generalizations reflect typical realities of pluralist, nonprofit sectors. This chapter reviews the positive and negative aspects of how nonprofits (1) attain their goals, (2) provide accountability, (3) affect the higher education system overall, and (4) contribute beyond that system. Along the way, the evaluation of patterned achievements and limitations includes parallels between academic and political or financial factors. A pivotal notion, sustained in each chapter, is of PRCs as specialist organizations. While such organizations exist within the public sector, they are especially associated with private sector pluralism.[1]

What follows, then, is a concluding response to the book's main evaluative question: On balance, are PRCs positive for higher education and overall development? Given the salient characteristics of PRCs, what follows also constitutes an evaluation of a pluralist nonprofit sector, a major chapter in the history of international philanthropy, and an unprecedented Latin American research effort. Of course, the main answer is already clear: the evaluation is mostly positive. A "balanced" summary should be fair and inclusive but should not, a priori, assign equal weight to the positive and negative sides.

The Positive Side

Attaining Goals

PRCs do well on several criteria that organizational sociologists and others use to evaluate performance (Kanter and Summers 1987: 157–58). At a basic level, organizations try to survive. PRCs manage that and more: great growth in the overall sector and growth within individual organizations. Many of the specific explanations for growth involve positive evaluations by outsiders as well as insiders.

The attainment of goals is impressive, as PRCs usually accomplish what they set out, or promise, to do. Most of those nonprofit organizations, formed in part because of perceived public failure, continue to offer true alternatives. Most of those formed to meet new demands have done that. On the political side, for example, PRCs have protected individuals, scholarship, and freedom; and they have provided diverse actors with choice, with institutional options that suit particular political beliefs that do not capture majority support or that do not conform to rulers' beliefs. On the academic side, PRCs also meet or surpass expectations. They are leaders in social research. At least most standard indicators suggest that. These include the weight and seriousness of graduate instruction; staff credentials, such as advanced degrees held; the quantity of output; the international stature of people, publications, and centers; competitions; and attractiveness to employers, governments, and international agencies. PRCs also provide policy-relevant studies for various actors in the public, for-profit, and third sectors, thus defying many dependency critiques. In fact, PRCs often contribute considerably to policy and politics, even when their conventional academic performance is not so impressive.

PRCs are organizationally well positioned to attain their own goals. They typically select and pursue their tasks with considerable autonomy from any overarching, systemwide authority and with considerable freedom from the centrifugal pulls generated by conflict. This helps individual PRCs tailor their research undertakings, excluding alternatives where success would be less likely. Of course, financial dependence undermines the autonomous selection of tasks, but most funders match up with PRCs more than they control them, and they turn to those PRCs that appear capable of handling the task. PRCs sometimes broaden their scope by adding tasks—as by mixing research with service, consulting, or training—as they respond to market or societal needs. A more impressive breadth, including sectoral pluralism (i.e., both academic tasks and political perspectives), emerges from the accumulation of undertakings by specialized individual centers.

Accountability

The natural dynamics of these nonprofit organizations means that in attaining their own goals they satisfy another criterion often used to measure organizational success: accountability. PRCs earn high ratings by users. They serve their constituencies. Free from systemwide authority, individual PRCs are less autonomous from their own donors, contractors, or group affiliates, ranging from religious to partisan. Instead, PRCs are, by choice or necessity, very accountable to their own communities. As voluntary organizations within a pluralist system, PRCs usually do not view this accountability as antithetical to autonomy. Individual PRCs are not, after all, accountable to most societal interests. They are rarely accountable to hostile interests or authorities. Their accountability is narrow. But it is deep; PRCs serve their matched communities. In general, PRCs reshape the basic contours of accountability in Latin American social research.

When we include all PRC communities and the interests they represent, the breadth of accountability is impressive. It includes many who are dissatisfied with the public alternatives. Businesses, social movements, political parties, governments, and international agencies draw on information, analysis, and training not otherwise available or not available at the same high level. They find their abilities, power, or legitimacy enhanced. All this obviously gratifies very powerful interests. At the same time, however, PRCs serve many underprivileged groups as well. Nor should we overlook how well PRCs serve the researchers themselves if the public sector is either too politically restrictive or too small to accommodate them. The work conditions, productive possibilities, and rewards are superior in PRCs: researchers are allowed the leeway to pursue their own priorities, as when they mix academic research with social service or policy work.

Given the voluntary nature of support for PRCs, their success is identifiable in market terms. If PRCs were not accountable—if they did not perform well in the eyes of those capable of sustaining them—they would fail. Market tests are especially attractive gauges of performance when more objective data are lacking or limited or ambiguous in their meaning, as in so much educational evaluation. The ability of PRCs to survive, grow, proliferate, and flourish is striking. Their graduate programs attract good students and their research programs attract good scholars. PRCs also attract unprecedented voluntary financial support: international, private (domestic), and even governmental (from decentralized agencies handling discretionary funds much more than from encumbered ministerial budgets).

Impact on Higher Education

As they attain their goals and satisfy their constituencies, PRCs contribute to the higher education system. In the simplest terms, virtually all their academic achievements constitute contributions. Many enlarge on the activities of universities and other institutions. Other PRC activities are not found elsewhere in the system, or not at the same quality level, or not linked to the same social or political visions. Accordingly, PRCs add breadth academically, politically, and financially to Latin America's higher education systems and intellectual life. Most dramatic is their rescue of social research under repressive conditions. More common is their provision of the bulk or of a major share of the social research. Much of this is related to the failure of the rest of the system. But the quantitative and qualitative revolution in social research led by PRCs in a region where research and graduate education have not been well served should be cast in more positive terms than public failure alone. PRCs represent a huge private success, which adds greatly to Latin American higher education. In any case, PRCs add much that actual alternatives have not and that realistic alternatives probably could not, in the foreseeable future, given the weaknesses of the state, the economy, and the university.[2]

Another PRC contribution to the higher education system is the way they serve as models for universities. Of the two major alternatives to inadquate public enterprises—reform and privatization (Heath 1990)—PRCs have obviously represented mostly the latter. But they may also stimulate the former. Though PRCs do not shape the bulk of the systems, they do influence many leading pockets, precious points of excellence and reform. Affected places include URCs, leading faculties and departments, and other formal or informal units within universities. Influences include internationalization (reaching both within and beyond the Latin American region), ties to the business world and government, an interest in alternative funding, accountability and evaluation, norms of productivity and efficiency, and new methodologies; more generally, influences include a concern for research, both basic and applied.[3] That influence is political-economic as well as strictly academic.

PRCs thus pioneer many aspects of the new modernization agenda for Latin American higher education. A new wave of university reform increases the chances for PRCs to serve as models. PRCs escape many of the basic and valid criticisms of Latin American higher education (Winkler 1990). Sustained reform could of course undermine PRCs as alternatives to failing institutions, but it could also strengthen university-PRC interaction—and set PRCs within a much healthier higher education environment.

Impact Beyond Higher Education

PRCs are not isolated academic institutions. They do not pull intellectuals into ivory towers. On the contrary, their research concentrates on pressing concerns as PRCs prove accountable. The research is problem oriented. Much work has direct social or applied ends. If any adjective remains in question, it is *academic* more than *practical.* Further still, practicality is repeatedly infused with progressiveness. PRCs directly serve marginal populations, peasants, unions, cooperatives, small producers, and consumer, environmental, and other grassroots social groups operating largely in the third sector. In my view, most PRC service to the public sector, as well as to the relevant international agencies, is also progressive; certainly most of the governments in question are much more progressive than those that PRCs have not served.

PRC contributions to freedom are at least as noteworthy as their other contributions. Individuals have been protected from violence, repression, and exile. They have not simply retreated to safety, however. Many have heroically engaged danger and uncertainty. PRCs have been sanctuaries but also have been active opponents of authoritarian rule. They have fortified democratic resistance beyond their walls. And their contribution to democratization has continued with the advent of elected government. PRCs are instrumental in empowering various groups, encouraging, counseling, and arming their participation. They are providers of knowledge for a variety of organizations, strengthening the plurality and viability of civil society and horizontal ties among its parts. Like their accountability, their constituencies are extensive.

PRCs also present valuable information, advice, personnel, and contacts to governments forging democracy under trying socioeconomic circumstances. Yet they present similar help to the opposition forces found in society, often building the alternative store of data and ideas. PRCs have bolstered political moderation and a Western-oriented internationalism at the expense of political extremism. They probably also help effect a more positive view of pluralist, nonprofit sectors. A more neutral conclusion is that PRCs have without doubt promoted political change.[4]

Related Contexts

The PRC impact should be further appreciated in four major arenas of both policy and scholarly concern: international philanthropy, comparative higher education, the nonprofit sector, and pluralist sectors. PRCs outpace the typical performance in the first two arenas and fulfill many of the grand claims made by champions of the other two.

Regarding international philanthropy, in the postwar decades, foreign agencies poured unprecedented funds into projects for university development. Conventional wisdom highlights the unmet objectives (Dye i), but even a more charitable view acknowledges that, like many attempts at major policy reform, these attempts disappointed with their highly incomplete patterns of implementation (Levy forthcoming). The frustration was especially sharp in many areas where PRCs have since shone—the social sciences, research, administrative coherence, academic quality, and full-time staff.[5]

Both participants and outside observers usually consider grants to PRCs as successes. Few projects fail, and most avoid the bewildering mixes of exported model and entrenched tradition that characterize assistance for university development. Instead, donors are usually happy with what they have bought academically (quality, methodology, substantive orientation, innovation, institutional differentiation and managerial strength, internationalization) and politically (freedom, support for civil society, moderation, Western-oriented internationalism). And recipients are usually pleased with what they accomplish with their grants. In fact, quite unlike universities (Sutton 1986), PRCs often exceed donors', recipients', and observers' expectations regarding impact both within and beyond academia. An excellent illustration lies in the PRC contributions to democratization.[6] Insofar as much assistance for PRCs has been philanthropic, their successes support the claim that foundations can advance significant innovation, whether or not they usually do (Ylvisaker 1987: 371–74).

Positive answers thus emerge to the questions posed, in the introductory chapter, about international philanthropy. First, philanthropy has promoted major, innovative, and even imaginative change, though not of course radical anticapitalist change. Second, donors have cooperated with mutually matched partners more than they have imposed agendas, though they have steered them. Third, philanthropy has fostered political and academic pluralism and progressiveness, less by acting apolitically than by avoiding partisanship and supporting moderate democratic positions. Fourth, while philanthropy has done much for which democratic Latin American governments and the U.S. government should be thankful, it has at crucial times done so by going where government cannot or will not go, supporting alternatives to repressive host governments. Fifth, contrary to claims by many critics, philanthropy has had great public impact; critics may interpret the impact as adverse to the public interest, but I find the balance favoring the public good.

Such a positive evaluation of international philanthropy is still more remarkable for its contrast to prevailing tendencies in assessment of comparative higher education, especially for developing nations. Both common discourse and serious study (Clark and Neave 1992; Altbach 1991) speak mostly of disappointment. They speak of crises, problems, frustrated reforms, and deteriorating standards. How different is the vocabulary that characterizes PRCs. This characterization should, in turn, help modify generalizations about Latin American higher education.

PRCs also earn a positive assessment in the context of nonprofit sectors. Nonprofits face basic challenges regarding mission, finance, power, effectiveness, and governance (Simon 1980). PRCs assume and fulfill significant missions that are either neglected or poorly pursued elsewhere, notably in the public sector. PRCs attract enough finances to function and grow in various environments, while maintaining a reasonable degree of autonomy. Regarding power, they prove unexpectedly influential in both the state and society, if not in the public sector of higher education. Measures of effectiveness in research and other tasks lend some of the strongest evidence of success; this evidence is integrally tied to several factors, including successful governance: stable, coherent rule that produces accountability sufficient to please many important actors and thus to sustain growth. Whether that accountability is achieved along with pluralist governance depends on structural level (more at the sectoral than the institutional level). Overall, PRC endeavors and results furnish substantial evidence consistent with claims often made for nonprofit performance.

Finally, as PRCs are nonprofits that form a pluralist sector, their successes also contribute to a positive evaluation in the context of pluralism. Although this summary sticks to those claims strongly sustained by the evidence, other claims are also probably sustained.[7]

Great diversity, both academic and ideological, exists among PRCs. So does organizational adaptability and flexibility. PRCs are free to differ from one another in structure, commitment, approach, and orientation. A corollary is choice for actors, from researchers to consumers to donors. Another corollary is protection from unified, central control, whether from dictatorial repression or majority will. This protection in turn sustains tolerance for autonomy, freedom, dissent, and differing values and approaches. Furthermore—reaching into an area less explicit in most pluralist theory—narrow, focused authority structure and commitments promote an effectiveness and accountability that allows PRCs to dedicate themselves coherently to their own market rather than to disperse their efforts uncertainly toward broader, vaguer targets (Chubb and Moe 1988; Levy 1987; 270–71). Such pluralism is especially compelling as it fits the modernization model now dominant in the political-economic arena.

The Negative Side

Without contradicting the validity of these positive points, there are negative or troubling features. The idea is not to graft a neutral evaluative conclusion onto the mostly positive analysis developed throughout the book. Much of the negative side is a qualification of a success story. It is a substantial but not equal counterweight.

Nor is the idea to grade, or to denigrate, PRCs. The goal is understanding and realism, not blame. In fact, some shortcomings are counterparts to the very successes just discussed, more than faults of bad or misguided PRCs; some are results of external dynamics that conspire to limit PRCs. Still, these and other shortcomings are part of the total package. That package lends support for those who emphasize the complexity of assessments of organizational effectiveness (Kanter and Summers 1987) and, more explicitly thematic to our study, of privatization (Gormley 1991b; Levy 1986). Accordingly, the package helps us construct a mixed profile of identifiable patterns of nonprofit performance. The result is at once rewarding for knowledge and disappointing for polemical or simple bottom-line judgments.

The negative evaluation returns to the four criteria of (1) attaining goals, (2) accountability, (3) impact on the higher education system, and (4) impact beyond higher education (reversing the order of the last two). Although it does not return in parallel form to the four related contexts of international philanthropy, comparative higher education, nonprofits, and pluralism, it analyzes problems with the latter two and obviously removes some luster from identified accomplishments in all those arenas.

Attaining Goals

PRCs attain most of the goals they set for themselves and that others set for them, but the goals tend to be limited in significant ways.[8] Neither unimportant nor unworthy, they are substantially' less than the goals that higher education must meet. There are notable similarities to the mixed performance of Latin America's private universities, which avoid research and graduate education. Although PRCs engage in these areas, they do so in social studies, with little presence in natural sciences or other expensive fields. Like private universities, PRCs are scarce in poor regions, compared to public universities.[9] Overall, PRCs are specialist institutions that undertake few tasks within the gamut of higher education possibilities or even of research possibilities. Many devote their efforts to one or two major problems, or perhaps to one or two at a time, and only to the jobs they feel ready to handle.[10] The ideological and methodological range within given PRCs likewise tends to be small.

PRCs' tasks are usually feasible. This is not to belittle them. The critique that voluntary organizations succeed because they select tasks freely or bask in isolation is not fair here. Their agendas depend partly upon intense relations with other nonprofit as well as for-profit and public agencies, domestic and foreign, and upon their obligations to the donors. Nor are PRC tasks inherently easy; PRCs do a lot that the public university and other institutions cannot. But PRCs are more likely to undertake tasks they can handle, while public universities may assume broad and contradictory tasks as different groups or units within the institutions choose according to different values and interests; some push universities into tasks without any realistic assessment of feasibility. Extrauniversity interests, too, foist tasks upon the hapless universities, interests that may be driven more by political or social agendas than by feasibility considerations. In contrast, among PRCs internal consensus and hierarchy may guard against the selection of contradictory or infeasible tasks.[11] For their part, donors usually fund PRCs that are fit to manage the proposed activities; contractors have a self-interest in giving PRCs tasks they can handle. And as PRCs assume certain tasks, they may leave public universities with other, intractable ones—a common criticism of how the nonprofit choice leaves the public sector disadvantaged. In short, by both what the organizations choose for themselves and what their environments push on them, a selectivity bias adds to PRCs' comparative effectiveness.[12]

By sticking mostly with what is feasible for them, PRCs are less impressive in scope than in effectiveness. In fairness, some of the restrictiveness is imposed. Wary agencies, from public universities to repressive governments, deny PRCs certain desired activities (e.g., graduate education). Also important, however, are PRCs' limited abilities. PRCs cannot take on much more without risks to their own sense of community and coherence. Their narrow financial, physical, personnel, and academic bases are tangible constraints. In fact, finance is crucial to most limits; donors and contractors limit PRCs to certain programs, projects, and approaches, which has some negative effects on innovation and diversity. Simply in terms of the sums available, PRCs typically can undertake only certain missions. And the fragility of the financial base is a signal preoccupation. Although PRCs have proven more capable of attracting resources than one might have imagined, this fragility undermines wider goal attainment.

Accountability

Just as PRC success in attaining goals means service to sponsoring and targeted groups, so the goals' restricted scope means limits to that service. Accountability stretches only so far. A skeptical perspective on market tests emphasizes the relative ease of pleasing clients, much easier than pleasing the clients of failing public institutions, especially as the nonprofits assume only certain tasks. An analogy holds for the success of international philanthropy to nonprofits compared with official development assistance to larger public agencies.

Beyond the empirical limits of PRC accountability lie normative problems. The ensuing paragraphs focus on those concerning the public interest and equity.

An essential doubt about pluralist systems—and, one might add, nonprofit sectors—is whether they serve the public interest. Following the common pluralist pattern, the PRCs sector does not identify and pursue a given public interest; the public interest is, tacitly, whatever mix emerges from a marketplace of diverse pursuits, a marketplace that is especially evident as piecemeal contract work for "users" increasingly influences the research agenda. But attaintment of plural interests by PRCs does not guarantee attainment of broader higher education or societal interests. Fulfillment of a public interest depends on an invisible hand. These weaknesses fit Lowi's (1979) critique of pluralist dispersion and its lack of an adequately coordinating hand, as well as more recent critiques of "contracting out" and other forms of privatization. PRCs also fit Salamon's (1989b) critique of nonprofits' lack of accountability to broad, democratic authority. And they specifically fit critiques of U.S. think tanks as amoral, serving particular clients rather than the public interest (Orlans 1972: 18).

A particular concern is that society's underprivileged groups do not become integral parts of the pluralist or nonprofit mosaic (McConnell 1966; Dahl 1982: 40). Consider the role of PRCs' financial suppliers. Those that have money can contract with, sponsor, or even help create, a PRC sympathetic to their interests and concerns. Such links then facilitate substantial accountability. But what about those unable to finance a center? Granted, the equity issue is mixed for PRCs. Research often benefits society more than a particular interest; even advocates of high university tuition, on the grounds that individual students reap the rewards, usually favor public subsidization of research on the grounds that most research benefits are public. However, the case for public subsidization of research also stems from concern that privately sponsored research (prevalent at PRCs) could have more selfish and inequitable payoffs. Finally, while overlap with social action centers helps some PRCs enormously on the equity question, other PRCs may not score as high as their brethren elsewhere in the third sector.

A PRC balance sheet regarding equity in accountability should include the following considerations. On the positive side, major sponsors, notably foreign foundations, are institutionally rather disinterested and their philanthropy goes to groups in need—political and academic need as well as financial need. Other important sponsors are simultaneously clients, and are not the elite. And much PRC research is applied and mixed with social action in favor of groups traditionally underprivileged and further hurt by both repressive government and democratically managed austerity. Furthermore, PRCs increasingly work with democratic governments to deliver assistance to the poor. On the negative side, privileged groups have the most assured access through their sponsorship of "their" centers; PRC proliferation yields a rising percentage that are more oriented to meeting their sponsors' or clients' own interests than to meeting philanthropic interests. Relatedly, the financial trend moves PRCs away from philanthropy and toward contracts. The evidence suggests, then, that pluralism among PRCs does not inevitably mean inequitable access and service or the opposite. Instead, access and service are concerns that warrant ongoing evaluation.

Apart from whom or what nonprofit plural sectors exclude, normative concerns also involve whom or what they include. As nonprofits serve some, they injure others. For those on the right, most PRCs are objectionably on the left; for those on the radical left, most PRCs objectionably uphold the status quo; for those sympathetic to one political party (or no party), other party PRCs are antagonists. Those sympathetic to authoritarianism may disparage the PRC contribution to democracy, just as many democrats may disapprove of pluralist systems based on internally undemocratic organizations. And so on, for a range of PRCs that serve government, religious, business, or grassroots associations, interests, or values. Moreover, if most individual PRCs—like other nonprofit organizations—represent a rather narrow or specialized view or group, then the general public may oppose what they pursue; more commonly, the general public remains largely indifferent, while some are opposed.

Thus, beyond mere neglect, PRCs can actually inflict damage. As Dahl writes (1982: 31): "The problem of democratic pluralism is serious, however, precisely because independent organizations are highly desirable; and at the same time their independence allows them to do harm." Responses to harm range from counteraction—proscription, regulation, or the formation of opposing organizations—to toleration based on either a realistic resignation or an acceptance of diversity. Naturally, more powerful groups have more recourse to action and counteraction.

Finally, even for those represented by PRCs, democratic accountability is not assured. Instead, the internal governance process restricts political participation. PRCs tend to be hierarchical as well as homogeneous.

Impact Beyond Higher Education

Circumscribed accountability translates into limitations, already adequately established, on contributions beyond the higher education system. Although this study finds the PRC contribution is overwhelmingly positive, legitimate reservations also arise. For example, while questions persist about PRC responsiveness to international agendas, questions intensify about "hired gun" responsiveness to domestic contractors. One fair concluding statement is that PRCs contribute much beyond higher education, but that contribution is uneven and not always positive.

Impact on Higher Education

Problems with service beyond higher education also arise when service comes at the expense of higher education's own interests. PRCs serve some interests beyond academia better than some within it. This point holds despite PRCs' academic achievements.

For the higher education system, the narrowness of individual PRCs is but partly compensated for by the sectoral breadth resulting from the proliferation of diverse entities. That proliferation may work more for political and perhaps financial pluralism than for academic breadth. PRCs disappoint insofar as their specializations are not complementary pieces which, placed side by side, compose a viable academic system or a full social research system. While some forces work toward healthy interaction among these nonprofit centers, others work toward hyperproliferation. New ideas, tasks, topics, funds, and leaders routinely lead to the creation of new centers rather than to the strengthening of existing ones. One result is that academic excellence with breadth develops almost nowhere. Lacunae include disciplinary development, vibrant debate, and anonymous peer review by scholars holding different perspectives. Nor do we see much integrated training capacity or infrastructure that protects long-term, basic, and complex academic work from the short-term accountability of the PRC marketplace.

Consequently, the best PRCs are limited. Even an excellent PRC is an inadequate substitute for a good university, and even an excellent PRC sector is an inadequate substitute for a good university system.[13] For all the similarities found between Latin America's PRCs and U.S. think tanks, a crucial difference concerns the extent to which institutions form a part of, or the core of, a social research system.

Notwithstanding their contributions to system and societal pluralism, typical PRCs are narrow more than they are pluralistic. This characteristic has captured our attention mostly regarding political affiliation but also regarding finances, tasks, and goals. Diversity at the work site is exceptional. So is the kind of liberal discourse among conflicting philosophies and ideas that can enlighten and persuade both participants and listeners. Narrowness is not an accidental or incidental characteristic; it is intrinsic to most PRCs' internal functioning, order, coherence, and attractiveness and accountability to external actors. This narrowness is reinforced by internal hierarchy. Parallels with Latin America's private universities are again compelling. So are generalizations about how private nonprofit contributions to societal pluralism and democracy may emanate from institutions that are themselves rather narrow and undemocratic.

Additionally, the evaluation of pluralist sectors tends to emphasize the most important institutions. Here, that has meant the best-known PRCs, which tend to be the broadest as well as the ones that do the best research and that advance the highest level policy advice. In contrast, most "no name" institutions, which score lower on almost all gauges of academic quality, are narrower.[14] Whereas public sectors may be known by their average member, private nonprofit sectors are better known by their peaks.

It is almost always possible to challenge such criticisms of nonprofits' limited contributions by depicting the contributions as welcome additions: without them, the system would be only what the public sector delivers—a correspondingly smaller and narrower system. This evaluative approach has validity. It throws us into crucial but foggy "what if" issues. If PRCs did not exist, which of their activities would be undertaken elsewhere, and how well would they be done? Under authoritarian conditions, alternatives were weak; this remains largely so, but the picture today is more mixed and debatable. Alongside push factors, pull factors increasingly account for PRC growth, and these factors carry us beyond necessity alone to preferences and advantages for researchers, donors, and clients from all three sectors. It would be disingenuous to assert that a higher education system without PRCs would be a system without any of the contributions PRCs now make.[15] It is more reasonable to highlight where PRCs are positive models for the broader public system; yet the mixed conclusions on that score also include

PRCS' inability to transform the bulk of the higher education system, even in the area of social research.[16]

In any case, progress by PRCS while public universities suffer grave problems is partly self-limiting. To build a broader base of support, even PRC researchers depend on the academic profession. If it is not valued, not nourished and recreated, those in the PRCS can escape just so far. And it is hard to build broad political legitimacy when the student base is small. Without that legitimacy, financing is precarious.

Furthermore, as is typical in private-public considerations, the third sector's success may hurt the public sector in significant ways. The question of harm has already been considered regarding normative impacts beyond higher education.

Regarding substantive impacts on the higher education system, PRCS add to stratification. The previous chapter shows the effect of PRCS as models for mostly the university peaks, raising them higher above the mainstream. Also important is the gap between universities in general and leading PRCS. Stratification may mean a loss of public university prestige, talent, resources, and self-esteem. Complaints along these lines emerged about FLACSO back in the 1960s and were aggravated for the Argentine and other branches by the 1980s (Balán 1982: 217; Mollis i). Complaints abound in Brazil that Rio's PRCS undercut even the good universities of São Paulo, just as they abound where the public universities live in dire conditions, as in the Dominican Republic and, for years, in Chile (Miceli i; Sánchez M. i-2; CINDA 1986: 18–19).[17]

The evidence shows a mixture, in which PRCS prosper by several means: picking up what is no longer viable in public universities, adding undertakings previously not found in the system, and simply outcompeting universities in many areas. Whether *robbery* is an apt term depends a good deal on one's perspective and emphasis. Although I would not choose it, it is not a wild criticism.

Much again comes down to counterfactual speculation about where universities would be if PRCS were not prominent.[18] No one can be sure exactly what public universities would otherwise look like, but PRCS do attract resources that universities need. Much also depends on how universities respond to the challenges posed by agile and attractive PRCS. If PRCS stimulate university reform, they could simultaneously become more successful for that contribution and comparatively less attractive themselves.

In sum, an analysis of Latin America's nonprofit research organizations yields a classic profile of pluralist strengths and weaknesses. To take both seriously is to appreciate why a virtual standoff often exists between the pluralist school and its critics. Without revising pluralist theory, this analysis has used it to conceptualize a significant change in Latin America's state-society relations.[19] In the process, it has perhaps expanded the empirical base for literature on pluralism by region, field (research), and sector, all cross-nationally.

Policy Implications

Many factors account for the relative lack of a policy debate over PRCs.[20] None, however, justifies it. There should be increased reflection on how to make PRCs best serve academic as well as political, social, and economic ends. In that connection, the comparative weight, shape, and performance of PRCs and related institutions should be continually reassessed. At the same time, my view of the private, pluralist contours and roots of PRC performance—successes and limitations—argues against any single general policy formulation, a formulation that would be neither easy nor wise.

Evaluation of PRCs leaves difficult dilemmas for policymakers. Appreciation and applause are warranted, yet so are reservation and skepticism. For example, depending on time and place, PRCs help universities in some ways and hurt them in others. And because much of what is troubling about PRCs relates to their very nature as specialist, private organizations within a pluralist nonprofit sector and to their very strengths, policy aimed at remedying PRCs' problems while preserving their contributions is often elusive.[21] Choices between PRCs and universities may reflect classic policy choices between specialist, private institutions that appear to perform their tasks reliably well and generalist public institutions that appear more problem ridden. To push the nonprofit specialists to broaden themselves may be to jeopardize their efficiency, effectiveness, tranquility, cohesiveness, their match with domestic and foreign constituencies and supporters, and so forth. To bypass the specialists is to surrender major terrain that works in social science and policy research. But to settle in comfortably with the specialists is to accept many of the system's shortcomings. The central, difficult policy challenge is to address problems without destroying PRCs' compelling characteristics.[22]

A related policy implication stemming from the interwoven positive and negative aspects highlighted in this evaluation is that comprehensive policy reform is unlikely. One reason is the success of so many PRCs, combined with the strength of their constituencies. This involves self-interest. If it does well, gains support, and serves its ends, a PRC finds its niche. Its concerns may then concentrate on that niche. Meanwhile, external pressures on the system come from sources that likely treat aspects of the system, more than from centralized action aimed at comprehensive reform. Thus, while a debate may be expected on how to readjust the juxtaposition of PRC and university, and while some government initiatives are likely, individual PRCs and universities have already been working out their own agreements, as have individual researchers.[23]

A dynamic of pluralist systems composed of nonprofit specialists is that most decisions are made by individual institutions or actors. Thus, a PRC determines how to mix its academic research with other tasks, how much to bend to attract what resources, what influence to pursue at the expense of autonomy, how partisan to be, and so forth. Individuals within PRCs confront many of the same decisions—as well as others, such as whether to remain within an existing PRC or found another for greater specialism, greater personal leadership opportunities, or any other reason. Additionally, policy in this sort of market-oriented, pluralist system intertwined with the world beyond higher education is largely determined by decisions made, and events transpiring, outside the system per se.

All that still leaves room for consequential policymaking by actors who reach beyond a single PRC. This mostly relates to financiers. Many face trade-offs between PRCs and universities, just as they face trade-offs within the PRC sector itself (e.g., disciplinary development versus applied tasks). The relevant funders increasingly include domestic government as well as international philanthropy. Some systemic dilemmas are in fact most intense for governments, in that they have a direct obligation to their national higher education system and the public universities. International and indigenous philanthropy, and both foreign and indigenous contractors, have no comparable obligation. Yet leading donors such as Ford and SAREC are among the few actors that can affect the shape of Latin America's PRCs beyond a single nation. Nonetheless, no funder—domestic or foreign, private or public—basically governs the PRC sector. None basically fixes its policy, dictates its contributions, or addresses its major shortcomings.

These perspectives on policy allow a concluding response to the book's introductory question on whether PRCs should be promoted, left alone, regulated, or curbed. The ample success of PRCs argues against a need for general public policy to promote their growth or effectiveness. Such a policy could jeopardize their positive performance, based on pluralist dynamics with an emphasis on the private side. Nonetheless, more specific policies could promote a presence by PRCs where limitation has been the norm. Tasks might include increased graduate programs and basic research, though affected PRCs might then come to resemble public research centers more. To minimize risks and maximize impacts, it is crucial that most promotional policies target only certain PRCs and not the sector as a whole.

Targeted promotional policies like these go beyond a pure laissez-faire approach. Calls for government regulation or the curbing of PRCs would go much further. They could flow from the negative evaluation, including the deleterious effects of certain successes by PRCs on the broader system. Though these calls are increasingly heard regarding private university expansion, they have not surged regarding PRCs. For instance, few people push to incorporate PRCs under the general legislation on the higher education system. The reasons include the lack of debate over PRCs, an ideological rejection of state regulation, and favorable views of PRCs' overall performance along with a reticence to tamper with it. This is fortunate: this analysis of the essentially private, pluralist base of PRC performance suggests that such government regulation would indeed jeopardize success. On the other hand, unlike public funders, private funders cannot regulate PRCs. But they can curb them. A more appropriate conception of what they properly and typically do is influence through incentives; governments can do likewise.[24]

BUILDING PRIVATIZATION

However one evaluates it, or pursues policy in response to it, privatization is a major reality in Latin American higher education and society. A whole new area, research, is open to private nonprofit organizations, and these, in turn, bolster related nonprofits. This chapter's final sections assess the findings on privatization's extent and shape. They consecutively consider the qualitative privateness, quantitative expanse, persistence, and pluralism that characterize privatization. Supportive evidence outweighs reservations on each count.

Although privatization has most clearly referred to a large empirical shift in the quantitative balance of activity handled by nonprofit and public sectors, qualitative dimensions have also been important in our considerations. This is notoriously murkier terrain. If *privatization* sometimes carries connotations such as clean private-public distinctions or government-private separation, that has not marked the usage in this book.[25] Nevertheless, the findings show a strong privateness. Short of clear-cut separation from publicness, privateness ranks high within the context of third sectors generally—high enough to conclude that true privatization is at play.

For all their ambiguities, finance and governance both show substantial privateness. Most income for PRCs has been nongovernmental, despite rising government finance. Moreover, much of the government finance comes through contracts, often from decentralized entities rather than ministerial subsidies. Regarding governance, PRCs enjoy extraordinary autonomy from state control. It is unmatched in Latin American higher education. It is rare in comparative higher education. PRC-government cooperation notwithstanding, PRCs are truly nongovernment organizations. PRCs do not fit the civil law pattern of a state-oriented third sector where nonprofits resemble government institutions (Anheier and Seibel 1990b: 384).

Still, PRC service to the state, or more broadly to the public, raises doubts about privateness in function. Service includes contractual research; taking on some of the government's difficult responsibilities; lessening brain drain; attracting foreign funds; providing legitimacy, political ideas and change, policy suggestions, and technical aid. Sometimes the PRCs' researchers are recruited into high governmental positions. Nonprofits may serve the state in such ways while paradoxically undermining it in other ways, diminishing its stature and that of its public university. In any case, PRCs' service to the state has soared with the ascension of democratic regimes.

Indeed, PRC-state relations increasingly involve partnership. Additionally blurring private-public lines, the partnership destroys simplistic notions of unambiguous privatization: the third sector does not replace the public sector in zero-sum fashion. The blossoming partnership with democratic government analyzed in chapter 3 has been fleshed out with details on government finance, political alliances, relevant policy research, ties between PRCs and public universities, and so forth. This sort of partnership neither erases private-public concepts nor destroys realistic notions of privatization. Instead, it fashions a new shape in privatization involving a qual-ified private expansion. It makes nonprofit-state patterns consistent with those prevalent beyond Latin America. As Latin America's PRCs increasingly work with government and receive its funds, they become more—not less—typical nonprofits, at least judged by literature on developed nations (Kramer 1981).

For all this complexity, PRCs point to a shrinking state. They take on many functions once located in the public sector as well as new functions that the public sector either does not want to assume or cannot assume. PRCs are not simply antistate, but they are part of a historic abandonment of the concept of a central, development, benefactor state. Even public-nonprofit partnership patterns and nonprofit roles that represent mostly continuity in the U.S. context (Salamon 1990) may represent privatization in Europe or Latin America. Third-sector growth compatible with public growth is part of the story, but most of the privatization involves propor-tional expansion of the third sector. Alongside new state-society coopera-tion comes a substantial expansion of societal initiative in rejection of the state.

By comparison with once-dominant notions of modernization based overwhelmingly on the state and its public sector, viable notions must now involve three sectors, all heavily interrelated. Like many institutions in the third sector, PRCs get help from government but also from for-profit and other nonprofit institutions. They serve the state, but they also serve for-profit and other nonprofit institutions. No sector is fully private or fully public, but the overall development mix takes a major private step with the role played by nonprofits such as PRCs.

In a less tangible but related vein, PRCs play a role in reshaping the political culture regarding private action. They help make private action, including nonprofit private action, seem more legitimate, natural, and even desirable.[26] After all, PRCs successfully perform many important and visible tasks. This success reflects positively on private finance, international phi-lanthropy, market mechanisms, and nongovernment policymaking. The weight of privatization again goes beyond what numbers alone might sug-gest.

Quantitative Dimensions

In quantitative terms also, the evidence favors highlighting the privatiza-tion. Of course, most research, including some social research, remains in public universities and GRCs. And other tasks undertaken by PRCs are also undertaken by public organizations, though PRCs may proceed and perform differently. Then too, one could recite all the conceivably related tasks that PRCs do not undertake, especially those still handled by public institutions. Finally and crucially, variation by nation is large.

But few endeavors worldwide fall within just one sector nearly as naturally as zealous advocates often suppose. That said, one must be struck by how much PRCs displace public institutions, especially universities, in significant ways. Moreover, they charter and capture new terrain, where social research previously did not venture. The propelling forces for privatization through displacement on old turf and conquests of new turf are powerful. These forces are diverse, though they are susceptible to conceptualization in such categories as public failure, push and pull factors, and supply and demand. The extent of privatization can be appreciated by its presence in varied times, places, and circumstances: where social science is most advanced and least advanced, where economies stagnate and where they grow, where regimes are authoritarian and where they are democratic, and so forth. Flowering under varied conditions, PRCs assume many forms. As Vega (1989: 49) puts it for Central America, "the designation *privatization* is not a monolithic or rigid process." The privatization is, instead, multidimensional.

Two comparisons shed added light on the extent of privatization effected by PRCs. One involves privatization in foreign assistance. Compared to the funds aimed at Latin American university development earlier, funds received by PRCs are much more likely to be private. And contrasts regarding recipients prove more decisive than those regarding donors: although foreign assistance went disproportionally to private over public universities, most of the total funds went to the latter and institutional form was not nearly as determinative as it is in assistance to research centers, where privateness predominates.[27]

The second comparison involves private universities. Their growth and influence mark extraordinary privatization (Levy 1986), but PRCs extend this privatization. In terms of higher education's grand functions, what private universities do for teaching, PRCs do for research. More accurately, the one's privatization in mostly teaching and, to a lesser extent, research and service is paralleled by the other's privatization in mostly research and, to a lesser extent, service and graduate teaching.

The privatization in research involves a quieter revolution, despite its astonishing reach into broad social, political, and economic territory. University privatization came first and required bitter battles against public monopolies sustained by tradition, power, and even constitutional guarantees. Creation of private universities was a visible event, easily recognized by supporters and foes alike as a historic and permanent change. Creation of PRCs often initially appeared to be a marginal and temporary event, and it was quite unplanned. A key difference was the involvement at universities of the student body, along with teaching and professional training, which have long been the core of university activity and which dwarf research. Another factor was the greater religious involvement at universities, especially until the mid-1960s, an involvement that evoked fear and antagonism. Additionally, university privatization erupted when ideologies of state-led development were preeminent. But PRC growth increasingly fits a decline of those ideologies. If the rise of private universities evoked exaggerated concern and conflict, the rise of PRCs has aroused inadequate debate.

The private university-PRC comparison is also sustained in our earlier qualitative terms. PRCs are usually more private than private universities. This holds even though the universities score very high on privateness. Regarding finance, the conclusion is foggy, as increasing government funds for PRCs may offset the government subsidies that have gone to a minority of private universities; the main contrast in finance lies between dominant private sources of philanthrophy for PRCs versus tuition for private universities. Regarding governance, however, PRCs clearly outdistance private universities in privateness. They escape state regulations regarding matters ranging from fees to standardized curriculum to tutelage under public universities.

But whether more privatization stems from private universities or PRCs is not the main issue. One does not supplant the other. On the contrary, PRCs indirectly help private universities as they make the political culture and economy of higher education friendlier to private institutions and activities.[28] Whatever their effects on universities, PRCs add significant privatization to higher education and to society.

Together with private universities and the many other private service and advocacy organizations that have proliferated in recent decades, PRCs contribute greatly to building the nonprofit and for-profit privatization now rampant in Latin America. The juxtaposition of these sectoral trends, including the many mutually reinforcing interrelationships identified in earlier chapters, allows us to see PRCs as part of a massive and multifaceted regional privatization.[29] The conclusion is not that the third sector is more important or even as important as the public and for-profit sectors. Comparisons of that nature depend on the particular activity under consideration. And they lose meaning as intersectoral relations blossom. What is clear in our area of study and beyond is that three important, interrelated sectors are at work.

Persistence

Privatization is a persisting phenomenon. Of course, the future is not simply the present. The short time during which PRCs have been prominent shows pronounced twists and turns, including unforeseen ones. A near certainty is future uncertainty.

Accordingly, no one can be sure that PRCs will retain their present robustness. Many of the empirical limitations characteristic of PRCs mark vulnerabilities. So do the normatively controversial characteristics. Politically, individual PRCs face dangers from opposition forces or from an indifference that is linked to their limited power base in enrollments and professional training. Financially, PRCs suffer vulnerabilities stemming from political vulnerabilities. They show a fragility common for nonprofit organizations but exacerbated by their existence in economically poor and unstable environments and by their unusual reliance on philanthropy, foreign sources, and contracts rather than fees and state subsidies. Pullbacks by foreign foundations present an especially worrisome prospect. Academically, a sad historical reality is that structural breakthroughs for Latin American research often have terminated in decay rather than maturity (Schwartzman 1991). Today's inability to produce an intergenerationally self-sustaining base or a broadly viable academic profession and higher education system increases the risks of PRC isolation. Nor is there much solace for PRCs in the realization that much of this precariousness affects Latin American higher education generally. On the other hand, where university recovery proves feasible, PRCs may well shrink in relative size and importance.[30] Persistence need not mean predominance.

An additional perspective on precariousness could emphasize the continued fragility of PRCs despite the advent of democratic government, economic growth in some nations, and an established academic reputation. If PRCs looked surprisingly strong in hostile and pioneering environments, perhaps they look depressingly fragile for their inability to establish a secure and stable existence in more benign circumstances.[31]

But accumulated evidence has mostly highlighted a PRC ability to survive and sometimes flourish. Many have achieved a "remarkable operational stability" (Cariola 1994: 89). The natural dynamics of private nonprofit pluralist sectors suggest that some PRCs will die or transform and that the size and shape of the sector will change. This change will flow from the internal dynamics of PRCs and especially from their interactions with changing environments, including new policy initiatives. Nonetheless, the sector will likely remain strong.

To begin with, the demise of authoritarian regimes has not brought the PRC decline that most observers, including researchers themselves, had expected. For one thing, many factors (including university failures) that have contributed to PRCs' vitality are only partly or indirectly related to activity by the regime in power. For another, authoritarian regimes leave legacies that reinforce PRCs and other nonprofits. There is a fear of subsequent authoritarian rule. Argentines, Guatemalans, and most others familiar with their nation's political history cannot dismiss the possibility. PRCs have proven themselves safer places to be than universities, in such situations. Another legacy of authoritarian rule is the exposure (the initial exposure, for many) to nonprofit institutions, international ties, alternative financing, and so forth. More broadly, by the time authoritarian regimes fall, formidable allegiances and interests have established themselves around PRCs. Regime change has proven neither irrelevant nor crippling to PRCs; nor has change from initial to subsequent democratic governments. Instead, PRCs respond to all this change. They adapt with a dexterity quite equal to the enthusiastic claims made for nonprofit, pluralist sectors.[32]

Further, in regard to allegiances and interests, the pull factors introduced in chapter 3 have found potent elaboration in subsequent treatments of finances, politics, and academics. Researchers, donors, contractors, and other users perceive PRCs as comfortable, supportive, trustworthy, efficient, productive, and accountable. They need not see PRCs in general that way: reflecting common patterns of choice within plural systems, they see their "own" PRC that way. The attraction is strong. In contrast, there is proportionally less identification with one's "own" university, and the evaluative tone of the identification tends to be more mixed. Given an option, most of the relevant actors connected with PRCs continue to select PRCs over universities. Not given a PRC option, many others still spurn the university, even in Brazil (Miceli i), turning instead to government employment, international organizations, or emigration. Once a pluralist option has arisen and achieved the success the PRC has, a great amount of coercion, incompatible with democracy, might be necessary to close the option; less drastically, a policy to alter the incentive structure remains possible but faces formidable counterforces. The realization sets in that PRCs probably will continue to be important institutions within the newly important third sector.

Put another way, PRCs have a prominent future because they have been so successful. Whatever the points that compromise it, the success is considerable and it is decisive for many connected to it, who in turn nurture and protect it. As is often the case with critiques of pluralist nonprofit sectors, alternatives base themselves largely on counterfactual assumptions, such as how universities might benefit if PRCs receded. Even plausible assumptions may run up against the reality of interests and groups well served by the existing pluralist order.

Pluralism

The nonprofit privatization in question is markedly pluralist. Allowing for the nonpluralist nature of individual PRCs, pluralism triumphs in broader arenas. These include the PRC sector and its wider role in extending pluralism for both higher education and society in general.[33]

Of course, conclusions about higher education cannot be simply generalized to Latin American politics and society. The findings do not show that Latin America is pluralist rather than corporatist. They do not invalidate the lament that even the democracies are hierarchical, "delegated," suppressively centralized, and otherwise weak in pluralism and participation or in the way they touch peoples' lives (O'Donnell 1992; Gamarra 1993). But the findings showcase a more positive face of reality: pluralistic democratic dynamics. The findings are especially significant when considered as part of the broader nonprofit privatization that PRCs both represent and promote—a privatization generally ignored in the bleaker portrayals. Wherever one had been inclined to fix the pluralist-corporatist balance, the new evidence might modify the assessment. And the evidence obviously challenges the still vigorous claim that corporatism remains the accurate overall characterization.[34]

Interactions within the PRC sector typify pluralist systems. Most of all, organizations operate separately, interacting more with their own constituencies and donors than with each other. This does not rule out a coordination that might preferably be labeled cooperation, competition, or copying. PRCs sometimes work with one another on given tasks, just as they sometimes work with universities. Common donors, and constant efforts to attract them, help produce common agendas, as does work with similar constituencies. Linking also results from a flow of personnel among institutions as well as from shared experiences, including study abroad, government service, and repression. Norms of professions and disciplines play a role. So does the perception of success elsewhere and the optimism surrounding its emulation. Isomorphism springs from many sources. All such dynamics, however, come in bits and pieces. Central coordination is sparse; no single controlling authority or hand dictates the action systemwide. None structures the system. PRC forces are multiple, continually evolving, and largely market driven. As Martin Trow has repeatedly observed for pluralist systems in higher education, the question for government policymakers is less, What sort of system should we design? than What is going on there and how can we benefit from it and influence it?

The classic operationalization of pluralism and corporatism cited in chapter 1 (Schmitter 1974: 93–94) helps summarize the characteristic pluralism.[35] It applies to the PRC sector and its relation to the state and society. Once again, PRCs add to the enormous nonprofit contribution already made by private universities; though private universities fit the pluralist model much more than the corporatist model (Levy 1986: 323–28), PRCs incline still farther toward the pluralist side.

First, PRCs burst forth spontaneously or from private initiative. State cooperation is usually absent or secondary, though increasing; creation in opposition to the state is more common than in cooperation with it. Private universities, in contrast, usually needed explicit state approval to break public monopolies. Second, PRCs then proliferate freely. None receives a state grant of monopoly, none is forced, like many private universities, under the (at least temporary) authority of a public university, none is blocked by decrees halting private proliferation, like those in the 1970s for Peruvian and Brazilian private universities—even though PRCs show comparable hyperproliferation of low-quality private institutions. Third, PRCs compete in an open-ended system without centrally directed efforts at functional ties among institutions. Unlike private universities in some countries, they are not even formally incorporated into official coordinating boards, seminars, or data collection, and sometimes not even into voluntary associations.

Fourth, central regulation, limited enough for most private universities, hardly touches PRCS. Fifth, state subsidization and accompanying controls are also less common for PRCS than for private universities, and multiple funders are more common. Sixth, in relation to governments, PRCS are more autonomous than are private universities, which themselves enjoy ample autonomy; internal governance and leadership selection are usually free from government influence.

In sum, the greater privateness of PRCS than of even private universities fits pluralism and defies corporatism. On all these counts, for PRCS to match private universities, let alone to surpass them, means great approximation to the pluralist model.[36]

Fortification of this pluralist model marks a change in state-society relations. In fact, the state's own involvement with PRCS shows pluralist tendencies. This expresses itself in the lack of a more central or controlling state role. It further expresses itself where the state does act: funding through decentralized, competitive mechanisms or working with multiple, diverse private organizations. But of course pluralism takes fuller form when PRCS build up the nonstate sectors, interacting with and contributing to the growth and vibrancy of both for-profit and nonprofit institutions. Nonprofit private pluralism has even affected political culture, as well as structure and policy. The increased legitimacy of diversity, competition, markets, specialist institutions, and nonprofits marks an important evolution in both the academic and political-economic worlds. All in all, PRC and nonprofit pluralism alters the balance and interrelationships between public and private sectors.

SUMMARY

Once a scattered few, PRCS now either tower over universities in social research and related areas or do well alongside them. PRCS thrive not just because of push factors connected to public sector failures but, increasingly, also because of pull factors that make them attractive to researchers, donors, contractors, and clients. PRCS produce formidable innovations and contributions in myriad academic as well as political, social, and financial ways. They are remarkable successes, surpassing any reasonable expectations. Yet they also show patterned weaknesses and limitations—many that are typical for pluralist nonprofit sectors—leaving flaws in the higher education system and challenges for ongoing policy.

As befits nonprofit, pluralist privatization, no grand plan has guided PRCs' development. It has arisen unannounced, more as pragmatic reaction than proclaimed ideology. It has, in fact, often arisen in the face of a hostile state. But ascendent democratic neoliberalism is much friendlier to pluralism and privatization. Although they remain significant alternatives to the public sector, PRCs influence it and operate in partnership with it. More than ever, PRCs and other development-oriented nonprofits swim with the current. More than ever, they contribute to mainstream political-economic tendencies. Indeed, swimming with the stream involves vigorous work with all three sectors.

PRCs add substantially to nonprofit privatization. The effect is great on higher education, society, and the state. We have before us evidence of important activity in the third sector. The closing hope here is that this book has helped identify and conceptualize that activity and will help guide our understanding of its future evolution.

Appendixes

Notes

References

Index

A Interviews

Alcalde, Salvador. Chapingo, secretary general. Feb. 1989, Chapingo.

Aldana, Eduardo. Institute SER, former director. July 1991, Kuala Lumpur.

Altbach, Philip. SUNY-Buffalo, professor. Nov. 1990, telephone.

Araya, Manual. FLACSO-Costa Rica, director, international relations program. (1) Aug. 1988, San José; (2) Apr. 1991, Washington, D.C.

Arregui, Patricia de. GRADE, executive director. May 1989, Lima.

Balán, Jorge. CEDES, director. (1) May 1989, Buenos Aires; (2) Sept. 1992, Los Angeles.

Barnés, Dorotea. UNAM, director general, academic exchanges. Feb. 1989, Mexico City.

Barquín, Manuel. UNAM, general council. June 1987, Mexico City.

Basáñez, Miguel. CEOP, director. Feb. 1989, Mexico City.

Beltrán, Jesús. Autonomous University of Baja California, professor. May 1991, Albany.

Black, Joseph. Rockefeller Foundation, former head, Education for Development Program. Feb. 1988, telephone.

Briones, Guillermo. National University of Colombia, former dean. Apr. 1989, Santiago.

Brunner, José Joaquín. FLACSO-Chile, director. (1) Mar. 1989, Santiago; (2) Apr. 1989, Santiago.

Cano, Daniel. Ministry of Education and Culture, administrator. May 1989, Buenos Aires.

Cano Valle, Fernando. UNAM, director of medical faculty. Feb. 1989, Mexico City.

Carmichael, William. FF, director, Latin American program. Dec. 1987, New York.

Carvajal, Iván. National Council of Universities and Polytechnic Schools, secretary general. Feb. 1993, Bogotá.

Catterberg, Edgardo. Argentine Radical Party, pollster. May 1989, Buenos Aires.

Cavarozzi, Marcelo. CEDES, former director. May 1989, Buenos Aires.

Chaparro, Fernando. IDRC, regional coordinator for Latin America. Nov. 1990, New York.

Contreras, Manuel. UDAPSO, executive director. Feb. 1993, Bogotá.

Correa, Jorge. Universidad Diego Portales, dean of law school. Mar. 1989, Santiago.

Cosse, Gustavo. FLACSO-Argentina, director. May 1989, Buenos Aires.

Cotler, Julio. IEP, director. May 1989, Lima.

Cox, Stephen. FF, representative in Mexico and Central America. Feb. 1989, Mexico City.

Croxatto, Héctor. Catholic University of Chile, researcher. Mar. 1989, Santiago.

Cueto, Mario. GRADE, researcher. (1) May 1989, Lima; (2) Mar. 1991, New York.

Cuneo, Andrés. Institute of Legal Teaching and Research, president. Apr. 1989, telephone.

Davidson, Ralph. Rockefeller Foundation, former representative. Feb. 1988, telephone.

D'Etigny, Enrique. AHC, president. Mar. 1989, Santiago.

Díaz, Heliodoro. Chapingo, academic vice rector. Feb. 1989, Chapingo.

Dore, Carlos. CERESD, former researcher. (1) Oct. 1991, telephone; (2) Oct. 1991, telephone.

Drysdale, Robert. World Bank, researcher. Nov. 1988, telephone.

Dye, Richard. FF, former administrator. Nov. 1988, telephone.

Eisemon, Thomas. World Bank, researcher. (1) July 1991, Kuala Lumpur; (2) Nov. 1992, telephone.

Escala, Miguel. INTEC, dean, special programs. Feb. 1990, Santo Domingo.

Esteva, Luis. UNAM, director, engineering institute. Feb. 1989, Mexico City.

Estévez, Federico. ITAM, director, social science departments. (1) Dec. 1990, telephone; (2) Jan. 1991, telephone.

Estrada, Luis. UCR, director, graduate studies. Aug. 1988, San José.

Ettedgui de Betancourt, Corina. Technological University of the Center, academic vice rector. Jan. 1992, Caracas.

Facundo D., Angel. Pedagogical University of Colombia, professor. May 1991, Caracas.

Figueroa, Gonzalo. Institute of Legal Teaching and Research, executive secretary. Apr. 1989, Santiago.

Fischel, Astrid. UCR, researcher. (1) Aug. 1988, San José; (2) Apr. 1991, Washington, D.C.

Fruhling, Hugo. AHC, researcher. Apr. 1989, Santiago.

Fuente, Juan Ramón de la. UNAM, director, science institutes. Feb. 1989, Mexico City.

García Guadilla, Carmen. CENDES, professor. May 1991, Caracas.

García, Rolando. UBA, former dean, science faculty. Feb. 1989, Mexico City.

Garita, Luis. UCR, rector. Feb. 1993, Bogotá.

Garza, Beatriz. El Colegio, director, literature and linguistic studies center. Jan. 1989, Mexico City.

Geithner, Peter. FF, director Asia programs. Apr. 1991, telephone.

Godoy, Oscar. CEP, researcher. Apr. 1989, Santiago.

González, Ignacio. University of Concepción, former rector. Apr. 1989, Santiago.

Grannel, Elena. USB, former professor. Jan. 1992, Caracas.

Harrison, John. Rockefeller Foundation, former administrator. (1) Mar. 1988, telephone; (2) Oct. 1988, telephone.

Hernández, Alicia. El Colegio, director, history center. Jan. 1989, Mexico City.

Hidalgo, Cecilia. CECI, researcher. May 1989, Santiago.

Himes, James. FF, former director, International Division. Mar. 1988, telephone.

Ibarrola, María de. DIE, former director. June 1987, Mexico City.

Jiménez, Leobardo. Chapingo, director. June 1987, Chapingo.

Kelly de Escobar, Janet. IESA, director, research. Jan. 1992, Caracas.

Kent, Rollin. DIE, researcher. Nov. 1990, New York.

Kovacs, Karen. El Colegio, researcher. June 1987, Mexico City.

Krotsch, Carlos. UBA, director, social science graduate studies. Aug. 1990, Buenos Aires.

Larraín, Hernán. Andes foundation, administrator. Mar. 1989, Santiago.

Latorre, Ramón. CECI, researcher. June 1989, Santiago.

Lavados, Iván. CINDA, director general. (1) Mar. 1989, Santiago; (2) May 1989, Santiago.

Livingston, Duncan. AHC, former vice president. (1) Mar. 1989, Santiago; (2) May 1989, Santiago.

Lladser, María Teresa. AHC, former academic coordinator. (1)Apr. 1989, Santiago; (2) May 1989, Santiago; (3) June 1989, Santiago.

Llerena Quevedo, Rogelio. Catholic University of Peru, professor. May 1989, Lima.

Lomnitz, Larissa. UNAM, professor. (1) Apr. 1987, New York; (2) Feb. 1989, Mexico City.

Lungo, Mario. CSUCA, researcher. Aug. 1988, San José.

Macaya, Gabriel. UCR, professor. Aug. 1988, San José.

Machado de Sousa, Edson. Ministry of Science and Technology, deputy minister. July 1991, Kuala Lumpur.

Marrou, Estuardo. Universidad del Pacífico, rector. May 1989, Lima.

Meyer, Lorenzo. El Colegio, academic coordinator. June 1987, Mexico City.

Miceli, Sergio. IDESP, director. Nov. 1990, New York.

Miguel, José A. de. INTEC, director, Office of Professorial Development. Feb. 1990, Santo Domingo.

Molina, Fernando. Catholic University of Chile, former vice rector. Apr. 1989, Santiago.

Mollis, Marcela. FLACSO and UBA, researcher. Aug. 1990, Buenos Aires.

Morelos, José. El Colegio, director, demographic studies center. Jan. 1989, Mexico City.

Muga, Alfonso. Chile, education ministry, director of higher education. Dec. 1991, Albany.

Mundet, Eduardo. Ministry of Education and Culture, subminister for universities. Feb. 1993, Bogotá.

Muñoz, Humberto. UNAM, director, humanities institutes. Feb. 1989, Mexico City.

Muñoz, Oscar. CIEPLAN, researcher. Apr. 1989, Santiago.

Muñoz Izquierdo, Carlos. CEE, researcher. June 1987, Mexico City.

Nadal, Alejandro. El Colegio, director, science and technology project. Jan. 1989, Mexico City.

Navarro, Juan Carlos. IESA, professor. (1) Aug. 1991, Albany; (2) Jan. 1992, Caracas.

Ojeda, Mario. El Colegio, president. Feb. 1989, Mexico City.

Oliveira, Orlandia de. El Colegio, director, sociological studies center. Feb. 1989, Mexico City.

Ornelas, Carlos. U.S.-Mexico Council on Educational and Cultural Exchanges, executive director. Aug. 1988, Mexico City.

Orozco, Luis Enrique. Universidad de Los Andes, vice rector. Sept. 1994, Bogotá.

Padua, Jorge. El Colegio, researcher. Jan. 1989, Mexico City.

Pantojas, Emilio. SUNY-Albany, professor. Feb. 1992, Albany.

Pérez, Manuel Elías. Centro Médico Docente la Trinidad, director, research and education. Jan. 1992, Caracas.

Piñango, Ramón. IESA, academic director. Jan. 1992, Caracas.

Post, David. Pennsylvania State University, professor. Feb. 1991, telephone.

Puryear, Jeffrey. FF, representative, Andean region. May 1989, Lima.

Quezada, Tirsis. AVEDIS, former researcher. Feb. 1992, telephone.

Ratinoff, Luis. IDB, administrator. May 1987, Washington, D.C.

Reñero, Ignacio. UNAM, administrator. Feb. 1989, Mexico City.

Reséndiz, Daniel. UNAM, director, engineering faculty. Feb. 1989, Mexico City.

Reyna, José Luis. FLACSO-Mexico, former director. Feb. 1989, Mexico City.

Roces, Carlos. El Colegio, director, economic studies center. Jan. 1989, Mexico City.

Ronfeldt, David. RAND, researcher. Dec. 1991, telephone.

Sada, Pablo. CERPE, coordinator, graduate education. Jan. 1992, Caracas.

Sánchez M., Julio. INTEC, professor (1) Oct. 1991, Albany; (2) Nov. 1991, Albany; (3) June 1991, Albany.

Saurkhán, José. UNAM, coordinator, science institutes. June 1987, Mexico City.

Scherz, Luis. Independent scholar. Apr. 1989, Santiago.

Schiefelbein, Ernesto. World Bank, researcher. May 1989, Santiago.

Schmidt, Samuel. UNAM, director, general office of academic projects. June 1987, Mexico City.

Schwartzman, Simon. NUPES, director. (1) Mar. 1988, New Orleans; (2) Aug. 1990, Buenos Aires; (3) Sept. 1992, Los Angeles.

Segovia, Rafaél. El Colegio, academic coordinator. Feb. 1989, Mexico City.

Serrano, Mariana. IEPRI, researcher. Aug. 1990, Buenos Aires.

Serrano, Sol. CERC, researcher. May 1989, Santiago.

Silva, Jorge. El Colegio, director, African and Asian studies center. Jan. 1989, Mexico City.

Stavenhagen, Rodolfo. Mexican Academy of Human Rights, dircector. Feb. 1989, Mexico City.

Stitchkin, David. University of Concepción, former rector. Mar. 1989, Santiago.

Sutton, Frank. FF, former deputy vice president, international division. Jan. 1987, New York.

Székely, Gabriel. El Colegio, professor. Jan. 1989, Cuernavaca.

Tedesco, Juan Carlos. CRESALC, former director. Mar. 1989, Santiago.

Teitelboim, Claudio. CECI, director. Apr. 1989, Santiago.

Tierney, James. FF, former representative. Nov. 1988, telephone.

Torres, Blanca. El Colegio, director, international studies center. Jan. 1989, Mexico City.

Treviño, Javier. El Colegio, director, public administration program. Jan. 1989, Mexico City.

Tyler, Lewis. LASPAU, executive director. Feb. 1988, telephone.

Urquidi, Víctor. El Colegio, former president. (1) Jan. 1989, Mexico City; (2) Feb. 1989, Mexico City.

Vera, Manuel. IDB, former administrator. Nov. 1988, telephone.

Vessuri, Hebe. IVIC, head, science studies department. Jan. 1992, Caracas.

Vielle, Jean-Pierre. CREFAL, researcher. Feb. 1989, Mexico City.

Walker, Chuck. Bartolomé de la Casas Center of Andean Regional Studies, former researcher. Mar. 1991, telephone.

Wessman, James. SUNY-Albany, professor. Sept. 1991, Albany.

Wolf, Alfred. FF, program director for Latin America; IDB, program advisor to the president. Nov. 1988, Washington, D.C.

Zorrilla, Juan Fidel. CESU, researcher. Feb. 1989, Mexico City.

B Personal Correspondence

Albornoz, Orlando. Nov. 29, 1994, UCV, Venezuela.

Aldana, Eduardo. (1) Feb. 26, 1992; (2) Mar. 24, 1992; (3) Aug. 26, 1992. Instituto SER, Colombia.

Alvarez, Virgilio. (1) Feb. 6, 1993; (2) Feb. 6, 1993; (3) May 25, 1993. FLACSO-Brazil.

Arregui, Patricia de. Apr. 17, 1992. GRADE, Peru.

Balán, Jorge. Nov. 25, 1994. CEDES, Argentina.

Balvé, Beba. Apr. 16, 1991. CICSO, Argentina.

Bejarano, Javier. Nov. 26, 1990. Fundación Santillana, Colombia.

Brunner, José Joaquín. Mar. 1, 1993. FLACSO-Chile.

Buxedas, Martín. Mar. 26, 1991. CIEDUR, Uruguay.

Cerna, Manuel. Aug. 14, 1991. CIRD, Paraguay.

Cobo, Alex. Jan. 1983. FES, Colombia.

Cosse, Gustavo. Apr. 10, 1992. FLACSO-Argentina.

Cotler, Julio. Feb. 28, 1992. IEP, Peru.

Court, David. Apr. 3, 1991. Rockefeller Foundation, Africa.

Cruz, Anabel. (1) Oct. 28, 1991; (2) Feb. 21, 1992. ICD, Uruguay.

Cunha, Luiz Antonio. Jan. 10, 1992. Universidade Federal Fluminense, Brazil.

Escobar, Natalia. (1) Jan. 10, 1991; (2) Nov. 21, 1990; (3) Feb. 26, 1991. FEDESARROLLO, Colombia.

Gandásegui, Marco. May 2, 1991. CELA, Panama.

García Guadilla, Carmen. Jan. 11, 1991. CRESALC, Venezuela.

Garita, Luis. Jan. 11, 1991. University of Costa Rica.

Gerhart, John. Mar. 8, 1991. FF.

Gurgulino de Souza, Heitor. Jul. 26, 1991. United Nations University.

Ibarrola, María de. (1) Mar. 12, 1991; (2) May 17, 1992; (3) June 17, 1992.

Leis, Raúl. Apr. 2, 1991. CEASPA, Panama.

Lladser, María Teresa. (1) May 15, 1992; (2) Dec. 12, 1994. AHC and CIPMA, Chile.

Martínez, Astrid. Apr. 10, 1991. CRESET, Colombia.

Melián, María Mercedes. May 14, 1991. CEPEP, Paraguay.

Mollis, Marcela. (1) Feb. 22, 1991; (2) Nov. 9, 1991; (3) Apr. 10, 1992.

Moreno, Juan Carlos. Apr. 10, 1991. CDE, Paraguay.

Morgan, Hyacinth. Feb. 19, 1991. UNDP, U.S.

Navarro, Juan Carlos. Nov. 29, 1994. IESA, Venezuela.

Norori, María Teresa. Aug. 28, 1991. INIES, Nicharagua.

Ornelas, Carlos. Jan. 28, 1993. U.S.-Mexico Council on Educational and Cultural Exchanges.

Ortoll, Servando. Aug. 31, 1991. University of Colima, Mexico.

Palau, Tomás. June 26, 1991. BASE-IS, Paraguay.

Paniagua, Carlos. Aug. 25, 1988. University of Costa Rica.

Rojas, Elsa. Jan. 2, 1991. CCRP, Colombia.

Rubio, Luis. (1) Jan. 7, 1991; (2) Feb. 12, 1991. CIDAC, Mexico.

Schwartzman, Simon. (1) Sept. 1, 1987; (2) Feb. 18, 1991; (3) Mar. 7, 1991; (4) Oct. 19, 1991; (5) Jan. 26, 1993. NUPES, Brazil.

Serrano, Mariana. (1) Sept. 15, 1990; (2) Mar. 12, 1992. IEPRI, Colombia.

Silié, Rubén. Aug. 22, 1991. FLACSO-Dominican Republic.

Smith, James. Feb. 14, 1992. Independent researcher, U.S.

Unger, Kurt. Feb. 18, 1992. CIDE, Mexico.

Vessuri, Hebe. Mar. 1, 1993. IVIC, Venezuela.

Zaid, Gabriel. Feb. 26, 1991. Independent researcher, Mexico.

Zelaya, Raquel. Mar. 26, 1991. ASIES, Guatemala.

Notes

1. Breakthroughs

1. Universities remain far more important with regard to numbers—and therefore professional training, expenditures, and many political and sociological concerns—and within research itself, with regard to areas outside social research.

2. There are also NGDOS or nongovernmental development organizations. Most references to NGDOS do not encompass PRCs, but the exclusion appears arbitrary. It usually emerges de facto, not through explicit exclusion; in fact, PRCs are both "nongovernment" and "organizations." This work uses *nonprofit organization* as the encompassing term, thereby avoiding repeated jarring clashes with extant connotations of NGDOS, while still linking with a broad conceptual literature on those NGDOS.

3. The term *think tank* came into popular U.S. usage in the 1960s. Think tanks are institutions that allow for interactions between academic research and policy; however, other traits sometimes put forward as definitional need not be (e.g., multidisciplinarity or requisite minimum size). Dickson (1971: 27–28) includes nonprofit, and public institutions. He emphasizes the ill-defined nature of the term, noting that many small institutions find it flattering while many large ones find it demeaning. Rough synonyms include *policy research institutes* and *independent nonprofit research institutes* (Orlans 1972) and *advisory corporations*. J. Smith (1991) documents the massive U.S. think tank growth in recent years. Although PRC and think tank are largely overlapping terms, several factors promoted PRC for our thematic use. Among these were a desire to avoid the trendy phrase, especially one that might carry trivializing connotations on the academic side or that might otherwise understate the centers' importance beyond just politics. Moreover, the term PRC directs attention toward both the private-public dimension and to parallels to other research institutions.

4. Of course, the contrast is relative. There never have been only two sectors, even though dual- (or single-) sector analyses work for many contemporary activities. Furthermore, although few scholars explicitly deny the third sector's activities, elements of which appear in references to civil society, they rarely identify or analyze the sector. They obscure this sector by omission.

5. A reasonable case can be made for either term: *third sector* or *nonprofit sector*. Seibel and Anheier (1990: 7) push the former in introducing their pioneering comparative study. They see *nonprofit* as mostly a U.S. term and *third sector* as the more common term in Europe. In fact, both terms are amply used in their book and beyond, and *nonprofit* is more common than *third sector* in Latin America. I use the terms interchangeably. *Third sector* has special appeal in emphasizing relations with the other two

sectors, as *nonprofit* has when emphasizing sectoral characteristics or links to the pertinent literature (which uses *nonprofit* more than *third sector*). Here as elsewhere, nonprofit is the preferred term in references to organizations rather than sectors. Other labels for the sector include *voluntary* and *independent*. Gidron, Kramer, and Salamon (1992) also advocate *third sector* over *nonprofit* for their comparative usage.

6. Nonprofits may also be designated *fundaciones* (foundations). This designation may bring more preferential treatment than that gained simply by the status of civil association (AC), as in Colombia and Mexico. But *fundación* carries somewhat different meanings across nations. In Venezuela and Brazil it need not signify private; there and in Argentina it is more common than in Mexico. Other nonprofits may be *sociedades de profesionales*, as with Chile's socially committed professionals (A. Thompson 1992).

7. For documentation of both the lack and the rapid progress, a solid single-volume work is Powell (1987). Also from Yale University's pioneering PONPO is a large working paper series and a book series with the Oxford University Press. Many other academic centers have also sprouted (Independent Sector, n.d.). Meanwhile, Jossey-Bass has been an exceptionally active book publisher. The Association for Research on Nonprofit Organizations and Voluntary Action is the leading professional association.

8. Leading comparative volumes are Anheier and Seibel 1990c; McCarthy, Hodgkinson, Sumariwalla 1992; Gidron, Kramer, and Salamon 1992; James 1989). The pioneering journal, *Voluntas*, appeared in 1990. Its coeditors noted that restriction to articles that truly compare would yield "a very slim" publication (Anheier and Knapp 1990: 3). Yet the other major scholarly journal on nonprofits, the *Nonprofit and Voluntary Sector Quarterly*, is less comparative. We may simultaneously lament the truth of Lohmann's claim (1992: 2) that research on nonprofits bases itself on twentieth-century U.S. experience and take heart from fast-increasing exceptions. The International Society for Third-Sector Research was founded in 1992.

9. To the extent that PRCs in fact represent a wider Latin American pluralism, observers can decide if and how much either to discredit corporatist analyses or to downgrade them as dated in certain key respects. Additionally, some pluralist tendencies across sectors are mutually reinforcing, as exemplified by the growth of nonprofits interacting with municipalities (Reilly 1994).

10. As Gormley (1991a: 4) admonishes polemicists worldwide, privatization cannot be understood or evaluated without studies on a variety of private-public combinations as well as policy fields and nations. Although a few PRCs were once part of the public sector, many more illustrate other forms of privatization identified in the literature (Glade 1991; Gidron, Kramer, and Salamon 1992): a shrinking state, contracting out, private-public partnerships, deregulation, or movement from public toward hybrid organizations in terms of governance or finance. Above all, as with private universities, the PRCs show a privatization in which new activities emerge disproportionally in the private nonprofit sector and personnel and resources shift there from the public sector.

11. Other estimates for grassroots organizations in Latin America, Asia, and Africa exceed 100,000 (Fisher 1992: 70). And large growth appears even where it has been rather unheralded. With "very little publicity," Colombian NGOs have "multiplied" and "fortified" their legal standing (Lemos 1994). For national directories of Latin America's NGOs, see IAF (1990). Some nations are building centers to study as well promote the growing area of nonprofits and philanthropy (e.g., Mexican Center on Philanthropy).

12. I follow conventional usage in referring to institutional efforts to better humankind through sustained development, although this overlaps with alleviation of immedi-

ate suffering (Payton 1989: 30). Expansive usage would include public as well as private aid, in that foreign giving is voluntary giving (Levy 1991: 6–7), but I do not press that usage here.

13. For a classic history of U.S. foreign philanthropy, see Curti (1963); a major recent source is McCarthy (1984).

14. Levy (forthcoming) analyzes the massive public and private U.S. assistance aimed at Latin American universities, especially in the 1960s and early 1970s. It depicts that assistance as voluntary, selective, targeted efforts that still ran up against entrenched forms. Results have included failure, hybrids from the interaction of model and indigenous form, and pivotal influences upon the local balance of power in leading reforming pockets while the higher education system overall has shown discouragingly little change. In short, it depicts a complex pattern that shows more positive impact than conventional wisdom holds but more disappointment than that seen in international philanthropy's more focused efforts with PRCs.

15. For example, the populist and anticapitalist critique that Karl and Katz (1981: 248–56) note within the United States has a strong international counterpart, like Leninism's addition of an international dimension to Marxist critiques.

16. Ambiguity attaches to the use of terms like *scientific* and *technological research* and *science research (investigación científica)* because they may refer to only certain "hard" areas (e.g., physics) or they may refer to all research that claims to use scientific or systematic methods, including the social sciences. Even where analysts prefer to be inclusive, they may be stymied by the restrictiveness of citation indexes. The problem is not as severe when money (as opposed to number of projects or researchers) is the measuring unit, since hard research dominates even when social science is included.

17. Research is widely accepted as a necessary activity, although debate continues on how much and what kind Latin America should do, as well as where it should be housed. See, for example, the debate in *Interciencia* vol. 8, numbers 2 and 3, 1983. Critics often favor adaptation and application over what they call luxurious, costly, infeasible, or basic research, tied to foreign research interests but not society's needs (Fuenzalida 1973: 196–210; Fuenzalida 1984). Some argue that nonuniversity research is more appropriate.

18. Government overshadows university, as the 60 percent versus 25 percent figures show. The Chilean case is interesting because it is now labeled unique for the university's greater than 50 percent share, but that is down from 80 percent in 1985 (Schiefelbein 1992: 136). Research inside government institutions cries out for more study (Adler 1987).

19. Numerous works have recently documented the development of social science in individual Latin American nations, such as Brazil (Miceli 1989b), Chile (CPU 1983), and Mexico (Bolio 1990). Two regional studies attentive to institutional setting are CLACSO (1991) and SSRC (1991). We should emphasize the more inclusive concept of social research, with its policy and applied orientations alongside academic social science.

20. Alongside its half dozen universities that do significant research, Colombia has built about two dozen estimable research centers; almost half are private. Some broke off from the leading universities. Striking features of Colombia's PRCs include a major presence in exact sciences and in research for businesses. In Ecuador the absence of sustained, brutal military repression contributed to incredible growth in university size, and universities do some social research, largely within URCs. But several PRCs also account for a major percentage of the total presence. This is reflected in CLACSO data, especially if we count the FLACSO, which is growing in importance. Chapter 2 maps out how the size of the PRC sector depends on our definition of PRCs.

21. An inexact but indicative index of PRC strength lies in a nation's receipt of Ford grants. Venezuela has received just one grant for roughly every ten received by Peru. Although this ratio concerns various higher education institutions, a greater percentage of Peru's funds have been for PRCs; Venezuela's only large Ford grant was for IESA.

22. Reasonable qualifications pertain to most nations. For example, Guatemala outdistances most of its neighbors for having a more varied institutional fabric (Alvarez pc-3). Mexico has few classic PRCs but great weight in graduate research centers as well as borderline cases involving consulting or links to wider private institutions; chapter 2 sketches the Mexican case more fully. The Dominican Republic might approximate the third category because of CERESD at the UASD, but PRCs are more extensive. Similarly, some Bolivian universities have many social science professors, but productivity comes mostly from the PRCs, flanked by one fine URC in the Catholic university and two fine public research centers.

23. A council of science and technology is found in every Latin American nation, whereas only three existed in 1966, eight in 1972 (IDB 1985: 7–8). Much national research money is now theirs, not the university's; councils do give to universities, but they also give to other research settings, including many GRCs; PRCs get less, as councils give only a small percentage to social research. Overall, the councils are generally disappointing outside Brazil. Aside from other problems, two errors in the UNESCO European model relate to an overestimation of the degree of autonomy research achieves. One assumption was that the creation of an expanded supply of research would stimulate internal demand for it, an especially shaky assumption for dependent economies. A second assumption was that research decisions could be effectively taken outside the policymaking core surrounding the presidency; autonomy has more often meant impotence (Lavados i-2). In comparison, the pluralist PRC sector breaks new ground as it meets expanded demand and is not tied to a presidential core.

24. Chapter 2 maps the definitional area, but here I note that PRCs, engaged in academic research though not first-degree education, may be part of higher education—as may colleges that do teaching but not research; besides, some PRCs offer graduate teaching or various nondegree postsecondary teaching.

25. The Brunner and Barrios book concentrates on Argentina, Brazil, Chile, and Uruguay under military rule. It also deals with some topics beyond the scope of this book, such as the history of social science there. The CLACSO study is considered in chapter 2. Beyond surveys, the national analyses I have identified are A. Thompson (1994) on Argentina, Spalding (1991) on Peru, and Lladser (1988a) (and Raczynski, Vergara, and Vergara, 1993) on Chile. Further neglect shows in the chapters on Latin America in the four-volume encyclopedia on higher education (Clark and Neave 1992); a few cite PRCs as major institutions but then say no more, whereas others completely ignore PRCs even in nations where they are prominent.

26. Hellman (1990: 8) finds that the much larger literature on grassroots organizations suffers from an "intensely protective attitude" by researchers, but Carroll (1992: 152) finds that scholars do criticize these NGOs.

27. Two citations that provide multiple leads are World Bank (1987) and the literature review in Carroll (1992: 15–24).

28. For one review essay, see Jaksić (1985), and for further sources and delineation and analysis of the literature's limits and achievements see Levy (1986: 11–12, 360–61). The Ford Foundation has sponsored a novel comparative effort involving five nations. Revealingly, the authors work mostly at PRCs (Argentina, Chile) or URCs (Brazil, Colom-

bia, Mexico). Some parallels gaps exist in the separate literatures on nonprofits and higher education: neither, for example, has paid due attention to research institutions or to comparative analysis.

29. Among the foreign agencies, the Ford Foundation contemplates expansion and reorientation in its activities in Latin American higher education. More important in terms of funds available is the Inter-American Development Bank, with renewed concern for higher education as part of its broad initiatives in the social arena. The World Bank, hitherto largely absent in this arena, contemplates initiatives that could have a major impact and has recently turned attention to the question of where research is housed, as have others (Alvarez and Gómez 1994). Both banks have joined other private and public donors in discovering distinct attractions of working with nonprofit private organizations.

30. Spain boasts research in university departments and URCs but also in the state's High Council of Scientific Research and its constituent institutes (García Garrido 1992: 667). As it often does in higher education, Great Britain falls between the continental and U.S. patterns; in research it falls closer to the latter. In both nations, most higher education institutions historically have concentrated on teaching and later have incorporated research. GRCs and industry also play important roles. In both nations, graduate education occurs at the department level but with less priority in Great Britain than in the United States (Rothblatt 1990: 69; Henkel and Kogan 1993). Great Britain also has a number of think tanks, such as the Royal Institute of International Affairs, the Centre for Policy Studies, and the Adam Smith Institute, several of them linked to the conservative surge of the 1980s.

31. Baltic republics moved quickly against the Soviet-imposed structure of research academics. In East Central Europe, both universities and academies have lost ground and "public policy-oriented research is adapting new forms," some aided by international philanthropy and some housed in think tanks linked to political parties (Siegal and Yancey 1992: 26).

32. Geiger (1990b) estimates there were 2,140 URCs in 1985; the figure could be much higher with a more liberal definition. Some of these research centers have been called "bureaus of governmental research" for their linkage and service to particular agencies (Feller 1986: 73–80). Most major U.S. URCs relate to the university overall, whereas European URCs relate more to a given faculty or other unit (Ben-David 1971: 155).

2. Mapping the Center and Periphery

1. This reality faces students of U.S. PRCs as well; see, for example Orlans (1972) on nonprofit research institutes and Weaver (1989) on think tanks.

2. Obviously, this book cannot deal in depth with the totality of research institutions or of nonprofits; in the Latin American context, PRCs are an especially significant component of each.

3. Chile's VECTOR has also been viewed as an umbrella organization for constituent PRCs, and CIPMA and CENECA have been called "research confederations" (E. Fox 1980: 11–12).

4. Research centers are only one type of nonprofit created by for-profits. For example, U.S. businesses create charitable organizations (Hall 1989: 222).

5. More than some Latin American nations, Mexico labors under a popular concep-

tion that, even in research, "private" means of and for business; with that comes a disinclination to distinguish between nonprofit and for-profit (Rubio pc-2). Argentina is probably another example. Indeed, a reasonable generalization is that Latin Americans, like most people outside the Anglo-American world, lack a clear concept of private nonprofit activity—but that familiarity is increasing (A. Thompson 1992; Seibel and Anheier 1990: 7). Perhaps the idea of "private" as both for-profit and nonprofit has taken root in the Dominican Republic since the fall of dictator Trujillo (1961) spurred development of an extensive nonprofit sector.

6. The Foundation for Economics and Development illustrates how these trends intersect. The foundation is juridically freestanding but is linked to a business in the Dominican Republic; the foundation's key figure (who has a Ph.D. from the University of Chicago) is son of a major importer.

7. Ambiguity may linger, however. Though considered a separate institution, Hoover still lies within Stanford University's "framework of governance" and reports to the university's board (J. Smith 1991: 280). Stanford's board of trustees helped create the Stanford Research Institute in 1946 as a "wholly owned subsidiary" of the university; a 1970 separation agreement sold the institute to its directors, ended the university trustees' ownership, and gave the institute five years to shed the university's name. But the institute had substantial autonomy prior to the break, and personnel overlap continued after it (Dickson 1971: 204).

8. Mission (or function, task, or output) could also be considered, though that introduces notoriously ambiguous definitional terrain. Privateness could then refer to such matters as service and ties to nongovernment actors and organizations. PRCs' contributions to beliefs in private action as opposed to a dominant state would constitute further privateness in mission. We will find such privateness at PRCs but, also, increasing service and ties to government—epitomizing the inter-relationships between the nonprofit and public sectors.

9. Many of Brazil's "foundations," in research and other areas, are juridically ambiguous: public with lots of privateness or private with lots of publicness (Schwartzman pc-5). The Joaquim Nabuco Foundation, an organ of the educational ministry, enjoys its own juridical and administrative identity and academic autonomy; it concentrates on social research and cultural promotion to improve the quality of life in north and northeast Brazil. Created in 1980, with roots back to 1948 as a government institute, the foundation is similar in major ways to PRCs.

10. Thus Brunner and Barrios (1987) refer to "centros académicos independientes"; Fruhling (1985: 58–77) uses "private" in his title but "independent" in the heart of his analysis. Hall (1992) emphasizes the dependence of nonprofits in his broad treatment of the U.S. nonprofit sector.

11. Spalding (1991: 43, 48, 80, 93) finds economics the largest and strongest field among Peru's PRCs, followed by sociology. These PRCs also include an unusual amount of anthropology and history, however, and some Ford-sponsored PRCs deal with traditional Andean music. Urrutia (1994: 82) confirms that PRCs do a "large proportion" of Latin America's economic research. CLACSO's count deals only with social science, and its inclusion of large centers that are not PRCs, coupled with its exclusion of many of the smaller or less academic PRCs, elevates the disciplinary proportions within the social area. In any case, its personnel also specialize much more in sociology (24 percent) and economics (23 percent) than any other discipline: 6–7 percent each for political science (which, however, accounts for 14 percent of those with doctorates), history, and anthro-

pology; 2–4 percent each for law, administration, education, social communication/ journalism, philosophy, architecture/urban studies, demography, and social psychology; 1 percent each for agricultural sciences, engineering, and linguistics; and 10 percent other (Calderón and Provoste 1990: III-5).

12. Some of these Colombia PRCs focus on basic science, such as the CIF and the CIB in physics and biology, respectively. Others work more in applied areas, notably agriculture; alongside PRCs working on sugar and water, the most important is CENICAFE, on coffee. Money comes largely from business, but U.S., Japanese, and German sources and the Colombian government are also sources. The fact that half or more of the projects and funds from Colombia's science and technology council goes to research centers reflects the importance of PRCs as well as public centers in these fields (Aldana pc-1; Orozco I).

13. One could add short-term training, which partly overlaps the tasks mentioned. Brunner and Barrios (1987: 111–12, 170–79) provide a categorization by tasks.

14. Philanthropy has helped a few institutions to blend undergraduate education and research. A good example is the Dominican Republic's ISA, in agriculture. ISA displays several features in common with most PRCs: privateness, research prominence, and a low student-to-faculty ratio (314 to 44). Other features, not tied to the PRC definition, are foreign assistance (in this case, especially AID and Ford, followed by Kellogg); a lack of stable income sources; research that is dependent on available sources; and tasks built around problem areas. Nonetheless, the institution's "primary mission is undergraduate teaching" (Hansen, Antonini, and Strasma 1988: 9). Another agricultural example is EARTH, where Kellogg and especially AID have been the key funders.

15. Except for Costa Rica and to a lesser extent Nicaragua, Ford has not found many suitable Central American targets. But Honduras's Advisors for Development pursues varied tasks alongside research (e.g., on women). And the relatively greater role of AID over Ford further illustrates the lack of research weight in Honduras.

16. Those include the Center for Women's Advancement and Services and the Social Aid Foundation of Christian Churches. And recipient professional colleges such as the Medical College of Chile are also not PRCs. The Group of Twenty-four, which worked courageously for redemocratization, was mostly a professional lobby of lawyers, doctors, geographers, and others; the Human Rights Commission did little academic research, though it gathered facts on violations and published a monthly bulletin. The AHC had the only human rights program that did academic studies (Lladser pc-1).

17. The definitional borders of PRCs can thus be blurred on more than one end at a time. Both CISOR and Guatemala's AVANCSO mix research and social action, but despite strong ties to a grassroots nonprofit, AVANCSO retains the freestanding status that CISOR surrendered. And social action outstrips nonprofit research in the Eastern Caribbean, as research remains mostly in the university.

18. Other URCs emerge to protect academic oligarchs. In any case, the line between faculty and URC can also be vague. U.S. medical schools at universities often function like URCs (Geiger 1992).

19. We have more complete listings of GRCs than PRCs but still lack a study of GRCs (Roper and Silva 1983).

20. CINVESTAV is tied to the IPN in some ways, however. Because it is by law an auxiliary unit of the IPN, it could be a URC. Ambiguity and controversy have persisted regarding its relation with the IPN. The institutions share some professors and facilities, and the IPN's budget includes CINVESTAV's construction and electricity.

21. The IICA is a specialized agricultural institution of the inter-American system, including Canada, the United States, twelve Latin American nations, plus some smaller Caribbean ones. It receives considerable international money, as from the World Bank. Among the relevant sources on agricultural IRCs in Latin America are Cano Gallego (1981), CIAT (1990), and K. Thompson (1974).

22. The line between a national center and an IRC is not always firm. For example, CLEPI is generally considered a Chilean PRC, but it calls itself a Latin American organization with its "campus" *(sede)* in Santiago (Lladser 1986: 122). A different domestic-international mix arose in 1990 when an IRC took root within IDEA, then a public research center: the International Simón Bolívar Center of Scientific Cooperation, tied to UNESCO, engages in interchanges, research, and graduate education.

23. One different international look arises where foreign foundations open research affiliates in Latin American nations, such as the Naumann Foundation in Paraguay and the Santillana in Colombia. Another arises with centers tied to U.S. universities; a center on administrative justice at Florida International University has a branch in Costa Rica. Centers merely affiliated with foreign universities better meet the criteria of separate structures. CIAPA (N.d.), founded with help from the Costa Rican government and Tulane University, is a PRC affiliated with Tulane.

24. The UN University, created in 1975 and including five Latin American units, is really an IRC. It has no students in degree programs. Instead, it concentrates on research, training, and dissemination (Gurgulino de Souza pc).

25. Consistent with Collier's (1991) view of the research cycle and mix, this study takes an approach that is neither a single case study nor a comprehensive statistical sampling; instead, it aims for systematic qualitative comparisons and a nourishing contextualization.

26. Thompson places Argentina's "private academic centers" at 70, but "clearly academic think tanks" at about half that, whereas a less focused survey finds more than 200 "foundations" doing research, but most are outside the social fields and many are tied to larger institutions (A. Thompson 1992: A. Thompson 394; 1994: 13; FJMA 1980: 268–73).

27. One center on this list (but not on lists limited to classic PRCs) is the CPU, a relatively open forum. It holds numerous conferences, with a national or Latin American slant, on such matters as health, housing, and education. It also has an academic department of four people (as of 1986), though it more frequently hires academics as well as members of professional colleges (e.g., architecture) to do particular studies.

28. Listed elsewhere in the chapter are IESA, CEDICE, CERPE, CISOR, AVEDIS, and the Trinidad medical center, as well as institutions on the second periphery, especially public research centers. INVESP is a PRC doing research as well as training and consulting on international policy and politics (Navarro pc; Albornoz pc). Mexico's PRC count could be limited to a few, yet inclusion of centers focused on consulting or simple documentation, or linked with larger private organizations, or otherwise in the second periphery and beyond could push the nation's total private and public count over 500 (Zaid pc; Zaid 1992; CONACYT 1984).

29. Some current signs indicate an interest in cooperation with at least the Asian counterpart to CLACSO: ADIPA (1989) created in 1973, encompasses seventeen nations and more than 100 centers. Unlike CLACSO, it includes many industrial and scientific ones. Loose counterparts also exist in Africa, the Middle East, and Europe.

30. These points are not criticism of the survey, which is a pioneering contribution and logically deals with CLACSO's constituent centers. The problem here is that those centers do not otherwise represent a clearly delineated group, certainly not of PRCS.

31. CIDE has no undergraduates, though that will change; El Colegio has few (roughly 20 to 60, depending on the year). Each has roughly 200 graduate students and 100 faculty (ANUIES 1989). These data underscore their status as research institutions.

32. El Colegio's own officials maintain that their institution is legally public and point to its listing as a parastatal in the government's *Diario Oficial*. It gets the legal treatment of public institutions regarding its budget, patrimony, and workers, and although El Colegio is admittedly a Civil Association, an A.C. may be seen as public if its founders were public. Such points make ours a close call which could legitimately go either way; even in terms of juridical status, let alone broader criteria of identifying private and public, this is an institution most accurately regarded as mixed. Although our approach demands labeling as one or the other, this does not justify a dogmatic or otherwise exaggerated stance.

But the bible on higher education listings and data is ANUIES' annual statistical yearbook and, needing to place institutions dichotomously, ANUIES chose private for El Colegio, CIDE, and the provincial colegios. This is especially noteworthy since it lists as public other social research institutions, such as CINVESTAV, CIESAS, Chapingo, and even FLACSO (listed as private in other nations). Only starting in 1994 has ANUIES listed all the previously private ones as public, explicitly because El Colegio solicited that, whereas ANUIES officials still maintain that they are juridically private. (Whether or not it figures into El Colegio's motivation, a public listing may carry benefits in terms of legitimacy and finance.) In any event, the listing was private for virtually the entire period of time discussed in this book.

For ANUIES, the following points are determinative. Above all, A.C. indicates private legal status, supplemented by the fact that the institution has its own "juridical personality" and its "own patrimony." All this has been replicated even by the most recently created provincial colegios, such as the Mexiquense. Of course, there is great publicness and the institutions come under certain public laws because they receive the majority of their funds from government, but being like a public institution is not being a public institution. Additionally, El Colegio (though not the other institutions in question) earned a presidential decree in 1962, giving it formal status as a free school *(escuela libre)* and a key idea there is to allow private institutions (such as ITAM) the same autonomy that public universities enjoy to set their own programs. However close a CINVESTAV may come to El Colegio in such respects, it was designated as public when created and was not, like El Colegio, registered before a notary public.

33. For example, many perceive Brazil's Getúlio Vargas Foundation as public. It has a line in the government budget, and the government asserts that some rights flow from this. But FGV personnel are not civil servants, and the FGV is legally private. The listing of such institutions as private does not artificially inflate private weight in Latin America; more weight lies in public centers with considerable privateness. Moreover, the private designation grates less once the nonprofit concept is established; many who would balk at "private" would easily accept a "nonprofit" designation for places like El Colegio and the FGV.

34. Additionally, I am familiar with El Colegio from three separate visiting research

associateships: in academic year 1975–1976, the spring of 1987, and the winter of 1988–1989. Research for this project was conducted during the last two visits.

3. Growth: Public Failure and Beyond

1. The theoretical argument of this chapter, with fewer details on specific countries and institutions, appears in Levy (1995a).

2. Intranational analysis confirms the effects of repression. Among Chile's universities with the most social science, the Catholic universities of Chile and Valparaíso were initially less affected by the repression and therefore contributed less to the growth of PRCS. By 1976, the former succumbed but the latter made more cosmetic changes, sending social scientists to different units within the university itself; when faculty returned from scholarships abroad, the university likewise incorporated them. In contrast, the University of Chile contributed immediately to PRC growth, as the University of Concepción did to a lesser degree.

3. If the Argentine regime installed in 1976 had a retarding effect on nonprofit creation for some time, it was because state terror was so prevalent that it allowed little space even in the private sector (Fruhling 1985: 37–40).

4. Calderón and Provoste (1990: VII 2–3) use stability along with level of social science development to construct their four-part categorization of CLACSO's national membership. High on both measures are Brazil and Mexico, followed by Colombia and Venezuela. Low on both measures are Central America without Costa Rica, the Dominican Republic, Bolivia, and Paraguay. High on stability but not on development are Cuba and Costa Rica. High on development but not on stability are Argentina, Chile, Uruguay, and Ecuador. The most striking correlation to my four-part categorization (chapter 1) is the lack of stability in those nations where PRCS predominate.

5. Weisbrod (1977: 51) acknowledges that the public failure theory is "essentially static." The dynamic, empirical approach used in the present work avoids the triviality that the nonprofit sector is always the second choice if one defines the function broadly and the first choice if one defines it narrowly (as the niche the public sector did not fill).

6. Salamon (1990: 229) effectively criticizes public failure theory for its inability to explain government finance of nonprofit activities; beyond that, such finance need not require majority approval.

7. Aware of its bureaucracy's reputation and of confrontation between ministries and municipalities, the Colombian government asked the prestigious SER to assess the metro system. Returning to the Dominican case, CIEA receives contracts from the central bank and provides it with regular economic analysis. Each of the three full-time researchers previously worked with the bank, and the three other researchers likewise worked within the government; some also worked at the public university (CIEA 1991).

8. U.S. examples are RAND and the Urban Institute; the TDRI is an Asian example. The Thai government wanted a private agency, outside the bureaucracy, to do research on economic and social issues and to mobilize talent toward that end (Geithner i). Malaysia's ISIS is another example.

9. One could attribute nonprofit growth with democratization to the failure of authoritarian government, but that would be stretching theory in an exaggerated effort to save it.

10. Costa Rica and Brazil, where the university did not disintegrate, held up unusu-

ally well in Ford's funding. And some countries never had been important Ford recipients for higher education. In Mexico, El Colegio captured more than 25 percent of total Ford money, versus less than 10 percent for universities in 1972–1980 (Moller and Flores: 1985: 89), but this was not a sharp break from prior years. Chile was the extreme of the more common shift from university to PRC.

11. Outside the six nations that received most Ford Foundation money, the foundation's recipients in the 1970s were still mostly universities (ibid., 48). This suggests a leadership of large nations in the PRC surge. Demonstration effects also came from outside Latin America, especially from donor nations that were hosts to graduate students who already or subsequently worked at PRCs. Colombia's CRESET is modeled on the French economics observatory. The effects of academics from the developed world on the region's PRCs is pursued in chapter 6. Many demonstration effects provide evidence of internationalization through PRCs.

12. Given the universities' weaknesses, alternatives developed early, as with INCAP in Panama. By the late 1950s, universities implored governments to hand more tasks over to them (Tünnerman 1972: 101).

13. This politicization has encouraged the creation of "advanced centres," including PRCs, in India. These alternatives increase the chances of purposive research (Datta 1989: 82).

14. Standardization has also been blamed for research problems in European universities, but the rationale for separate research centers has less often been translated into action, as Mommsen (1987) shows for Germany. The Colombian case shows how standardization goes hand in hand with endogenism, so that even the largest public university, according to a sympathetic insider, fails to attract top researchers (Kalmanovitz 1989: 77).

15. Just the transient rise of U.S. student activism in the late 1960s led to fears of research migration from universities to PRCs, but basic university strengths ensured there would be nothing comparable to the Latin American dynamic (Orlans 1972: 141–49).

16. With this perspective, Venezuelans concerned about health policy created AVEDIS and CIES in the 1980s (Quezada i). Of course, this failure is not the university's alone.

17. My calculations, based on educational research centers listed by CRESALC (1984: 1–37), perhaps lend support for the view that URCs, like PRCs, are alternatives to the university mainstream. The mean for year of foundation for fourteen centers within faculties is 1963; for thirty-one URCs at public universities it is 1971–1972; for fourteen PRCs (excluding IRCs), also 1971–1972. Private URCs have an even later average, whereas IRCs appear about as early as faculty centers, and GRCs earliest of all.

18. CEDE is an interesting case because it broke from one of the Dominican Republic's few academically elite (private) universities, which usually escape the problems plaguing the nation's public university. The very creation of CEDE (and another, short-lived, URC) marked a retreat from INTEC's aspiration to integrate research with teaching in the mainstream (Sánchez M. i-1).

The powerful CEDE (which included about half of INTEC's founding members) clashed with the central administration and turned more to "committed" rather than "pure" research, and to grassroots action. It took specific political stands, denouncing repression in barrios and unions, while INTEC preferred an apolitical posture. Conflict also arose over whether the university had the authority to command CEDE to administer a high school. In one way or another, basic tensions always involved the URC's autonomy. Both sides finally agreed to a formal separation—to the creation of CEDEE. So difficult had the experience been, however, that "the ghost of CEDE" has dissuaded others from establishing another major URC.

19. Thus La Plata's physics institute, after notable achievements, suffered from problems such as budgetary insecurity, student preference for the greater employment opportunities in engineering, and the politicization brought by the Córdoba reform of 1918 (Pyenson 1978: 92–101).

20. Sometimes arrangements allow for cooperative faculty-center relations, as at the Autonomous University of Baja California (Beltrán i). In Ecuador, although the national university's URCs are inside faculties, Cuenca has one URC alongside its social science faculties—which do not control it, though they exert influence through broad university bodies (Carvajal I).

21. Rare units that do mix research and graduate education also have a hard time finding a niche. Such was the history of Chile's ESCOLATINA at the UCH, which achieved some successes but was weakened by severe university political conflict, personnel turnover, a need to offer remedial education, and problematic ties to the economics faculty (FF #61372, especially Peter Hakim to William Carmichael, Jan. 2, 1974; and Lovell Jarvis to Peter Bell, Jan. 2, 1974). Where special universitywide graduate units emerge, as at the University of Costa Rica, they also can be constrained by the mainstream—for example, by a lack of financial incentives (UCR 1987: 27, 60).

22. Policy-oriented URCs may encounter special difficulties in establishing a comfortable position. This is particularly pertinent because policy is a PRC priority. The UCR's CESPO, specializing in Costa Rican population studies, received support from AID, the UN, and Ford. Ford's grant became one of its most-studied (FF #68230, Richard Dye, Oct. 20, 1975, to William Carmichael; and John Nagel, Sept. 8, 1975, to Carmichael). Ford pushed the policy orientation hard, which it often does with PRCs, perhaps too hard for a URC. The university mainstream rebelled against interference as well as stratification. CESPO received insufficient university support, and its staff lacked university tenure. By 1975 the battered center was absorbed into various departments of the university.

23. These problems appear applicable to URCs beyond Latin America. The Ethiopian national university has failed with URCs such as the Institute of Science and Technology: teaching remains the university's major emphasis, the financial base is shaky, and repression has taken a toll (Wagaw 1990: 168–70).

24. Work produced at a prominent ITAM URC has led critics to denounce not just the work, the researcher, and the URC but also the ITAM in general, presenting difficulties for the many ITAM alumni in high government positions (Estévez i-2).

25. Earlier examples obviously come from those few private universities that achieved significance before the mid-1960s. These include Colombia's Andes, with CEDE linked to its economics faculty. As Ecuador and Chile show, however, most examples come from the earliest Catholic universities.

26. This point complements the chapter's earlier criticism of zero-sum approaches that fail to see how public and nonprofit sectors can grow together as social welfare expands. Just as one sector's activity need not mean another's inactivity, one sector's inactivity need not mean another's activity.

27. Such heightened demand also contributes to URC growth, particularly private URCs. The Center of International Studies (Centro de Estudios Internacionales 1990) at Colombia's Universidad de Los Andes explains its formation in 1983 as stemming from

the internationalization of the world and Colombia; in 1986 it moved from dependency on a faculty to direct accountability to the rectorate. Perhaps no nation surpasses Mexico for heightened demand. In leading cities, private URCs are notable responses; in some small cities lacking top private universities, state universities and technical institutes respond (de Ibarrola pc-1).

28. Even where public failure adequately explains the exodus, we must account for relocation to PRCs rather than to other institutions, not to mention relocation outside the national research world. Whatever attractiveness PRCs have in social research, they offer little opportunity in most other research areas.

29. I have not systematically explored whether change comes more through the creation of new organizations rather than the reform of extant ones (Hannan and Freeman 1984).

30. For example, where URCs incline toward long-term research, it is natural that clients would first choose PRCs that comfortably do short-term research. Georgetown cut loose its Center for Strategic International Studies, now a PRC, when an outside review found it lacked academic soundness (J. Smith 1991: 211–12).

31. In other cases, centers' organizers sought but did not secure government funds. IESA had hoped its emphasis on public administration would entice the Venezuelan government; its committee of business executives saved the day with private money and the cooperation of U.S. management schools (Gómez and Bustillo 1979: 83–84). By the same token, Chile's GIA formed as a PRC after it could no longer secure funds as part of a University of Wisconsin undertaking. If IESA is a government failure, GIA is an assistance failure; but such usage is too vague.

32. Funding supply is likewise a direct cause for the creation of many URCs, particularly at private universities. In Mexico since the 190s this has complemented heightened demand for contract research, connected with Mexico's economic opening. The Monterrey Technical Institute opened its Center of Strategic Mexican-U.S. Studies in 1990 with Hewlitt Foundation support; a key to ITAM's URC formation was the desire to tap available foreign funds and the government's desire to tap into World Bank and other funds via an active research center (Estévez i-1). Among public URCs formed partly to pull in available funds are some at the University of Costa Rica (Vega 1989: 42).

33. Chapter 5 analyzes the domestic political forces that provide a crucial supply of opportunities, and chapter 6 treats the international role in supplying ideas, forums and linkages. Most of all, chapter 4 emphasizes the financial supply.

34. Mexico's limited number of PRCs owes partly to the lack of political instability or great repression but, partly, also to the nation's reluctance until recently to accept foreign funds for educational or cultural affairs. In turn, knowing how sensitive the point is, and how readily such assistance (along with its recipients) is denounced, international philanthropy has often refrained from extending its hand (Basáñez i).

35. The trend was clear by the 1970s and 1980s—and for many endeavors (Carroll 1992: 1; B. Smith 1990: 5; Anheier 1990b: 363; Meyer 1993: 203). These endeavors include higher education and go beyond Latin America alone (Eisemon and Kourouma 1991: 22).

36. The concept of trust as an explanation for the use of nonprofit organizations usually refers to clients (Hansmann 1986a), but we can include donors and members. Donors may trust in PRCs and appreciate how grassroots groups trust more in nonprofits than government, as is the case with Central American PRCs (Vega 1989: 41). Researchers typically join PRCs where a feeling of mutual trust exists from past associa-

tions and political affinity (see chapter 5). Recognizing donors' trust in PRCs, political party and government officials sometimes set up PRC fronts for their operations (see chapter 4).

37. The FDN arose partly out of frustration with the politicization and bureaucratization of Peru's agrarian agencies but partly from the desire of professors at the Molina agricultural university to make more consultancy income than they could at the university, and partly from the opportunity (financial supply) offered by AID (Carroll 1992: 199).

38. In less dramatic times too, PRC expansion meant absorption of those trained in the social sciences by university faculties. Coombe's (1991: 41) depiction of African PRCs as "of but not in the university system," is pertinent. URCs (and GRCs) have also welcomed home returning scholarship holders, as at Costa Rica's UCR and Mexico's UNAM (Macaya i).

39. An example from the developed world is the Swedish Collegium for Advanced Studies in the Social Science, a nice setting for a research respite from ongoing university pressures that are not, however, disabling. Some African and Asian scholars resented international philanthropy's generosity with Latin American PRCs in situations less grave than theirs (Eisemon i-1); grounds for resentment arguably became firmer with Latin America's democratization.

40. In Mexico, for example, Víctor Urquidi, a long-time leader of El Colegio, founded the Tepoztlán center; and Pablo Latapí, once the CEE's leading figure, established his Prospective University (a PRC). Both men then used their reputations to seek foundation funds for their new centers.

41. The point holds even more where universities are strong and pay fairly well. Spain is a pertinent example. In Puerto Rico two major consulting centers head the list of those that pull professors from the main public university's planning school. Or professors continue at the university but with their major time commitment outside. The frequent political conflicts and policy changes that plague the university account for part of the shift in personnel, but so does a more than two-to-one salary differential (Pantojas i).

42. Another exceptional supply factor in Venezuela concerns international philanthropy. Even where PRCs might resemble their counterparts in other nations, they have trouble raising funds because of the external view that Venezuela could make do on its oil money (Sada i).

43. If push factors alone were determinative, URCs might cluster in the worst universities. Yet URCs stand out at places like Brazil's USP and UNICAMP (e.g., the centers on population and public policy). The University of Costa Rica's "Research City," geared to the needs of private enterprise, is a good example of public universities, like private universities, using URCs to compete for researchers who are free to choose. Throughout Latin America, URCs' competition includes GRCs that attract social scientists by offering more (better salaries, etc.) than what is available in faculties.

44. Guatemalan intellectuals who had fled into exile looked to URCs and increasingly to PRCs to make their return feasible, but then others opt for PRCs over universities to reap better rewards and security. Argentine scholars shifted to PRCs to escape the government repression of universities; they now choose PRCs that flourish as part of a broader process of democratic privatization (Vega 1989: 38–39; Mollis pc-3).

45. However much alternative theory based on partnership with government fits U.S. experience (Salamon 1990), it is only a partial substitute in assessing third-sector growth in Latin America; public failure theory cannot be abandoned.

46. Even a too-brief summary shows such patterns and tendencies over time as (1) early demand and supply by religious groups, (2) a huge push in the 1970s from military repression, complemented by supply from prior university development and international philanthropy, while under civilian regimes university failure and positive macropolitical factors counted for more, and (3) the surge in the 1980s due to broader privatization, increased government contracts, and researchers' preferences. For some broad parallels to Latin American nonprofits generally, see A. Thompson (1992); within a single nation, others have also seen fit to use a mix of nonprofit concepts to explain growth (Anheier 1990c).

4. Finances: Philanthropy, Diversification, and Control

1. Evidence from nations such as Paraguay and Peru (Duarte 1991: 18; Spalding 1991: 29) shows the sector receiving ample foreign funds, without quite the foundation presence found for PRCs. Human rights nonprofits join Latin America's PRCs on the high side, whereas environmental nonprofits that do little research exemplify nonprofits that rarely attract such funds (A. Thompson N.d.: 51).

2. At home, U.S. foundations concentrate heavily (though decreasingly) on education and, especially, higher education (Ylvisakar 1987: 370). With respect to the latter, research has occupied a special place. The same holds for foundations' international work. Yet the literature on that work hardly deals with research specifically. This is partly because, unlike PRC assistance, university assistance tended to mix research with teaching and overall institutional development.

3. A less detailed piece dealing with sources of funding and not with control is Levy 1995b.

4. Total figures vary widely, however. One estimate is that $50 million to $60 million of total Peruvian NGO annual income of $200 million goes to social studies (Andean Report 1992: 32). For Chilean PRCs, Puryear (1994:52) hazards an admittedly conservative estimate of $3 million a year, 1980–1988, up from $1 million, 1975–1980, whereas Lavados (1987: 129) reports closer to $7 million a year in the mid-1980s.

5. Argentina's CEDES counted on foreign contributions for 95 percent of its needs when the military was in power (Fruhling 1985: 68). Ecuador's PRCs likewise depend on international philanthropy (Carvajal i). Central America's CRIES (1991) relies heavily on the Dutch NOVIB.

6. Ford's total to Brazilian higher education exceeded $50 million from 1960 through the late 1980s, based on data from computer printouts prepared by the Ford Foundation archives. Miceli (N.d.) analyzes Ford funding of the PRCs.

7. The ICEG's president (Nicolás Ardito Barletta), who holds an economics Ph.D. from the University of Chicago, is a former World Bank vice president as well as former Panamanian president. The ICEG reportedly works with more than 240 economic policy institutes in ninety-four nations. Latin American centers include places like Peru's ILD though nonPRCs like ITAM also participate (Mutch 1992).

8. While the IDB keeps a data base on all its projects for universities, science and technology councils, and agricultural agencies, it has no counterpart for its comparatively small but numerous technical assistance and other projects that involve PRCs (Vera i). Computer printout from the UNDP's Management Information Services, searching under "Research Centers and Private Sector," shows just four projects in Latin America,

totaling under $700,000 (data provided in Morgan pc), yet many PRCs list the UNDP as a source. The World Bank is the main funder of African social science research, but that is mostly for universities; Ford, the IDRC, and SAREC lead for African PRCs.

9. Centers doing a lot of social action also draw on foundations but alongside a wider array of churches and European donors. For Chile, Brunner and Barrios (1987: 138) contrast the PRC list (Ford, SAREC, the IDRC, the French government) to a social action list featuring the three German party foundations, the Italian government, and the IAF. Many of CLACSO's social action nonprofits draw on European funds (Calderón and Provoste 1990: V-10). NGOs in appropriate technology receive major support from UN agencies after having received more from German, Dutch, and U.S. governments (Baquedano 1989: 115). Another higher education institution funded significantly though not mostly by foreign sources is the institute geared to private sector management (but little research). It often counts on foreign support to supplement tuition, as AID and the USIA do for INCAE.

10. Despite the difficulties, the IDB helped save economics from authoritarian regimes through its work with ECIEL (F. Herrera 1985: 317–21).

11. CSUCA is a revealing example. A union of universities in the 1960s, it got its heavy financing from AID. As CSUCA turned into more of a PRC, it moved toward support for special programs more than for a general budget. New funders included Ford, the IDRC, and West Germany's DAAD (FF #62109; Lungo i).

12. Ford directed just 35 percent of its Latin America giving to universities; GRCs took 16 percent; but 49 percent went to research centers and private organizations (Moller and Flores 1985: 31–33). Naturally, the 49 percent would go much higher were we to limit ourselves to Ford's social science money (47 percent of the foundation's total). For Rockefeller, see Bustamante 1985: 34).

13. Analysis of research centers on education shows how strong the tie is, in firm contrast with the public funding dominating GRCs, URCs, and university faculties. Private URCs are second in private income profiles. IRCs join PRCs as the leading recipients of multilateral funds:

14. Between 1983 and 1987, even as redemocratization was already bringing fresh

Income Sources of Research Centers

Type of Center (number)	Private		Multilateral		Government	
	total	part	total	part	total	part
PRCs (14)	5	8	0	9	0	3
Private URCs (9)	3	3	1	1	2	2
Public URCs (31)	0	7	0	3	24	5
Faculties (14)	2	2	0	1	9	1
GRCs (7)	0	0	0	2	5	2
IRCs (8)	0	3	5	3	0	1

Source: Based on CRESALC (1984: 1–37); also see Myers (1981): 27–28.

government funds in some nations, both the total amount and percentage of CLACSO centers' income coming from international sources increased (Calderón and Provoste 1990: VII-1). This reflects PRC growth within CLACSO and the continued heavy dependence of the most academically inclined PRCs on international philanthropy.

15. Ford has given, for example, to Brazilian GRCs, including the National Institute for Amazonian Research, the Brazilian Center of Physics Research, the Casa de Rui

Barbosa Foundation, and even to more direct agencies of government, such as CAPES and the agriculture ministry of São Paulo state. For health research, the majority of Latin America's funding is foreign, mostly from government and industry, while government accounts for almost all domestic funding (Carrasquilla 1994: 143).

16. This mixed pattern appears to have strong parallels in other regions. Indian URCS in social and natural sciences draw foreign assistance for projects while fulfilling most of their needs through domestic sources, including the Indian Council for Social Science Research, which, like its Brazilian and U.S. counterparts, gives to projects on merit-ocratic criteria, regardless of the institutional type housing them (Altbach i). The United States also shows a strong trend toward URCS that must attract project money, though obviously not much from foreign sources, while counting on their universities for infra-structure and salaries (Geiger 1989).

17. Government funds are from the science and technology council, the treasury ministry, the presidency, and other official units. Local private donors are the National Association of Industrialists and Nestles of Colombia. Multinationals are the World Health Organization, the FAO, ILPES, the IDB, the World Bank, and the UN University. U.S. foundations include Ford, Rockefeller, and Tinker. The list, in fact, was even longer both within these four categories and beyond (e.g., the Ecuadorean Development Bank and the University of Toronto). Also at the Andes, the CEI has recently drawn on the OAS, the UN, Ford, and Tinker, among others.

18. The new receptiveness stemmed from a generalized opening to U.S. contacts, a lack of alternatives in the midst of domestic economic tragedy, and a desire to add advanced programs. The CLACSO survey also suggests that its URCS increasingly seek international financing (Calderón and Provoste 1989: 76). This shift is a further reason to understand the PRC experience.

19. This tendency, alongside rising international funds for URCS, suggests increasing overlap in funding sources for PRCS and URCS.

20. The Getúlio Vargas branch in Rio has received roughly 10 percent of its income from private contributions, and the São Paulo branch has done well with its state's corporations (FGV 1977: 5). Foreign donations also greatly exceed what goes to typical higher education institutions in Brazil.

21. INCAE fits here like an IRC. AID has been vital. From 1972 to 1977, for example, $3.9 million promoted expansion and a full-time staff (AID #596044). The IDB, World Bank, the IAF, the IDRC, Ford, and Germany's Hanns Seidel Foundation have also helped. Other sources are tuition and corporate donations, including from multination-als such as Esso (INCAE N.d.).

22. Puerto Rico's consulting firms get the great majority of their money from gov-ernment contracts. Indeed, many former public officials move to jobs in these firms through a "revolving door." Whereas government earlier worked largely through big U.S. firms such as Arthur Little, which then subcontracted to Puerto Ricans, it now directly contracts more to proliferating Puerto Rican centers (Pantojas i).

23. Costa Rica shows how much PRC flavor FLACSO has when it is not a teaching center. Though government (including the Mexican government) helps cover adminis-trative costs of the regional secretariat, money from places like Ford funds projects (Araya i-2).

24. Reflecting regional changes in types of government and PRC work, the fraction of CLACSO centers receiving government funds jumped from one-quarter to nearly one-half between 1983 and 1987 alone (Calderón and Provoste 1990: III-14).

25. Whereas governments struggle to set just small parts of their university budget aside for distribution based on competitive performance among institutions, they give to PRCs mostly on a discretionary basis. At least in Chile and Brazil, project competition has gained respectability. U.S. think tanks have long competed intensely for government grants (Orlans 1972: 123–39). A sense of privatization even amid increased government funding also applies where recipient PRCs work on neoliberal projects, as in Central America (Vega 1989: 42).

26. These examples show that no simple line separates the researcher from the institution. Income for the former helps the latter subsist. PRC researchers gain income from several sources. Teaching at universities brings money from indigenous sources, usually public; Brazil is the leading case. Consultancies and project grants targeted at individuals bring money from sources private and public, domestic and foreign. In any case, these sources allow researchers to remain at PRCs. Seen the other way around, PRC work and affiliation often bring the credibility and contact that lead to personal financial opportunities.

27. The pertinence of councils as domestic support for PRCs is limited by a few factors, however. One is that councils are themselves major recipients of funds from the IDB, AID, the World Bank, the OAS, and other foreign agencies (Segal 1986b: 150). Others are the councils' concentration on science and technology and their greater financial support for GRCs and URCs than for PRCs.

28. Another obstacle in nations like Argentina is the perception of corruption, which makes it hard for PRCs to get a budget line, the way Bariloche and IDES did decades ago (Balán i-2).

29. ITAM, a leading private university in Mexico, is raising substantial funds to endow chairs for periods of three to four years, renewable, to retain top researchers at its URCs and thus limit the brain drain to business and government (Estévez i-2).

30. It is too soon to see how much Latin American corporations may create conservative foundations to support research. The Lilly Endowment and the Olin and Smith Richardson foundations are U.S. precedents (Nielsen 1985: 37–58).

31. Paralleling certain categorizations developed for the U.S. foundation world, Venezuela has all five foundation types: general and special purpose, corporation and family sponsored, and community interest (Spear 1972: 31).

32. A survey of these foundations shows 59 percent financed mostly through gifts and 41 percent mostly through their own income (FJMA 1980, 1983, 1989); the 41 percent is probably exaggerated, given that respondents came disproportionally from larger foundations. Also, the Illia and Fundeco foundations show that some engage heavily in political party activities.

33. Of course, the United States too has private organizations that must receive before they can give; the SSRC, though a "council," is an example for the funding of social research.

34. Such foundations, therefore, appear to go beyond the U.S. "company-sponsored foundation" (Ylvisaker 1987), which, though accountable to its corporation, aims its philanthropy beyond its own institution.

35. Argentina also has foundations connected to individual faculties of public universities, as with the foundation of the UBA's agronomy faculty, and to private graduate institutions, as with the School of Advanced Economics and Business.

36. FES also undertakes joint work with foreign donors, including the Ford and Kellogg foundations. Not tied to any family or corporate fortune, FES engages in about $4

million of philanthropic giving per year. It is one of Colombia's two nonprofit investment companies serving nonprofits (FES 1989: 2–5; Cobo pc; B. Smith 1985: 33–34).

37. Great variety characterizes pay at PRCs. Regular salaries are less common than at
U.S. think tanks (Orlans 1972: 74). At one extreme, for example, Chile's CIPMA (E. Fox
1980), there is no remuneration, just donated services. Short of that, dedicated individuals often accept very little pay. Other researchers depend fully on projects, whether
money goes through the PRC or directly to them. This is the fate of many assistants
outside the PRC's core and of nearly everyone at weak PRCs. But leading figures at top
PRCs usually draw a fixed salary, as do some others designated as permanent staff. Institutional salaries are the rule at PRCs that include graduate teaching and use indigenous
funds. A typical senior researcher salary at a SAREC-supported PRC without such teaching
was estimated at $1,000 a month in the mid-1980s (Spalding, Taylor, and Vilas 1985: II-
1). A prior estimate for researchers at IDRC-supported PRCs was $650–$2,500 (Tillett
1980: 35). Grants and consultancies increase the real income in most nations. Finally,
conditions are different at prosperous consulting centers and struggling centers tied to
grassroots work.

38. Peru illustrates how income at institutionally solid PRCs such as DESCO and Bartolomé, at about $500 a month, is far below First World standards yet far above the
perhaps $60 for some university professors or the $200 for full-timers at the national
university (Walker i; Spalding 1991: 23); the ILD can do still better. CIPAF (Dominican
Republic) shows how PRC researchers outearn their university counterparts yet fall short
of professional counterparts in business (León and Spalding 1992: 36). Taken along with
travel and other perks, rewards at top PRCs may allow a bourgeois life. On the other
hand, lack of health and other insurance benefits may make for a precarious life.

39. The breakdown for CLACSO funds is as follows: 44 percent from private philanthropy, usually international; 8 percent from self-generated income; 14 percent from
government donations or contracts; and 32 percent from the university or other academic institution of which the center is a part (Calderón and Provoste 1990: III-13). The
32 percent component would disintegrate for PRCs, and the 44 percent component
would be much larger.

40. A good example of such a PRC is Colombia's CRESET. Formed in 1984, it has
already received support from Ford, the World Bank, the IMF, the European Community, CEPAL, and several government agencies, including treasury and planning. Some of
this support is in the form of donations, while some is payment for services. Its economic analyses also allow it to earn money from sales of a monthly newsletter.

41. Early assistance might go to the national universities, but with proliferation the
vast majority of undistinguished public and private universities would be ignored (Levy
1991: 41–42). As marginal PRCs with little research multiply, foreign assistance becomes
much less commonplace.

42. Recognizing the problem, Peru's GRADE recently instituted new guidelines. The
center, not the individual, makes the proposals. It pays salaries based on experience and
responsibilities more than simply individual projects. It cross subsidizes to maintain
unprofitable tasks. In short, it consciously tries to build institutional coherence against
powerful market forces (Arregui pc). Peru's Bartolomé in Cusco also stresses cohesion
to the point of discouraging individuals from pursuing funds on their own (Walker i).

43. Even CLACSO data show the majority of grants to be by project. Institutional
grants account for only 21 percent, a figure replicated when we zero in on the three
largest grants per center to PRCs. Half the centers report program grants averaging under

1.5 years; 14 percent are for more than 2.5 years. Shorter term grants are still more typical if the focus is PRCS (Calderón and Provoste 1990: II-17–18, IV-7).

44. However noncontrolling it wants to be, SAREC periodically reviews the performance of the centers it funds and decides on whether, and how, to continue. While they are generally supportive, its evaluators do criticize and suggest—for example, that funding be equalized among the three SAREC-supported Uruguayan PRCS. Not all research efforts get high marks for academic quality. Some topics are seen as interesting but outside SAREC's priorities. In rare cases, doubts are raised about the political appropriateness of certain topics. The most vigorous criticism concerns underrepresentation of women in research and authority positions (Spalding, Stallings, and Weeks 1990: 92–93, 106; Spalding, Taylor, and Vilas 1985: I-5–6).

45. This tendency must be balanced against the specialization tendency noted above, wherein PRCS seek some comparative advantage. Whatever the exact balance, the tendencies are not limited to PRCS, though they appear especially powerful there. The region's URCS may also skew their agendas the more they seek international philanthropy. African and Asian research centers are also susceptible, as the growth of women's studies centers appears to suggest (Eisemon and Kourouma 1991: 21).

46. The Dominican case is illustrative. The most academic PRCS, Fondo and FLACSO, depend on international philanthropy. Such philanthropy also goes to PRCS with more applied social action, such as CIPAF and CEPAE (the latter also drawing from its ecumenical ties with North America.). In contrast, the consultancy PRCS, led by CIEA, depend mostly on domestic contracts. Among the foreign donors, Europeans have inclined toward social action and leftist political parties, priorities promoted by exiles from the Southern Cone who work in the donor agencies (Dore i-1).

47. PRCS receive in each of the five research funding patterns outlined by Becher (1985: 175–80): *proprietorship,* when organizations fund their own centers; *purchasing* through contracts; *prescription,* with strong guidelines; *persuasion,* based on milder indications of priorities; and a *pluralism* that tacitly accepts researchers' own priorities.

48. Although one can always presume that unwelcome findings could lead to diminished chances for further funding, this does not appear to be a major concern of researchers, at least those who have received funding. Besides, such fear could exaggerate the thoroughness or specificity of funders' evaluations.

49. Sometimes foundations cope with such partisan use by at least pursuing pluralism. Although the Luis Muñoz Marín Foundation is a political front more than a real PRC, Ford also has funded the proindependence Puerto Rican Institute of Civil Rights.

50. Also, foundations provided a minority of total income for El Colegio, even in the early decades, though their money was crucial for research development. By 1969 foreign funds fell to one-fifth of the budget, three-quarters of that from Ford and Rockefeller (FF #68229). That was still a major amount, especially for voluntary funds, and the juxtaposition with government will allow us to draw reasonable comparisons about the risks of dependence on foundation versus other income sources; the analysis will also allow comparison to more recent behavior by foundations.

51. I found only one exception in the archives, where El Colegio was compared to an adolescent who needs to show independence. At times, a foundation representative would criticize the policy of El Colegio's president of not publicizing its Ford grants; CIMMYT, too, would shy away from the media for fear of inspiring jealousy for its special status and criticism over its ties to foreign donors (Richard Magat memo to William Carmichael, May 20, 1974, FF archives).

52. Brazil is the major example where government picked up on work previously promoted by foundations, AID, etc., in both the natural and social sciences (Moreira and Copeland 1976: 139–45; Schwartzman 1979).

53. One type of evolution occurs when PRCS welcome domestic funding that covers some of their ongoing needs; the PRCS then use their international funds rather in the way good universities use "soft money"—for innovation. U.S. philanthropy was once crucial to El Colegio's existence, then to its academic credibility, and now to its high standing and international activity (Ojeda i; Garza i).

54. The major exceptions are PRCS with graduate programs. Several FLACSOS figure in here, buoyed also by FLACSO's intergovernmental status. The Mexican government has been a steadier provider than the Ecuadoran or Argentine governments (Reyna i). But budgetary instability hurts in Mexico too. El Colegio sometimes suffered greater instability in its government funding than in its foundation funding (FF #68229). *Colegios* modeled on El Colegio de México depend mostly on their state governments, which makes for major funding instability (Meyer i).

55. Critics of foundations concede such points, though they tend to minimize them in referring to the larger picture, in which foundations serve as the liberal arm of international capitalism (Arnove 1980a: 309).

56. Research on U.S. assistance to universities shows that foundations also allow more autonomy than do bilateral agencies (Levy: forthcoming). The basic conclusion regarding PRCS is consistent with at least two separate studies on centers specializing in education research; each finds greater autonomy, academic freedom, and criticism at foundation-supported than at government-supported institutions (Myers 1981: 22; Vielle 1975).

57. Lacking substantial studies of public research centers, one can only make broad, tentative comparisons. Those centers often enjoy much more autonomy than typically found in public agencies, but compared to philanthropy for PRCS, government funds less political pluralism and allows less leeway once funds are disbursed. Vessuri (1984: 216) draws a direct connection between IVIC's dependence on funds from the Venezuelan health ministry and its political identification with the government. El Colegio is a useful PRC example because it gets so much government funding and because we have examined the limited control exercised by foreign foundations. Not only does the government push for what it wants, (e.g., applied research), it pushes in directions others push it. In the 1980s the government did not take the academic side when worker demands of the sort that have so disrupted public universities threatened El Colegio (Urquidi i-2). Government is susceptible to widespread political pressure. More broadly, government initiatives to fund research and teaching separately stem largely from a desire for increased control over the research agenda, otherwise hidden from direct accountability (Clark 1993a).

58. There is a striking if loose similarity between discretionary government funding of nonprofits in the United States and other industrialized democracies: the evidence shows surprisingly little outside control coupled, however, with the uncertainties, emphasis on grantsmanship, and fragmentation of activities that short-term foundation funding means for PRCS (Kramer 1989: 226–31; Salamon 1987: 113–15). Many of the factors that minimize control by foreign donors over PRCS parallel points found in Kramer (1981: 160–62): mutual dependency, valued nonprofit provision, lack of information, a pay-for-services form, and plural sources. A more direct comparison can be made between Latin America's PRCS and its human rights organizations; also heavily dependent

on foreign philanthropy, the latter have apparently enjoyed considerable autonomy (Fruhling 1987: 35–37), with significant mutual matching.

59. Kohler (1991) appears to go further in shunning the concept of donor infringement on recipient autonomy by conceptualizing patronage as integral to scientific production rather than as a necessary problem. Still, his study parallels the present one in emphasizing complementarity while nonetheless identifying instances of patron-recipient ent conflict.

60. From another perspective, PRCs lead a return to reality when they do research barred or evaded elsewhere and deal with social and political issues suppressed in public debate. And the previous chapter shows how PRC growth increasingly fits rather than escapes mainstream trends.

61. This chapter's findings on control seem consistent with depictions of quantitative resource dependency as a constraint but one that leaves organizations the latitude to deal actively with their environment (Pfeffer and Salancik 1978).

5. Politics: The Two Faces of Pluralism

1. For example, the leading handbook's twenty-four chapters include little on macropolitics, especially beyond the issue of how nations divide tasks among the sectors. Like the massive working paper output of Yale's PONPO, the handbook shows greater representation by sociologists and economists than by political scientists in studies of the third sector. See also the comparative volume in PONPO's book series (James 1989; McCarthy, Hodgkinson, and Sumariwalla 1992). There is change, however (Salamon 1989b; Anheier and Seibel 1990b; Gidron, Kramer, and Salamon 1992), and many treatments of related matters, like public policy and intrainstitutional management. Micropolitics remains sparsely studied (Seibel and Anheier 1990: 9).

2. Leftist, authoritarian regimes are especially intolerant of private institutions, either nonprofit or for-profit, but they are also less common than rightist authoritarian regimes in Latin America.

3. Nonprofit insecurity is illustrated by the repression of church-affiliated NGOs, accused of Marxism, by governments in Singapore, Malaysia, and Indonesia (McCarthy N.d.: 2–6). Nonprofit pockets of freedom under authoritarianism are documented in Togo, Mali, Niger, and other African nations (Anheier 1989: 344).

4. Brutal political repression also comes from nongovernment groups. Peru's Shining Path bombed, murdered, issued "soft death threats," and forced cutbacks, suspensions, and relocations (M. Smith 1992).

5. In contrast, Mexican one-party rule has contributed to a feeling that once you are out of government you have little opportunity for opposition work with expectations of a return to power. This is one reason that those who leave El Colegio for government rarely return (Ojeda i).

6. The sciences at public research centers, which do not benefit from the sanctuary offered by private centers, may seek sanctuary partly through geographical isolation, whereas social science PRCs concentrate more in the capital city. Science examples include Venezuela's IVIC, which is placed out of easy reach of Caracas's students and faculty, and perhaps Argentina's Bariloche in the far south. Agricultural centers, such as Chapingo and Costa Rica's Turrialba, also follow the rationale, along with the more obvious rationale of the need for work sites in rural areas.

7. B. Smith (1990: 230, 247–49) is more inclined than I am to find the answer in nonprofits' lack of challenge to the system.

8. An extreme comes when intergovernmental IRCS transcend Latin America; UN IRCS are the main examples. The experience of regionbound intergovernmental IRCS appears more mixed. CEPAL, a Latin American organization, though UN affiliated, sacrificed its early spirit of free criticism as it turned increasingly into a representative of government in the late 1960s (Ansaldi and Calderón 1989: 10, 36).

9. The work PRCS do with unions and social service nonprofits touches on at least two significant political questions about nonprofits generally. One is how they contribute to the fabric of pluralist, civil society. The other concerns the power or influence of one nonprofit over other nonprofits.

10. Although some authorities show how grassroots nonprofits bolster local government (Fisher 1992: 70–89) and serve as contractors for a privatizing state, others argue that they make less policy impact than PRCS and advocacy nonprofits (Carroll 1992: 125).

11. Some URCS also promote democratization. IEPRI of Colombia's National University consults with government on pertinent policies, including human rights and pacification. Outside Latin America, as well, URCS cooperate with democratic government. U.S. think tanks such as the Urban Institute are examples paralleled by India's CPR in political science; the TDRI in Thailand is an influential PRC (Geithner i). Another comparative note: PRCS' cooperation with democratic government is not totally new for Latin America (e.g., Chile's CIDE in the 1960s).

12. The proliferation and institutionalization of PRCS, including on the right, increases the odds that some will serve future authoritarian governments.

13. A key difference between nations where PRCS dominate in social research and those where they share the scene with universities is shown by the initial recruitment in Argentina and Chile versus that in Brazil. Whereas the first two relied on PRCS, Brazil drew on universities (USP, UNICAMP, PUC-Rio), along with PRCS such as CEBRAP and the Getúlio Vargas Foundation. Because PRCS lack a mass base, they cannot of course match universities in staffing the bureaucratic rungs; the emphasis here is on high posts.

14. CIEPLAN illustrates a particular pluralist triumph. In economics, AID's university assistance project with the University of Chicago and the Catholic University of Chile helped produce the "Chicago boy" leadership for economic policy under the junta (Valdés 1989). Economics looked nonplural at government and university sites. But CIEPLAN's activity upheld pluralism in economic thought and, with the return of democracy, showed how strong alternative development had been. Elsewhere, too, the flow of centrists and moderates into government undermines the critique that internationally sponsored scholarships targeted conservative people, fields, and institutions (Arnove 1980b). In fact, foundations strained for diversity in training (R. Hellman 1988). They simply did not control which former trainees would then have access to government.

15. These are familiar patterns at U.S. think tanks. Former officials in Latin America have sometimes sought advice at places like RAND for promoting opposition PRCS (Ronfeldt i). Think tanks thus become indispensable for aspirants to office. As A. Thompson (1994: 3) remarks on Argentina: "Any politician or bureaucrat with ambition, any high-level policymaker, counts on a 'think tank' to provide ideas, help him formulate proposals, connect him with international thinking, and help him with data and information for political debate." In this sense, the centers can become more like political foundations than academic institutions.

16. Although the ILD had consulted for both the Belaúnde and García administra-

tions, the election of Fujimori in 1990 introduced a strikingly visible PRC-government connection; most affiliated PRC talent had gathered around the candidacy of novelist Mario Vargas Llosa. ILD head Hernando de Soto would be a peerless help to President Fujimori, providing ideas, legitimacy, and access to powerful international agencies and to Washington's Republican administration, and gaining affirmation that Peru was truly trying to end production of illegal drugs. Peru's ambassador to the United States and its minister of economics were associated with the ILD. Jealousy and resentment ran strong among others in the government, however, and in 1991 these people prevailed on Fujimori to back away from the major policy he had publicly supported on de Soto's advice. De Soto retreated to less institutionalized advice. The tight, personal ILD-government association ended (*Caretas* 1991; Brooke 1990; Cueto i-2).

17. Petras's account is fundamentally correct about the leftist decline, but in my view it is faulty on several grounds: its implications about the motivations of PRC members are unfairly derogatory; it skips too facilely over PRCs' antiauthoritarian courage and contribution; it greatly understates the efforts made in research, outreach, and political activity aimed at helping the poor; it ignores the heightened academic quality of work at PRCs, as it romanticizes the organic intellectuals; and it confuses the Southern Cone with all Latin America in failing to take into account both the continuation and the partially changing leftist intellectual activity in public universities and in other arenas (e.g., some print media); and it fails to account for international forces.

18. Depending upon nation, it is difficult to assess how much a positive ideology that boosts nonprofits has taken hold. In Peru there is basic acceptance of nonprofits as a reality, a necessity (Cueto i-1; Post i). Many question how much the state will ever recover; moreover, its priority should then be direct service to the poor rather than rebuilding a public higher education system. Some who still consider themselves social-ists regard the Peruvian state as deeply hierarchical, corrupt, and nepotistic; they there-fore grudgingly accept nonprofits as an alternative (Walker i).

19. Puryear (1994) provides an illustrative case. Insightful Chilean scholars describe a change from their prior intellectual role of sharpening ideological and political differ-ences to one of promoting social, psychological, and ultimately political reconciliation. An example of leftist moderation achieved through think tanks was the acceptance that those who had been sympathetic to the military were not necessarily fascists and that many citizens opposed the military on practical more than ideological grounds. Despite considerable reluctance by party leaders, such views helped move the opposition away from its faltering mobilization strategy to a more moderate, nuanced, and successful approach. One constant, however, has been intellectuals' involvement in politics.

20. How PRCs compare to other nonprofits and their related social movements is unclear. J. Hellman (1990: 7–8) finds these often to be anti-Marxist, opposed to class approaches to change, and even antileftist. But B. Smith (1990: 280) finds them often enough on the left to cause problems with their international donors. By contrast, I have found PRCs usually compatible with their donors; of course, this apparent differ-ence between sets of nonprofits might relate in part to differences between sets of do-nors. Díaz-Albertini (1990: 15) reports a pointed distance between NGOs and political parties, including those on the left.

21. The decline of a national left sometimes played a major role; this occurred with CERESD, "the voice of the Dominican Republic's intellectual left," a URC unreceptive to Ford funds (Dore i-2).

22. Intergovernmental IRCs also show some intermediate traits. Although radicalism

is limited, a statist ideology of planning has contrasted with thinking at mainstream PRCs (Calderón and Provoste 1990: V-3).

23. In Peru, not only the Shining Path but also some less radical groups denounce PRCs and other nonprofits as counterrevolutionary, as being tied to imperialism and a regressive state ("Los ONGS" 1992). To draw another comparison, the ideological gap between PRCs and universities finds some parallel between public research centers and universities. This further demonstrates a similarity between PRCs and public research centers. A Mexican example involves the Chapingo center versus agricultural universities. Venezuela's IVIC is likewise alternately denounced by the UCV as too cozy with government or too aloof from issues of change that the UCV champions (Vessuri 1984: 213–14).

24. By comparison, the UN-affiliated CEPAL is far larger and heterogeneous, with PREALC in between, and they lack the uniform profile (and quality) of the more classic PRC (CIEPLAN).

25. The PDC side also includes CIEPLAN, CED, the Chilean Institute of Humanistic Studies, and ILADES, while the renovating left also includes FLACSO, SUR, and PET.

26. Related to the *uso combinado* mentioned in the previous chapter, suspicion runs deep in Peru, Costa Rica, and other countries that parties create "PRCs" to attract international philanthropy, whose donations they then recycle to party activities.

27. Similarly, Forum was more a loose association than a PRC when it used Ebert's funds to bring together Dominican communists, centrists, businessmen, and others in the late 1970s to discuss policy issues. Even then, many saw an effort to bolster the party in power (Dore i-2).

28. In Mexico, for example, despite the lack of the vibrant interparty competition that sets the pluralist pattern in many other Latin American (and European) nations, observers know the political orientation behind even the intellectually leading periodicals and book publishing houses. The nation's main sociology journal, *Revista Mexicana de Sociología*, is published by a URC (Institute of Social Research) with a marked political position rather than by a politically diverse national professional association. In 1991, *Este País* proclaimed itself a pioneer among Mexican magazines for its commitment to present a plurality of political views.

29. Kanter (1977) stresses the importance of trust and homogeneity in recruitment into for-profit organizations.

30. A leading example of Ford's efforts to promote pluralism in the university sector concerned the University of Chile and the Catholic University of Chile. Such balancing was tricky but less so than efforts to insist on pluralism within institutions. ESCOLATINA, in the University of Chile, was seen as probably the only graduate research center in economics that mixed the two leading tendencies of Marxism and neoclassicism (Peter Hakim to William Carmichael, Jan. 2, 1974, in FF #61372). Chilean diversity was based on balances of power more than on a commitment to pluralism per se (Puryear 1983: 3).

31. One exception occurred when Ford pushed Foro to add Dominican leftists, including a prominent communist. This Foro did not do, probably could not do, and Ford's funding dried up. Ford's motivation could have been a pluralist conviction or a bid to shore up its image in the face of leftist charges that it was an agent of the U.S. government and the CIA, dealing in intellectual terrorism.

32. Consider the effects in terms of the donor's political effectiveness. Grants to internally diverse universities, such as Colombia's Nacional, always ran the risk that

funds intended for one part and purpose would merely free up other university funds for other parts and purposes; PRCs are more unified structures, with many fewer divergent orientations. Also, opportunities for surer, more immediate, more visible impacts are attractive, given donors' own politics and the need to show results to boards or publics.

33. While UNAM's social science URCs tend to have identifiable political profiles, IEPRI at Colombia's National University prides itself on a pluralistic respect for political differences.

34. An exception is Brunner and Barrios (1987: 106–09), but they dismiss the hierarchy as natural for knowledge organizations.

35. General assemblies are rare and are more associated with PRC networks; even there, formal authority may yield to real power exercised by a board (CRIES 1991: 9–10).

36. It is unusual for leaders to be deposed at PRCs, and examples do not always show power from below. At Peru's IEP, it took alleged scandal and resolute action by the center's other main figures. Furthermore, placing two leaders in one PRC can be dangerous. The Dominican Republic's CIDOS imploded from personality clashes between two figures—one CERESD's *padrino*, the other prominent in CLACSO and FLACSO—and personnel felt pressured to choose sides. Problems between Bolivar Lamounier and Fernando Henrique Cardoso at Brazil's CEBRAP contributed to Lamounier's departure and the growth of IDESP.

37. In its PRC system as in its university system, Colombia shows an affinity for boards with external representation. CRESET's board boasts members of national prestige, and internal committees include representation by some organizations that provide contract research (Martínez pc). FEDESARROLLO attributes its quality largely to the stability of its twenty-four-person directive council, with its heavy tilt toward government and business; academics are a small minority. FES's board shows twice as many business as higher education representatives. At Chile's CIDE, Jesuits nominate the head council.

38. Marcia Rivera has ruled at Puerto Rico's CEREP. A challenge by personnel with doctoral degrees reportedly led to their replacement by less advanced personnel who were willing to give major credit to the person that lines up the money.

39. Naturally, exceptions and variations exist among other PRCs as well. León and Spalding (1992: 47) find more internal democracy in women's centers than in other PRCs supported by SAREC.

40. For contracts and applied research, funders may care little about the ability of leaders to build their institution's long-term academic development, but certainly they care about the likelihood that the institution will deliver on the immediate commitments it undertakes.

41. Hierarchy might therefore help PRCs to defy generalizations about weak management at nonprofits (Hodgkinson and McCarthy 1992: 20). But the lack of participation might parallel reality at other nonprofit recipients of philanthropy. Carroll (1992: 92–93, 116, 141, 158) describes Latin America's grassroots NGOs as less participatory than often assumed from their role in promoting societal democratization—though more participatory than government or business organizations. Those NGOs, like PRCs, rely on loyalty and shared values and purposes. In fact, intellectuals are major founders, directors, and staffers of those NGOs.

42. Similar patterns can be detected at URCs. In the Dominican case, Luis Gómez was the key figure at UASD's CERESD because of the authority he acquired in the struggle

against Trujillo, which in turn made him the person with direct and powerful access to the UASD officials who distribute the budget. Thus Gómez could bypass the formal lines of authority controlled by the university's faculties.

43. Many of these explanations for hierarchy at PRCS apply to certain other non-profits, including PRCS elsewhere. Asian PRCS are very hierarchical, with very little participation; indeed, they go further in these respects than many public research centers in the same nations (Geithner i). Malaysia's ISIS has a governing board of twenty-one, with nine directors selected by the nation's prime minister.

44. The "chair" (*cátedra*) has traditionally represented hierarchy within university research fields. Departmentalization challenges such hierarchy, but it has been a difficult reform to implement, as have other efforts to supplant hierarchy in research settings. When they tried elections, under glastnost, Soviet research institutes fell into disorder and political conflict (NSF 1990: 6).

45. Scattered evidence from elsewhere further indicates that successful URCS, such as NUPES at Brazil's USP, do not get stuck in common faculty governance patterns. The Center of International Studies at Colombia's Andes has shifted from dependence on faculties to more direct dependence on the rectorate, which allows greater leeway for governance distinctive from that usually found in the faculties.

46. I have explained much in terms of PRCS' interactions with their environment, which deflects "blame" from PRCS. But since PRCS cannot be separated from these interactions, such explanations do not make the limitations incidental to PRCS. A changing environment could affect institutional governance, but many crucial environmental factors will probably not change fundamentally.

47. Within the higher education system itself, politically as well as academically, PRCS promote interinstitutional decentralization based on intrainstitutional centralization. My conclusions in this regard must be weighed against contrasting conclusions reached by some other scholars of nonprofits. Fisher (1993), for example, stresses high intrainstitutional democratic participation. She also stresses the need for international philanthropy to promote that, whereas my account highlights trade-offs between institutional restrictiveness and broader sectoral or societal democratic pluralism.

48. If, as Kalman Silvert repeatedly observed, Ford's Latin America program led the foundation—indeed foundations—in thinking about democracy, freedom, and human rights, PRCS have been indispensable partners. The foundation was proud of its role (Sutton i).

49. Evidence comes from sources on other nonprofits in Latin America and beyond (Reilly 1994; McCarthy, Hodgkinson, and Sumariwalla 1992). In East Central Europe (Siegal and Yancey 1992: 15–45), parallels include nonprofits' role in expanding civil society in late authoritarian and postauthoritarian eras, a movement from activity against authoritarian regimes to partnership or squabbling with their democratic successors, and contributions to pluralist over statist approaches—but also ambiguity over partisan versus nonpartisan roles and a meager level of intrainstitutional democracy.

6. Combining Quality and Relevance

1. Chapter 1 identified the PRCS' leadership role in social research; chapter 2, the mix between academic and other tasks; chapter 3, how universities' academic failures and shortcomings contribute to the rise of PRCS; chapter 4, funders' control over research

agendas; and chapter 5, the significance for freedom and democratization of much work produced at PRCs and disseminated by them.

2. Prior chapters note exceptions, where personnel wear two hats or return from government to less than total commitment at PRCs. More commonly, just as universities hire individuals to teach a given course, so PRCs hire for particular research projects; universities more often consider part-timers as staff, whereas PRCs hire their part-timers as temporary contractees.

3. All calculations are made from data in El Colegio de Postgraduados (1985: 53–302).

4. Many of those with the most advanced training at the agricultural ministry have followed a similar path: work at Chapingo preceding U.S. study.

5. The U.S. weight is commonly less than in the PRCs. The distribution of the fourteen doctorates (held or pursued) at the IEPRI of Colombia's National University is not unusual for a top URC: four were from U.S. institutions, eight were from European ones, and two were from Latin American ones (IEPRI 1990: 29–30).

6. This observation runs counter to my view of PRCs' readiness to scamper to wherever financial opportunity beckons. On the other hand, El Colegio may well signal that PRCs that are relatively large, publicly subsidized, and active in teaching will stay the academic course more than other PRCs.

7. The explanation for high productivity lies mostly beyond this analysis. But leading accounts (Israel 1987; Alvarez 1994) often refer to factors identified here as salient among PRCs: specificity, external pressure, links to the environment, competitiveness, adaptation, and management.

8. *Colombia Internacional* at the Universidad de Los Andes is an example of a leading journal by a URC; CINTEFOR's *Boletín* is an IRC example.

9. IRCs often lead in agriculture, with their well-trained and up-to-date staff, stability, sound finances, and flexibility. Successes in Mexico led Rockefeller and other sponsors to follow the model in Colombia, Peru, Central America, and nations outside Latin America (Cano Gallego 1981: 30).

10. Two caveats. One is that UNAM's graduate teaching follows the U.S. model more in the natural than in the social sciences. The other that Americanization is not inevitable. For example, a 1990 reform moved doctoral study at Brazil's IUPERJ (1991: 3) away from formal course work and toward more tutorials, even as formal course work increased at the master's level.

11. Or PRCs pick up where aborted university efforts leave off. Gino Germani had promoted empirical work, case studies, and statistics over impressionistic work at Argentina's UBA, as counterparts had with scientific sociology in Chile's universities. Several IRCs have also promoted such methodological change. ECIEL did so in economics (F. Herrera 1985: 321). A significant case of Americanization via URCs occurred in the Center of Social Research at the University of Puerto Rico, thereby contributing to the academic needs of the dominant political party (Quintero N.d.: 31–32).

12. All this is enough to invite charges that PRCs excessively mimic U.S. practices (Spalding, Taylor, and Vilas 1985: I-2). What constitutes excessive is subjective, but my view is that the reality does not significantly undermine academic performance. PRCs do not strictly follow a foreign model, let alone a pure U.S. model.

13. My count of Latin American participants listed in the program for the Sixteenth International Congress of the Latin American Studies Association (LASA 1991: 2–77) shows 193 from PRCs, 117 from universities, and 20 from URCs. Without Brazil the numbers are 175, 81, and 14, or roughly a two-to-one PRC over university lead. Some partici-

pants who list only their university are from URCs. Additional ambiguity results as scholars affiliated with both PRCs and universities list only one institution. To take another illustration, a 1993 conference on Peru at the Wilson Center in Washington hosted seven speakers from Peru: five from PRCs, one from a private university, and one journalist.

14. The CLACSO survey finds two-thirds of its centers with international links, mostly with the United States, followed by Europe (Calderón and Provoste 1990: IV-11, VIII-9).

15. Ford purposefully set out to build local capacities to study higher education and to link up those localities. Multilaterals, including the IDB, the World Bank, the UN, and the OAS, have also contributed. The dominant thrust of the research and consultancies thereby promoted has clearly favored such key elements of internationalization or Americanization as private funding and frequent evaluations. Among the key PRCs are FLACSO, CEDES, and GRADE, in Chile, Argentina, and Peru, respectively.

16. Such relevance need not mean exclusive preoccupation with local interests. Rockefeller's role in Peru health problems in the 1920s emphasized concrete applications (e.g., beating back yellow fever) to the point of subordinating research per se, but protection of U.S. commercial interests was also an objective (Cueto 1989).

17. Several URCs make relevant contributions, like those made by PRCs. For example, at Colombia's National University, IEPRI focuses on democratization, violence, peace, and economic development.

18. The findings on PRCs thus also further the case of those who argue that Latin American social science has been development oriented (Balán 1982: 239). An essential change, however, is away from the broad theorizing characteristic of university-based work to the greater policy and pragmatic focus of most PRC work. In education studies, for example, PRCs usually beat universities in timely research for policy makers; if they account for about a third of all education research in the region, the figure increases to about a half if IRCs that resemble PRCs are added, and goes higher if the focus is on policy or the poor (Cariola 1994).

19. A pointedly progressive evaluation of SAREC-funded PRCs reports that "even the most technically oriented and methodologically conservative of the centers carry out research that manifests considerably more social conscience and relevance to the goals of mass participation and social justice than we have found in analogous centers in the Western developed countries" (Spalding, Stallings, and Weeks 1990: 24). Of course, it depends on what is chosen for analogy. Government, think tanks, advocacy agencies, and interest groups in Western democracies conduct a great deal of research relevant to everyday and underprivileged lives. The comparison does work, however, if we focus on the institutional centers doing the majority of social research: universities in developed countries, PRCs in Latin America.

20. Practical, local, and national focuses help explain in a positive way why Latin America scores even lower in the social than the natural sciences on international publication indexes; the social scientists concentrate more on problems of local interest and publish more in Spanish and Portuguese (IDB 1988: 101, 306–07).

7. The Subordination of Scholarship

1. The greater length of the present chapter could also deceive. By and large, PRCs' academic strengths are easier to spell out and understand. Further, the present chapter includes more topics (e.g., models), where PRC performance is mixed, and it makes

more sense to consider both the problems and the achievements together than to split them between two chapters.

2. Even works that consider problems of financial and programmatic dependency usually do not consider academic limitations in terms of quality, disciplinary development, or teaching (Calderón and Provoste 1990).

3. There is insufficient information to say whether PRCs become less or more academically specialized over time. My impression inclines toward the former, as organizations seek stability and opportunities in uncertain environments. This seems to hold for many U.S. think tanks, such as the Hudson Institute (J. Smith 1991) and for Latin America's own private universities (Levy 1986). Against that is the hyperproliferation of institutions and the tendencies toward specialization identified in this and other chapters. (If we consider the addition of social and political tasks, diminished specialization would be clear.)

4. Thirty-one percent of centers have fewer than fifteen full-time researchers, while 24 percent have more than forty, accounting for eight percent and 62 percent of CLACSO's researchers. PRCs appear to be small to middle sized in budget, also (Calderón and Provoste 1990: II-5–8, III-9).

5. CRESALC (1984: 1–37) has gathered data on research units working on educational issues. My calculations show PRCs comparable in size to public URCs and IRCs but smaller than GRCs and, especially, than university faculties. The means for full-time personnel are 11 for fourteen PRCs; 12 for thirty-one public URCs; 9 for eight IRCs; 24 for seven GRCs; and 192 for fourteen faculties. If we use the median, faculties are still three times larger than PRCs, though GRCs lose their advantage in size, as they do when we look at part-timers.

6. PRCs range from cohesive, with personnel working in the same specialized area, to those that are loose homes for whatever individuals might do. Centers like Di Tella boast of researcher autonomy and diversity, while critics decry the absence of coherence and community.

7. Geographical scope is relevant to academic performance in the sense that PRCs pursue their tasks in only certain places.

8. Interviews at Chapingo suggest academic cohesiveness within centers, though no research was done on cohesiveness across centers. Personnel at UNAM's science URCs also generally regard the existence of "teams," heavily influenced by the United States, as conducive to the group work required in science (Barnés, i; de la Fuente i).

9. A further GRC-PRC similarity lies in links to university teaching. The GRC presence on the campus of Rio's Catholic university is extraordinary. Though GRCs maintain their juridical separateness from the university, some of their personnel supervise theses, while students can work on research projects (Machado de Sousa i). Argentina's atomic energy center is another example.

10. But initiative and control by URCs is also rare. It has occurred at the CEDE, in the Dominican Republic's INTEC, due to the unusual prestige of the initial personnel, who were cofounders of the university and who controlled the master's program; they held faculty membership but tended to see it as a second job (Sánchez M. i-3). Where URCs try to create strong graduate programs, as at the International Studies Center of Colombia's Universidad de Los Andes, they are swimming against the tide.

11. A rare UNAM exception underscores the lack of connection between research and undergraduates. Mindful of the gulf, the biomedical institute became, in 1974, UNAM's only institute to offer formal studies. It marked the first time UNAM had research scien-

tists, rather than practicing professionals, teach undergraduates. By international measures of quality, the program has far outpaced typical UNAM education: professors hold
foreign postdoctoral degrees; the program is very selective and, after that, very demanding; and the scientific ethos of questioning is advanced by vigorous student-professor
interaction. But the numbers are tiny for this huge university. Only four to eight students are admitted annually. No other institute has managed a similar program. Because
institutes cannot give diplomas, the institute solicited three faculties for help. Each refused (Fortes and Lomnitz 1991).

12. At the University of Puerto Rico such institutional problems, combined with
commonwealth status, explain why some researchers at URCs prefer to do undergraduate
teaching stints at U.S. mainland universities.

13. Faculty-URC relations appear more cooperative in some places, including certain
Mexican universities where faculties and institutes give some joint graduate studies.

14. Further evidence comes from agricultural IRCs created with hopes of emulating
the land-grant teaching-research-extension concept but often winding up with only
training on the teaching side (Cano Gallego 1981: 26–29).

15. Twenty years after opening its master's program and ten after opening its doctoral program, Brazil's IUPERJ (1991: 3) had graduated only 140 of 406 master's degree
students and 6 of 108 doctoral students.

16. CLACSO also offers degree programs, including a master's degree in rural sociology that has had impact in Costa Rica, but it mostly facilitates offerings in affiliated and
other centers.

17. A large initiative in Ecuador, begun in 1989, seeks to break the pattern with an
intensive two-year master's program projected to attract 150 resident students and
twenty-five full-time faculty by 1993. FLACSO-Chile had been the leading hope until
academic training was stripped from it.

18. Where universities are strong, we can also envision more of what is found between the *colegio* and the public university in Baja California, where university professors teach at the PRC (Beltrán i). The university's full professors do not carry massive
teaching loads at their own institution and thus have time in their schedule, which
assists the PRC in escaping some of the limitations of small size and scope. Yet the
most important potential duo, El Colegio and UNAM, is disheartening for the antipathy,
ideology, fear, and pride that have often divided them.

19. In addition to the prominent programs discussed above, others also have respectable histories. IDES, though it is an association of social scientists, has been active since
the 1960s in producing good graduate students as well as a fine journal (Balán 1982:
237–38). Central America benefits from some regional programs, including ICAP's master's degree program in public administration, CSUCA-coordinated courses, some limited
to three weeks, and CLACSO's master's program in rural sociology (Vega 1989: 29; Fernández 1989: 84). Other Latin American regional nonprofits offering notable graduate education include ILPES and IICA. CLAF contributed education and disciplinary development
in physics, with a pronounced impact through the CBPF in Brazil (Vessuri pc).

20. The Chilean case suggests that early PRCs, established to do research not done in
universities, did very little teaching. CEPAL, an IRC, was an exception (Brunner 1990b).

21. Even in some rather propitious circumstances, reluctance remains. Chile's CECI
has contributed to the UCH in graduate science through thesis supervision, workshops,
employment of students as research assistants, etc., especially as the university remained
better in science than in politically sensitive fields. But CECI wants no dependency on

the university and wants, for example, its own laboratory facilities (Teitelboim N.d.: 2; Latorre i).

22. PRCs outside the social fields most repressed by military regimes could offer teaching earlier. In population studies, virtually all of CENEP's researchers taught courses at Argentina's Universidad de Belgrano (E. Fox 1980: 38).

23. Yet redemocratization lessens the teaching contribution of some PRCs. CIEPLAN's teaching diminished in the years leading up to Chile's regime change, and the small "research school" training program closed, as preparation for political posts consumed more time (CIEPLAN N.d.: 3; O. Muñoz i).

24. The university shares facilities and personnel in sociology and anthropology. The program confers an importance on FLACSO-Brazil, which it lacks in research and policy (Alvarez pc-2). That is, the institutional link helps the PRC's prestige, whereas links between FLACSO and universities in other nations would often help the universities more.

25. Brazil, the leader, has retreated from a major commitment to increased integration, making the PRC-university duality look more permanent. Similarly, Argentina and Chile, into their second postmilitary governments, have felt little official push toward integration or toward reattracting researchers back from their centers to the universities. At least outside Brazil, governments prefer to finance social as well as scientific and technological research outside the university; PRCs function well for the applied social work they seek. Another alternative to integration occurs where PRCs convert into universities, sometimes to complement consultancy research with business education. Probably the two most notable new universities carrying old PRC names are Chile's AHC and Argentina's Di Tella. But there is less conversion here than one might imagine. The AHC is basically a new undergraduate teaching institution, a venue for part-time teaching by researchers from the centers that once composed the AHC's large PRC network. Some U.S. research centers have converted into research universities (for example, the Rockefeller University), whereas others have tried to broaden themselves by incorporating additional fields of research (for example, the Hudson Institute).

26. In India, top URCs have gained the right to award degrees in physics and some social sciences (Altbach i). Indian PRCs mostly avoid teaching, but some have teaching "wings" (Datta 1989: 83).

27. CLACSO's centers should on average surpass PRCs in research focus, yet only 26 percent of directors rate it as the only focus—though 29 percent rate it as paramount alongside occasional social action, and another 17 percent rate it as paramount alongside regular social action. That leaves 15 percent rating research over social action, only 8 percent rating social action over research, and none rating social action as the only focus. (5 percent answered "other"; see Calderón and Provoste 1990: V-9). Of some 6,000 research centers in the region's seven leading nations in 1985, probably not much more than a tenth qualified as high quality (Alvarez 1994: 10).

28. CLACSO has barely more personnel with graduate degrees than with undergraduate degrees (Calderón and Provoste 1990: III-2). Ecuador's CIUDAD (N.d.) has no faculty with doctorates, three are doctoral candidates, seven have master's degrees, and four have undergraduate degrees.

29. Of fourteen PRCs, two cite only basic research as their task, while four cite only applied research, and the rest cite both. GRCs, followed by IRCs but not by universities, appear most often devoted to basic research: of seven GRCs, five cite only basic research and two cite only applied research; of eight IRCs, the respective figures are three and

two, with the others mixed. Of forty URCs, only six cite only basic research, while four-teen cite only applied research; for fourteen university faculties, the respective figures are zero and five. See CRESALC (1984: 1–37). Of course, such comparisons are suspect due to the varying interpretations and motives of respondents. Parenthetically, many Jesuits think the creation of their specialized PRCs in education was a mistake because of the centers' consequent isolation from social science (Myers 1981: 27).

30. Insofar as the shunning of generalizations reflects a secular trend away from the savant, or grand intellectual, tradition, whether to regret it depends on one's view of the appropriate political and critical role of scholarship.

31. The market for Chilean social science books reportedly wilted during the years of military rule after 1973 (Fruhling i). Where books written in PRCs are published out of the country, including elsewhere in Latin America, one can both praise the productive internationalism and lament the barriers to publication within some nations.

32. Exceptions occur where PRCs strike agreements with a separate press. Here too, though, an open review process is circumvented. An example is Mexico's CIDAC. Brazil's CEDEC works with both *Vozes* and *Paz e Terra*. URCs usually publish through their own university's press; indeed, as at UNAM, the publisher is often a university unit. At Colom-bia's Andes, CEDE publishes its own books, working papers, and the journal *Desarrollo y Sociedad;* and one of the first actions of the National University's IEPRI was to intro-duce its journal, *Análisis Político.* Other PRC-URC similarities exist regarding publication weaknesses, but they require further study.

33. The CLACSO survey finds that much productivity rests on the work of only a few institutions (Calderón and Provoste 1990: IV-10–11). An evaluation of top Argentine PRCs found "notably uneven" quality at one and high-level work at another "directed and published by the same small corps" (Spalding, Stallings, and Weeks 1990: 47, 49). And just as some nations rank high for the overall quality of their PRCs, others trail, such as Honduras within the Central American context.

34. A gap between publications and high prestige can be identified at particular institutions. IESA, Venezuela's most important PRC, is a good example. It has improved its publication quality, staff, and curriculum, but probably not enough to account for its soaring prestige. Another part of the explanation lies in voguish privatization—an invigorated for-profit sector and a revamped state value IESA's output. The mirror-image decline in prestige at CENDES, a public URC, must likewise be understood in reference to how its traditional concern with administrative planning and the public sector suddenly seemed irrelevant, or worse, to many government, private, and interna-tional actors (Vessuri i; Navarro i-1).

35. A few top think tanks do large-scale research with massive empirical content, but most research is short term. The oldest think tank still operating, the Russell Sage Foundation, established in 1907, is rare for its emphasis on basic social science research, though it is still policy oriented. The Brookings Institution publishes prominent book-length studies, whereas the AEI typifies the move toward shorter, policy pieces aimed at government officials, journalists, and business leaders (J. Smith 1991: 183; Weaver 1989: 568).

36. The findings on PRCs' academic weaknesses support a major conclusion of Ben-David's (1971: 161) acclaimed comparative study of scientific development. In fact, Ben-David found specialist organizations not only limited but inferior. The "superiority of large multipurpose organizations" relates to their ability to share experiences and innovations and to their diverse stimuli, whereas "in a small, specialized and segregated

institution the atmosphere may easily become extremely homogenous." Of course, many differences exist between Ben-David's subject matter and ours. PRCs partly escape the stereotype of specialist institutions, and the alternatives to them hardly approach Ben-David's multipurpose universities.

37. The case relates to political orientations at UNAM's URCs versus El Colegio. El Colegio is more internationalist, the URCs more nationalist, though it is a matter of degree—and URCs follow French influences more. On matters of language, culture, legislation, history, and sociology, the URCs do good work on Mexican issues, and the decline of Marxist dogma helps (Lomnitz i; Kovacs i; Zorilla i).

38. An interesting example occurs in a SAREC review of the women's centers it has funded in Latin America (León and Spalding 1992: 44). It acknowledges weaknesses in quantitative output and disciplinary rigor but does not lay responsibility at the door of those PRCs. Instead, while praising them for breakthroughs in their research area, the report cites problems of small size, poor working conditions, responsibilities for social promotion, and pressures from funding agencies.

39. Chapter 4 shows the mix between long-term academic development and immediate application promoted by international philanthropy. In the 1960s, Ford pushed for academic development at centers like IESA, focusing on doctoral training where none had existed and on academic social science. In recent years, however, the emphasis has shifted toward policy. IESA members who claim their PRC surpasses any Venezuelan university in publications on social research topics temper their claims by noting that all forces press for analysis of the present rather than for reflective or disciplinary work (Navarro i-1; Gómez and Bustillo 1979: 84–85). Carroll (1992: 205) notes the detrimental consequences for Peru's FDN, a PRC in agronomy, because the center's personnel, as well as its contractors, have fallen into a project mentality.

40. A similar complaint about foundations' zeal for continual affirmation of productivity and legitimacy through short-term, visible results echoes in Africa (Court 1980: 136). A shift in U.S. university research funding from steady federal money to private and contract money has probably purchased relevance at the expense of infrastructure, graduate training, and other academic needs (Geiger 1990a: 31).

41. Whether these activities or university teaching blends better with research is an open and important question.

42. Lagos (1982) traces PRC relevance to a need for small, private, and initially unknown institutions to build legitimacy through direct policy contributions, whereas universities often enjoyed a legitimacy that did not depend on direct contributions.

43. Harrison (N.d.: 16–18) makes the exceptional but reasonable argument that centers need not be models, nor do they need to prove long-term success, if they produce important direct results. He cites the Rockefeller-supported Mexican Literature Center in the middle of twentieth century.

44. Within the comparative literature, Kramer (1981) reaches discouraging conclusions on social science agencies, whereas findings are mixed or positive for Latin America's grassroots NGOs (Annis and Hakim 1988; Carroll 1992: 119) and for its private universities (Levy 1986: 318).

45. Similarly, the numbers are not impressive at other centers. FLACSO-Argentina has only thirteen foreign students, of which six are from neighboring Uruguay (FLACSO 1987: 13).

46. The suggestion to locate outside the state's major city is a page out of the political history of U.S. higher education in the sense of trying to avoid the caldron of politics.

But insofar as Mexican state universities are in the capitals, the placement of *colegios* elsewhere is also meant to avoid antagonizing the universities.

47. Demography tells the tale well, as places like El Colegio and CELADE, an IRC, have excelled while university research disappoints (Harkavy and Diescho 1988: 9).

48. A good example of a university unit's historic impact is the UCH's ESCOLATINA. Between 1961 and 1966 more than half its students came from outside Chile; they received solid training and later had major impacts in their own nations (FF #61372; Davidson i; Coleman and Court 1992).

49. The inability to do more may come from the characteristics of the university or the PRC, or it may come from their interaction. Obstacles also originate in the environment, as when governments repress university social science. But the new environment of privatization and a revamped state could mean strong pressures for universities to emulate PRCs.

50. My main approach has been to treat parallels between PRCs and other research centers as adding to the importance of the PRC phenomenon. One could, alternatively, give more emphasis to the points that show PRCs as just one component in a complex research configuration outside the university mainstream.

8. Conclusion

1. Without going as far, this conclusion echoes Kramer's (1981: 259) on specialization as the "first salient attribute of a voluntary agency." My finding comes particularly close to Carroll's (1992: 13, 143) on Third World grassroots organizations; while they spread out across points along a specialist-generalist continuum, most incline toward the former, though they often cluster several tasks around a single purpose. Kramer pushes for intrainstitutional democratization and formal accountability to government; my findings on the positive as well as limiting features of specialism leave me wary of such proposals.

2. Also, by encouraging researchers to stay in their country and to work in social science—and by training others—PRCs have produced a supply of people to work part-time in the universities. Ironically, PRCs initially once depended on the prior success of universities in providing a supply of researchers, but now some universities depend on a supply flowing from PRCs.

3. Salutary effects are sometimes half forced on universities. For example, Colombian and other public universities that seek international funds now offer incentives, ranging from research resources to administrative flexibility, to attract top PRC people to part-time university posts (Facundo i).

4. The positive findings on PRCs' contributions beyond the higher education system contrast at least in emphasis with much literature that depicts nonprofit organizations, from foundations to social service providers, as disappointing in their inability (or disinclination) to change the power structure with which they interact. This is the case, for example, of a landmark work on Latin American grassroots nonprofits (B. Smith 1990). PRCs, I find, play an important role in political and social change. This finding is more consistent with Fruhling's (1989: 366–74) on how human rights nonprofits helped build a new political landscape. Much obviously depends on the nonprofit type in question, as well as on factors that vary across nations and time.

5. The characteristics of PRC projects parallel, or go beyond, those of the more suc-

cessful university assistance projects. These include selective targeting, with mutual matching or at least limited opposition; attempts at change through new structures more than through the reform of traditional ones; and large external assistance as a portion of total resources for recipient institutions.

6. Chapter 5 notes that the literature on democratization has generally minimized the positive effects of U.S. influence; likewise, the literature on assistance has undermined ringing claims. Attention has focused mostly on public assistance. In contrast, PRCs provide a major example of private U.S. and other international philanthropy, where the impact has been major (while the claims were more modest).

7. Examples include the idea that pluralist options increase the stability of the system by avoiding the stakes of monopoly power. For some of the strongest claims about pluralism, I have explored both why and how the results appear. For others, we see at least a persuasive correlation between a structurally pluralist system and other sectoral characteristics.

8. The notion that nonprofits avoid "failure" by committing to values more than performance standards (Seibel and Anheier 1990: 15–16) probably applies to some peripheral PRC-social action centers, but there is considerable evidence that PRCs pass rather demanding performance tests. Still, as is often so with nonprofits, it is hard to know how many new or weak efforts fail outright. In the Dominican Republic efforts to build PRCs have sometimes failed despite the involvement of estimable scholars; a group runs a few conferences and publishes a few papers, but after a year or two the organizing effort dwindles (Sánchez M. i-3).

Consulting centers and other less academic centers probably disappear more frequently than academic ones. Moreover, some centers that are "extra" homes may be vulnerable, as happened with Mexico's Center for Ecodevelopment. It faded when CON- ACYT halted funding, arguing that authors listed other institutional affiliations as well as the center on their works (Ornelas pc). ECIEL is an IRC that faded as funds vanished (Brunner pc). Other centers survive but fall short of their goals. Many must compromise their academic goals, and some of the best have slipped from their pinnacle. Argentine examples include Di Tella, Bariloche, and CISEA. Peru's IEP is one of those that have suffered setbacks, though not necessarily secular declines, in recent years; several regional *colegios* in Mexico have failed to attain their goals.

9. However, PRCs are much more involved with the poor than private universities are. This is obviously true for PRCs involved in social action.

10. The addition of goals, or changes in goals, poses a problem in assessing organizational effectiveness. So does the vagueness of ongoing goals. While I emphasize the evidence of attained goals, insistence on more precise specification of standards and results could lead to less conclusive judgment, at least on the academic side.

11. Put more generally, those that act voluntarily can choose tasks for which their prospects of success are high. Private organizations are more associated with such voluntary roles; governments have obligatory roles. On the other hand, governments sometimes off-load intractable problems onto nonprofits (Seibel 1990: 114–15); this would seem more pertinent to nonprofit service organizations than to research organizations. The U.S. federal government sometimes chooses for itself tasks that carry political consensus and good prospects for success, while delegating tougher tasks (Leman 1989: 76–77); the federal government is also a rather voluntary actor when it comes to foreign aid (Levy forthcoming).

12. Whereas the literature on selectivity bias focuses on how the selection of top

talent makes an elite institution appear excellent, the ability to select—and to specialize, limit, and exclude—is central to success more generally. It involves tasks, personnel, and constituencies, as well as clients.

13. Parallel debates have already developed in Africa, despite the much more limited presence of PRCS. In response to those who would give up on research in the universities (almost all public), Coombe (1991: 32, 44–45) points not only to the good university pockets that persist but also to the ultimate weakness of dependence on consultancies and specialized PRCS. Doubts likewise emerge about the effects of GRCS' achievements on overall academic development (World Bank 1985: 29).

14. Studies that focus on a representative sample of nonprofits are likely to be less flattering. Note, for example, Kramer's (1981: 257) conclusions about social service nonprofits; his association of innovation with big bureaucracy rather than with small nonprofits does not find a parallel in my research. There are good reasons, however, to focus some studies on key nonprofits more than on a representative sample; Carroll (1992: 119) reports a mixed record in innovation by key grassroots nonprofits.

15. The PRC experience transcends, in some sense, the dual-sector debate about how private affects public: PRCS in several nations have held a near monopoly in areas of social research. There, PRC limitations are system limitations. Although this study has usually taken the more charitable view that PRCS contribute above point zero, one could emphasize that PRCS are severely limited even where no wider pertinent institutions exist.

16. This is a natural difficulty for specialist institutions of an organizational type different from the mainstream. For example, India and Pakistan's good specialist institutes in areas such as theoretical physics form "small oases" incapable of fertilizing the area around them and facing the danger of withering amid a weak environment (Salam 1966: 464).

17. In India as well, there is university resentment of their position alongside thriving freestanding research centers (Ganesh and Sarupia 1983).

18. For a typical criticism along these lines, see Hachette (1990: 256) on how PRCS present problems for university research development and fund-raising in Chile. To take a less common example, would absorption of PRCS such as Venezuela's IESA and Brazil's Getúlio Vargas enhance universities' finances or ruin the nations' best business schools? Similar claims and rebuttals arise regarding U.S. universities and research centers. They also arise regarding international philanthropy and its retreat from large institution building to work with smaller nonprofits.

19. Obviously, pluralism is not reserved for private sectors. Despite recent diversification within Latin America's public university sector, however, its traditionally weak pluralism has contributed to the growth and success of PRCS. In contrast, each chapter has demonstrated an extraordinary pluralism within the PRC sector, a private nonprofit sector.

20. These factors are (1) the growth and prominence of PRCS are fairly recent, (2) almost nobody expected such persistence and evolution, (3) repression or other realities have often obviated alternatives, (4) continued PRC growth results from no explicit overarching plan, (5) the PRC sector is markedly private or nongovernmental, (6) PRCS serve the self-interest of many researchers as they serve many others as well, and (7) PRCS do not match most people's notion of higher education.

21. A search for complementary relationships between multitudinous nonprofit organizations and public structures finds parallels in many fields beyond research (e.g., Downs and Solimano 1989).

22. A theoretical approach developed by Salamon (1989a) could help orient policy on PRC-university coexistence. The government and its public institutions enjoy special strengths in having a steady income and in setting broad public priorities (propositions that weaken in the face of economic crisis and political fragility). Nonprofits, on the other hand, normally suffer problems in finding adequate funds and in particularism (or specialism). At the same time, nonprofit advantages in coherence, flexibility, choice, and so forth, provide attractive alternatives to government. Similarly, Orlans (1972: 80) finds U.S. nonprofit research institutes good for concentrated attacks on policy problems but weak in political legitimacy and financial security. One might envision a research system with increased government funding and agenda setting for some PRCs, even as universities recover from decay. In fact, such an orientation is relevant to the Latin American nonprofit sector in general, which is likewise impressive for its growth, persistence, and myriad accomplishments but weak in funding and democratic legitimacy (A. Thompson 1992: 403–04). On the other hand, the U.S. and European experience (Gormley 1991b: 312: DiMaggio and Anheier 1990: 152) shows how difficult it is for the government to steer and monitor what it delegates or contracts out to nonprofits.

23. Those concerned with improving the PRC-university dynamic in Latin America can consider both the common problems and the arrangements reached elsewhere. Africa's best PRCs hire recent university graduates as research assistants and their professors as visitors; they also channel travel funds and other resources to university faculties. Some split-site degree programs exist, and scholarly organizations are trying to build graduate education at the best PRCs. Nevertheless, a need exists for increased PRC-university "twinning," which foreign foundations are well placed to promote. Meanwhile, an exodus of professors to PRCs hurts university research, while PRCs remain inadequate substitutes for universities (Coombe 1991: 41–49). Also see Pereira (1971: 41–44) on the need to better link the university and the GRCs of Africa. In Thailand, the TDRI was to mobilize research forces without promoting an exodus from the university, but such an exodus has hurt university teaching (Geithner i).

An alternative to linking institutional types is diversification within each. This is the French tendency: instead of encouraging personnel overlap between any two of its three sectors (university, CNRS, and *grandes écoles*), the higher education system demands that careers be made within a sector; yet top young university professors combine research with their teaching, and universities develop URCs that parallel the *grandes écoles* in their selectivity, autonomy, management, et cetera, while the CNRS adds graduate education to its traditional concern with research (Friedberg and Musselin 1987). Within the Soviet higher education system, academies came to offer degrees as early as the 1930s, and universities continued to do some research (M. Adams 1990: 57). In Latin America, PRCs offer graduate courses, and universities expand URCs.

24. In more subjective, prescriptive terms, my analysis pushes me in the following general directions. Major philanthropic actors should restrain their turn away from PRCs in their pursuit of social action, attention to other regions, or shifting responsibility to host governments. Their help is too desperately needed while PRCs face crises related to economic recovery, state budget cuts, and perhaps democratic consolidation and generational change. In the longer run, foundations might maintain pivotal help for a select group of leading PRCs spread across various areas. Mostly, they can continue to give for projects they value. Governments, meanwhile, should continue to contract for chosen projects while increasing incentives and rewards to benefit PRC infrastructure. They should address the major shortcomings of PRCs less by curbing them directly than

by helping to rebuild the finances, political security, and research base of their promising universities. Both governments and foundations should offer incentives for improved linkages between PRCs and universities, including an academically responsible but large increase in graduate education. All this would involve increased and improved partnerships between government and the third sector.

25. See Salamon (1989b: 256–57), who also cites a connotation of preference for private over public action.

26. The building of legitimacy for the growing nonprofit sectors is an important challenge in other parts of the world as well, as in postcommunist Europe (Siegal and Yancey 1992: 29–43).

27. Such points run a risk of tautology, as funds to PRCs are of course funds fully to private institutions; given how foreign philanthropy has swung from universities to separate research centers, however, and how PRCs predominate among these centers (outside of agricultural IRCs, which have been major recipients all along), the notion of a privatization of targets makes sense.

28. PRCs also directly help some private universities and serve as models; on the other hand, private universities might do more research, with more qualified people, were PRCs to disappear. And whatever distinctions exist between the university and the PRC, higher education's overall privatization is impressive. Much of this privatization preceded the regional and worldwide ideological leap toward privatization; it accelerated when that leap initially meant more in rhetoric than in real change in other fields (Coburn and Wortzel 1986).

29. This conclusion is much stronger than what I felt comfortable with earlier, when considering university privatization in the context of a then more dubious political-economic privatization (Levy 1986: 331–34).

30. The analysis contrasts Argentina, Paraguay, and Central America (outside Costa Rica), where little university option challenges PRCs, with nations where universities share the research role (e.g., Brazil) or may have the overall strength to stage a comeback (e.g., Chile).

31. Where one observer might emphasize PRCs' persistence through change, another might emphasize their fragility where PRCs need to be rescued from the outside. An example is SAREC's entry into Peru in the 1990s, when PRCs were reeling from the nation's crises.

32. It would be interesting to compare this to the adaptation made by other nonprofits. Fruhling (1985: 76) points out that they would be forced to greater redefinition than would the PRCs; this is obvious for human rights organizations.

33. Just as I am emboldened regarding privatization, so I am on pluralism. I hedged on the pluralist label in characterizing the university world several years ago (Levy 1986: 323–28), preferring to emphasize the inadequacies of the corporatist concept. Now I am comfortable with the pluralist label—increasingly, if incompletely, for higher education overall; strongly for the PRC sector.

34. Wiarda (1992) depicts an organic, top-down corporatism that stresses harmony and either maintains a remarkable persistence or erodes without any viable replacement emerging; he explicitly rejects the idea that U.S. or other pluralistic models emerge. This study runs counter to each of these particulars. As it finds a pluralism that lies far from an idealized form, it echoes the pluralism realistically identified elsewhere, including a role for government, conflicts with the broad public interest, and inequality in access, participation, and influence (Waste 1987: 13–17).

35. In turn, where societal shifts occur from corporatism toward pluralism, PRCs that are linked to certain groups and organizations assume increased privateness (e.g., serving labor unions that have become more autonomous).

36. Each of the cited pluralist characteristics undercuts the state corporatist notion most associated with Latin America. Two characteristics listed in the literature on corporatism are prominent at PRCs, however: clientelism and hierarchy. They undercut pluralism at the institutional level but not beyond. "Societal corporatism" (Schmitter 1974: 103–04), which lacks the centrality and repressiveness of the state, would present a more mixed picture overall. Depending on how far one wanders toward the periphery where PRCs are not convincingly freestanding, some PRCs have ties with corporate entities, including churches, businesses, and unions. Societal corporatism may well gain relevance as democratic governments work closely with various types of private organizations. But some fundamental tendencies of PRCs run counter even to societal corporatism, with its functionally integrated systems, planned pursuit of a common public interest, directed coordination, and state sanctioning and subsidization.

References

Acosta U., Mariclaire, and Yolanda Alvarado E. 1984. "El subsistema de investigación científica." In Dirección General de Asuntos Personales 1984.

Adams, Mark. 1990. "Research and the Russian University." In NSF 1990.

Adams, Richard, and Charles Cumberland. 1960. *United States Cooperation in Latin America*. East Lansing: Michigan State University Press.

ADIPA. 1989. *Handbook*. Kuala Lumpur: ADIPA.

Adler, Emanuel. 1987. *The Power of Ideology: The Quest for Technological Autonomy in Argentina and Brazil*. Berkeley: University of California Press.

Albornoz, Mario. 1992. "Incentivos al investigador en Argentina." *Interciencia* 17(6): 324–28.

Albornoz, Orlando. 1979. *Teoría y praxis de la educación superior venezolana*. Caracas: Ediciones de la Facultad de Humanidades y Educación, UCV.

———. 1993. *Education and Society in Latin America*. London: Macmillan.

Altbach, Philip. 1987. *The Knowledge Context: Comparative Perspectives on the Distribution of Knowledge*. Albany: State University of New York Press.

———, ed. 1991. *International Higher Education*. New York: Garland.

Alvarez, Benjamin. 1994. "Institutions and Their Context." In Alvarez and Gómez 1994.

Alvarez, Benjamin, and Hernando Gómez, eds. 1994. *Laying the Foundation: The Institutions of Knowledge in Developing Countries*. Ottawa: IDRC.

Andean Report. 1992. "NGOs Target the Private Sector for Future Funds." *Andean Report* (Mar.): 32–33.

Anderson, Dole. 1987. *Management Education in Developing Countries: The Brazilian Experience*. Boulder: Westview.

Anheier, Helmut. 1989. "Private Voluntary Organizations and Development in West Africa: Comparative Perspectives." In James 1989.

———. 1990a. "Institutional Choice and Organizational Behavior in the Third Sector." In Anheier and Seibel 1990c.

———. 1990b. "Private Voluntary Organizations and the Third World: The Case of Africa." In Anheier and Seibel 1990c.

———. 1990c. "A Profile of the Third Sector in West Germany." In Anheier and Seibel 1990c.

Anheier, Helmut, and Martin Knapp. 1990. "Voluntas: An Editorial Statement." *Voluntas* 1(1): 1–12.

Anheier, Helmut, and Wolfgang Seibel. 1990a. "Introduction." In Anheier and Seibel 1990c.

———. 1990b. "The Third Sector in Comparative Perspective: Four Propositions." In Anheier and Seibel 1990c.

———. eds. 1990c. *The Third Sector: Comparative Studies of Nonprofit Organizations*. Berlin: Walter de Gruyter.

Annis, Sheldon, and Peter Hakim, eds. 1988. *Direct to the Poor: Grassroots Development in Latin America*. Boulder: Lynne Rienner.

Ansaldi, Waldo, and Fernando Calderón. 1989. "La búsqueda de América Latina: Entre el ansia de encontrarla y el temor de no reconocerla." Paper prepared for the Conference on International Academic Relations and Institutional Development of the Social Sciences in Latin America, Montevideo, Aug. 17–19.

ANUIES. 1989. *Anuario estadístico 1988: Posgrado*. Mexico City: ANUIES.

Arango, Marta, and Glen Nimnicht. 1987. *El caso de CINDE*. Medellín: CINDE.

Ardila, Jorge. 1994. "Institutional Failure or Success: Variables Affecting Agricultural Research." In Alvarez and Gómez 1994.

Arregui, Patricia de, and Máximo Torero C. 1991. *Indicadores de ciencia y tecnología en América Latina, 1970–1990*. Lima: GRADE.

Arnove, Robert 1980a. "Foundations and the Transfer of Knowledge." In Arnove 1980b.

———, ed. 1980b. *Philanthropy and Cultural Imperialism*. Boston: G. K. Hall.

ASIES. N.d. "ASIES." ASIES, Guatemala City.

Atcon, Rudolph. 1966. *The Latin America University*. Bogotá: ECO Revista de la Cultura.

Badelt, Christopher. 1990. "Institutional Choice and the Nonprofit Sector." In Anheier and Seibel 1990c.

Bailey, John. 1988. *Governing Mexico*. New York: St. Martin's.

Balán, Jorge. 1982. "Social Sciences in the Periphery: Perspectives on the Latin American Case." In Stifel, Davidson, and Coleman 1982.

———. 1990. "The State of Graduate Social Sciences in Latin America and the Role of Independent Research Centers." Paper prepared for Ford Foundation, Meeting on Higher Education in Latin America, City, Nov. 16.

———. N.d. "El impacto de la asistencia externa en la institucionalización de las ciencias sociales: El caso argentino." Paper prepared for SSRC. (See SSRC 1991.)

Baquedano, Manuel. 1989. "Socially Appropriate Technologies." In Downs et al. 1989.

Barreiro, Fernando, and Anabel Cruz. 1990. *Organizaciones no gubernamentales de Uruguay: Análisis y repetorio*. Montevideo: ICD and Agencia Española de Cooperación Internacional.

———. 1991. *Entre diversidades y desafíos: Organizaciones no gubermentales de Uruguay*. Montevideo: ICD and Agencia Española de Cooperación Internacional, and Comisión de las Comunidades Europeas.

Bartholomew, James. 1990. "The University, Industry, and Research in Japan." In NSF 1990.

BASE-IS. N.d. "Presentación institucional." BASE-IS, Asunción.

Becher, Tony. 1985. "Research Policies and Their Impact on Research." In Wittrock and Elzinga 1985.

Ben-David, Joseph. 1971. *The Scientist's Role in Society: A Comparative Study.* Englewood Cliffs, N.J.: Prentice-Hall.

———. 1977. *Centers of Learning—Britain, France, Germany, United States.* New York: McGraw-Hill.

Berman, Edward. 1983. *The Influence of the Carnegie, Ford, and Rockefeller Foundations on American Foreign Policy: The Ideology of Philanthropy.* Albany: SUNY Press.

Beyerchen, Alan. 1990. "Trends in the Twentieth-Century German Research Enterprise." In NSF 1990.

Blair, Calvin, and Kalman Silvert. 1969. "El Colegio: An Evaluation." Report, Dec. 4. Ford Foundation, New York.

Bolio, Francisco José Paoli, ed. 1990. *Desarrollo y organización de las ciencias sociales en México.* Mexico City: CIIH-UNAM.

Borón, Atilio. 1990. "Higher Education in Latin America." Paper prepared for Ford Foundation, Meeting on Higher Education in Latin America, New York, Nov. 15.

Brañes, Raúl. 1991. *Institutional and Legal Aspects of the Environment in Latin America, Including the Participation of Nongovernmental Organizations in Environmental Management.* Washington, D.C.: IDB.

Bromley, Ray. 1990. "A New Path to Development: The Significance and Impact of Hernando de Soto's Ideas on Underdevelopment, Production, and Reproduction." *Economic Geography* 66(1): 328–48.

Brooke, James. 1990. "Peruvian with a Vision Gets Power." *New York Times,* Nov. 27.

Brunner, José Joaquín. 1988a. "Las funciones de la universidad: De la retórica a la práctica." *Opciones,* no. 13: 98–108.

———. 1988b. *Un espejo trizado.* Santiago: FLACSO.

———. 1990a. "La educación superior en Chile, 1960–1990: Evolución y políticas." Paper prepared for the meeting of the Regional Project on Comparative Higher Education Policy, Buenos Aires, Aug. 13–15.

———. 1990b. "Educational Reform in a Democratic Chile." Paper prepared for Ford Foundation, Meeting on Higher Education in Latin America, New York, Nov. 16.

———. 1990c. "Graduate Social Sciences and the Role of Independent Research Centers."

———. 1991a. "Comentario final." In CLACSO 1991.

———. 1991b. *Investing in Knowledge: Strengthening the Foundation for Research in Latin America.* Ottawa: IDRC.

Brunner, José Joaquín, and Alicia Barrios. 1987. *Inquisición, mercado y filantropía: Ciencias sociales y autoritarismo en Argentina, Brasil, Chile y Uruguay.* Santiago: FLACSO.

Bustamante, Maclovia Eugenia. 1985. "Fundaciones norteamericanas en América Latina y el Caribe: Educación superior, prioridades y tendencias (1972–1980): El caso de la Fundación Rockefeller." Thesis for licenciatura thesis, Autonomous University of Guadalajara.

Calderón, Fernando, and Patricia Provoste. 1989. "La construcción de las ciencias en América Latina." *David y Goliath* 43(5): 66–79.

———. 1990. "La construcción institucional de las ciencias sociales en América Latina." CLACSO Buenos Aires. (See CLACSO 1991.)

Camp, Roderic. 1984. *The Making of a Government: Political Leaders in Modern Mexico.* Tuscon: Univ. of Arizona Press.

———. 1985. *Intellectuals and the State in Twentieth-Century Mexico.* Austin: Univ. of Texas Press.

———. 1989. *Entrepreneurs and Politics in Twentieth-Century Mexico.* New York: Oxford Univ. Press.

Campesino Romeo, Enrique, Rubén López-Revilla, and Miguel Angel Pérez-Angón. 1985. "Estado de la investigación científica." *Avance y Perspectiva,* no. 22–23: 22–30.

Cano, Daniel. 1985. *La educación superior en la Argentina.* Buenos Aires: Grupo Editor Latinoamericano.

Cano Gallego, Jairo A. 1981. "Formation of Human Resources for Agricultural Research in Latin America and Participation in Research Networks: The Case of Former CIAT Trainees." Ph.D. diss., Michigan State Univ.

Caretas. 1991. "¿Quién entiende al presidente? Hernando de Soto, posiblemente." *Caretas* (Mar. 11): 11–14.

Cariola, Patricio. 1994. "Institutional Development of Educational Research: Institutional Development of Educational Research." In Alvarez and Gómez 1994.

Carrasquilla, José Gabriel. 1994. "Health Research Institutions." In Alvarez and Gómez 1994.

Carroll, Thomas. 1992. *Intermediary NGOs: The Supporting Link in Grassroots Development.* West Hartford, Conn.: Kumarian.

Cassen, Robert, and Associates. 1986. *Does Aid Work?* New York: Oxford Univ. Press.

Cayuela, José. 1988. *CEPAL: 40 años (1948–1988).* Santiago: CEPAL.

CEASPA. 1989. *CEASPA.* Panama City: CEASPA.

CEBRAP. N.d. CEBRAP. flyer. CEBRAP, São Paulo.

CEDE. 1977. *Poder e información.* Bogota: CEDE.

CEDEC. 1990. "Relatório de atividades 1990." CEDEC, São Paulo.

———. N.d. "CEDEC" Pamphlet. CEDEC, São Paulo.

CEE. 1974. *Diez años de investigación educativa, 1963–1973.* Mexico City: CEE.

CELADE. 1990. "CELADE." Pamphlet. CELADE, San José.

Centro de Estudios Internacionales. 1990. "Centro de Estudios Internacionales, Universidad de los Andes." CEI, Bogota.

Cepeda, Fernando. 1978. "La cooperación internacional y la universidad: Aproximaciones al caso de Colombia." In Iván Lavados, ed., *Universidad y desarrollo.* Santiago: CPU.

CEPEP. 1991. *Encuesta nacional de demografía y salúd, 1990.* Asunción: CEPEP.

CERES. N.d. "CERES." Pamphlet. CERES, Montevideo.

Chalmers, Douglas, Maria do Campello de Souza, and Atilio Borón, eds. 1992. *The Right and Democracy in Latin America.* New York: Praeger.

Christian, Shirley. 1990. "Where Perón Lived." *New York Times,* Jan. 18.

Chubb, John, and Terry Moe. 1988. "Politics, Markets, and the Organization of Schools." *American Political Science Review* 82(4): 1065–87.

CIAPA. N.d. "Pamphlet. CIAPA, San Jose.

CIAT. 1990. "CIAT." Report. CIAT, Cali.

CICCSB. 1990. *Estatutos.* Caracas: UNESCO and IDEA.

CICE. 1977. *Memoria 1977.* Buenos Aires: CICE.

CICSO. 1990. *1966-CISCO-*1990: Programa y reseña. Buenos Aires: CICSO.

CIDE. N.d. "Centro de Investigación y Docencia Económicas." CIDE, Mexico City.

CIEA. 1991. *Breve descripción del Centro de Investigación y Económia Aplicada.* Santo Domingo: CIEA.

CIEDUR. N.d. "CIEDUR se presenta, 1977–1987." CIEDUR, Montevideo.

CIEPLAN. 1988. *Publicaciones, 1976–1988. Santiago:* CIEPLAN.

————. N.d. "Informe de actividades 1988." CIEPLAN, Santiago.

CINDA. 1986. "Cooperación internacional y universidad." *Boletín Informativo,* no. 70: 15–21.

————. 1987a. "Financiamiento." *Boletín Informativo,* no. 71: 4–9.

————. 1987b. "Seminario Cooperación Internacional." *Boletín Informativo,* no. 72: 9–13.

CINTEFOR. 1977. *Documentos y resoluciones.* Montevideo: CINTEFOR.

CIPMA. 1992. *Objectivos, actividades, estructura.* Santiago: CIPMA.

CIRD. 1990. *Directorio de organizaciones privadas de desarrollo en el Paraguay.* 2d ed. Asunción: CIRD.

CIUDAD. N.d. *CIUDAD: Centro de investigaciones.* Quito: CIUDAD.

CLACSO. 1991. *Autonomía y estabilidad: Los desafíos de las ciencias sociales en América Latina.* Buenos Aires: CLACSO. (This is the final version of Calderón and Provoste 1990. It is almost the same except for fourteen pages of final commentary by José Joaquín Brunner and Jorge Balán.)

CLACSO and OECD. 1984. *Directory of Development Research and Training Institutes in Latin America.* Paris: OECD.

Clark, Burton, ed. 1984. *Perspectives on Higher Education: Eight Disciplinary and Comparative Views.* Berkeley: Univ. of California Press.

————. 1987. *The Academic Profession: National, Disciplinary, and Institutional Settings.* Berkeley: Univ. of California Press.

Clark, Burton. 1993a. "Conclusion." In Clark 1993c.

————. 1993b. "Introduction." In Clark 1993c.

————, ed. 1993c. *The Research Foundations of Graduate Education: Germany, Britain, France, United States, Japan.* Berkeley: Univ. of California Press.

Clark, Burton, and Guy Neave, eds. 1992. 4 vols. *The Encyclopedia of Higher Education.* Oxford: Pergamon.

Cleaves, Peter. 1987. *Professions and the State: The Mexican Case.* Tuscon: Univ. of Arizona Press.

Coatsworth, John. 1989. "International Collaboration in the Social Sciences: The ACLS/SSRC Joint Committee on Latin American Studies." Paper prepared for SSRC. (See SSRC 1991.)

Coburn, John, and Lawrence Wortzel. 1986. "The Problem of Privatization in Developing Countries." In William Glade, ed., *State Shrinking: A Comparative Inquiry into Privatization.* Austin: Institute of Latin American Studies, Univ. of Texas.

Colegio de Postgraduados. 1985. *Catálogo, 1986–1987*. Chapingo: Colegio de Postgraduados.

Coleman, James S., and David Court. 1992. *The Development of Universities in the Third World: The Rockefeller Foundation*. Oxford: Pergamon.

Collier, David, ed. 1979. *The New Authoritarian in Latin America*. Princeton: Princeton Univ. Press.

———. 1991. "New Perspectives on the Comparative Method." In Dankwart Rustow and Kenneth Erickson, eds., *Comparative Political Dynamics*. New York: HarperCollins.

Comissão Nacional para Reformulação da Educação Superior. 1985. *Uma nova política para a educação superior*. Brasilia: Ministry of Education.

CONACYT. 1984. Directorio nacional de instituciones y unidades que realizan investigación y desarrollo experimental. Mexico City: CONACYT.

———. 1991. *Indicadores: Actividades científicas y tecnológicas*. Mexico City: CONACYT.

Coombe, Trevor. 1991. "A Consultation on Higher Education in Africa. London: A Report to the Ford Foundation and the Rockefeller Foundation."

Cotler, Julio, Romeo Grompone, and Fernando Rospigliosi. 1988. "El desarrollo institucional de las ciencias sociales en el Perú." Paper prepared for SSRC. (See SSRC 1991.)

Courard, Hernán, ed. 1993. *Políticas comparadas de educación superior en América Latina*. Santiago: FLACSO.

Court, David. 1980. "The Growth of Social Science in East Africa: Notes on the Development of University-based Knowledge." In Irving Spitzberg, ed., *Universities and the International Distribution of Knowledge*. New York: Praeger.

———. 1982. "The Idea of Social Science in East Africa." In Stifel, Davidson, and Coleman 1982.

———. 1991. "The Development of University Education in Sub-Saharan Africa." In Altbach 1991, vol. 1.

CPDOC. 1991. *Perfil do CPDOC*. Rio: CPDOC

CPU, ed. 1983. *Las ciencias sociales en Chile: Análisis de siete disciplinas*. Santiago: CPU.

CRESALC. 1984. *Directorio de centros de investagación y unidades de información sobre educación superior en América Latina y el Caribe*. Caracas: CRESALC.

CRIES. 1991. *Memoria 89–90, Programa 90–91*. Managua: CRIES.

CSUCA. 1989. *Catálogo de instituciones de enseñanza superior e investigación en centroamérica*. San José: CSUCA.

Cueto, Marcos. 1989. *Excelencia científica en la periferia*. Lima: GRADE-CONCYTEC.

Curti, Merle. 1963. *American Philanthropy Abroad: A History*. New Brunswick: Rutgers Univ. Press.

Dahl, Robert. 1982. *Dilemmas of Pluralist Democracy: Autonomy versus Control*. New Haven: Yale Univ. Press.

Datta, Bhabatosh. 1989. "Social Science Research: Universities and Autonomous Institutions." In Amrik Sigh and G. D. Sharma, eds., *Higher Education in India*. Delhi: Konark.

Dent, David. 1990a. "Introduction: Political Science Research on Latin America." In Dent 1990e.

————. 1990b. "Major Reserch Centers and Institutes in Latin America and the Caribbean." In Dent 1990c.

————, ed. 1990c. *Handbook of Political Science Research on Latin America.* Westport, Conn.: Greenwood.

DESCO. 1990. *25 años de quehacer institucional.* Lima: DESCO.

DESEC. 1990. "D.E.S.E.C." DESEC, Cochabamba.

"Los ONGS y su papel." 1992. *El Diario,* Feb. 12.

Díaz-Albertini, Javier. 1990. "Development as Grassroots Empowerment: An Analytical Review of NGDO Programs in Lima, Peru." Working Paper 157, Program on Non-Profit Organizations, Yale University.

Dickson, Paul. 1971. *Think Tanks.* New York: Atheneum.

DiMaggio, Paul, and Helmut Anheier. 1990. "The Sociology of Nonprofit Organizations and Sectors." *Annual Review of Sociology* 16:137–59.

Dirección General de Asuntos Personales (UNAM), ed. 1984. *Diagnóstico del personal académico de la UNAM. Mexico City:* UNAM.

Dooner, Patricio, and Iván Lavados, eds. 1979. *La universidad latinoamericana: Visión de una década,* Santiago: CPU.

Douglas, James. 1987. "Political Theories of Nonprofit Organizations." In Powell, 1987.

Downs, Charles, et al., eds. 1989. *Social Policy from the Grassroots: Nongovernmental Organizations in Chile.* Boulder: Westview.

Downs, Charles, and Giorgio Solimano. 1989. "Toward an Evaluation of the NGO Experience in Chile." In Downs et al. 1989.

Duarte, Rosalino. 1991. "¿Existen manos negras de las organizaciones no gubermentales?" *Noticias* (Asunción), Mar. 31.

Durand, Francisco. 1992. "The New Right and Political Change in Peru." In Chalmers, Campello de Souza, and Borón, 1992.

Eisemon, Thomas. 1981. "Scientific Life in Indian and African Universities: A Comparative Study of Peripherality in Science." *Comparative Education Review* 25(2): 164–82.

Eisemon, Thomas, and Moussa Kourouma. 1991. "Foreign Assistance for University Development in Sub-Saharan Africa and Asia." Paper prepared for World Bank, Seminar on Improvement and Innovation in Higher Education in Developing Countries, Kuala Lumpur, July 1–4.

El Colegio de México. 1987a. "Actividades del Departamento de Publicaciones durante 1986." *Boletín* 11: 8–9.

————. 1987b. *Una idea de casi medio siglo.* Mexico City: El Colegio de México.

————. N.d. "Requisitos de factibilidad mínimos para el establecimiento de institutos de investígacion académica y enseñanza de postgrado en los estados de la República. (Elaborados en base a la experiencia de varios colegios creados a partir de 1979.)" El Colegio de México, Mexico City.

EURAL. N.d. "EURAL." EURAL, Buenos Aires.

Evans, Peter, Dietrich Rueschemeyer, and Theda Skocpol. 1985a. "Towards a More Adequate Understanding of the State." In Evans, Rueschemeyer, and Skocpol, 1985b.

———. 1985b. *Bringing the State Back In.* New York: Cambridge Univ. Press.

Fajnzylber, Fernando. 1987. "Reflexiones sobre ciencia, technología y sociedad." In Pablo González Casanova and Héctor Aguilar Camín, eds. *México ante la crisis.* 3d ed. Mexico City: Siglo XXI.

Favaloro, René. 1991. "No privatizar la ciencia." *Futuro,* May 4.

FEDESARROLLO. 1990. *Pensar para el país.* Bogotá: FEDESARROLLO.

Feller, Irwin. 1986. *Universities and State Governments.* New York: Praeger.

Fernández, Rodrigo. 1989. "El surgimiento de las ciencias sociales en la región centroamericana." Paper prepared for SSRC. (See SSRC 1991.)

FES. 1989. *Informe anual.* Cali: FES.

FGV. 1977. "Relatório geral y prestação de contas exercício de 1977." FGV, Rio.

Fisher, Julie. 1992. "Local Governments and the Independent Sector in the Third World." In McCarthy, Hodgkinson, Sumariwalla 1992.

———. 1993. *The Road from Rio: Sustainable Development and the Nongovernmental Movement in the Third World.* New York: Praeger.

FJMA. 1980. *Primer directorio de fundaciones de la República Argentina.* Buenos Aires: FJMA.

———. 1983. *Fundaciones argentinas: Encuesta, 1983.* Buenos Aires: FJMA.

———. 1989. *Primer directorio de fundaciones de la República Argentina. Suplemento: Nuevas fundaciones.* Buenos Aires: FJMA.

FLACSO. 1987. "Programa Buenos Aires, 1986–87." FLACSO, Buenos Aires.

———. 1990. "Informe de actividades." FLACSO, Quito.

———. N.d. "FLACSO." FLACSO, n.p.

Ford Foundation. Various years, 1959–1987. *Annual Report.* New York: Ford Foundation.

Fortes, Jacqueline, and Larissa Lomnitz. 1991. *La formación del científico en México.* Mexico City: Siglo XXI.

Fosdick, Raymond. 1952. *The Story of the Rockefeller Foundation.* New York: Harper and Brothers.

Foweraker, Joe, and Ann Craig, eds. 1990. *Popular Movements and Political Change in Mexico.* Boulder: Lynne Rienner.

Fox, Elizabeth, (with Nina Manitzas). 1980. "Support for Social Sciences Research in the Southern Cone. Evaluation report. IDRC, Ottawa.

Fox, Robert. 1990. "Research, Education, and the Industrial Economy in Modern France." In NSF 1990.

Franco, Augusto, and Carlos Tünnermann. 1978. *La educación superior de Colombia.* Cali: FES.

Freeman, Howard. 1973. "The Social Sciences and their Utilization in Mexico." FF card catalogue #4059.

Friedberg, Erhard, and Christine Musselin. 1987. "The Academic Profession in France." In Clark 1987.

Friedman, Ray. 1980. "The Role of Non-Profit Organizations in Foreign Aid: A Literature Review." Working Paper 32, Program on Non-Profit Organizations, Yale University.

Fruhling, Hugo. 1985. "Nonprofit Organizations as Opposition to Authoritarian Rule: The Case of Human Rights Organizations and Private Research Centers in Chile." Working Paper 96, Program on Non-Profit Organizations, Yale University.

———. 1987. "Nongovernmental Human Rights Organizations and Redemocratization in Brazil." Working Paper 124, Program on Non-Profit Organizations, Yale University.

———. 1989. "Private Voluntary Organizations and Development in West Africa." In James 1989.

Fuentes, Olac, Manuel Gil, and Rollin Kent. 1990. "Proyecto de investigacion sobre políticas comparadas de educación superior en América Latina: El caso de México." Paper prepared for Meeting of the Regional Project on Comparative Higher Education Policy, Buenos Aires, Aug. 13–15.

Fuenzalida, Edmundo. 1970. "La dependencia de América Latina en el saber superior." *Revista Paraguaya de Sociología* 7(18): 98–114.

———. 1973. "La universidad chilena no debe hacer investigación científica." In CPU, ed., *Desarrollo científico-tecnológico y universidad.* Santiago: CPU.

———. 1982. "The Contribution of Higher Education to a New International Order." In B. C. Sanyal, ed. *Higher Education and the New International Order.* Paris: UNESCO.

———. 1983. "The Reception of Scientific Sociology in Chile." *Latin American Research Review* 18(2): 95–112.

———. 1984. "Institutionalisation of Research in Chile's Universities: 1953–1967." In R. M. Gassett, ed. *Education and Development.* London: Croom Helm.

———. 1987. "La reorganización de las instituciones de enseñanza superior e investigación en América Latina entre 1950 y 1980 y sus interpretaciones." *Estudios Sociales* 52(2): 115–38.

Fundación Santillana. 1989. *América: El lugar donde fondean los sueños.* Bogotá: Fundación Santillana para Iberoamérica.

Gaillard, Jacques. 1991. *Scientists in the Third World.* Lexington: University of Kentucky Press.

Gamarra, Eduardo. 1990. "Bolivia." In Dent 1990c.

———. 1993. "Market-Oriented Reforms and Democratization in Latin America." In William Smith, Carlos Acuña, and Eduardo Gamarra, eds. *Latin American Political Economy in the Age of Neoliberal Reform.* Miami: North-South Center.

Ganesh, S. R., and Dalpat Sarupia. 1983. "Explorations in Helplessness of Higher Education Institutions in the Third World." *Higher Education* 12(2): 191–204.

García, José María. 1990. "El desarrollo del posgrado en México." *Revista Latinoamericana de Estudios Educativos* 20(1): 107–30.

García Garrido, José-Luis. 1992. "Spain." In Clark and Neave 1992, vol. 1.

García Guadilla, Carmen. 1989. "Temas relevantes para el estudio de la educación superior en América Latina." *Educación Superior* (Caracas) 27–28: 104–36.

Garretón, Manuel Antonio. 1981. "Las ciencias sociales en Chile al inicio de los 80." Working Paper 113. FLACSO, Santiago.

Gatti, Bernadette, and Jorge Chateau. 1988. "Program Support: CIDE." In IDRC 1988.

Geiger, Roger. 1986. *To Advance Knowledge: The Growth of American Research Universities in the Twentieth Century, 1900–1940.* New York: Oxford Univ. Press.

———. 1989. "La investigación académica en los Estados Unidos." In CPU, ed., *Tendencias de la educación superior.* Santiago: CPU.

———. 1990a. "The American University and Research." In NSF 1990.

———. 1990b. "Organized Research Units: Their Role in the Development of University Research." *Journal of Higher Education* 61(1): 1–19.

———. 1992. "The Institutional Fabric of the Higher Education System." In Clark and Neave 1992, vol. 3.

Gellert, Claudius. 1993. "The German Mode of Research and Advanced Education." In Clark 1993c.

Gellert, Claudius, Erich Leitner, and Jurgen Schramm, eds. 1990. *Research and Teaching at Universities: International and Comparative Perspectives.* Frankfurt: Peter Lang.

Gibson, Edward. 1990. "Democracy and the New Electoral Right in Argentina." Working Paper 12, Institute of Latin American and Iberian Studies, Columbia University.

Gidron, Benjamin, Ralph Kramer, and Lester Salamon, eds. 1992. *Government and the Third Sector: Emerging Relationships in Welfare States.* San Francisco: Jossey-Bass.

Glade, William, ed. 1991. *Privatization of Public Enterprises in Latin America.* San Diego: U.S.-Mexico Center, Univ. of California-San Diego.

Gómez, Henry, and Iván Bustillo. 1979. "IESA: Shaping a Viable Strategy." In David Korten, ed., *Population and Social Development Management.* Caracas: IESA.
Gormley, William. 1991a. "The Privatization Controversy." In Gormley 1991c.

———. 1991b. "Two Cheers for Privatization." In Gormley 1991c.

———, ed. 1991c. *Privatization and Its Alternatives.* Madison: Univ. of Wisconsin Press.

GRADE. 1990. *Memoria, 1980–1990.* Lima: GRADE.

Grobet, Paulina, and Norah Schlaen Novick. 1984. "Las figuras académicas del personal docente de posgrado." In Dirección General 1984.

Gumport, Patricia. 1993. "Graduate Education and Organized Research in the United States." In Clark 1993c.

Hachette, Dominique. 1990. "Financiamiento de la investigación universitaria." In Carla Lehmann, ed., *Financiamiento de la educación superior.* Santiago: CEP.

Hall, Peter. 1989. "Business Giving and Social Investment in the United States." In Magat 1989.

———. 1992. *Inventing the Nonprofit Sector and Other Essays on Philanthropy, Voluntarism, and Nonprofit Organizations.* Baltimore: Johns Hopkins Univ. Press.

Hammack, David, and Dennis Young, eds. 1993. *Nonprofit Organizations in a Market Economy.* San Francisco: Jossey-Bass.

Hannan, Michael, and John Freeman. 1977. "The Population Ecology of Organizations." *American Journal of Sociology* 82(5): 929–64.

———. 1984. "Structural Inertia and Organizational Change." *American Sociological Review* 49(2): 149–64.

Hansen, David, Gustavo Antonini, and John Strasma. 1988. *Dominican Republic: The Superior Institute of Agriculture.* Project Impact Evaluation Report 167. Washington, D.C.: AID.

Hansmann, Henry. 1986a. "The Role of Nonprofit Enterprise." In Rose-Ackerman 1986.

———. 1986b. "Why Do Universities Have Endowments?" Working Paper 109. Program on Non-Profit Organizations, Yale University.

Harkavy, Oscar, and Letticia Diescho. 1988. "Case Report: PISPAL." Report, Aug. 26. Ford Foundation, New York.

Harrison, John. N.d. "Observations on External Support of the Humanities in Latin America: The RF [Rockefeller Foundation] Experience since 1955." Photocopy. New York.

Harrison, John, Joseph Burnett, and George Waggoner. 1967. *A Report to the American Academic Community on the Present Argentine University Situation.* Austin: LASA.

Heath, John, ed. 1990. *Public Enterprises at the Crossroads.* London: Routledge.

Hellman, Judith Adler. 1990. "Latin American Social Movements and the Question of Autonomy." *LASA Forum* 21(2): 7–12.

Hellman, Ronald. 1988. "The Impact of the Ford Foundation on the Economic Sciences in Chile." Bildner Center, City University of New York. (Paper reproduced from 1971 original.)

Henkel, Mary, and Maurice Kogan. 1993. "Research Training and Graduate Education: The British Macro Structure." In Clark 1993c.

Herrera, Amilcar. 1973. "Social Determinents of Science Policy in Latin America." In Charles Cooper, ed., *Science, Technology, and Development.* London: Frank Cass.

Herrera, Felipe. 1985. *Experiencias universitarias: Escenarios nacionales e internacionales.* Santiago: Pehuén.

Hickson, David, et al. 1971. "A Strategic Contingencies' Theory of Interorganizational Power." *Administrative Science Quarterly* 16(2): 216–29.

Higley, John, and Richard Gunther, eds. 1992. *Elites and Democratic Consolidation in Latin America and Southern Europe.* Cambridge: Cambridge Univ. Press.

Hodgkinson, Virginia, and Kathleen McCarthy. 1992. "The Voluntary Sector in International Perspective: An Overview." In McCarthy, Hodgkinson, Sumariwalla. 1992.

IAF. 1990. *A Guide to NGO Directories.* Rosslyn, Va.: IAF.

Ianni, Octavio. 1967. "Sociology in Latin America." In Manuel Diegues Jr. And Bryce Wood, eds., *Social Science in Latin America.* New York: Columbia Univ. Press.

Ibarrola, María de. 1986–1987. "La formación de investigadores en México." *Avance y Perspectiva* 29: 3–21.

IDB. 1985. "Enfoque y contribuciones del BID en ciencia y tecnología." IDB, Washington, D.C.

———. 1986. "Distribution of IDB Education Financing, by Areas, 1962–1985. Photocopy. IDB, Washington, D.C.

———. 1988. *Economic and Social Progress in Latin America: Science and Technology Section.* Washington, D.C.: IDB.

———. 1992. "Extra: Environment." IDB *Newsletter,* June.

IDEA. 1989. *Estatutos.* Caracas: IDEA.

IDRC. 1986. "Institutional Support to the Southern Cone." Working paper. IDRC, Ottawa.

———, ed. 1988. *Evaluation Report: Program Support in Chile.* Ottawa: IDRC.

IEPRI. 1990. *Memorias, 1986–1989.* Bogotá: Universidad Nacional de Colombia.

IME. 1991. *SIE México.* Brochure. IME.

INCAE. N.d. *Expansión and diversificación.* Brochure. Mexico City: IME.

Independent Sector. N.d. *Academic Centers and Programs.* 3d ed. Washington, D.C.: Independent Sector.

Israel, Arturo. 1987. *Institutional Development Incentives to Performance.* Baltimore: Johns Hopkins Univ. Press.

ITDT. 1990. "Actividades de docencia e investigación." ITDT, Buenos Aires.

IUPERJ. 1991. *Relatório anual, 1990.* Rio: IUPERJ.

Jaksić, Iván. 1985. "The Politics of Higher Education." *Latin American Research Review* 20(1): 209–21.

———. 1989. *Academic Rebels in Chile.* Albany: SUNY Press.

James, Estelle, ed. 1989. *The Nonprofit Sector in International Perspective.* New York: Oxford Univ. Press.

Jänicke, Martin. 1990. *State Failure: The Impotence of Politics in Industrial Society.* Trans. Alan Braley. Cambridge, U.K.: Polity.

Jenkins, J. Craig. 1987. "Nonprofit Organizations and Policy Advocacy." In Powell 1987.

Jiménez, Leobardo, Ramón Fernández, and Jorge Galindo. 1978. *Trajectoria y perspecti-*

vas del Colegio de Postgraduados. Chapingo: Secretaría de Agricultura y Recursos Hidraúlicos.

Jiménez M., Fernando. 1982. *El autoritarismo en el gobierno de la UNAM.* Mexico City: Ediciones de Cultura Popular.

Kalmanovitz, Salomón. 1989. "Sigamos hablando de la Universidad Nacional." *Análisis Político,* no. 6: 72–79.

Kamerman, Sheila, and Alfred Kahn, eds. 1989. *Privatization and the Welfare State.* Princeton: Princeton Univ. Press.

Kanter, Rosabeth Moss. 1977. *Men and Women of the Corporation.* New York: Basic Books.

Kanter, Rosabeth, and David Summers. 1987. "Doing Well While Doing Good: Dilemmas of Performance Measurement in Nonprofit Organizations and the Need for a Multiple-Constituency Approach." In Powell 1987.

Karl, Barry, and Stanley Katz. 1981. "The American Private Philanthropic Foundation and the Public Sphere, 1890–1930." *Minerva* 19(1): 236–70.

King, Kenneth. 1981. "Dilemmas of Research Aid to Education in Developing Countries." *Comparative Education* 17(2): 247–54.

Klenner, Arno, and Humberto Vega. 1989. "Support for Income Generation in an Economy of Poverty." In Downs et al. 1989.

Kohler, Robert. 1991. *Partners in Science: Foundations and National Scientists, 1900–1945.* Chicago: Univ. of Chicago Press.

Kramer, Ralph. 1981. *Voluntary Agencies in the Welfare State.* Berkeley: Univ. of California Press.

———. 1989. "The Use of Government Funds by Voluntary Social Service Agencies in Four Welfare States." In James 1989.

Labadie, Gastón, and Cristina Filardo. 1989. "Tendencias en la expansión de la educación universitaria en Uruguay entre 1955 y 1966." Working paper. CERES, Montevideo.

Lagos, Ricardo. 1982. "Algunas reflexiones sobre las ciencias sociales en Chile." Paper prepared for FLACSO, Seminar on Intellectuals, University, and Society, Santiago, May 17–19.

Larraín, Hernán. 1985. "Nivel académico en Chile." In María José Lemaitre and Iván Lavados, eds. *La educación superior en Chile.* Santiago: CPU.

LASA. 1991. *Program, Sixteenth International Congress.* Pittsburgh: LASA.

Lavados, Iván. 1987. "Financiamiento de actividas académicas." *Estudios Sociales* 51(1): 119–34.

Leman, Christopher. 1989. "The Forgotten Fundamental: Successes and Excesses of Direct Government." In Salamon 1989c.

Lemos, Carlos. 1994. "Las ONG." *El Tiempo,* Sept. 21.

León, Magdalena, and Hobart Spalding. 1992. "An Evaluation of SAREC's Support to Three Women's Research Institutions in Latin America." SAREC, Stockholm.

Levy, Daniel. 1979. "The Private-Public Question in Higher Education: Distinction or Extinction." Working Paper 37. Higher Education Research Group, Yale University.

———. 1980. *University and Government in Mexico: Autonomy in an Authoritarian System.* New York: Praeger.

———. 1981. "Comparing Authoritarian Regimes in Latin America: Insights from Higher Education Policy." *Comparative Politics* 14(1): 31–52.

———. 1986. *Higher Education and the State in Latin America.* Chicago: Univ. of Chicago Press.

———. 1987. "A Comparison of Private and Public Educational Organizations." In Powell 1987.

———. 1991. "Targeted Philanthropy: How U.S. Donors Selected Latin American Universities." Working Paper #170. Program on Non-Profit Organizations, Yale University.

———. 1992a. "Recent Trends in the Privatization of Latin American Higher Education: Solidification, Breadth, and Vigor." *Higher Education Policy* 6(4): 12–19.

———. 1992b. "Private Institutions of Higher Education." In Clark and Neave 1992, vol. 3.

———. 1995a. "Latin America's Think Tanks: The Roots of Nonprofit Privatization." *Studies in Comparative International Development* 30(2): 3–25.

———. 1995b. "Novel Funding for a Novel Nonprofit Sector: Latin America's Private Research Centers." *Nonprofit and Voluntary Sector Quarterly* 24(1): 41–58.

———. Forthcoming. "To Export Progress: U.S. Assistance to Latin American Universities" (tentative title).

Lida, Clara. 1988. *La Casa de España en México.* Mexico City: El Colegio de México.

Linz, Juan. 1975. "Totalitarian and Authoritarian Regimes." In Fred Greenstein and Nelson Polsby, eds., *Handbook of Political Science.* Vol. 3. Reading, Mass.: Addison-Wesley.

Lladser, María Teresa. 1986. *Centros privados de investigación en ciencias sociales en Chile.* Santiago: AHC and FLACSO.

———. 1987. *Directorio de investigadores.* Santiago: AHC.

———. 1988a. "The Emergence of Social Science Research Centers in Chile Under Military Rule." Occasional Paper 159. Center for Studies in Higher Education, University of California-Berkeley.

———. 1988b. "Formación académica." Santiago. Photocopy.

Lohmann, Roger. 1992. *The Commons: New Perspectives on Nonprofit Organizations and Voluntary Action.* San Francisco: Jossey-Bass.

Loveman, Brian. 1991. "NGOs and the Transition to Democracy in Chile." *Grassroots Development* 15(2): 8–19.

Lowenthal, Abraham. 1991. "The United States and Latin American Democracy: Learning from History." In Abraham Lowenthal, ed., *Exporting Democracy: The United States and Latin America*. Baltimore: Johns Hopkins Univ. Press.

Lowi, Theodore. 1979. *The End of Liberalism: The Second Republic of the United States*. 2d ed. New York: Norton.

McCarthy, Kathleen. N.d. "The Voluntary Sector Overseas: Notes from the Field." Working paper. Center for the Study of Philanthropy, Graduate School and University Center, City University of New York.

————, ed. 1984. *The International Foundation Perspective*. Philadelphia: Univ. of Pennsylvania Press.

McCarthy, Kathleen, Virginia Hodgkinson, Rosey Sumariwalla, and Associates, eds. 1992. *The Nonprofit Sector in the Global Community: Voices from Many Nations*. San Francisco: Jossey-Bass.

McConnell, Grant. 1966. *Private Power and American Democracy*. New York: Knopf.

Magat, Richard. 1979. *The Ford Foundation at Work*. New York: Plenum.

————, ed. 1989. *Philanthropic Giving: Studies in Varieties and Goals*. New York: Oxford Univ. Press.

Malloy, James, ed. 1977. *Authoritarianism and Corporation in Latin America*. Pittsburgh: Univ. of Pittsburgh Press.

————. 1987. "The Politics of Transition in Latin America." In James Malloy and Mitchell Seligson, eds., *Authoritarians and Democrats: Regime Transition in Latin America*. Pittsburgh: Univ. of Pittsburgh Press.

Malo, Salvador. 1992. "El sistema nacional de investigadores en México." *Interciencia* 17(6): 344–47.

March, James. 1982. "Studying Abroad: The Fundación Gran Mariscal de Ayacucho." Photocopy. Pittsburgh.

Marschall, Miklos. 1990. "The Nonprofit Sector in a Centrally Planned Economy." In Anheier and Seibel 1990c.

Massi, Fernanda. 1989. "Franceses e norte-americanos nas ciências sociais brasileiras (1930–1960)." In Miceli 1989b.

Medina, José. 1992. "El sistema de promoción de investigador en Venezuela." *Interciencia* 17(6): 354–57.

Meneses, Manuel. 1987. "Inciertos, los apoyos de CONACYT." *La Jornada* (Mexico City), June 5.

Merkx, Gilbert. 1979. "Argentine Social Science: CICSO." *Latin American Research Review* 14(1): 228–33.

————. 1992. "Editor's Forward." *Latin America Research Review* 27(1): 3–5.

Meyer, Carrie. 1993. "Environmental NGOs in Ecuador." *Journal of Developing Areas* 27: 191–210.

Miceli, Sergio. 1989a. "A ilusão americana: Relações acadêmicas entre Brasil, Estados Unidos e Europa." Paper prepared for Fifteenth Latin American Studies Association Convention, Miami, Dec. 3–6.

———, ed. 1989b. *História das ciências sociais no Brasil.* São Paulo: Edições Vértice, IDESP.

———. 1990. "The State of Graduate Social Sciences in Latin America and the Role of Independent Research Centers." Paper prepared for Ford Foundation, Meeting on Higher Education in Latin America, New York, Nov. 16.

———. N.d. Paper prepared for SSRC. (See SSRC 1991.)

Moller, Mónica, and Ana María Flores. 1985. "Fundaciones norteamericanas en América Latina y el Caribe: Educación superior, prioridades y tendencias (1972–1980): El caso de la Fundación Ford." Thesis, for licenciatura UAG, Guadalajara.

Mommsen, Wolfgang. 1987. "The Academic Profession in the Federal Republic of Germany." In Clark 1987.

Moock, Joyce. 1980. "Ford Foundation Assistance to University-Level Education in Developing Countries." Paper prepared for Review Advisory Committee Meeting, Rockefeller Foundation, Education for Development Program, New York, Apr. 6–8.

Moreira, Frota, and B. K. Copeland. 1976. "International Cooperation in Science: Brazil-US Chemistry Program." *Interciencia* 1(3): 138–46.

Mosher, Arthur. 1957. *Technical Cooperation in Latin American Agriculture.* Chicago: Univ. of Chicago Press.

Muñoz, Humberto, and Herlinda Suárez. 1984. "El personal académico de la coordinación de humanidades." In Dirección General 1984.

Muñoz Izquierdo, Carlos. N.d. "CEE: Veinticinco años de investigaciones." Mexico City.

Mutch, David. 1992. "Economic Policy Group Networks for Free Markets." *Christian Science Monitor,* Apr. 23.

Myers, Robert. 1981. *Connecting Worlds: A Survey of Developments in Educational Research.* Ottawa: IDRC.

———. 1983. "External Financing of Foreign Study: The Ford Foundation in Peru." *Prospects* 13(4): 503–13.

Nagel, John, and Conrad Snyder. 1989. "International Funding of Educational Development: External Agendas and Internal Adaptations—The Case of Liberia." *Comparative Education Review* 33(1): 3–20.

Naim, Moisés. 1992. "The Launching of Radical Policy Changes: The Venezuelan Experience." World Bank, Washington, D.C.

Navarro, Juan Carlos, ed. 1994. *Community Organizations in Latin America.* Washington, D.C. IDB.

Neave, Guy. 1993. "Separation de Corps: The Training of Advanced Students and the Organization of Research in France." In Clark 1993c.

Nielsen, Waldemar. 1972. *The Big Foundations.* New York: Columbia University Press.

———. 1985. *The Golden Donors.* New York: Dutton.

NSF, ed. 1990. *The Academic Research Enterprise within the Industrialized Nations: Comparative Perspectives.* Report of a Symposium. Washington, DC: National Academy Press.

NUPES. 1990. "NUPES da USP: O primeiro ano." Photocopy. NUPES.

Ocampo, Alfonso. 1987. "The Privatization of Higher Education in Colombia." Paper prepared for Wingspread Conference on Private Higher Education, Racine, Wis., June 15–18.

Odendahl, Teresa. 1989. "Independent Foundations and Wealthy Donors." In Magat 1989.

O'Donnell, Guillermo. 1988. *Bureaucratic Authoritarianism: Argentina, 1966–1973, in Comparative Perspective.* Berkeley: Univ. of California Press.

———. 1992. *Delegative Democracy?* Working paper 172. Notre Dame: Kellogg Institute.

O'Donnell, Guillermo, Philippe Schmitter, and Laurence Whitehead, eds. 1986. *Transitions from Authoritarian Rule: Prospects for Democracy.* Baltimore: Johns Hopkins Univ. Press.

O'Neill, Michael. 1989. *The Third America.* San Francisco: Jossey-Bass.

Orellana R., Mario. 1986. "Reflexiones sobre las ciencias sociales y del comportamiento." In CPU, ed. *Conocimiento, educación superior y desarrollo nacional.* Santiago: CPU.

Orlans, Harold. 1972. *The Nonprofit Research Institute.* New York: McGraw-Hill.

Packenham, Robert. 1973. *Ideas in Foreign Aid and Social Science.* Princeton: Princeton Univ. Press.

———. 1992. *The Dependency Movement: Scholarship and Politics in Development Studies.* Cambridge: Harvard Univ. Press.

Payton, Robert. 1989. "Philanthropic Values." In Magat 1989.

Pereira, H. C. 1971. "The Integration of Research Agencies for African Agricultural Development." *Minerva 9(1): 38–45.*

Petras, James. 1989. "La metamorfosis." *La Jornada* (Mexico City), Jan. 4.

———. 1990. "The Redemocratization Process." In Susanne Jonas and Nancy Stein, eds., *Democracy in Latin America.* New York: Bergin and Garvey.

Pfeffer, Jeffrey, and Gerald Salancik. 1978. *The External Control of Organizations.* New York: Harper and Row.

Piña, Carlos. 1990. "Las organizaciones no gubermentales en el ambiente local urbano." *Estudios Sociales* 63(1): 47–51.

Portes, Alejandro. 1975. "Trends in International Research Cooperation: The Latin American Case." *American Sociologist* 11(3): 131–40.

Powell, Walter W., ed. 1987. *The Nonprofit Sector: A Research Handbook.* New Haven: Yale Univ. Press.

Powell, Walter, and Rebecca Friedkin. 1987. "Organizational Change in Nonprofit Organizations." In Powell 1987.

Przeworski, Adam. 1986. "The Lambert Report." *PS* 19: 78–83.

Puryear, Jeffrey M. 1983. "Higher Education, Development Assistance, and Repressive Regimes." Report. Ford Foundation, New York.

———. 1994. *Thinking Politics: Intellectuals and Democracy in Chile, 1973–1988*. Baltimore: Johns Hopkins Univ. Press.

Pyenson, Lewis. 1978. "The Incomplete Transmission of a European Image: Physics at Greater Buenos Aires and Montreal, 1890–1920." *Proceedings of the American Philosophical Society* 122(2): 92–114.

Quintero, Angel. N.d. "El desarrollo institucional de las ciencias sociales en Puerto Rico." Paper prepared for SSRC. (See SSRC 1991.)

Raczynski, Dagmar, Pilar Vergara, and Carlos Vergara. 1993. "Políticas sociales: Prioridades de investigación y necesidades de capacitación en Chile." Santiago: CIEPLAN, Notas Técnicas, #156.

Reilly, Charles, ed. 1994. *Nuevas políticas urbanas: Las ONG y los gobiernos municipios en la democratizacion latinoamericana*. Arlington, Va: IAF.

Remmer, Karen. 1991. "New Wine or Old Bottlenecks? The Study of Latin American Democracy." *Comparative Politics* 23(4): 479–96.

Resource Center. 1990. *National Endowment for Democracy: A Foreign Policy Branch Gone Awry*. Alburqurque: Resource Center.

Reveló, José, and Eugenio Tironi. 1988. "Program Support: PIIE." In IDRC 1988.

Reyna, José Luis. N.d. "La educación superior en México: Tendencias y perspectivas dentro de los marcos institucionales e internacionales existentes." Paper prepared for SSRC. (See SSRC 1991.)

Rhoades, Gary. 1991. "Graduate Education." In Altbach 1991, vol. 1.

Rodrigues, Leôncio Martins. 1982. "Ciências socais, universidade e intelectuais no Brasil." Paper prepared for FLACSO-Chile, Conference on Intelectuales, Universidad y Sociedad. Santiago, May 17–19.

Rodríguez, Mariano. 1986. "Recursos humanos para la investigación: El caso de Costa Rica." Centro Internacional de Investigaciones para el Desarrollo, San José.

Roett, Riordan. 1972. *The Politics of Foreign Aid in the Brazilian Northeast*. Nashville: Vanderbilt Univ. Press.

Roper, Christopher, and Jorge Silva, eds. 1983. *Science and Technology in Latin America*. London: Longmans.

Rose-Ackerman, Susan, ed. 1986. *The Economics of Nonprofit Institutions*. New York: Oxford Univ. Press.

Rothblatt, Sheldon. 1990. "Research and British Universities." In NSF 1990.

Ruiz Massieu, Mario. 1987. *El cambio en la universidad*. Mexico City: UNAM.

Sagasti, Francisco. 1979. "Subdesarrollo ciencia y tecnología: Una apreciación del rol de la universidad latinoamericana." In Dooner and Lavados 1979.

———— et al. 1984. "Ciencia y tecnología en América Latina." *Comercio Exterior* 34(12): 1163–79.

Salam, Abdus. 1966. "The Isolation of the Scientist in Developing Countries." *Minerva* 4(4): 461–65.

Salamon, Lester. 1987. "Partners in Public Service: The Scope and Theory of Government-Nonprofit Relations." In Powell 1987.

————. 1989a. "The Changing Tools of Government Action: An Overview." In Salamon 1989c.

————. 1989b. "Conclusion: Beyond Privatization." In Salamon 1989c.

————, ed. 1989c. *Beyond Privatization: The Tools of Government Action.* Washington, D.C.: Urban Institute.

————. 1990. "The Nonprofit Sector and Government: The American Experience in Theory and Practice." In Anheier and Seibel 1990c.

Saloma, John. 1984. *Omnibus Politics: The New Conservative Labyrinth.* New York: Hill and Wang.

Schamis, Hector. 1991. "Reconceptualizing Latin American Authoritarianism in the 1970s: From Bureaucratic Authoritarianism to Neoconservatism." *Comparative Politics* 23(2): 201–20.

Schiefelbein, Ernesto. 1978. "Educational Research in Latin America." *International Review of Education* 24(4): 483–501.

————. 1992. "Chile." In Clark and Neave 1992, vol. 1.

Schmitter, Philippe. 1974. "Still the Century of Corporatism?" In Frederick Pike and Thomas Stritch, eds., *The New Corporatism.* Notre Dame: Univ. of Notre Dame Press.

Schoijet, Mauricio. 1979. "The Condition of Mexican Science." *Minerva* 17(3): 381–412.

Schwartzman, Simon. 1979. *Formação da comunidade científica no Brasil.* Rio de Janeiro: FINEP.

————. 1984. "Higher Education and Scientific Research: A View from Latin America." In Clark 1984.

————. 1985. "The Quest for University Research." In Wittrock and Elzinga 1985.

————. 1991. *A Space for Science: The Development of the Scientific Community in Brazil* University Park: Pennsylvania State Univ. Press.

————. 1992. "The Future of Higher Education in Brazil." Working Paper 97. Woodrow Wilson International Center for Scholars, Washington, D.C.

Schwartzman, Simon, and Cláudio de Moura Castro. 1986. *Pesquisa universitária em questão.* São Paulo: UNICAMP/Icone, CNPQ.

Segal, Aaron. 1985. "Higher Education in Latin America and the Caribbean: An Overview." *Interciencia* 10(4): 196–98.

———. 1986a. "From Technology Transfer to Science and Technology Institutionalization." In John R. McIntyre and Daniel S. Papp, eds., *The Political Economy of International Technology Transfers.* New York: Quorum.

———. 1986b. "Science, Technology and Development in Latin America." In Jack Hopkins, ed. *Latin American Contemporary Record*, vol. 4. New York: Holmes and Meier.

Seibel, Wolfgang. 1990. "Organizational Behavior and Organizational Function: Toward a Micro-Macro Theory of the Third Sector." In Anheier and Seibel 1990c.

Seibel, Wolfgang, and Helmut Anheier. 1990. "Sociological and Political Science Approaches to the Third Sector." In Anheier and Seibel 1990c.

SELA. 1990. "Survey of Intergovernmental Organizations, Institutions, and Agencies Active in the Regional and Inter-American Spheres." Paper prepared for Sixteenth Regular Meeting of the Latin American Council, Caracas, Sept. 3–7.

Selvaratnam, Viswanathan. 1988. "Higher Education Co-operation and Western Dominance of Knowledge Creation and Flows in Third World Countries." *Higher Education* 17: 41–68.

Shafer, Robert. 1973. *Mexican Business Organizations.* Syracuse: Syracuse Univ. Press.

Siegal, Daniel, and Jenny Yancey, 1992. *The Rebirth of Civil Society: The Development of the Nonprofit Sector in East Central Europe and the Role of Western Assistance.* New York: Rockefeller Brothers Fund.

Silié, Rubén. 1988. "Educación superior dominicana: Situación y perspectiva." Photocopy. Santo Domingo.

Simon, John. 1980. "Research on Philanthropy." Paper prepared for Twenty-fifth Anniversary Conference of the National Council on Philanthropy, Denver, Nov. 8 (printed as an Independent Sector research report).

Skloot, Edward. 1987. "Enterprise and Commerce in Nonprofit Organizations." In Powell 1987.

Smith, Brian H. 1983. "U.S. and Canadian Nonprofit Organizations (PVOs) as Transnational Development Institutions." Working Paper 70. Program on Non-Profit Organizations, Yale University.

———. 1985. "Nonprofit Organizations and Socioeconomic Development in Colombia." Working Paper 93. Program on Non-Profit Organizations, Yale University.

———. 1990. *More than Altruism: The Politics of Private Foreign Aid.* Princeton: Princeton Univ. Press.

Smith, James. 1991. *Idea Brokers: Think Tanks and the Rise of the New Policy Elite.* New York: Free Press.

Smith, Michael. 1992. *Entre dos fuegos: ONG, desarrollo rural y violencia política.* Lima: IEP.

SOLIDARIOS. 1981. *Catálogo de instituciones de desarrollo sin fines de lucro en América Latina.* Santo Domingo: SOLIDARIOS.

Sommer, John G. 1977. *Beyond Charity: U.S. Voluntary Aid for a Changing Third World.* Washington, D.C.: Overseas Development Council.

Soto, Hernando de. 1989. *The Other Path.* Trans. June Abbott. New York: Harper and Row.

Spalding, Hobart. 1991. "Peru, a Country in Crisis: A Report on the Social Sciences and Social Science Research Centers." Report. SAREC, Stockholm.

Spalding, Hobart, Barbara Stallings, and John Weeks. 1990. *An Evaluation of SAREC's Latin America Programme.* Stockholm: SAREC.

Spalding, Hobart, Lance Taylor, and Carlos Vilas. 1985. *SAREC's Latin American Programme (LAP): An Evaluation.* Stockholm: SAREC.

Spear, Nat. 1972. "Venezuela's Philanthropic Climate." *Foundation News* (Nov.–Dec.): 31–35.

SSRC. 1991. Project on International Scholarly Relations in the Social Sciences. (The project was linked to CLACSO, *Autonomía y estabilidad,* but the SSRC papers were not collectively published; 1991 is the year the project ended, and the dates for individual papers vary by nation.)

Stepan, Alfred. 1978. *The State and Society: Peru in Comparative Perspective.* Princeton: Princeton Univ. Press.

Stepan, Nancy. 1976. *Beginnings of Brazilian Science: Osvaldo Cruz, Medical Research, and Policy, 1890–1920.* New York: Science History Publications.

Stifel, Laurence, Ralph Davidson, and James Coleman, eds. 1982. *Social Sciences and Public Policy in the Developing World.* Lexington, Mass.: D.C. Heath.

Stromberg, Ann, ed., 1968. *Foundations in Latin America.* Washington, D.C.: Pan American Development Foundation and Russell Sage Foundation.

Suárez, María Herlinda. 1984. "Diagnóstico del personal académico." In Dirección General 1984.

Sutton, Francis. 1986. "Foundations and Higher Education at Home and Abroad: A Tale of Heroic Efforts Abandoned." Working paper. Center for the Study of Philanthropy, City University of New York.

Tedesco, Juan Carlos, and Hans Blumenthal. 1986. "Desafíos y problemas de la educación superior en América Latina." In Juan Carlos Tedesco and Hans Blumenthal, eds. *La juventud universitaria en América Latina.* Caracas: CRESALC.

Teitelboim, Claudio. N.d. "CECI." Santiago.

Thompson, Andrés. 1992. "Democracy and Development: The Role of Nongovernmental Organizations in Argentina, Chile, and Uruguay." In McCarthy, Hodgkinson, and Sumariwalla 1992.

———. 1994. *"Think Tanks" en la Argentina: Conocimiento, instituciones y política.* Working Paper 102. Buenos Aires: CEDES.

————. N.d. "Philanthropy and Ecology in South America." Working paper. Center for the Study of Philanthropy, City University of New York.

Thompson, Kenneth, and Colleagues. 1974. "Higher Education and National Development: One Model for Technical Assistance." In F. Champion Ward, ed. *Education and Development Reconsidered: The Bellagio Conference Papers.* New York: Praeger.

Tillett, A. D. 1980. *Social Science Research in the Southern Cone.* Ottawa: IDRC.

Timerman, Jacobo. 1987. "Reflections: Under the Dictator." Trans. Robert Cox. *New Yorker,* Nov. 2, 113–35.

Tiramonti, G., et al. 1994. "La nueva universitaria." *Revista del Instituto de Investigaciones en Ciencias de la Educación, UBA* 2(3): 4–17.

Todd Pérez, Luis Eugenio, and Antonio Gago Huguet. 1990. *Visión de la universidad mexicana.* Mexico City: SEP.

Tünnermann, Carlos. 1972. "Planificación y autonomía." In Ana Herzfeld, Barbara Ashton Waggoner, and George Waggoner, eds., *Autonomía, planificación, coordinación, innovaciones.* Lawrence: Univ. of Kansas Press.

UCR (Consejo Universitario). 1987. *Documentos para ser conocidos por las asembleas de las unidades académicas.* San José: UCR.

UNAM. 1988. *Institutes and Centres for Scientific Research.* Mexico City: UNAM.

Urrutia, Miguel. 1994. "Institutional Development of Economics." In Alvarez and Gómez 1994.

Valdés, Juan Gabriel. 1989. *La escuela de Chicago: Operación Chile.* Buenos Aires: Grupo Zeta.

Vega, José Luis. 1989. "Pauta del desarrollo de las ciencias sociales en centroamérica." Paper prepared for SSRC. (See SSRC 1991.)

Vessuri, Hebe. 1983. "El papel cambiante de la investigación científica académica en un país periférico." In Elena Díaz, Yolanda Texera, and Hebe Vessuri, eds., *La ciencia periférica: Ciencia y sociedad en Venezuela.* Caracas: Monte Avila.

————. 1984. "The Search for a Scientific Community in Venezuela: From Isolation to Applied Research." *Minerva* 22(2): 196–235.

————. 1986. "The Universities, Scientific Research, and the National Interest in Latin America." *Minerva* 14(1): 1–38.

Vielle, Jean-Pierre. 1975. *Las instituciones Mexicanas de investigación educativa.* Mexico City: Ministry of Public Education.

Wagaw, Teshome. 1990. *The Development of Higher Education and Social Transformation: An Ethiopian Experience.* East Lansing: Michigan State Univ. Press.

Waste, Robert. 1987. *Power and Pluralism in American Cities.* Westport: Greenwood.

Weaver, R. Kent. 1989. "The Changing World of Think Tanks." *PS: Political Science & Politics* (Sept.): 563–78.

Webb, Richard. 1991. "Prologue." In Carlos Paredes and Jeffrey Sachs, eds., *Peru's Recovery Plan.* Washington, D.C.: Brookings.

Weisbrod, Burton. 1977. *The Voluntary Nonprofit Sector: An Economic Analysis.* Lexington, Mass.: Lexington Books.

———. 1988. *The Nonprofit Economy.* Cambridge: Harvard Univ. Press.

White, John. 1974. *The Politics of Foreign Aid.* New York: St. Martin's.

Wiarda, Howard. 1992. "Conclusion: Toward a Model of Social Change and Political Development in Latin America." In Howard Wiarda, ed., *Politics and Social Change in Latin America: Still a Distinct Tradition?* 3d ed. Boulder: Westview.

Winkler, Donald. 1990. *Higher Education in Latin America: Issues of Efficiency and Equity.* Discussion Paper 77. Washington, D.C.: World Bank.

Wittrock, Bjorn. 1985. "Before the Dawn: Humanism and Technology in University Research Policy." In Wittrock and Elzinga 1985.

Wittrock, Bjorn, and Aant Elzinga, eds. 1985. *The University Research System: The Public Policies of the Home of Scientists.* Stockholm: Almqvist and Wiksell.

World Bank. 1980. Education Sector Policy Paper. Washington, D.C.: World Bank.

———. 1985. "Peru: Higher Education Subsector." World Bank, Washington, D.C.

———. 1987. *World Development 1987.* Supplement. New York: Oxford Univ. Press.

Ylvisaker, Paul. 1987. "Foundations and Nonprofit Organizations." In Powell 1987.

Young, Dennis. 1983. *If Not for Profit, for What?* Lexington, Mass.: D. C. Heath.

Zaid, Gabriel. 1992. *Directorio de centros de información.* 10th ed. Mexico City: Ibcon.

Zald, Mayer, and John McCarthy. 1987. "Organizational Intellectuals and the Criticism of Society." In Mayer Zald and John McCarthy, eds., *Social Movements in an Organizational Society.* New Brunswick, N.J.: Transaction.

Index

Academic freedom, 135
Accountability, 125, 241–42, 246–50
ADIPA, 284*n29*
AEI (U.S.), 20, 95, 155, 309*n25*
Africa, 21, 137, 288*n23*, 292*n8*, 298*n3*, 310*n40*, 313*n13*
AGRARIA (Chile), 32
Agrarian development, 82, 146
Agriculture, 13, 39–43, 70–72, 91–92, 233, 304*n9;* funding of, 95, 110; studies of, 205–06
AHC (Chile), 62, 85, 118, 168, 206, 308*n25;* funders of, 115, 128; political impact of, 56–57, 141, 143; tasks at, 49–50, 121, 215, 218, 283*n16*
AID (U.S.), 21, 33, 61, 93–95, 97, 100, 102, 155; and applied research, 192; and IRCS, 43; and URCS, 77
ALAHUA (Ecuador), 32
Alfonsín, Raúl, 102, 131, 144
Americanization, 76, 186, 304*n10*, 305*n15*
ANICS (Nicaragua), 63, 189, 217
Anthropology, 31, 232, 282*n11*
Architecture, 32, 39, 57
Argentina, 31, 33, 37, 46–47, 63–64, 203, 221, 294*n28;* Americanization in, 186; funding in, 83, 92–93, 98, 104, 108–11, 113, 131, 162, 294*n35;* GRCS in, 39–40; IRCS in, 45; NGOS in, 10; political orientation in, 152, 156, 163; repression in, 57–58, 63, 65, 135–36, 138, 143, 262, 286*n3;* research in, 13, 15, 72, 85, 106, 182, 299*n13*, 309*n33;* researchers in, 84, 146–47; teaching in, 179, 208–09, 217–18; universities in, 72, 74, 78, 110, 219, 288*n19*, 308*n25;* URCS in, 26–27, 74–75. *See also* UBA
Asia, 20–21, 298*n3*, 303*n43*
ASIES (Guatemala), 188; funding of, 113, 115; and politics, 147, 159, 161–62; tasks of, 62, 143, 181, 184, 197
Authoritarianism, 8, 244. *See also* Regimes, repressive
Autonomy, 122–25, 257, 265; and funding, 90–92, 103, 112–34, 241, 297–98*nn58–59;* and

governance, 166; and markets, 103, 107; and research centers, 40, 43, 87
AVANCSO (Guatemala), 161, 181, 283*n17*
AVEDIS (Venezuela), 32, 287*n16*

Bariloche Foundation, 24, 31, 203, 206, 229, 312*n8;* funding of, 101–02, 136; tasks at, 197, 214
Barros Sierra Foundation, 36, 102, 106, 110, 145, 182, 205
Bartolomé Center, 31, 93, 106, 133, 209, 229, 295*n42;* quality of, 183–84, 221
BASE-IS (Paraguay), 78, 85, 113, 214
Belaúnde, Fernando, 144–45
Bolivia, 10; funding in, 92–93; politics in, 58, 143; research in, 15, 182–83; research centers in, 42, 75, 280*n22;* social action in, 35, 81; universities in, 68–69, 77
Brain drain, 147–48, 210
Brazil, 10, 92–93; Ford and, 28, 36; foundations in, 110, 282*n9;* funding in, 99, 102–04, 109–10, 113, 117, 291*n6*, 292*n15*, 297*n52;* graduate education in, 179–80, 215; politics in, 57–58, 63–64, 72–73, 138, 147, 152, 162; research in, 13, 15, 122, 182, 187, 299*n13;* research centers in, 31, 42, 46, 48–49, 75–76, 190; researchers in, 84; teaching in, 217; universities in, 77, 99, 160, 209, 219, 253, 286*n10*, 308*n25*
Brookings Institution, 20, 25, 107, 204, 213, 309*n35*
Brunner, José Joaquín, 147
Business, 2, 25–26, 65, 80, 161, 294*n30;* as field of study, 31, 33, 186, 198. *See also* For-profit organizations
Bustamante, Jorge, 168, 232

CAAP (Ecuador), 182, 196
CAIE (Mexico), 26–27
CAPIDE (Chile), 31
Caputo, Dante, 146
Cardoso, Fernando Henrique, 147
Caribbean, 283*n17*
Caritas, 36

341

Carlos Chagas Foundation (Brazil), 36, 93, 110, 196
Carvallo, Domingo, 147
Casa, Gilberto, 159
CATER (Ecuador), 32
Catholic University of Chile, 56, 76–77, 99
CATIE, 33, 43–45, 220
Cato Institute, 20, 25, 155
CCE (Mexico), 26
CCRP (Colombia), 25, 32, 65, 102–03, 198, 203
CDE (Paraguay), 102, 145, 169, 183–84, 197, 223
CEA (Cuba), 40
CEAP (Cuba), 40
CEAS (Brazil), 25, 81
CEASPA (Panama), 181, 197, 200, 203
CEBEM (Bolivia), 69, 113, 118, 183
CEBRAP (Brazil), 36, 85, 204; cooperation at, 188–89, 218; funding of, 93, 102, 107, 109, 115; political impact of, 57; research of, 182, 199, 209
CECI (Chile), 31, 64, 85, 168, 184, 188; funding of, 123, 129; and graduate education, 307n21
CED (Chile), 30, 143
CEDE (Colombia), 99, 182, 189, 309n32
CEDE (Dominican Republic), 87, 122, 125, 159, 287n18, 306n10
CEDEC (Brazil), 57, 93, 162, 182, 189, 218, 309n32
CEDEE (Dominican Republic), 288n18
CEDEP (Peru), 61, 102, 152, 184, 199
CEDES (Argentina), 85, 168, 188, 204; funding of, 93, 131, 291n5; political impact of, 144, 146; tasks of, 14, 199, 209
CEDICE (Venezuela), 29
CEDLA (Bolivia), 70, 196
CEDLADE, 45, 96, 204, 220, 311n47
CEDOH (Honduras), 61, 184, 197
CEE (Mexico), consulting of, 34; funding of, 36, 93, 102, 104, 114–15, 124; leadership in, 167; research in, 182, 187, 198
CEESP (Mexico), 26, 105
CEESTEM (Mexico), 36
CELA (Panama), 113, 181, 184, 198, 204, 217, 228
CELADU (Uruguay), 162, 183
CEMA (Argentina), 156, 179, 213
CEMAT (Guatemala), 32
CEMLA, 44, 96
CENDES (Venezuela), 74, 189, 309n34
CENECA (Chile), 31, 50, 183, 281n3
CENEP (Argentina), 308n22
CENICAFE (Colombia), 283n12
Central America, 15, 64, 113, 283n15
CEOP (Mexico), 29
CEP (Chile), 30, 95, 108, 156, 163, 204
CEPAE (Dominican Republic), 25, 81, 153, 296n46
CEPAL, 45, 150, 198, 204, 299n8, 301n24, 307n20
CEPEI (Peru), 157
CEPEP (Paraguay), 96, 198, 204

CEPES (Peru), 102, 152
CEPLAES (Ecuador), 98, 113
CERC (Chile), 50, 143, 162, 183–84
CEREP (Puerto Rico), 197, 302n38
CERES (Bolivia), 69, 113, 188, 196, 209
CERES (Uruguay), 64, 144, 157, 166, 176; and research, 183, 187, 204
CERESD (Dominican Republic), 39, 130, 159, 189, 300n21
CERPE (Venezuela), 25, 202, 220
CES (Uruguay), 197
CESPO (Costa Rica), 288n22
CET (Argentina), 44, 85
CETAL (Chile), 32, 198
CEUR (Argentina), 76, 85, 93, 98, 146, 166
CGIAR, 43
Chapingo, 41, 43, 70, 149, 171, 178, 304n4; and El Colegio de México, 52, 233–34; criticism of, 301n23; funding of, 100–01, 104, and Plan Chapingo, 100, 178; research and, 190, 194
"Chicago economics," 156, 161, 299n14
Chile, 10, 46–50, 82, 203, 221, 301n30; funding in, 83, 92–93, 102–03, 109–10, 113–15, 133, 292n9; political orientations in, 151–52, 157, 161; political impacts in, 56–57, 63, 65, 72, 141, 147–48, 163; publications in, 184; research in, 13, 15, 121, 158, 182–83, 199, 299n13; research centers in, 39–40, 74–75, 77; researchers in, 30, 75, 84, 149, 175; sanctuary in, 138, 140; social action in, 36, 144, 190; social science in, 223, 309n31; teaching in, 214; universities in, 75, 234, 253, 286n2, 308n25, 313n18. See also Catholic University of Chile; UCH
China, 21
Church, 2, 25, 82, 105–06, 138, 141
CIAPA (Costa Rica), 65, 155, 166, 188, 284n23
CIAT, 43, 97
CIB (Colombia), 101, 283n12
CIBIMA (Dominican Republic), 39
CICSO (Argentina), 57, 115, 124, 183, 196, 203
CIDAC (Mexico), 26, 182, 204–05, 309n32
CIDCA (Nicaragua), 40
CIDE (Chile), 25, 36, 82, 141, 203, 209; funding of, 93, 114; governance of, 166, 302n37
CIDE (Mexico), 41, 51, 204; and El Colegio de México, 33, 50–51; 232–33; funding of, 100, 102; governance of, 168, 170; personnel at, 63, 177; tasks at, 182, 184, 212–13, 285n31
CIDEIM (Colombia), 32
CIDOS (Dominican Republic), 302n36
CIEA (Dominican Republic), 34, 85, 115, 196, 204, 286n7, 296n46
CIEDUR (Uruguay), 57, 81, 144, 146, 168; funding of, 101, 114; research of, 183, 197
CIEF (Uruguay), 25
CIEN (Guatemala), 181

Donors, 114–16, 119–21, 123–24, 161, 163. *See also* Foundations, foreign; Funding; Philanthropy, international

EARTH, 283*n14*
ECIEL (Brazil), 36, 44, 96, 292*n10*, 304*n11*, 312*n8*
Economics (as field of study), 30, 119, 145, 182, 199, 233, 282*n11*; in Chile, 38, 76, 158, 183, 223
Ecuador, 75, 219, 279*n20*; funding in, 92, 104; graduate education in, 307*n17*; scholars in, 63; social action in, 35; social research in, 15, 182
Education (as field of study), 5, 39, 75–76, 82, 191, 205; funding of, 110, 292*n2*. *See also* Graduate education; Higher education; Undergraduate education
El Colegio de México, 24, 36, 50–52, 124, 206–07, 229, 304*n6*, 312*n8*; autonomy of, 125–27; Center for International Relations, 146; disciplines, 31, 199, 205, 311*n97*; funding of, 93, 97, 100, 102, 104, 107, 296*nn50–51*; 297*nn53–54*, 57; governance of, 162, 167, 171; and government, 145, 149; and graduate education, 33, 70, 180; and internationalism, 186, 310*n37*; juridical status of, 285*n32*; as model, 168, 231; and other research centers, 41, 237; personnel at, 158, 177; and politics, 63, 157; publications of, 185, 225–26; research in, 14, 33, 70, 182, 194, 200; teaching in, 212–13, 216, 285*n31*; and UNAM, 51, 67, 72, 159, 307*n18*
El Salvador, 58, 181
Endowments, 107
Engineering (as field of study), 38–39, 71, 193, 212
Enrollment, 10, 261
Environmental programs, 30, 32, 70, 153; funding for, 82, 96, 108, 291*n1*
ESCOLATINA (Chile), 38, 288*n21*, 301*n30*, 311*n48*
EURAL (Argentina), 98, 114, 162, 199, 218
Europe, 19–20, 217, 296*n46*; Eastern, 9, 64, 281*n31*, 303*n49*; Western, 91, 94, 153

Fals Borda, Orlando, 48
FAO, 39
FDN (Peru), 32, 162, 166, 196, 290*n37*, 310*n39*
FEDESARROLLO (Colombia), 47, 110, 189, 203, 221; funding of, 102–03, 106, 114; governance of, 302*n37*; personnel at, 217, 222; and politics, 64–65, 157; tasks at, 34, 37, 182, 184, 199, 205, 214–15, 228–29
FES (Colombia), 83, 109, 111, 204, 294*n36*; governance of, 302*n37*
FESCOL (Colombia), 37, 99, 109, 144, 162
FIEL (Argentina), 156
Fields of Study, 39, 78, 204–06, 215, 282*n11*
FINEP (Brazil), 104, 117
FLACSO, 43–44, 94, 131, 136, 203, 206, 217, 235;

in Argentina, 57, 102, 114, 146, 148, 213, 220, 310*n45*; in Brazil, 308*n24*; in Central America, 113, 215, 293*n23*; in Chile, 93, 101, 127–30, 143, 147–48, 162–63, 168, 182–83, 204, 224; funding of, 96, 115, 141, 296*n46*, 297*n54*; in Mexico, 41, 102, 170, 213; and other institutions, 220, 231, 253; tasks at, 48–50, 184, 199, 213, 228
Flora Tristán Peruvian Women's Center, 144, 196, 203–04
Fondo, 94, 110, 115, 156, 159, 167, 296*n46*
Ford Foundation, 28, 35–36, 66, 83, 93, 95, 97, 99–100, 255; and autonomy, 123; in Central America, 283*n15*; and democratization, 143, 146; in Dominican Republic, 115; endowments of, 107; evaluations of, 228; and FLACSO, 127; and higher education, 163, 280–81*nn28–29*, 287*n11*, 292*n12*; and IRCS, 43–44; in Mexico, 36, 41, 125, 169, 233; and other donors, 128; outside Latin America, 21, 303*n8*; political orientation of, 162, 164, 301*nn30–31*, 303*n48*; programs of, 113, 117–19, 181, 192; in South American countries, 49, 57–58, 97, 280*n21*, 288*n22*
For-profit organizations, 2, 20, 52
Foundations, 12, 27, 91–94, 110, 154–56, 278*n6*, 284*n23*; 294*n31*. *See also* Donors; Funding; Philanthropy, international
France, 39
Frei, Eduardo, 144
Friedrich Ebert Foundation (Germany), 94, 98, 109, 115
Friedrich Naumann Foundation (Germany), 94–95
FUNDAEC (Colombia), 37
Funding, 82–83, 90–134, 154, 218, 225, 292*n13*, 296*n47*, 297*n56*; domestic, 103, 109–111; private, 105–112, 259; public, 50, 98–100, 103–05

Gallup-Argentina, 29
García, Alán, 144
GEA (Chile), 32, 50
Generation gap, 209
Germani, Gino, 48
Germany, 19, 97
Getúlio Vargas Foundation, 25, 33, 36, 110, 206, 285*n33*, 313*n18*; funding of, 93, 100, 103, 293*n20*; tasks at, 50, 180, 199, 216
GIA (Chile), 32, 50, 196, 216, 229, 289*n31*
Gómez, Emeterio, 29
González Casanova, Pablo, 171
González González, Luis, 232
Governance, 27, 165–71, 202, 246, 257, 269, 302*nn34–36*
Government, 81, 141, 148, 161, 213, 256; and funding, 90–91, 99–100
GRADE (Peru), 25, 162, 189, 203–04, 234; fund-

ing of, 93, 115, 295n42; personnel at, 176, 217; tasks at, 37, 209, 214, 221

Graduate education, 14, 149, 208; funding of, 20, 99; and research, 38–39, 71, 107; at research centers, 32–34, 40–41, 48–49, 70, 77, 214, 235. *See also* Higher education, Graduate education

Grassroots organizations, 9, 35, 37, 54, 196, 278n11, 299n10, 313n14; influences on, 82, 151; study of, 16, 280n26

GRCS, 14, 56, 140, 170, 283n19, 306n9, 313n13; and other research centers, 20, 39–42

Great Britain, 281n30

GRECMU (Uruguay), 85, 115, 183, 196, 217

Guatemala, 103, 145, 159; funding in, 92; politics in, 58, 64, 139, 143, 196, 262; research centers in, 280n22; universities in, 74, 78, 139, 159, 183

Haiti, 15, 39, 113

Harvard University, 33, 130

Hayek, Friedrich, 156

Health research, 32, 39, 192

Heritage Foundation, 20, 155, 204

Herrera, Felipe, 48

Hierarchy, 169–70, 252, 302–03nn41–44

Higher education, 3, 5–6, 15, 17–18, 27, 29, 313n20, 314n23; funding of, 83, 90–91, 95, 103–04, 111, 131, 279n14, 280–81nn28–29; impacts on, 238, 242–43; 251–54; studies of, 45. *See also* Graduate education, University

History (as field of study), 31, 39, 126, 128, 183, 205, 232, 282n11

Honduras, 61, 68, 92, 95, 103

Hoover Institute, 20, 27, 107, 155, 282n7

Humanities, 31, 38–39, 128, 233

Human rights, 30, 54, 119–20, 283n16, 291n1

Humboldt, Wilhelm von, 19, 208

IAF (United States), 94–95

IBAFIN (Mexico), 26

IBGE (Brazil), 42

ICAL (Chile), 31

ICAP, 45, 307n19

ICEG, 95, 291n7

IDB, 91, 95–96, 102, 186, 192, 281n29, 291n8, 292n10; and Plan Chapingo, 100

IDEA (Venezuela), 40, 284n22

IDEC (Argentina), 156

IDES (Argentina), 57, 213, 307n19

IDESP (Brazil), 36, 85, 189, 204, 218, 302n36

IDRC (Canada), 44, 77, 83, 117–18, 123, 189, 192, 295n37; in individual areas, 93, 94–95, 97, 100, 115, 292n8

IEP (Peru), 118, 169, 189, 205, 221, 302n36, 312n8; funding of, 93, 115; personnel at, 217; and politics, 141, 152; tasks at, 14, 36–37, 81, 107, 196, 199, 214

IEPRI (Colombia), 75, 189, 211, 299n11, 302n33, 304n5, 305n17; journal of, 309n32

IESA (Venezuela), 25, 33, 80, 103, 166, 204, 309n34, 310n39; Americanization of, 186; and funding, 280, 289n31; and government recruits, 148; tasks at, 50, 180, 182, 216, 229; and universities, 313n18

IICA, 44, 284n21, 307n19

ILADES (Chile), 50, 82, 214

ILD (Peru), 95, 148, 166, 170, 203, 223, 199n16; political orientation of, 156–157; tasks at, 182, 225

ILDIS (Ecuador), 115

ILET, 44–45, 64, 85, 117, 143, 148, 183

ILO (Switzerland), 45

ILPES, 45, 307n19

IME (Mexico), 34

IMES (Mexico), 100, 182

IMF, 96

INCAE, 33, 176, 188, 199, 293n21

INCAITI, 44

INCAP, 287n12

India, 21, 287n13, 293n16, 308n26

Indigenous groups, 120, 167

Industry, 20, 195

INIES (Nicaragua), 63, 85

INPROA (Chile), 82

INTEC (Dominican Republic), 161, 287n18

Intellectuals, 1, 45, 150

Intercentros, 189, 228

Internationalization, 54, 155, 185–89, 289n11

International research centers. *See* IRCS

INVESP (Venezuela), 284n28

IPDE (Panama), 33

IPEA (Brazil), 42

IPN (Mexico), 29, 41, 211, 283n20

IRCS, 42–45, 96–97, 198, 204, 233–34, 299n8, 304n9, 307n14

ISIS (Malaysia), 21, 286n8

ITAM (Mexico), 78, 86, 288n24, 294n29

IUPERJ (Brazil), 36, 57, 169, 189, 204; degrees of, 176, 307n15; funding of, 93, 117; tasks at, 14, 81, 180, 182, 184, 199, 229, 304n10

IVIC (Venezuela), 40, 67, 190, 204, 210, 297n57, 301n23

Jaguaribe, Helio, 48

Japan, 20–21

Joaquim Nabuco Foundation, 282n9

Jorge Blanco, Salvador, 148

Journals, 184, 188, 226–27

Juridical status, 52, 285n32

Kellogg Foundation, 77, 94

Konrad Adenauer Foundation, 94, 113, 115, 127

Labor, 36, 105–06; unions, 25, 72, 106, 170, 299n9

Lamounier, Bolivar, 218

Lampadia Foundation, 109, 111
Law (as field of study), 71, 119
Libraries, 228–29
Lobbying, 33, 35
Luis Roche Foundation, 32, 67, 109, 204

MacArthur Foundation, 94
Macropolitics, 55–59, 88
Malaysia, 39
Management (as field of study), 31, 199, 210
Manhattan Institute, 20
Marketed research, 105–07
Markets, 103, 132, 224, 230, 242, 264
Marxism, 75, 150, 152, 158
Max Planck Institute, 19, 217
Medicine (as field of study), 13, 39, 71, 101, 119
Mediterranean Foundation, 108–09, 131, 147, 156
Menem, Carlos, 147
Mexico, 25–27, 34, 40, 47, 206; funding in, 92–94, 97, 100–02, 109, 113, 120, 289*n34*; personnel in, 86, 146, 177–79; politics in, 58, 62–63, 138, 147, 149, 298*n5*, 301*n28*; research in, 13, 15, 80, 182, 190, 193–95, 210; research centers in, 10, 39, 41, 74–75, 280*n22*; teaching in, 179, 211–15; universities, 38, 67, 71, 86, 110, 158, 167, 170, 233. *See also* UNAM
Miceli, Sergio, 218
Military, 39–40. *See also* Regimes, repressive
Mission, 213, 245–46, 282*n8*
Modernization, 13, 243, 258
Moya Pons, Frank, 159, 170

National Endowment for Democracy, 95
NGOS, 2, 10, 21, 35, 95, 291*n4*
Nicaragua, 40, 63, 92, 102, 181
Nonprofit organizations, 6, 10, 90, 202, 234, 277*n2*, 278*n5*, 313*n14*, 314*n22*
Nonprofit sector, 4, 79, 303*n45*. *See also* Third sector
NUPES (Brazil), 303*n45*

OAS, 37, 44–45, 49, 95–96, 100, 192
Oswaldo Cruz Institute, 42, 210

Panama, 74–75, 78, 103, 181
Paraguay, 10, 47, 110; funding in, 61, 92, 110, 114; politics in, 58, 64, 143; social research in, 15, 30, 182, 237; universities in, 78
PDC (Chile), 301*n25*
Peronism, 57
Peru, 10, 47, 61, 119, 141, 282*n11*, 300*n18*; funding in, 92–94, 97–98, 109, 194, 280*n21*, 305*n16*; personnel in, 84, 217–18, 295*n38*; politics in, 63, 143–45, 152, 155, 162, 169; research in, 15, 36–37, 80, 182–83, 197, 206; research centers in, 28, 42, 75, 78, 93;

unions in, 105; universities in, 68–69, 78, 158
PET (Chile), 36, 50, 141, 166, 184, 214
Philanthropy, corporate, 108–09
Philanthropy, indigenous, 108–11
Philanthropy, international, 3, 11, 66, 83, 91–131, 188, 244–45; criticism of, 150; decline of, 230; targets of, 70, 73–74, 77, 99, 192, 313*n18*. *See also* Donors; Foundations, foreign; Funding
PIIE (Chile), 50, 75, 122, 147, 203, 214
PISPAL, 44
Pluralism, 2, 68, 151, 160–65, 254, 263–65, 315–16*nn33–36*; and donors, 114–15, 162–65; intrainstitutional, 172, 246; problems of, 250; sectoral, 59, 237, 241, 313*n19*
Policy, 2, 14, 141, 241, 254–56, 266; and research, 29–30, 120, 198, 200, 227
Political orientation, 31, 155, 157, 161, 165, 241, 300*nn19–20*; leftist, 63, 136, 150, 152–54, 158, 300*n17*, 301*n25*; moderate, 149–52; rightist, 60, 105, 151, 154–57, 266
Political parties, 25, 65, 86, 105–06, 125, 140, 161, 301*n26*
Political science (as field of study), 30–31, 158, 182–83, 199, 205, 282*n11*
Politicization, 67–68, 86, 287*n13*
Population studies, 32, 44, 188, 194, 198
Poverty, 104, 110–11, 120, 196, 249–50
PREALC, 45
Prebisch, Raúl, 48
PRI (Mexico), 25
Privatization, 3–4, 8–11, 54, 62, 231, 256–61, 290*n44*, 291*n46*; assessments of, 247, 278*n10*; forms of, 60; in individual countries, 42, 61, 86; and PRC funding, 105–12; in research, 80, 83; in universities, 68, 315*n28*; and URCS, 73
Progressiveness, 195–97, 243
Publications, 106, 183–85, 224–26
Public failure theory, 55, 58–59, 62, 286*n5*, 290*n45*
Public opinion, 2, 120, 143, 145
Public research centers, 51, 204
Puerto Rico, 75–76, 99, 290*n41*, 293*n22*, 304*n11*, 307*n12*

R&D, 12–14
RAND (United States), 20, 51, 286*n8*
Recruitment, government, 146–49
Redemocratization, 60–61, 218, 221
Regimes, repressive, 101–02, 146, 215, 286*n2*, 290*n44*, 299*n12*, 313*n20*; leftist vs. rightist, 298*n12*; and research centers, 2–3, 55–59, 74, 136, 140–41, 262; scholars under, 63, 85
Regime types, 101–03, 144–46
Religious organizations, 9, 65, 81–82, 260
Research, 6, 10–13, 16, 29, 69–81, 138, 180–83,

229–30; applied vs. basic, 29, 38, 101, 107, 122, 191, 308*n29;* committed, 35; debate over, 279*nn17–18;* empirical, 186–87; geographical focus of, 197–98; quality of, 189–91, 220–30; relevance of, 144–45, 191–97; and teaching, 71–72, 208; and universities, 18–22, 70–73
Research centers, 18. *See also* IRCS, Public research centers, URCS
Researchers, 14, 82–87, 214, 294*n26,* 295*nn37–38,* 311*n2*
RIAL, 44, 96, 234
RIDALC (Argentina), 45
Rockefeller Foundation, 28, 67, 94, 97, 99, 128, 130, 192; and autonomy, 119, 123; in individual countries, 38, 70, 125, 169, 207; at IRCS and URCS, 43–44, 77; under repressive regimes, 136–37
Russell Sage Foundation, 20, 309*n35*
Russia, 19, 303*n44*

Sanctuary, 135–42, 202, 298*n6*
Sandinistas, 63, 86, 102, 139, 146, 153
SAREC (Sweden), 47, 95, 101, 113, 115, 255, 292*n8,* 295*n37,* 296*n44;* and autonomy, 117–19, 123; criticism of, 150; and government, 131; recipients of, 83, 96, 197
Scholars, 31, 62–63, 73, 85–87, 104, 123, 224
Science: applied, 39–40; in Mexico, 38, 193; natural, 31–32, 41–42, 51, 83, 119, 128, 185; and technology, 98, 101, 279*n16,* 283*n12;* and technology councils, 104, 280*n23;* at URCS, 39, 74, 78, 190. *See also* Technology
SER (Colombia), 4, 47, 72, 182, 189, 203, 221, 286*n7*
Shining Path, 43, 153, 189,298*n4,* 301*n23*
Silvert, Kalman, 125–26
SINAMOS (Peru), 61
SNI (Mexico), 104, 178, 190
Social action, 2, 33–37, 80, 98, 106, 221, 292*n9*
Social development, 62
Social research, 15, 89, 210, 237, 242, 313*n15,* 279*n19*
Social science, 30, 78, 185, 192, 219, 227, 209–10, 279*n19,* 305*n18;* and Ford, 128; at GRCS and URCS, 39, 99; in individual areas, 38, 57, 137, 233; under military rule, 56–58; and policy research, 13–15
Social scientists, 37, 84
Social services, 54
Sociology, 30, 119, 158, 182–83, 199, 213, 223, 235, 282*n11*
Soto, Hernando de, 157, 166, 170, 225
Southern Cone, 46–47, 56–57, 67, 137, 203, 235
Spain, 153, 281*n30*
Specialization, 119, 202–08, 306*n3,* 311*n1*
SSRC (United States), 93, 294*n33*
Standardization, 72, 76, 78, 287*n14*
Stratification, 236, 253

Students, 213, 231, 234, 287*n15*
Study abroad, 123, 180, 209
SUR (Chile), 50, 143, 183, 214

TDRI (Thailand), 286*n8,* 299*n11*
Teaching, 71–72, 85, 207–20, 237
Technology, 30, 98, 101, 145, 206; appropriate, 32, 205. *See also* Science
TEKHNE (Chile), 32
Think tanks, 2, 20, 30, 83, 227, 277*n3,* 299*n15;* and politics, 81, 95, 157; publications by, 106
Third sector, 2, 4–6, 52, 79, 253, 277*nn4–5,* 314–15*n24. See also* Nonprofit sector
Third World, 9, 91, 175, 191
THOA (Bolivia), 70, 183
Tinker Foundation, 94
Trinidad medical center, 32, 106, 216, 220

UBA (Argentina), 76–78, 128
UCH (Chile), 74, 77, 99
UDAPSO (Bolivia), 42
UDUAL, 44
UN, 44–45, 95–96
UNAM (Mexico), 70, 99–100, 211, 306*n11;* and El Colegio, 51, 67, 72, 159, 307*n18;* funding of, 104, 128, 131; and politics, 72, 302*n33;* tasks at, 193, 304*n10;* URCS at, 38, 74, 76–78, 158, 171, 178
Undergraduate education, 32, 211, 283*n14*
UNDP, 37, 39, 45, 61, 96
UNESCO, 37, 45, 48–49, 96
UNICEF, 37
Unions. *See* Labor
United States, 46, 60, 62, 72, 95, 153, 163, 210, 279*n14;* universities in, 19–20, 177, 313*n18*
University, 9–10, 13, 18–22, 38, 78, 83–85, 110, 138; failure of, 3, 65–70; personnel at, 175, 213, 216, 218; and PRCS, 3, 26–27, 158–59, 234–37, 243, 251–53, 255; private, 78, 159, 259–60, 288*n25;* public, 17, 67, 71–73, 313*n19;* reform of, 10, 68. *See also* Higher education, Graduate education
University research centers. *See* URCS
Urban Institute, 20, 51
URCS, 14, 20, 170, 204, 281*n32,* 287*n17,* 290*n43;* and autonomy, 74; funding of, 99–101, 289*n32;* personnel at, 178–79; politics at, 75, 158; and PRCS, 17, 38–39, 79; tasks at, 190, 211; university and, 68, 73, 283*n18*
Urquidi, Víctor, 48, 126, 167, 290*n40*
Uruguay, 10, 46–47, 61, 92, 102, 146; politics in, 57, 64, 143; tasks in, 81, 101, 181–83, 216–17, 237; universities in, 71, 219; URCS in, 75
Uso combinado, 124–25, 301*n26*
USP (Brazil), 57, 78, 218

VECTOR (Chile), 161, 281*n3*
Venezuela, 28, 40, 47, 75, 78, 80, 140; funding

in, 86, 92, 280*n21*, 290*n42;* tasks in, 13, 15,
37, 67, 182, 215–16; universities in, 29, 40,
78, 86, 110

Westernization, 186, 191–92
Women's centers, 36, 38, 70, 161, 302*n39,*

310*n38;* issues of, 30, 119–20, 144, 161, 167,
188, 196–97, 296*n44*
World Bank, 3, 96, 102, 281*n29;* in Africa, 21–22;
in South American countries, 42, 125,
292*n8*